Catholic post-secondary education in English-speaking Canada

Etudes sur l'Histoire d'Enseignement Supérieur au Canada
Studies in the History of Higher Education in Canada
Sponsored by the Association of Universities and
Colleges of Canada, with financial support from
the Carnegie Corporation of New York

Catholic
post-secondary education
in English-speaking Canada

A history

LAURENCE K. SHOOK

University of Toronto Press

© University of Toronto Press 1971
Toronto and Buffalo
Printed in Canada
ISBN 0-8020-1765-7
Microfiche ISBN 0-8020-0070-3

FOREWORD

In his preface Professor Shook notes that this book is his 'somewhat leisurely response' to an invitation extended to him eight years ago to write a history of the English-language Roman Catholic universities and colleges of Canada. He has no reason to be apologetic. The subject is a formidable one, extending in time over more than a century and a half and in space from one end of the country to the other, involving over thirty institutions and (as the index will testify) close to one thousand individuals, and embracing a wide range of issues – political, philosophic, economic, and psychological. Few readers will be surprised to learn that eight years of study and thought lie behind the appearance of this book, particularly when it is realized that relatively few of the institutions involved had anything resembling an adequate history upon which Professor Shook could build. We really are doubly in his debt; first, for providing accurate basic chronicles of each of the institutions involved, and second for presenting these chronicles to us in such a way that a series of interrelated patterns emerges which explains as much about the development of Canadian higher education as a whole as about the development of that portion of it which can be designated. It is a case where we now can see the trees but also the forest.

In one sense it is fortunate that the task did require eight years to complete. As it stands the record is now brought forward to the spring of 1970. Readers will discover that a substantial number of Professor Shook's pages are devoted to developments which have occurred since 1965 and a significant number to developments which have occurred since 1968. The events of the past five years indicate very clearly that something close to a crisis faces every one of the universities and colleges with which Professor Shook is concerned. His first 400 pages provide ample evidence of the wide-ranging and highly significant contribution which the Roman Catholic institutions have made to the intellectual life of Canada over a long period of time and in every province. His final 30 pages reveal that the continuance of this contribution is now in doubt. The old financial dispensation will no longer do. A new dispensation must be found if the work of Alexander Macdonell, Joseph-Henri Tabaret, Hugh Macpherson, Henry Carr, Athol Murray, and so many others of this honourable company is to be carried on and, more important, if it is to be developed in the new ways that the new Canada requires.

It will be apparent that the spirit of Vatican II has informed many of the English-speaking Roman Catholic colleges of Canada. That spirit, which in essence is philosophic rather than religious and which is certainly not sectarian, must inform Canadian higher education as a whole – the Protestant universities and colleges as much as the Roman Catholic, the French-speaking as well as the English-speaking, the public as well as the private. One of the great values of Professor Shook's book is its demonstration at many points of this spirit in action – Henry Carr would have been entirely at home at Vatican II; and this is one reason why the book should be read (and reread) by presidents, deans, professors, and students from Memorial to Victoria. Unless, however, it is also read by a good number of other people, the benefits may be small. For, as Professor Shook also makes clear in his concluding chapter, in 1970 universities in Canada as everywhere else are not in control of their destinies. Perhaps they were in 1962 when Professor Shook agreed to undertake his assignment, though a stronger case could be made if the date were moved back to 1958. Today, however, all universities are directly or indirectly dependent upon public funds, and it is government, whether provincial or federal, which calls the tune. The welfare of Canadian higher education may well depend upon how many members of parliament and government officials read this book.

Catholic Post-Secondary Education in English-Speaking Canada is the sixth volume in a series which has been made possible by the grant of $25,000 to the Association of Universities and Colleges of Canada, then called the National Conference of Canadian Universities and Colleges, by the Carnegie Corporation of New York in 1958. The Directors of the Corporation must at times feel that the Committee responsible for the implementation of this grant could in its turn be accused of being somewhat leisurely in its response to the Corporation's generosity. Not that Stephen Stackpole and his associates have complained. It is my belief that in the case of Professor Shook's volume they will agree that this was well worth waiting for and it is my hope that the remaining volumes in the series will also justify their patience.

ROBIN S. HARRIS, University of Toronto

PREFACE

This study of Canada's English Roman Catholic colleges and universities is my somewhat leisurely response to an invitation issued to me some eight years ago by the NCCUC's (now the AUCC's) Committee on the History of Higher Education in Canada. Donald Masters' companion study of Protestant Church colleges has already appeared, and Claude Galarneau's of French Catholic colleges is approaching completion. The three volumes will not much resemble one another in plan or method, shaped as each must be by the materials at hand, but they ought together to constitute a complementary and, I trust, valid analytic survey of the important and not easily understood contribution of church colleges to national life.

The special problems affecting my assignment have been these: the number of colleges to be dealt with is large and shifting; the history of very few of them has ever been recorded; the categories 'Catholic' 'English' 'college' escape precise definition. These problems account for the decision to proceed by way of individual chronicles while allowing for diversity of approach between one chronicle and another.

At one point this procedure turns out to be embarrassing. The chronicle of St Michael's, where I have such ready access at all times to archival material, is disproportionately long. I thought at one time of reducing it drastically but found that doing so would mean that I could nowhere else give adequate and accurate coverage to a number of shared institutional experiences: the coming of co-education, the separation of college and high school, the establishing of relations with seminaries, the conferring of civil degrees in theology, the dependence upon American students, extravagant attention to sport, the division of the headship between president and superior, university federation. In allowing the longer account of St Michael's to stand, I hoped thereby to provide an acceptable paradigm for chronicles whose patterns were not dissimilar.

Unwillingly, save for a word of gratitude to Eva de Graaf, who prepared the final manuscript and index, I refrain from acknowledgements. I am indebted to so many people from St John's to Vancouver for written and oral assistance, for encouragement and, yes, criticism, that any list I could either remember or reasonably include would be quite inadequate. The discerning reader knows that this kind of volume, like scholarship itself, is essentially collaborative.

This book has been published with the help of a grant from the Social Science Research Council of Canada, using funds provided by the Canada Council, and with the assistance of the Publications Fund of the University of Toronto Press.

LKS

CONTENTS

Western Ontario

IV WESTERN CANADA
Manitoba

Saskatchewan

Alberta

British Columbia

DIRECTIONS

Catholic post-secondary education in English-speaking Canada

I
ORIGINS

CATHOLIC POST-SECONDARY EDUCATION

An historical examination of Catholic post-secondary education in the English-speaking parts of Canada can only be made in the context of two arbitrary decisions. The first is the decision to make no rigid legalistic distinction between universities in the strict sense and colleges. When a bishop or a Catholic group had in mind the founding of a college, envisaged was something approximating the European *collège* – the kind of school which would accept children leaving the elementary school, would take them through Latin and into philosophy, would gain them admission to some professional institution – the Roman seminaries or the American law schools, for example – and which might provide them, in some informal way at least, with enough theological instruction to justify ordaining them. This was 'higher education' for most of Canada's Catholic constituencies in their pioneering days. It was not university education even in the view of the founders, administrators, and students of the colleges, but it was, or blended into, a level of instruction and study comparable with that pursued in Protestant colleges generally and in most of the first universities founded in English-speaking Canada.

This decision to deal with colleges almost as though they are universities appears valid and certainly less arbitrary in the context of the terminology followed by John Strachan, first Anglican bishop of Toronto and founder of the University of Toronto, in articles published in the *Christian Recorder*, April and July 1819. Strachan deals with Upper Canadian schools in four categories: common (grammar) schools, district (grammar) schools, the projected college or university, and schools not enjoying government bounty. Common schools were those set up in Upper Canada by government legislation in 1816; they were public in character and elementary or primary in academic level. District schools, also public in character, were established in Upper Canada in 1807; they were secondary schools teaching 'the higher branches of education, the classics, mathematics, etc.'; these district or secondary schools were from the beginning to be provided for financially out of revenues from an appropriation of crown lands made in 1798 to support higher education; in 1819 they were still eight in number, one for each of the eight districts into which Upper Canada was divided. The projected university, though not yet founded in 1819 when Strachan's brief history was put together, was very much under discussion, and was also to be financed out of revenues from the same crown lands; this university, described sometimes as a college sometimes as a university by Strachan, was to be set up as a King's College in the home district, that is, in York (Toronto after 1834), and was to admit qualified students without ecclesiastical restrictions.

These three categories, common or primary, district or secondary, and university or post-secondary, remain clear today. The fourth, schools not enjoying public bounty, is not clearly defined. Some of these schools 'not enjoying public bounty' corresponded academically to common schools, some to district schools, some to a combination of the two, and a few took on programmes of a post-secondary character. In practice, and especially in that they were not tied to the legislature of Upper Canada by a system of grants, these schools are best dealt with as a compromise between what they were intended to be and what they succeeded in becoming. Those more ambitiously conceived were usually, as in Europe, the United States, and the Maritimes, called 'colleges' by their founders, especially by ecclesiastical founders who often had in mind both preparing students for admission to professional faculties and introducing them to university studies whatever these, either then or now, can be determined to consist in. Roman Catholic bishops, and religious congregations and orders, have been quick rather than slow to establish such colleges. Not all Catholic institutions so established as colleges will be formally considered in the present work but only those whose development has been such that they are today recognized as functioning in a practical way at the post-secondary level.

The second decision to be made in examining Catholic post-secondary institutions is to maintain a clear distinction between maritime, central Canadian, and western foundations. Not to do so only leads to both inaccuracies and misunderstanding. Founders of colleges in the Maritimes had to cope with pre-emancipation laws: students and professors had to subscribe to religious oaths which Catholics and nonconformists could not take; and the setting up of Catholic schools was an offence punishable by imprisonment and fine. The founding of the first colleges in the Maritimes was an important blow struck for both civil and religious liberty. This no doubt goes far towards explaining why the maritime system of universities and colleges is still basically sectarian.[1]

1 See in general, Sister Francis Xavier, 'Educational Legislation in Nova Scotia and the Catholics,' *Report of the Canadian Catholic Historical Association*, 24 (1957), 63–74; and esp. n.4.

The situation was different in central Canada. The problem there was not to break through oppressive laws but to show reason why the sectarian colleges should not throw in their weight with the state institutions where their students were more or less welcome and sometimes badly wanted. The Catholic of central Canada was more deeply immersed in the ghetto complex than his co-religionist in the Maritimes. The central Canadian Catholic did not share his disabilities with Presbyterians and Methodists, even though like them he had no money and came from depressed European constituencies with which to maintain ties was not very helpful. The attempt to start a Catholic college at Kingston was perhaps an exception in that Bishop Macdonell operated rather like a member of the establishment. But the college at Toronto was largely a missionary effort. It only partly sprang from the awareness of need for a college among the Catholics of the area; it was much more an expression of the great missionary spirit still alive in France which led men to give themselves to the work of Christ and the Church among foreign peoples without resources of their own. The Toronto saga is one in which an isolated group of impoverished citizens allowed their college, gradually and incompletely, to be integrated into a public system of post-secondary education.

The situation in western Canada was something else again. Colleges came to the prairies anywhere from fifty to a hundred years later than in the east. They were established by transferring and adapting patterns already in existence within the nation as a whole; the independent sectarian institution of the Maritimes, the federated colleges of Ontario integrated into a provincial system, or the extra-provincial affiliations provoked by an inflexible one-province – one-university philosophy now more or less associated with schools and departments of education. Western foundations, however, took form in more sophisticated times and under more prosperous initial conditions which have made them in many ways more progressive than those of the east. It is not at all impossible that the successful structures of tomorrow are even now being produced in Winnipeg and Edmonton rather than in Toronto, Montreal, Halifax, or Antigonish.

MOTIVATION OF THE FOUNDERS

The chronicles of individual Catholic colleges, the story of their founding and development, which form the bulk of the present study, indicate how complex is the motivation for the founding of Catholic colleges in English-speaking Canada. A brief look at the contributing elements to this motivation at the outset will both clarify the issues which arise in the various stories and simplify the assessment or appraisal reserved for the final section.

General objectives can be said to lie behind every foundation, even the most utilitarian, pragmatic, and capricious. Of such objectives, the most general and the most real is the desire to give expression, in founding a college, to the right of a community to religious and civil liberty. Such an expression may be patent as when St Mary's College, Halifax, was conceived in a context of the penal laws and religious tests of Nova Scotia. Or it may be a sort of simmering under the surface against provincial or institutional inflexibility as when Catholic colleges on the prairies had to work out a precarious arrangement, a sort of *actio in distans*, with Ottawa University, or when St Mark's College in Vancouver had to penetrate the veritable plastic dome of exclusivity with which the University of British Columbia had covered itself. But the expression of social liberty is always a basic ingredient of the complex action by which a religious or any other kind of college is brought into existence. There are other general objectives which apply particularly to Catholic colleges, and they are these: the expression of an awareness that teaching has always been accepted as a proper function of christians and that they have as communities, or institutionally in the Church as a whole, provided the prototype of most contemporary forms of education; the expression too of the awareness that the Church has a twofold educational mission – to man, whose total development is her proper concern, and to learning itself as a necessary component in human culture. This last item, the mission to learning itself, was not a prominent motive in the founding of the first Canadian Catholic colleges, but it gradually became more noticeable as interest and means combined to make possible the building up of characteristic library holdings or the taking on of specialized research appropriate to Church-related institutions or the undertaking of special services for the Catholic and the general public.

Specific objectives are a more tangible and more readily identifiable motivating ingredient in the founding of Catholic colleges. First and strongest among these, certainly in the case of all the early foundations, and in the case of most men's colleges down to the present time, has been the task of preparing young men to enter theology and the priesthood. The histories of St Dunstan's, St Francis Xavier, and St Michael's make this abundantly clear. Other students were not excluded, indeed, they were wanted, but the colleges would not likely have been started for them alone. It was the bishop in every case who actually called the college into existence and he was specifically looking for priests to help him serve the Catholics who had come to Canada. So strong was this objective that the admission requirements for theology in Quebec and Rome exerted a total influence on the selection and training of faculty and on the structure of the curriculum. It was a long time before administrators gave much thought to what the Protestant colleges were doing or to the admission requirements of the professional faculties in Canadian and American universities. The importance given the preparing of candidates for the ministry in American colleges before the Revolution and of the first Protestant colleges may be a matter of some debate,[2] but there can be no debate about it in the case of the Catholic men's colleges of English Canada founded before the twentieth century.

Another specific objective always present in the founding of a Catholic college was the pastoral. This kind of motivation took two forms: the creating of an educational community which would promote morality and virtue among its members, and the locating in that community of a supply of priests to assist the bishop and parish clergy with the care of souls in the diocese. The pastoral fact in the life of Catholic professors is a difficult one to assess. Psychologically, professors in holy orders seem to require an apostolate of service wider than the strictly academic; practically, the dioceses have been so short of priests that such services have simply had to be demanded and rendered. The system, however, has created a built-in hazard handicapping from the beginning the full academic and scholarly development of Catholic colleges and their faculties, and producing among other anomalies, situations in which professors are appointed only because they are priests, and promoted by being given a parish; or in which the professional leisure which professors require is misconstrued by the bishop, by priestly colleagues, and even by the professor himself as neglect of duty toward the faithful.

Other motives of a more venal kind occasionally entered into the psychology of a given foundation. The founding of St Andrew's (eastern PEI) by Bishop MacEachern and of Iona College (eastern Ontario) by Bishop Macdonell was in part intended to demonstrate that the Maritimes and Upper Canada were ready to become new dioceses, separate from Quebec. The opening of St Michael's was expected to make the Catholics of Toronto eligible along with the Anglicans, the Methodists, and the Presbyterians, to say nothing of the Catholics of the older and smaller diocese of Kingston, for government

2 Edward J. Power, *A History of Catholic Higher Education in the United States,* Milwaukee: Bruce, 1958, 17; and D.C. Masters, *Protestant Church Colleges in Canada,* Toronto: University of Toronto Press, 1966, 5

grants. Sometimes, the opening of a college was to provide expansion for a religious order or congregation or to serve for the training of its own members. St Lawrence College, Loyola, and Marianopolis were to serve the interests of an English-speaking constituency in the province of Quebec. Motives like these were not primary or decisive but they entered into the public image of the institutions concerned and have introduced both sectarian and political angles into their history.

One such motive, rare among Catholic colleges, but common among Protestant, was the desire to strengthen and perpetuate British culture in the narrower sense and strong ties with the British government. Indeed, the Simcoe Papers indicate the existence of a policy on the part of the government to encourage such an attitude. Writing to Henry Dundas, Secretary of State for Colonial Affairs, Simcoe advises: 'The higher (education) must be indebted to the liberality of the British Government, as, owing to the cheapness of education in the United States, the gentlemen of Upper Canada will send their children there which would tend to pervert their British principles.'[3] Simcoe also speaks of coalescing 'the different customs of the various descriptions of settlers' into one nation, and he makes it quite clear what he meant by this expression: 'From these distinct parts would [we] there establish one nation – and thereby strengthen the union with Great Britain and preserve a lasting obedience to His Majesty's authority.'[4] Alexander Macdonell was one Catholic bishop who subscribed to these ideas firmly. He wanted the Catholic Church to be financially dependent upon the British government; he wanted to have Catholic school teachers who were 'educated in Britain, or at least by those who have been themselves educated in the genuine principles of the British Constitution.'[5] This theme runs in a convincing way through all his efforts to establish churches and schools in Upper Canada and explains in part the sympathetic treatment his Kingston college long received from the government of Upper Canada.

BEGINNINGS OF HIGHER EDUCATION IN NOVA SCOTIA

It is almost impossible to determine at what date the oldest Catholic universities of Nova Scotia, St Mary's of Halifax and St Francis Xavier of Antigonish, can properly be described as providing post-secondary education. It is almost equally difficult to draw a line of demarcation between secondary and post-secondary education. To rely entirely on

3 Hodgins, *Documentary History*, I, 11
4 Ibid., 12
5 H.J. Somers, *The Life and Times of the Honourable and Right Reverend Alexander Macdonell, D.D., First Bishop of Upper Canada, 1762–1840,* Washington, 1931, 169

the dates of government charters, 1841 for St Mary's and 1866 for St Francis Xavier, is almost meaningless since these charters only confer legal recognition on programmes already in existence and already regarded, with considerable justification by the administration concerned, as of college or university level. Certainly the programmes provided for those of their students who were to apply for admission to theology in Quebec or Rome were comparable with those of King's and Dalhousie. That St Mary's and St Francis Xavier were *de facto* essentially secondary schools with special advanced instruction for candidates seeking admission to theology makes a defensible but not an altogether fair thesis when proposed largely only to show that they were functioning at a somewhat lower level than King's or Dalhousie. They were not. Absolutely speaking, however, there was a developing sense of standards and function in the minds of bishops and college administrators, an awareness closely interwoven with the objective of having in Nova Scotia a major seminary in the Tridentine sense of the word.

The practical problem for the historian is to determine when the concept of major seminary in the minds of the bishops was in part met by actually existing schools of the province. An attempt will be made to do so by providing a brief pre-history of the circumstances out of which these two Catholic university colleges emerged.

1802

Between 1802 and 1808 Father Edmund Burke took positive steps towards founding in Halifax a college or seminary. These steps are sketched in O'Brien's *Memoirs of Rt. Rev. Edmund Burke.*[6] The opening of such a school, college, or seminary was an enormous financial undertaking for the small Catholic settlement in Halifax at the turn of the century. It also contravened the laws of both England and the colony, as the early (1766) statutes of Nova Scotia make quite clear: 'If any popish recusant, papist or person professing the popish religion, shall be so presumptuous as to set up any school within this province, and be detected therein, such offender shall for every such offense, suffer three month's imprisonment without bail or mainprise, and shall pay a fine to the King of ten pounds.'[7] Burke's project, then, called for funds, for relaxation or dispensation from the statutes, and for teachers.

Burke got funds for his school, though not all that he hoped for. These funds included a valuable property donated by a Mrs Blake. He

6 Cornelius O'Brien, *Memoirs of Rt. Rev. Edmund Burke,* Halifax, 1894, 79–86
7 'Act Concerning Schools and Schoolmasters,' 28 June 1766, *Anno Sexto Georg III, Cap. VII.* And for the problem generally, see A.A. Johnston, *A History of the Catholic Church in Eastern Nova Scotia,* Antigonish, 1960, I, 77.

also proceeded with the erection of a building on the corner of Barrington Street and Spring Garden Road: 'A house of two stories, with kitchen and dining room in the basement, as well as cellar and store-room. It is sixty feet by forty inside the walls.'[8] This building, which was to become known as the Glebe House, from the use to which the top part was put when it became apparent that the school could not open, has its own interesting story. It stood on the busy corner of downtown Halifax for 89 years and was a wellknown landmark. The lower part was rented out by Burke, before 1805, to a Mr Doyle, who dug the well in the basement which for many year supplied the Glebe House with the spring water for which it had a local reputation. It was also in this house that the first Catholic boys' school was located in 1818, and where a number of seminarians were prepared for ordination in 1819 and 1820.[9] After the death of Bishop Burke in 1820, the building was used as a residence by Lawrence O'Connor until 1829 when it was bought for St Mary's Church.[10]

Dispensation from the statutes proved a more difficult matter at first than the erection of a building. In 1802 Burke placed before Sir John Wentworth, lieutenant-governor of Nova Scotia, a memorial 'praying leave to establish a Roman Catholic seminary in Halifax.' This was duly forwarded to Lord Hobart, secretary of state, with the recommendation that it be refused. The memorial was resented by Bishop Inglis and other anti-Catholics who not only pressed for its denial but began to investigate the possibility of the presence of Catholic teachers in any Nova Scotia schools with a view to prosecuting them under the penal laws. Opposition of this kind in Nova Scotia with all its Methodists and Presbyterians, equally conscious of their inequality before the law, turned out not to be insuperable. More discouraging for Burke was the unwillingness of the bishop of Quebec to throw his weight behind the memorial lest he thereby risk the security of the Catholics of Quebec, who were not encumbered with similar penal restrictions. It is not surprising, however, in view of the generally hostile attitude to penal laws as such among Nova Scotians, that Burke had by 1805 reached some kind of understanding with officialdom and that he could write: 'Lord Selkirk has addressed the Secretary of State regarding the opening of our school, and there will be no difficulty in obtaining passports for teachers, but unfortunately none can be found.'[11]

8 O'Brien, *Memoirs*, 81
9 Ibid., 119
10 John L. Quinan, 'History of St Mary's,' in *The Gazette*, Halifax, NS, 24 June, 1926
11 O'Brien, *Memoirs*, 84

It was this last-mentioned factor, the difficulty of getting qualified teachers, that was decisive in this first attempt to open a college. Between 1805 and 1808 Burke sought teachers from the bishops of Ireland, the Sacred Congregation of Propaganda (*de propaganda fide*), Bishop Plessis of Quebec, and from Father Brzozowski, general of the Jesuits, who was, during the period of the suppression, carrying on the administration of the order from Russia. It looked for a while as though the Jesuits might come to Nova Scotia. Two priests of the Society, Fidelis Grivel and Felix Syglinski, were named for the Halifax college, but arrangements to have the ecclesiastical restrictions relaxed as requested by Bishop Plessis fell through when Pius VII, though himself personally sympathetic towards the Jesuits, preferred not to override the objections of Propaganda.

By 1808 the first attempt to open a Catholic college or seminary in Nova Scotia had failed. The project was something more than a dream in that a building went up, the penal laws were in some sense tested, and negotiations for a staff were carried on; but in so far as no administration got appointed, no students were enrolled, no classes held, no name so far as is known (though it could only have been St Mary's) was selected, it can hardly be said that an institution of Catholic higher education had yet been born.

1816

In 1816, shortly before either was named a bishop, Edmund Burke and Angus Bernard MacEachern discussed plans for a regional seminary at Arisaig to educate priests for the maritime provinces.[12] Their reasons for thinking this way are interesting. They had since the beginning of the century been concerned about the training of local boys for the priesthood. Burke, as already seen, planned his own seminary as early as 1802; the same year MacEachern sent to Quebec the first Nova Scotian seminarian, Donald MacGillivray, who did not complete his course. In 1807 a plan was proposed to provide for the education of priests by levying a tax of 20 shillings a year on the Scottish families of Prince Edward Island, Cape Breton, and the adjacent parts of Nova Scotia. The proposal, made in the first instance by Captain John MacDonald, the Laird of Glenaladale, was not kindly received by the people generally. The plan was modified in 1810 to a subscription campaign. From 1812 onwards there were seminarians in Quebec preparing to work in the Maritimes. The expense continued to be troublesome, partly because there was so little money available, partly because

12 Johnston, *A History*, 414

there was no convenient way of transmitting funds to Quebec. On one later occasion, Burke actually had two of his boys, William MacLeod of Arisaig and John Chisholm of Antigonish, dropped from the Quebec seminary for non-payment of fees. Only the personal charity of Bishop Plessis prevented their being sent home; they were placed instead, at Plessis' expense, in a smaller seminary at Nicolet.

So in 1816 there was a problem of expense. There was also an academic matter: MacEachern felt that his boys should be made to read Gaelic in the seminary so that they would be able on their return to minister properly to the needs of their Gaelic-speaking parishioners. It is thus quite understandable that Burke and MacEachern should in 1816 be thinking of a seminary in the Maritimes and that they should plan to locate it in the convenient parish of Arisaig where costs would be minimal and where Gaelic was spoken. This too, however, was a visionary plan never to be realized.[13]

1817-20

Burke was named bishop of Sion and vicar apostolic of Nova Scotia in 1817, and was consecrated during July 1818. He had succeeded in getting the ecclesiastical province of Nova Scotia separated from the archdiocese of Quebec and placed directly under the Holy See. There was an implied affront to Quebec in the memorial which he submitted directly to Rome in 1815 without passing it through the hands of his bishop. Such circumstances made him all the more anxious to be completely free of Quebec and to have in Halifax all the facilities of an independent diocese, particularly his own seminary.

Burke already had two children's schools: one of these, enrolling about 200 girls, was staffed at the expense of a society of Catholic women; the other, with about 100 boys, was located in his own house – the Glebe House built originally to house a college or seminary – and was staffed by a priest and two seminarians.[14] The seminarians were part of another project, the preparing of local candidates for the priesthood. It is not possible to say how many young men actually studied in this informal theologate, but it is known that five priests were ordained from it in 1819 and 1820. Burke died in November 1820. His seminary experiment, as it may fairly be called, seems not to have been continued

13 John C. Macmillan, *The Early History of the Catholic Church in Prince Edward Island*, Quebec, 1905, 189–201; Johnston, *A History*, 264–8; *Mémoire sur les Missions de la Nouvelle Ecosse, du Cap Breton, et de l'Ile du Prince-Edouard de 1760 à 1820*, Quebec: C. Darveau, 1895, 250–1

14 'History of the Institute, Chapter LXXXIV: St Mary's College, Halifax,' *The Christian Brothers' Educational Record* (1941), 12–17

during the six and a half years in which the see remained vacant after his death, nor to have been revived in any way by his successor, Bishop Fraser.

1824–32

The Grammar School Act of 1811 is a key event in the development of higher education in Nova Scotia. It provided aid for secondary or high school education without which there could be little call for colleges and universities. The development of Pictou Academy provides the pilot case. There was in Pictou a private school at the primary or common level from about 1808. Thomas McCulloch opened another school, also a private school, and also covering at least the more advanced part of the common school curriculum, but covering too the high school or grammar school programme. In opening the school McCulloch had in mind the qualifying of boys for admission into some future Presbyterian seminary. He ran a good school which provided an ideal base for one of the new grammar schools eligible for subsidy under the terms of the act of 1811. It was so qualified. Boys who were brought up to college admission level in this grammar school formed the nucleus of the Pictou Academy which emerged from it, and which is properly regarded as Nova Scotia's oldest institution of higher learning after King's College. Pictou Academy had an existence of its own by 1816, and received its first grant independent of the grammar school in 1819. The academy flourished through the twenties, but fell into financial difficulties at the end of the decade and had to be reorganized. A bill of 1832 carried out this reorganization by broadening the board of trustees (e.g. Bishop Fraser, among others, was added), providing a principal's salary, and strengthening the position of the grammar school division at the expense of the academy proper. The reorganized academy continued to operate until 1838 when Dr McCulloch yielded to the pressure put upon him to accept the presidency of Dalhousie.

The Pictou pattern – private school becoming subsidized grammar school then extending its work into the college level – reappears with variations in eastern Nova Scotia.

Rev. W.B. MacLeod of Arisaig, a native Nova Scotian, whose seminary training was, as has been seen, a matter of some financial embarrassment to Bishop Burke,[15] and who was ordained for Bishop Plessis and the archdiocese of Quebec, was appointed immediately after his ordination to the Bras d'Or missions. He undertook the private tutoring of boys at Grand Narrows. His letter of 21 June 1824 to his ordinary,

15 Johnston, *A History*, 377–9

Bishop Plessis, is evidence of his vision of something distinguishable from the common school and pointing towards the study of theology: 'For quite a while I have been thinking about great projects. My idea has been that, if I ever succeeded in getting the means and facility, I would have with me a certain number of chosen young men, to train them in the chant and the ceremonies of the Church, and also to teach them something of the rudiments of Latin ... I already have three young men under my care, learning Latin. One of them is here with me, and I am maintaining the other two in a Latin school at Antigonish. These, My Lord, are the fine plans of your poor child. I beg Your Lordship to deign to let me know what you think of them.'[16]

The one student working with MacLeod became nine students within a few months and these private pupils formed the nucleus of the more formal school opened a short time later at East Bay with the newly-arrived Scottish immigrant Malcolm MacLellan as schoolmaster. We have as yet little precise information about the East Bay school, and cannot properly describe it as a grammar school because it seems to have been the private project of a priest working out of Quebec rather than a project of the government of Nova Scotia. It was, however, known locally as 'the college,' and three of its 'graduates' – Colin Francis MacKinnon, Neil MacLeod, Robert MacEachern – were admitted to the Urban College of the Propaganda in Rome in 1828.

In this same year, 1828, Bishop Fraser succeeded in obtaining a grant of £50 from the Nova Scotia legislature for a grammar school at Antigonish, a grant which was renewed annually until 1832.[17] MacLeod of East Bay tried to obtain an *exeat* from the archdiocese of Quebec in order to be able to teach in this school.

It is from this point that one can enter properly into the history of St Francis Xavier College and University.

BEGINNINGS OF HIGHER EDUCATION IN UPPER CANADA

The earliest documents referring to the possible establishment of a Catholic seminary or college in Upper Canada are letters written by Alexander, later Bishop, Macdonell to Lord Drummond, Lord Bathurst, and Lord Durham between 1815 and 1817. Alexander Macdonell was by this time spokesman for the Catholic settlers of Upper Canada. He had come out to Canada in 1804, having previously been the organizer and for eight years chaplain of the then disbanded Glengarry Fencible Regiment. With many officers and men of that regiment he settled in

16 Ibid., 479–80.
17 *Provincial Archives of Nova Scotia*, Treasurer's Account Book, v.400

Glengarry County and became the third pastor of the mission of St Raphael. As a distinguished pensioner and pro-British spokesman, he maintained close contact with both the government in Canada and the colonial office in London, and was well informed on all aspects of developments in Upper Canada. By 1815 there was much talk about the need for higher education in the colony, talk which was to culminate in the chartering of King's College at York in 1827 and the incorporation of Upper Canada College in 1829.

It is not surprising that Macdonell should investigate the possibility of a seminary or college at St Raphael's. A particularly informative letter of of January 1817 written in London to Lord Bathurst, secretary of state for the Colonial Department, was intended to encourage the department itself to suggest the offering of such assistance rather than have himself and the Catholic settlers put in a position where they would have to apply for it through the legislature. This letter sets forth his plan to set up a seminary: 'It is my intention to establish the principal School at my own place of residence in the County of Glengarry, in order that it may be under my own superintendence and direction, and for this School, I wish to procure a few Masters in this country [i.e. England], of superior talents and learning, capable of educating gentlemen's sons upon a more liberal and extensive plan than would be necessary for the lower class of settlers. This would preclude the necessity of sending them to the United States, or to the French seminaries of Lower Canada, as has been the case hitherto.' Later in the same letter this 'principal School' is spoken of as 'this Roman Catholic Seminary.'[18] What Macdonell seems to have had in mind is a Catholic institution which might on the one hand qualify for the assistance provided under the bill of 1807 and subsequent bills for schools and teachers, and on the other serve in some capacity as a post-secondary school and a training school for priests.

This seminary did not become a reality right away. Macdonell brought out three schoolmasters, Richard Hammond, John Murdoch, and Angus McDonald, and three priests, Angus Macdonell (a nephew), William Fraser, and John MacDonald, placing them, however, in grammar schools and missions. He was a long time getting payments for them in spite of Bathurst's favourable reception of his request. Macdonell felt that Dr Strachan and Justice Powell were responsible for blocking payment. At any event when, late in 1825, after many rep-

18 Macdonell to Bathurst, 10 Jan. 1917, printed in J.G. Hodgins, *Historical and Other Papers and Documents*, Toronto, 1911, I, 10–11. See also Macdonell to Lord Durham in J.G. Hodgins, *Documentary History*, III, 146.

resentations and memorials, considerable payment did come through from English, not Canadian sources, Macdonell lost much of it through the failure of his London bankers Maitland Garden and Aldjo with whom it had been deposited.[19]

In 1819 Macdonell was named a bishop, vicar apostolic of Upper Canada and titular bishop of Rhosina, but his precise status within the ecclesiastical province of Quebec was not determined until shortly before his consecration in 1820. What with the delicate task of establishing a Roman Catholic hierarchy in Upper Canada and the withholding of promised funds, his proposed seminary received little attention. A start was made, however, in his own residence at St Raphael's in 1821 when he was able to report to Bishop Plessis that he had one student reading theology under Father John MacDonald and teaching 'the boys I have in the house.' He had, he said, ten boys studying Latin at the time. This college was effectively opened under the name of Iona College in 1826 with Father W.P. MacDonald, recently arrived in the diocese, as its first rector.[20] In 1827 there were seven students enrolled in theology and five preparing for it, and a small addition was made to the building. Rather interesting is the list of books he asked Bishop Weld to acquire for the college: several sets of the excellent Bossuet and Huet edition of the Latin classics *ad usum serenissimi delphini*, sets of Greek classics, Latin and Greek grammars and dictamens, books on natural and experimental philosophy, on mathematics and astronomy, Lingard's tracts, Crevier's *Roman Emperors*, Blair's *Lectures* and *Nature Displayed*, Duncan Logré's *Eloquence of the English Bar and Senate*, as well as the usual catechisms, prayer books, and spiritual and apologetic writings. The following year, 1828, he reported 'eight ecclesiastics' in the second year of their theology, one in the first year and two in philosophy, all excellent subjects although of ordinary talents.[21] In a letter to W.J. O'Grady, parish priest of York, 16 January 1830, Bishop Macdonell speaks of having spent over 3000 pounds on this building, plus 300 pounds a year on board, clothing, and other necessities of from seven to nine or ten young men.

This college, or seminary section of an academy, as the case may be, operated at St Raphael's for over ten years. Macdonell was not present to superintend the college as much as he thought he would be when planning it. On 26 January 1828, before the college was in full opera-

19 Somers, 50–64
20 Ibid., 81, 97
21 Macdonell to Weld, 26 Nov. 1828, Ontario Archives, *Macdonell Letters*, v.4, 508 and 6 May 1827, v.2, 273–4

tion, his diocese was cut off from Quebec and established with Kingston (Regiopolis) as the official see. This change removed the bishop from St Raphael's a great deal of the time. After the college was opened he visited England to raise funds and support. Following his return, he acquired a residence in York – still of course in his own diocese – where he spent much of his time until 1836.[22] In late 1829 or early 1830, he purchased a house and property in Kingston for a thousand pounds. He was already thinking of moving his college there because he wrote to Bishop Weld that the house 'is a very large and well built one and would make a very good place with very little expense for educating ecclesiastics.'[23] When Macdonell himself removed to Kingston in 1836 it was a foregone conclusion that a college would be placed there.

On 4 March 1837, an act of incorporation gave civil existence to the College of Regiopolis to be erected in Kingston.[24] On 10 October of the same year, at a meeting held in the bishop's residence, it was definitely decided to proceed with the college, to canvas funds for it in Europe, and to erect a substantial stone building. The plan to move Iona was delayed by the outbreak of the Rebellion and by the decision to put up the new buildings in stone. On 10 June 1838, the cornerstone was laid with the bishop and his coadjutor Bishop Gaulin present and Dr Rolph of Ancaster delivering the address.[25] The building was located on Sydenham Street and is now part of the Hôtel Dieu Hospital.

Bishop Macdonell's idea seems to have been that his college would, when opened, be full-grown: with buildings, a staff, and government financing. This idea persisted. It was also his idea that it be part of any major provincial university complex which might come into existence. In 1837 the King's College charter was amended and the way cleared for the establishment of a provincial university. Macdonell succeeded

22 Bishop Macdonell acquired a house at Nelson (Jarvis) and Duchess Streets. The house was known as Russell Abbey long before Macdonell bought it. Russell Abbey was the house of Peter Russell, an Irishman and half-pay veteran who came out with Governor Simcoe and acted as head of the government during Simcoe's absences. See Frank Norman Walker, *Sketches of Old Toronto*, Toronto, 1965, 62.

23 Macdonell to Weld, 10 Mar. 1830, Ontario Archives, *Macdonell Letters*, VI, 762–3

24 An Act to incorporate ... a Board of Trustees ... of a Roman Catholic College at Kingston ... 'The College of Regiopolis' ... (7 William IV, ch.56; 4 Mar. 1837).

25 Thomas Rolph, physician and author, practised medicine in Ancaster, Upper Canada, 1835–9. He was a member of the Royal College of Surgeons, England, and travelled much in America. See his *A Brief Account Together with Observations Made During a Visit to the West Indies, and a Tour Throughout the United States of America in Parts of the Years 1823–33, Together with a Statistical Account of Upper Canada*, Dundas, Upper Canada, 1836. After returning to England in 1839 he became a Canadian immigration agent.

in incorporating his college before King's College actually opened. King's College only opened in 1843, although its original charter had been obtained by Bishop Strachan in 1827, and had called for the opening of an Anglican college subject to no external control. The amendment of 1837 reduced the role of the church and gave the state some authority and control. All this before the college ever opened its doors.

The first rector of Regiopolis College was the bishop's nephew and vicar general, Angus Macdonell, who supervised the construction of the college and then took over its administration. Father Angus was one of the original trustees of the college, a member of the Council of Public Instruction for many years, and later a member of the first senate of the University of Toronto.

Bishop Alexander Macdonell went to the old country in 1839 to raise funds for his college. Father Angus and Dr Rolph accompanied him; Bishop Gaulin, coadjutor since 1833, remained in charge of things at home. The old bishop died abroad in 1840 and Gaulin succeeded him. The college at this stage was developing very slowly, but it opened its Kingston doors some time before 1843, largely if not entirely as a preparatory school with seminarians attached. Things were not easy. As if pioneer conditions and lack of funds were not enough, Gaulin became incapacitated. Although he lived on until 1857, his see had to be entrusted to a coadjutor, Bishop Patrick Phelan, who was brought to Kingston in 1843 from Bytown where he had opened and pioneered the city's original parish.

After 1843, however, things began to pick up and it looked for a while as if the 'rely-on-the-government' policy of the Macdonells, and now of Bishop Phelan too, might pay off. Phelan was anxious to have the Oblates replace him in Bytown. In December 1843 he was corresponding with Bishop Bourget of Montreal about the possibility of opening a college in Bytown too. He was at the same time busy trying to get his own Regiopolis included among the affiliated colleges of the projected Toronto university, and the Baldwin University Bill, which was introduced into the legislature in 1843, but not passed, included Regiopolis nominatim.

This bill of Baldwin's was an interesting one. It would have brought Queen's, Victoria, King's, and Regiopolis into a University of Toronto. The bill was perhaps more than generous to Regiopolis in relation to the other colleges in that Regiopolis was not yet effectively in operation as a university college. The bill would, moreover, have necessitated certain changes in the college's incorporation; it would, for example, have altered its structure, changing the name and format of its corporation to 'the President, Masters and Scholars of the College of Regiopolis in the University of Toronto.'

The Baldwin government did not last and the bill (1843) disappeared with it; but the bill was significant none the less because Regiopolis was henceforth given full consideration in every effort of the legislature to replace King's College with a full-blown provincial university. Thus when the governor-general sent around in March 1846 a questionnaire asking the colleges where they stood on the university question, the opinion of Regiopolis was polled along with the others. The opinion expressed on this particular occasion by Bishop Phelan and the other signatories was that Upper Canada did not yet need a university, that the University of King's College Bill ought therefore to be repealed, that four colleges (King's, Victoria, Queen's, Regiopolis) and colleges of law and medicine should be chartered, and that Regiopolis did not want a share of King's College grant but a legislative grant of its own.[26]

It was in the course of this university controversy that Bishop Phelan, Angus Macdonell, and the board of Regiopolis realized that they would have to get a distinguishable college department into operation. The opening of such a department during 1846 was a legal and structural change rather than an educational one. However, from the fall of 1846 on there existed a legally recognizable college, distinct from the preparatory school and the theological seminary and comparable with Queen's and Victoria so far as the legislature of Upper Canada was concerned. The Sir John A. Macdonald bills of 1847 recognized this fact and proposed grants for Regiopolis as well as for the other university colleges. The Macdonald bills met a stormy reception. Even the Regiopolis board, which welcomed the grant recommendation, opposed the bills because they would establish a university which endangered the autonomy of their college.

On 5 November 1847, before the Macdonald bills had been set aside, Bishop Phelan and the priests of Kingston issued a public Address on the 'university question' to the Catholics of Upper Canada. Immediately afterwards a new petition, based on this letter, was forwarded to the legislature. This petition said in part:

Since the opening of the College of Regiopolis (at Kingston) several of such persons have lost no time in placing their sons in the Institution. If, then, through the liberality of your Honourable House, either from the property of the University of King's College, Toronto, or out of the proceeds of the

26 Hodgins, *Documentary History*, VI, 109–11

Jesuit's Estates, or from other sources at the disposal of the Provincial Government, the College of Regiopolis be established on a permanent and respectable basis, so as to be able to support a staff of well-trained professors for the upper branches of learning, Catholic parents in both portions of the Province, will feel security and encouragement, in confiding their children to that Institution.

Signed: Patrick Phelan, coadjutor, and 25 other RC citizens – 5 November 1847. A short time after this petition was submitted, and when it became clear that no university bill would be passed during the 1847 session, the usual aid was voted for the approved colleges. For the first time Regiopolis was included, being granted a subsidy of 500 pounds.[27] The policy continued. In 1856 the amount was raised to 750 pounds and in 1858 it was changed to 3000 dollars. Grants to colleges continued annually until the passing of the Confederation Act.

Regiopolis College was, with its new eligibility for grants, in a financially viable if relatively impoverished situation. The board was determined to remain outside the university if it could possibly do so. Its great problem, of course, was the impossibility of acquiring a qualified teaching staff. The president, Angus Macdonell, and a few Kingston priests, looked after all instruction. Help was sought from the Jesuits in Montreal who were, however, equally embarrassed for men. In an attempt to help, they released one priest to Kingston in 1849, Remi Joseph Tellier, who became at once dean of the college, prefect of discipline, and professor of theology. Tellier remained only one year, moving on then to Toronto, where he thought for a time he might be useful in helping the newly arrived Bishop de Charbonnel set up a college of his own. Tellier seems not to have been impressed by the policy of the bishops of Upper Canada, who counted rather too heavily on government support in founding their colleges. Had the Jesuits the men and resources for such a project, Tellier would have established a more traditional Jesuit college somewhere in Upper Canada. Realizing this to be impossible in the circumstances of 1849 and 1850, he settled for a teaching post at the new Fordham University in New York.

Meanwhile the legislature of Upper Canada continued its efforts to establish its own university. In 1849 it passed the Baldwin University Bill, which transformed King's College into a non-denominational university with faculties of arts, law, and medicine and provision for representation of incorporated colleges on the senate. The incorporated colleges were presented with a dilemma by the new arrangement. All of them decided to remain outside the university; some of them decided

27 Ibid., VII, 65, 115

to become universities themselves. The latter was out of the question for Regiopolis, which had still to build itself up as an academically acceptable college, and this it proceeded with some success to do.

Regiopolis may have played some small role in keeping Queen's open and independent. The board of trustees of Queen's College, reporting in 1850, after the passing of the Baldwin University Act of 1849, to the Presbyterian Church of Scotland, and announcing the decision to keep Queen's open, gave as one of several reasons for their action the following:

The Roman Catholic Church has made Kingston the principal seat of their educational operation in Upper Canada, for which purpose it is admirably fitted by its central situation and the easy access to it from all parts of the Province. Should Queen's College be given up, as a Literary Institution, there would be no Protestant College in the whole vast distance from Montreal to Cobourg; and thus the whole of the superior education of those large sections of country, of which Kingston is the natural capital, would be made over to a Roman Catholic Seminary.[28]

During the fifties, students began to enrol in Regiopolis from various parts of Canada and from New York, Massachusetts, Vermont, New Jersey, and Michigan. A supplementary report submitted by the president, Angus Macdonell, to the government, and dated 26 April 1856, reads as follows:

What follows will, I believe, supply the deficiency: two of the students have received the BA in the University of Laval. Our present limited number of professors compels us for the present not to receive as boarders any but those who are intended for the ecclesiastical state, and, therefore, the number of boarders this year is limited to seventeen. There are 53 day scholars who are, I believe, all Roman Catholics.[29]

The rest of the Regiopolis story, so far as this introductory section is concerned, is the acquiring of a university charter in 1866 and the closing down of the college in 1869.

The Baldwin Bill of 1849 was replaced by a bill introduced by Francis Hincks and known as the University of Toronto Act (1853), an act which remained in effect until the Federation Act of 1887. By this act the university remained non-denominational but became a non-teaching examining body. The preparation of students for degrees was

28 Ibid., IX, 147–8
29 Ibid., XII, 288; six professors were listed for 1856, Ibid., XII, 242

handed over to University College. It was quite possible for other colleges in Ontario to affiliate and prepare students for examinations and degrees as well. The heads of Victoria, Queen's, Regiopolis – and also of new institutions: Knox 1844; Bytown 1848; Trinity 1851 – were given seats on the senate. The religious colleges took places on the senate, but they did not affiliate.

During 1862 the commissioners of the University of Toronto circulated questions to the religious colleges to ascertain what features they would look for in the university should they wish to affiliate. In principle, Trinity, Queen's, Victoria, and Regiopolis indicated approval of a system of affiliation which provided for a common university board, an equal curriculum, and a common examination.[30] Angus Macdonell replied for Regiopolis. He found the system of affiliation set up in 1853 inoperative, destructive of independence, and conferring no advantages on any possible participant. He would only lead his institution into an affiliation that assured equal standards through a common board of examiners, that supported a uniform curriculum, that apportioned monetary aid on a fixed rather than a fluctuating basis, that permitted affiliates to exercise university powers, and that functioned under a board of heads and delegates from all participating institutions large enough to outnumber government nominees two to one. Such terms were not likely to be met and his statement of them indicated no real sympathy for affiliation.

It is hardly surprising that Regiopolis should ultimately seek its own university charter. This happened on 18 August 1866 when the royal assent was given. The year 1866 was an active one for Catholic colleges: Regiopolis of Kingston and Ottawa College both acquired university status and two other Catholic colleges, St Jerome's of Berlin and the Ursuline Academy of Chatham, were incorporated. What lay behind all this activity was the special situation of the years between the Scott Act of 1863 which gave a quasi finality to separate Catholic public schools and the confederation achieved in 1867. Everyone felt that Confederation would tend to freeze the educational arrangements of the various provinces and that it would be wise to enter the new era in as firm and healthy a situation as possible.[31] For perhaps the first time the problems of separate schools and Catholic colleges became intertwined. A proposed petition to be circulated among Catholics in 1865 would seek for Ontario Catholics 'a university, normal school, numer-

30 Ibid., XVIII, 58
31 Franklin A. Walker, *Catholic Education and Politics in Upper Canada*, Toronto, 1955, 240–311

ous endowed academics and grammar schools,' all advantages enjoyed by Quebec Protestants.[32] The position of Angus Macdonell, president of Regiopolis and vicar general of the diocese was clear: 'Unless the Catholics of Upper Canada get fair play in school matters, they may as well close their separate schools. As long as they are compelled to have but schools of a low *grade*; as long as it will remain impossible for a Catholic child to enter a Catholic school and continue step by step from the primary school to the university out of which he would come and stand equal of his protestant neighbours; as long as Catholics are allowed to begin as Catholics but are forced to complete their education conducted on foreign principles and in a foreign language, or in one which, to all intents is Protestant, so long will the Catholics of Upper Canada have a just reason for discontent.'[33] In this spirit Lower Canadian Protestants and Upper Canadian Catholics somewhat feverishly sought new legislation, so as to be ready for the final passing of a Confederation Act. Such seems to be the context and the background of the incorporation of the University of Regiopolis in 1866.

Regiopolis had played the leading role in introducing Catholic higher education into Upper Canada. It was, however, the first victim of Canadian federation. Early in 1867 it became apparent that the province, now called Ontario, was going to discontinue its system of annual operating grants. A formal protest was lodged on behalf of the majority of the colleges in a strong letter to the secretary of state of the dominion government. The protest was signed by S.S. Nelles, president of Victoria College, William Snodgrass, principal of Queen's, and Bishop E.J. Horan, acting president of Regiopolis.[34] The protest was of no avail, and aid to denominational colleges was voted out in December 1868. The words of Dr McGill spoken in the Ontario house were strong, indeed. He rejected support for such colleges because it did 'a great deal of harm to University College,' was injurious in 'lowering the standard of higher education,' and precipitated and induced 'a large number of young men to run after a higher education.' Dr McGill, accordingly, recommended as follows: 'I have arrived at the conclusion that it would be a decided advancement to the cause of higher education, if these graduating bodies – as graduating bodies – were blotted out of

32 Ibid., 295, n.12
33 Ibid., 305–6
34 'Horan became bishop of Kingston in 1858, following the death of Phelan during the preceding year. Horan was brought in from Lower Canada where he had been in college work. He had supported Angus Macdonell in his drive for a university charter. It was a trial to him to have to preside over the new university's dissolution.' J.G. Hodgins, *The Establishment of Schools and Colleges in Ontario, 1792–1910*, Toronto, 1910, III, 155

existence. Let them all be transformed into good High Schools, and they would be incomparably more public benefit than at present.'[35] Not all subscribed to all these reasons. Certainly few would today. Denominational education at the university level continued. So far as Catholic higher education was concerned, leadership in Ontario was taken over by institutions like Ottawa College and St Michael's College of Toronto, which had the contributed resources of religious communities behind them. Regiopolis had to close its doors in 1869 and when it was able to re-open them it was as a secondary, not a post-secondary, institution.

The foregoing accounts demonstrate that preliminary and experimental activity, with the founding of a small seminary in mind, preceded the establishment of the first post-secondary institutions in the Maritimes and eastern Ontario. There was no comparable preparatory stirring in the Montreal area because pre-seminary instruction for English-speaking Catholics was available in the already existing *collèges*. There was a period of such preliminary activity in the Toronto area also, but it was much briefer there because the resources of religious communities were called on.

Toronto Catholics seem not to have been college-conscious before 1850. From 1826 on, Toronto was located ecclesiastically in the diocese of Kingston, which meant that the Iona-Regiopolis project was a Toronto project too. Toronto became a separate diocese in 1842. Its first bishop, Michael Power, was far too preoccupied with the immense problem of organizing his parishes spread out over the entire western portion of Upper Canada, and then of coping with local plague conditions, to think of setting up a seminary of his own. Power himself contracted the plague and died in 1847. The diocese was without a bishop until the appointment of Armand François Marie, comte de Charbonnel, in 1850. De Charbonnel was a Sulpician who had for a time worked in Montreal but who had returned to France where he was living in semi-retirement when asked to accept the appointment as second bishop of Toronto. Being a Sulpician, he had a seminary project in mind even before leaving France to take up residence in Toronto, and he brought several priests and ecclesiastical students to America with him. One of the priests to accompany him was Patrick Molony, the Irish-born Basilian, professor of English in the Little Seminaries at Feysin and Vernoux, near the Basilian college at Annonay where de Charbonnel himself had once been a student. Molony and de Charbonnel discussed plans for a Little Seminary in Toronto even as they

35 Hodgins, *Documentary History*, XXI, 50

crossed the Atlantic aboard the American steamer, the *Washington*, although Molony was not charged by Father Tourvieille to open a religious institution in Toronto but was only 'ceded to the bishop for a time.'[36] However, the first letters sent back to France by both de Charbonnel and Molony raised the question of the Basilians establishing a Little Seminary in Toronto. In fact it is clear that de Charbonnel had in mind not only the establishing of a Little Seminary, but of a secular college, and local missions as well, and that he expected the help of various religious orders in carrying out his plans. Four orders came to Toronto at this time: the Sisters of Loretto, the Sisters of St Joseph, the Christian Brothers, and the Basilian Fathers. There was talk of others coming too, the Sisters of Providence and the Jesuits. Had the Jesuits come it would have been for a college. Remi Joseph Tellier, described by Molony as a 'former rector of the Collège de Chamberry,' who had spent 1849–50 as dean of Regiopolis, spent the year 1850–1 in Toronto living with the bishop, Molony, and others in the cathedral palace. Tellier was offered some property by the Honourable John Elmsley to establish *un grand collège d'haut-Canada*, but the Jesuits had no men available for undertaking such a project. Tellier invited Molony to collaborate with him in opening a college for the bishop.[37] The project was abandoned partly because Molony was not eager for this kind of arrangement, partly because the Basilians were by now more or less committed to a Little Seminary.

During this year 1850–1, Molony's first year in Toronto, he improvised a kind of school or class in the palace. His school was neither a college nor a seminary. It was for young boys and seems to have taught mainly beginner's Latin and religion.[38] It was a kind of holding operation for the brothers, who were expected shortly. Indeed, five of them arrived during May 1851 and took up teaching in several places.[39] Molony's school could be construed as a forerunner of the college set up by the brothers in the cathedral palace in 1852; it was never thought of as related to the proposed Little Seminary.

Such preliminaries marked the first moves in the direction of post-secondary schools in Nova Scotia and Ontario. Similar stirrings preceded the opening of St Dunstan's College in Prince Edward Island, and the college at Bytown.

36 *Registre pour les copies des lettres de M. Tourvieille, 1850–1855*, Basilian Archives, Annonay, 13
37 Molony to Tourvieille, 15 Nov. 1851, Basilian Archives, Toronto
38 J.R. Teefy, 'The Life and Times of the Right Reverend Armand Francis Marie, Comte de Charbonnel,' in the *Jubilee Volume of the Archdiocese of Toronto*, ed. J.R. Teefy, Toronto, 1892, 205
39 Molony to Chavanon, 13 Nov. 1850, Basilian Archives, Toronto

BEGINNINGS OF HIGHER EDUCATION IN WESTERN CANADA

Western Canada had not the same kind of urgency to provide itself with an educated priesthood as central and eastern Canada. The immediate needs of the west were looked after by the older colleges and by the extension character of the seminaries and scholasticates set up in various eastern dioceses. The problem the west had to face was that Catholics were not adequately represented in the lay professions. The west needed Catholic colleges in order to encourage Catholics to go to university at all.[40]

Western Canada had also a special problem which central Canada and the Maritimes did not: whether, when colleges were actually being projected in Winnipeg and farther west, it might not be wiser to follow the pattern already set by the Catholic University of America. An opinion strongly expressed was that the west's best course was to avoid both eastern patterns; that is, local autonomy as established by St Francis Xavier, St Mary's, and Ottawa, and federation or affiliation as worked out by St Michael's. The west, it was said, should learn from Washington, Nijmegen, and Milan that the true future of Catholic higher education lay in the establishing of a Catholic University of Western Canada.[41]

Action to erect a Catholic university, that is, one set up by the entire American hierarchy, and intended to serve primarily the needs of the clergy, especially in the ecclesiastical or ecclesiastically-related disciplines of theology, canon law, and philosophy; and secondarily the general public in both these and other disciplines, was instituted by the American bishops in 1884 during the Third Plenary Council of Baltimore. Bishop Spalding of Peoria pushed this idea hard, as did Isaac Hecker, the Redemptorist who founded the Paulists. There was strong support of this idea of a Catholic University for the United States despite the rugged opposition of bishops McQuaid and Corrigan of Rochester and New York respectively.

The Catholic University was formally opened in Washington, 13 November 1889. It was at first a graduate school university only, limited mainly to ecclesiastically related disciplines. As interest and support grew, and as financial crises appeared, the university entered other fields, including undergraduate studies, in 1905.

This was not the direction taken thus far by higher education in Canada, where the pattern was not nearly so national in scope whether

40 See below on St Thomas More College, 350
41 George Thomas Daly, *Catholic Problems in Western Canada*, Toronto: Macmillan, 1921, ch.11, 196–236. See p.142 below for Teefy's attitude toward the affiliation of 1881.

in chartered institutions or in the federated college of St Michael's. Canadian institutions tended to emphasize higher education for Catholics under public auspices rather than higher Catholic education in the absolute sense projected in the American idea of a Catholic university. Rather naturally, those who were experimenting in federation were quick to point out the financial, ecumenical, and disciplinary advantages of a system of integrated collaboration with state universities over segregated and autonomous systems.

This difference of opinion led to one bitter exchange during the summer of 1916. The *Catholic Register* of Toronto ran in June a series of articles on the advantages of university federation. Although Henry Carr of St Michael's was not the writer of the series, his views were given a sympathetic airing. Federation was held up as the most viable pattern for future Catholic institutions of learning in Canada, the claims for federation constituted a kind of indictment of the national Catholic university as supported by the bishops of the United States. The experiment at Washington was described as not all that its supporters hoped it would be.

Bishop Michael Fallon took issue with the *Register's* articles. He wrote to Bishop Shahan, rector of the Catholic University of America, Washington, asking point-blank if in his opinion the Catholic University was a failure. Shahan replied that it was not a failure, that in fact the university's present staff, endowment, support, and academic development were by any standards good and augured well for the future of the national Catholic university in the United States. The university's thirty-four year history was, wrote Shahan, 'an irrefutable argument in favour of the ultimate success of a national Catholic university wherever and whenever undertaken.' Fallon sent his correspondence with Shahan to the *Register* and castigated that paper for its 'pernicious campaign to delude its readers into accepting a college federated with the University of Toronto as meeting the needs of the Catholic people in the matter of higher education.'[42]

Fallon's attitude made little impact in Ontario. His letter no doubt proceeded more from annoyance than conviction. At any rate, only three years later, he wrote personally to the board of governors of the University of Western Ontario requesting the affiliation of two colleges in his diocese.[43] The letter, however, reflected the existence of real opposition to federation, a resistance which was strongly voiced in western Canada by the Canadian Redemptorist, George Daly, in a spirited

42 *The Catholic Register*, Toronto
43 See below, 294

paper in his volume *Catholic Problems in Western Canada*. Daly hoped that the bishops of Manitoba, Saskatchewan, Alberta, and British Columbia would collaborate, as the bishops of Ireland had done in Newman's time and as the bishops of the United States were already doing, to establish a Catholic University of Western Canada.

In putting forth his suggestion, which was not especially realistic given the situation of higher education in Canada, Daly laid his finger on a weakness in the attitude of the governments of the western provinces to higher education: 'But no country in the British Empire has pushed the policy of monopolization of education so far as our western provinces. Under the specious plea of efficiency and the absurd reason of uniformity, they will not even grant charters to independent institutions of higher learning.'[44]

Daly was of the impression, however, that the Catholic University idea, if taken up, would extract a charter from some provincial government; he felt that one university would be quite enough: 'The Catholic population of western Canada is yet very limited. We cannot afford to scatter our forces and multiply our institutions. One university for all western Canada would be sufficient to meet the present requirements. The multiplication of inefficient universities is a calamity for genuine education.'[45]

Although some of Daly's points were incontrovertible, the practicability of a huge Catholic university was not. The only course humanly possible seems to have been the one followed for many years: affiliations with the provincial universities in the case of St Paul's, St Joseph's, St Thomas More, St Mark's, and Campion; affiliations outside the province by Notre Dame of Canada and Notre Dame of Nelson.

Many Catholic colleges in western Canada, both English and French, are indebted to Ottawa University for their very existence. Ottawa's generous policy to new institutions has sometimes been criticized both as a power play and as a failure to grasp the meaning of high academic standards. Since motives are always mixed, there could be some truth to these charges. But Ottawa's policy has on the whole been in the line of institutional liberty and academic non-conformity. History has accepted Ottawa's moves as a sort of anticipation of the direction higher

44 Daly, *Catholic Problems*, 219. On President Murray's fear in the early nineteen-twenties that the provincial government might grant a Roman Catholic institution a charter and thus withdraw the monopoly written into the University Act of 1907, see W.P. Thompson, *The University of Saskatchewan: A Personal History*, Toronto, University of Toronto Press, 1970, 56.
45 Ibid., 229

education was actually to take not only in the west but elsewhere in Canada.

Other factors entering the founding of Catholic colleges in the west are dealt with in the chronicles which follow in Parts II, III, and IV.

Moving into the chronicles of Canada's Catholic universities and colleges, east, centre, and west, it will become apparent how varied are the traditions and how unique the circumstances contributing to the making of each. As the chronicles are successively recorded, it will be seen that there is much in each that is never duplicated. It will also, of course, be seen that there are identifiable patterns running through them – transfer of emphasis from the providing of priests to the providing of lay leaders, separation of high school from college programmes, acceptance of controlled accreditation by provincial certificates, conscious awareness of degrees, admission of women, transfer from a structured classical to an elective programme, democratization of government, acceptance of the validity of high standards, and the dedication to the pursuit of learning for its own sake and God's.

In large part this development is to be explained by the personalities involved: Henry Carr, Athol Murray, Neil McNeil, Aquinas Thomas, Albert Zinger – the cheerful dreamers and impenitent gamblers of the founding generations; Banim, Malone, St James Hickey, Ruth, Sullivan, Somers, fighting fashioners of programmes and schools; Corona Sharpe, Judith Anne, Margaret Nims, Maura Geoffrey, Mueller-Carson, creative women of gentility and genius; McLuhan, Cummings, Pegis, the Monahans, Lynch, and MacNamara, brilliant, controversial, lovable-unlovable practitioners and scholars. But individuals do not explain the chronicles in their entirety. For this must be invoked the unquestioning dedication of the constituency at large.

II
EASTERN CANADA

St Dunstan's University

CHARLOTTETOWN, PEI

1831–1969

St Dunstan's University (now fully absorbed into the new provincial University of Prince Edward Island) was located on Malpeque Road, Charlottetown, Prince Edward Island, where the Trans-Canada Highway enters the city from the north. The St Dunstan campus was, at the time of its dissolution, composed of a group of eleven red brick buildings,[1] playing fields, and a college farm extending over a total area of 350 acres. The university had been offering degrees in arts, science, and commerce, diplomas or preliminary work in engineering, nursing, teaching, as well as pre-medical and pre-dental programmes.

ST ANDREW'S COLLEGE

Early in the eighteenth century, the Sulpicians seem to have seriously considered the suggestion of Father René Charles de Breslay that they establish a seminary on St John's Island not merely to provide priests for the Acadians of the Maritimes but because the island offered conditions ideal for the training of priests: a place of quiet among men of faith in an excellent agricultural area removed from the distractions of busy centres like Montreal and Quebec. The suggestion was not taken up. Indeed, so few priests were sent to the island to administer to its inhabitants that the need for a seminary early became impressed upon all who knew the situation. The settling on St John's Island in 1772 of Scottish Catholics from Uist did not change things. Frequently but one priest, at intervals two or three, looked after the island.[2]

1 These buildings are: a Main Building opened 1855, Dalton Hall residence 1919, the arena 1926, Science Building 1939, Memorial Hall residence 1947, chapel and dining hall 1950, heating plant and laundry 1950, gymnasium 1951, Marian College women's residence 1959, Kelley Library 1963, St Vincent Hall acquired for residence 1964.

2 The history of the early days of St Andrew's College and also of St Dunstan's during the nineteenth century comes largely from the following sources: John C. Macmillan, *The Early History of the Catholic Church in Prince Edward Island*, Quebec: Evénement, 1905; also his *The History of the Catholic Church in Prince Edward Island from 1835 to 1891*; *Mémoire sur les missions de la Nouvelle-Ecosse, du Cap Breton, et de l'Ile du Prince-Edouard de 1760 à 1820* (a reply to O'Brien's *Memoirs of Rt. Rev. Bishop Burke*, by a committee of priests of the diocese of Quebec), Quebec: Darveau, 1895; Lawrence Landrigan, 'Peter MacIntyre, Bishop of Charlottetown,' *Report of the Canadian Catholic Historical Association*, 21(1953), 81–92; Emmett J. Mulally, 'Religion and Educational Connecting Links between Prince Edward Island and Quebec Province, 1534–1948,' *Report of the Canadian Catholic Historical Association*, 15(1947–8), 15–21.

The first college or preparatory seminary came in 1831 when Angus Bernard MacEachern, first bishop of Charlottetown and New Brunswick, opened a secondary school in his home in the parish of St Andrew's. That the first advanced school or college should have opened in St Andrew's near the head of the Hillsborough River in the eastern part of the island, rather than in Charlottetown or some more populous area, came about as follows. The Catholic Scottish settlers of the island had provided in the first instance not a church building in which mass could be offered but a farm which if properly worked might be expected to support a priest, pay for the education of candidates for the priesthood and, when free of debt, provide a location first for a church, then for a school and eventually a college. It was thus that a farm was purchased at St Andrew's in 1794, a church built in 1805, a primary school opened in the parish house during the twenties and a secondary school or college in the same house in 1831. By the time St Andrew's College was opened, the larger centres of population were to be found elsewhere.

St Andrew's College was the first Catholic college in English-speaking Canada. The circumstances making its founding imperative are three in number: First, the thorny career of Catholic emancipation in Prince Edward Island revealed that the Catholic population had too few educated priests and laymen to cope effectively with problems which the drive for the removal of their civil disabilities entailed. The Catholic petition for ordinary enfranchisement was rejected in 1827 for a variety of reasons but prominent among them was the feeling that Catholics were not well educated. The failure of the petition made the founding of a college certain, and even though the British parliament enfranchised Catholics at home and abroad in 1829, and although the legislature of Prince Edward Island officially extended the franchise to the Catholics of the island 30 April 1830, the awareness of the need for a college had become so strong that its immediate founding was a certainty.

Second, in December 1826, the Cardinal Prefect of the Sacred Congregation of Propaganda (*de propaganda fide*) offered two full bursaries for theological students from the maritime missions who wished to pursue their studies at the congregation's Urban College in Rome. The offer made Bishop MacEachern painfully aware that the primary school which he was conducting in his own home at St Andrew's could not possibly qualify boys for these scholarships.

Third, the diocese had to have its own college, and if possible its own seminary, in order to demonstrate that it was in fact ready for its ecclesiastical emancipation from the archdiocese of Quebec. This emancipation took place 11 August 1829 when MacEachern's appointment was changed from titular bishop of Rosen to first bishop of Charlottetown, with jurisdiction over Prince Edward Island, the Magdalen Islands, and New Brunswick. An exchange of letters took place after the establishment of the new independent diocese in which Archbishop Panet of Quebec recommended the founding of a college and MacEachern made clear that he was already making preparations to found one. Indeed, he had invited the entire diocese, including New Brunswick, which was not very receptive, to rally to the support of a new college to be opened at St Andrew's.

When the opening of the college became a certainty, a qualified rector had to be found and induced to come. By good fortune, on a visit to Bishop Fraser in Halifax, MacEachern met and discussed his problem with Edward Walsh, an Irish priest who had been in Halifax for only a year and who had taught in an Irish college before coming to America. On the strong urging of the two bishops concerned, Walsh accepted the rectorship of the new St Andrew's College, which was formally opened in the parish house of St Andrew's 30 November 1831. The *Royal Gazette*, 20 December 1831, reports as follows: 'We understand that the new seminary called St Andrew's College, at the head of Hillsborough, was opened on the 30th November, 1831 being St Andrew's Day. The institution established under the patronage of the Roman Catholic Bishop of Charlottetown, and the Right Reverend Doctor Fraser, of Nova Scotia, is presided over by Reverend Mr Walsh, a Roman Catholic clergyman, of whose literary attainments report speaks very highly. A professor of mathematics has also been appointed.' Commenting on this report, the historian of the early history of the Church in Prince Edward Island points out that the college thus established was little more than a high school where young men were prepared to enter on their higher studies on foreign seminaries.[3] Nevertheless, the fact remains that the two maritime bishops had now taken a step in the direction suggested to the Sulpicians a century before by René Charles de Breslay.

Twenty students enrolled during the first term. Most followed a curriculum comprised of Greek, Latin, French, and mathematics, though a commercial course was also provided. The new college was provisionally incorporated by the colonial legislature on 6 April 1833. In preparation for incorporation the St Andrew's farm was turned over to a college board of trustees consisting of the two bishops, two priests, and four laymen. Interesting for the future role of St Andrew's and St Dunstan's in the life of Prince Edward Island is the specific statement in the request

3 Macmillan, *Early History*, 288

for incorporation that no religious test be required for admission, and that only Catholic boys would be compelled to assist at church services. The act of incorporation was delayed some time in London for technical reasons, but it became law in its revised form in 1835. Meanwhile the board successfully handled the affairs of the college on revenues from the farm which was being fully cultivated and on a small annual grant of 50 pounds from the legislature.

The academic affairs of the college were in the hands of its rector. He was hardly a free agent. He had not only to work under the close supervision of his bishop, but he had also to serve as parish priest of St Andrew's and its adjacent missions. Walsh remained in charge until 1835. MacEachern died in May of that year and was succeeded by Bernard D. MacDonald. In August Charles Macdonald, an Irish-born ecclesiastical student who had been teaching in the college, crossed to Antigonish for ordination. Young Macdonald was immediately appointed to St. Andrew's as rector of the college and pastor of the parish. The procedure became a pattern. In 1838 Macdonald was succeeded as college rector and parish priest by James Brady, who had read theology under Macdonald and taught on the staff of St. Andrew's concurrently. Brady was named rector the moment he received holy orders. In 1843 Pius McPhee became rector and the pattern was identical. It is no surprise in view of such procedures, regardless of how necessary they were, that the college had to close down in 1844. The fact that it was now located at some distance from a populous settlement had something to do with it, and, although Bishop MacDonald had expressed dissatisfaction that parish dances were being permitted to disturb seminary discipline, it was quite impossible for an academic institution to survive under such an administrative expedient. To the degree that St Andrew's had been founded to provide vocations, it had not done badly. Its alumni list includes a total of 22 priests and two bishops. 'Many prominent men,' we are told by J.B. in a not very accurate article in *The Prince Edward Island Magazine*, 'as Senator Perry, Alick Beaton, and Bishop Sweeny claimed it as their *Alma Mater*.'[4] The same J.B. goes on to say: 'Among the teachers of the old college were Rev. Messrs Brady and LeFrance, Mr Slattery and the great linguist Thomas Irwin, who there put together the alphabet of the Micmacs and wrote primary school books in that language.'[5] When St Andrew's was closed in 1844, plans were immediately prepared for the construction of a new college

4 J.B., 'Days of Bishop McEachern, 1790–1836,' *The Prince Edward Magazine*, 3(1901–2), 148–53
   5 Ibid., 151

on a farm, recently purchased by the bishop, on Malpeque road, a short distance out of Charlottetown. The new institution was slow abuilding, and Prince Edward Island was without a Catholic college for ten years.

ST DUNSTAN'S COLLEGE: 1855 TO ACCREDITATION

The new college, its name changed to St Dunstan's, was formally opened near Charlottetown on 17 January 1855. Preparations for the event had been going on slowly but more or less continuously ever since the closing of St Andrew's. The bishop had first purchased the large property on Malpeque Road, exhausting all available diocesan funds in doing so. By 1854 a wooden building, paid for largely with accumulating funds provided from France by the Society for the Propagation of the Faith, was completed. A pastoral letter of 21 September 1854, announced that the building was ready and would open in January. Difficult as had been the acquiring of land and erection of a building, still more difficult was the finding of suitable staff. Two theological students, Angus MacDonald and James Phalen, were finally assigned to the work, MacDonald being named rector even though not actually ordained when the college opened, and not to be until 21 November 1855. Phalen, his assistant, had been educated in Ireland but would not be ready for ordination until the summer of 1856. The young rector was a native Prince Edward Islander, had begun his theology at the seminary of Quebec and, forced by ill health, had completed it privately under Bishop MacDonald. Angus MacDonald was without any specialized academic training. Unlike his predecessors at St Andrew's, however, he was able to devote himself almost entirely to college work. It was his junior colleague, James Phalen who, following his ordination, had to do double duty as teacher and as an assistant in the cathedral of Charlottetown.

The college opened with 18 students, all it could take into residence. Bishop MacDonald followed its progress closely, himself driving regularly from his residence in Rustico to say mass for the students during the months preceding the young rector's ordination. The bishop actually moved into the college late in 1859 shortly before his death.

Angus MacDonald remained rector of St Dunstan's from 1855 to 1869, long enough to bring prestige and stability to the office. His rectorship was marked by the strenuous pursuit of two objectives: the endowment of the college and the public defence of the faith. In the first of these he was far from successful. St Andrew's had enjoyed a small annual government subsidy of 50 pounds a year over and above the students' fees and the revenue from the college farm. The government grant was discontinued when the college closed and not revived when St Dunstan's opened. MacDonald seems to have been hopeful that it would be revived and did not hesitate to lay a formal request for an annual grant before the legislature in 1858, even though the time was known to be inopportune for increased government spending. His request was turned down. A small *ad hoc* grant for the purchase of some college apparatus was made, but no regular subsidy voted. During 1861 the matter of endowment was discussed privately between Bishop MacIntyre and W.H. Pope, the colonial secretary, and others. The bishop and the college rector thought at the time that the government was ready to help the college, and they were both surprised and disappointed when told later that all discussions were predicated on the assumption that St Dunstan's would accept a secular status similar to that of Prince of Wales College. The unexpectedly rigid policy on this matter of government support for the college seems to have developed out of the so-called 'Bible Question,' a controversy which disturbed the free primary school system of the island in 1857, and in which Bishop MacDonald's celebrated letter on free education, dated Rustico, 7 November 1856, played a crucial part.[6] It became even more rigid in that, following the death of Bishop MacDonald, the rector of St Dunstan's seems to have fallen heir to the chore of speaking for the Church in public controversies. In fact, the rector's second request to the government came during the lull between his two bitter newspaper debates with Mr Pope on the subject of Roman Catholicism.

The first of these debates took place at the end of 1860 and the beginning of 1861. It began with an anti-Catholic letter of Pope's in the Tory paper *The Islander*, 7 December 1860, to which MacDonald replied in the issue of 1 February 1861. The exchange was continued with considerable acrimony throughout February and March.[7] It focused around the issue of the temporal power of the papacy. Whether the islanders approved or disapproved of the methods and arguments employed by the rector and the colonial secretary, everyone now realized that the college had to be regarded as the forceful mouthpiece of a constituency which the Tories found advantageous to oppose. The second debate took place in 1862, between MacDonald and David Laird, supported apparently by W.H. Pope, in a religious publication edited by Laird and known as *The Protestant*. It was occasioned by an editorial attack on the index of prohibited books and quickly extended to the Church generally and to Catholic education. In this controversy MacDonald went so far as to request both the lieutenant-governor

6 Macmillan, *History*, 123–5
7 See *The Islander* for 1 Dec. 1860 and 1, 8, 22 Feb. 1861 and 8, 25 Mar. 1861.

(George Dundas) and the colonial minister (the Duke of Newcastle) to remove Pope from office. These controversies had two effects: they strengthened the college in the affections of the Catholic constituency; they made, on the other hand, the question of the endowment of the college a treacherous one for any government to touch.

By the summer of 1862 repairs on the wooden building were already badly needed. Something of the rector's practical efficiency can be seen from Macmillan's account:

Father Angus thought it best to grapple with the difficulty right away, and about the middle of June he employed a number of men to make the necessary repairs. The cross-walls and floors were shored up so as to keep them in place, the outer walls were then removed piece by piece and replaced with solid walls of brick, and the whole work proceeded with such despatch that by the end of October the exterior was finished and the college was ready for the reopening of the classes on the 3rd of December 1862.[8]

MacDonald paid for this job by holding a picnic on the college grounds 28 July 1862. Although the government had turned him down, the people of the island, and particularly of Charlottetown, both Catholic and Protestant, saw him through his difficulty. Typical of the project is that the bricks used to enclose the old frame were baked in a kiln, earlier made at Tignish, when Bishop MacIntyre was parish priest there, under the supervision of Father Dougald MacDonald. The sturdy quality and homemade roughness of these bricks still adds charm to the old main building on the present campus and records at the same time a trying moment of the history of the college.

The course of studies provided in St Dunstan's was designed to prepare students to continue their clerical education in the seminaries of Quebec and Montreal. A particularly good student was sometimes awarded a free scholarship to the College of the Propaganda in Rome, as happened to Cornelius O'Brien in 1864. In general, it is fair to say that the course provided at St Dunstan's covered the equivalent of the work prescribed in a French classical college. Thus we read that Dugald J. MacIsaac was ordained by the bishop of Charlottetown on 20 August 1863; that he had been among the first students to enter St Dunstan's when it opened in 1855; that he had completed his classical studies there and had been admitted directly into theology in Quebec. Similarly, Patrick Boyle, born at Lot 7 in 1839, attended the village school at Tignish, studied classics, privately at first under his pastor, Peter MacIntyre, and then entered St Dunstan's where he spent

8 Macmillan, *History*, 249

five years of preparatory studies after which he spent three and a half years in theology in Quebec, where he was ordained 24 January 1864. Boyle acted as an assistant in St Patrick's Church, Quebec, for the four months following his ordination; he then returned to Prince Edward Island for the summer, and received his appointment to the staff of St Dunstan's during August 1864. Cornelius O'Brien spent seven years in Rome, taking philosophy and theology at the Propaganda before being granted the doctorate and raised to the priesthood in 1871. These cases, recorded by Macmillan, make it fairly certain that the college course at St Dunstan's could take a student to the end of the second year of philosophy.

Angus MacDonald continued as rector of St Dunstan's until 1869. In June of that year the first Vatican Council opened in Rome. When the bishop left for Rome he placed the rector in charge of the diocese, relieving him temporarily of his other duties. At the end of the summer he summoned him to Rome as his theologian and replaced him as rector with James MacDonald, the priest at Indian River and Summerside. The length of Angus MacDonald's term of office, attributable in part to his uncertain health, had served to stabilize the college programme. It was a significant term, too, in that during it the tradition was established that a large proportion of St Dunstan's men went on for the Church as diocesan clergy. No Catholic college in English-speaking Canada has a finer record of such vocations, nor has any college been more happy in its ecclesiastical orientation.

James MacDonald assumed the rectorship of St Dunstan's in the fall of 1869 and held it until 1880. These were lively years in the field of education, especially at the primary level, and in politics too because they included the year of the island's entry into confederation. MacDonald seems not to have played a key role in either of these movements, leaving negotiations as much as possible in the hands of Bishop MacIntyre.

The bishop's involvement in school controversies actually began a year before; that is, in 1868, with his celebrated memorial to the legislature. He hoped to obtain an adjustment of the Free School Act before the island became a province of Canada. The bishop favoured confederation although Catholics generally were divided on the issue. He was accordingly faced with two hurdles: one set up by Protestants who were opposed to the island's having separate schools; another set up by those Catholics who were opposed to confederation. It was a bitter disappointment to him that the Davies School Act of 1872, passed just prior to Confederation, made no provision for separate public schools for Catholic children. As a result of this act, Catholic schools in the confederated province were private schools. Religious instruction was not available for Catholic children in the schools save where local boards raised no objection. This unsatisfactory resolution of the problem at the primary level indirectly affected higher education as well. St Dunstan's was more than ever limited to the status of a completely private institution.

In other ways too the administration of James MacDonald was less than satisfactory. The student enrolment rose very little, fluctuating between 37 and 72 throughout his rectorship, and there were many complaints from the Catholic constituency. The college had still only its original sources of revenue: the fees of the students, the revenue from the farm at St Andrew's, and what occasional aid the diocese could provide. Moreover, there was still a large turnover of teaching staff: James Charles MacDonald, Michael J. Macmillan, Cornelius O'Brien, Stanislaus Boudreault, Allan J. MacDonald, and others held short appointments under MacDonald before proceeding to other posts. It is not surprising that an announcement came in 1880 that the three priests on the staff of the college, James MacDonald, Daniel MacDonald, and Edward Walker, had been appointed elsewhere and that the bishop had, during his *ad limina* visit to Rome in 1880, successfully petitioned the superior general of the Jesuits to supply a staff and administration for St Dunstan's.

The Jesuits are first mentioned in the diocesan annals of Charlottetown when, on 11 November 1877, Father Glackmeyer opened the first parish mission given in the diocese. It was a particularly effective mission in that Glackmeyer, with the support of Bishop MacIntyre, was responsible for the rapid spread of the total abstinence movement throughout the island. This success encouraged the hope that the placing of the college into the care of the Society of Jesus would meet general approval. Thus in the autumn of 1880 Father Kenny became rector of St Dunstan's and Father Racicot his assistant. The two Jesuits were accompanied by four scholastics and lay brothers. Although the college enrolment went up immediately, there was little real understanding between chancery and the new college authorities. The Jesuits withdrew from Charlottetown in 1881 after the close of the academic year.

Following the departure of the Jesuits, the administration of St Dunstan's returned to the diocesan clergy. The bishop appointed Jean Chiasson to the rectorship. He was a man of some experience, having passed many years in study between his days as a student of St Dunstan's, 1864 to 1866, and his ordination in Quebec in 1878. He held his doctorate in theology and had been three years on the staff of the cathedral in Charlottetown. He was given W.H. Grant as his assistant and some lay teachers. Chiasson remained rector only sixteen months, then replaced Cornelius O'Brien at Indian River when the latter became archbishop of Halifax. Grant succeeded Chiasson but held office for only one year, 1883–4, having to withdraw when stricken with a serious pulmonary illness.

St Dunstan's was not flourishing in these years. Its enrolment dropped to as low as 12 students, and many were of the opinion that it should be closed entirely. Bishop MacIntyre, however, made still another appointment to the rectorship, James Charles MacDonald, a good appointment as events proved because MacDonald possessed the kind of practical drive the institution needed. He added a commercial course to attract more students and brought in an outside professor of philosophy, P.J. O'Ryan of Quebec City. J.C. MacDonald's seven years in office saw a strengthening of academic standards and an increase in the student body to over a hundred. Something of the enthusiasm he engendered is preserved in the coat of arms of the college bearing the motto, *ex eodem fonte fides et scientia*, which goes back to 1886 and is the product of the ingenuity and interest of two professors, the P.J. O'Ryan already mentioned, and J.A. MacDonald, later pastor at Grand River. An advertisement carried in *Frederick's Prince Edward Island Directory 1889–1890* lists the teaching staff and their respective subjects as follows: J.C. MacDonald, professor of Greek and mathematics; J.A. MacDonald, physics and mental philosophy; J.A .Blaquiere, Latin and French; McDougall, English, Latin, and vocal music; Ronald MacDonald, history and mathematics; J.M. Sullivan, bookkeeping, business, and telegraphy; W.P. McNally, assistant professor of French and English; J.H. Cunningham, preparatory.[9]

In 1890 J.C. MacDonald was appointed coadjutor bishop of Charlottetown, remaining for the time being rector of St Dunstan's. When bishop MacIntyre died in April 1891, MacDonald withdrew from the rectorship and appointed A.P. Macmillan as his successor. Macmillan was a native islander, one year ordained, and a teacher on the college staff. He was twice rector of St Dunstan's. This, his first term, lasted only one year; he was succeeded in 1892 by James Morrison.

Morrison's appointment marks the end of the first or pre-accreditation period of St Dunstan's. The college had been founded to assure the

---

9 *Frederick's Prince Edward Island Directory 1889–1890*, 35; see also p. 68 for a glowing description of the college.

diocese of a supply of priests and it had done that rather well. It had placed its students in the seminaries of Quebec, Montreal, and Rome, and some 80 of them had been ordained, two of these having already been consecrated bishops. It had provided higher education to a total of about 780 young men, over 90 per cent of them from Prince Edward Island and the Magdalens. It had attracted not only students of Scottish and Irish background but a substantial number of Acadians too, binding together disparate elements of the population as no other institution, secular or religious, had succeeded in doing until that time. Many of its students remained for only one or two years, and a large proportion never really got beyond high school work. But a substantial number succeeded in completing their professional training elsewhere, and the complete alumni roster published in 1954 includes an impressive list of islanders from these early years: Judge A.E. Arsenault (1885–93), Judge Stanislaus Blanchard (1872–4), Mr Justice J.P. Byrne (1890–6), Hon. George E. Hughes (1867–9), Sir Roderick J. MacDonald, KCG (1875–8), Captain William Mockler (1857–8), Sir W.W. Sullivan (1860–2), and a long list of medical doctors who have served the island and of whom the following are only representative: Harry F. McLeod (1884–9), David MacNally (1889–90), John Salomon (1885–93), George and James Warburton (1867–9, 1867–71), Peter Conroy (1861–2), Thomas Cunningham (1866–70) and W.B. Cunningham (1894–6), John McDonald (1867–72), Isidore Gallant (1871–3), Richard Ledwell (1884–91).

None of these men, nor any of the priests mentioned earlier, carried a St Dunstan's degree, but they provide testimony that Prince Edward Island was not without respectable educational facilities for a large part of the nineteenth century.

LAVAL AFFILIATION: 1892–1940

On 15 September 1892, arrangements were made between the rector of St Dunstan's, James Morrison, and the rector of Laval University, Mgr B. Paquet, for the affiliation of St Dunstan's College. No change of academic programme was here involved, but henceforth a St Dunstan's graduate could carry a BA degree. From the point of view of Laval this meant recognizing St Dunstan's as a classical college; from the point of view of the English-speaking constituency of St Dunstan's it tended to mean something more – that the college now had a recognizable undergraduate department and was now clearly functioning at the university level. The new arrangement was both a recognition of past achievement and a step forward. The numbers to qualify for the BA were at first small: three in 1893 (Terence Campbell, William McKenna, Francis Murphy), and two in 1895, but adequate to raise the academic sights of the entire student body.

Peter Curran replaced Morrison as rector in 1895. His, too, was a short three-year term, but a hopeful one. He had a staff of six priests, large enough, that is, to give promise of academic growth. He was also in a position to think about the physical development of the college, and he actually established some new recreational facilities, erecting an enclosed rink – probably the first in Canada – and draughting plans for an addition to the original building. It was Curran's successor, A.P. Macmillan, who, in 1898, entered his second term as rector and who opened the new wing in 1899. About this time enrolment reached 120, and the college was making measurable progress.

In 1900 Thomas Curran was appointed rector, holding the post for nine years, a period of continuing development. In 1901 (11 June) the Alumni Association was established under the presidency of Dr Peter Conway. In the same year a community of sisters was brought from France to take over the domestic duties of the college, instituting a policy both economical and efficient, which has been continued to this day. The original community of sisters remained only six years. They were replaced in 1907 by nuns from Sherbrooke. These were in turn replaced in 1916 by the Sisters of St Martha of Charlottetown, who are still at St Dunstan's.

In 1905 the college held a fiftieth anniversary, sponsored mainly by the Alumni Association, the guest of honour being a former professor of the college, Cornelius O'Brien, archbishop of Halifax.

In 1909 Terence Campbell became rector. He held the post for six years. His years are remembered especially by the founding of the present college paper, the *Red and White*, in 1910, and because World War I broke out while he was rector and made an unforgettable impact upon the college. Campbell was replaced as rector by G.J. MacLellan in 1915.

MacLellan's rectorship must be regarded as a lively, significant, and preparatory period. In May 1916 he got the alumni working on an expansion and endowment fund. About the same time, or a little later, he opened negotiations with the government for a university charter, which was granted during 1917. The act was essentially an incorporation of the board of governors of the college under the name of St Dunstan's University; but it also conferred full university powers upon the college, powers which St Dunstan's was not prepared to use right away but held in abeyance until 1941. The pertinent part of the act of 1917 is as follows: 'The said St Dunstan's College shall be and taken to be an University with all and every the usual rights, powers and privileges of such an institution and the students of the said University shall have the liberty and privilege of taking the degrees of bachelor, master and doctor in the several Arts and Faculties, at the appointed time, and shall have power within themselves of performing all scholastic exercises necessary for the conferring of such degrees as shall be directed by the statutes, rules and ordinances of the said Institution.'[10]

In 1919 the residence facilities were substantially increased with the erection of Dalton Hall, which was built with a gift from Sir Charles Dalton and furnished by the alumni association.

With the return of war veterans in 1919 the enrolment increased to 292 students. In 1921, when K.C.M. Sills and W.S. Learned of the Carnegie Corporation examined educational facilities and methods in the universities and colleges of the maritime provinces, the following appraisal of St Dunstan's was made which, unflattering as it was, ranked the college as something more than a high school and worthy at least of a 'fuller reference' than could be afforded five other Catholic institutions examined and Prince of Wales College:

The last is St Dunstan's at Charlottetown, Prince Edward Island, which deserves a somewhat fuller reference.

The classrooms and recreation rooms are bare of equipment. There is no scientific apparatus of any description for any purpose. There is a small library (5000 to 6000 volumes) that appears to be used only by the priests. Aside from a brief commercial course for a score of boys, classics and mathematics are the staple subjects, succeeded by a course in scholastic philosophy. The college has never given its own degree, tho' recently empowered to do so by the legislature, and it does not intend to do so in the immediate future. Its candidates have hitherto taken the examinations and degree of Laval University at Quebec. About 30 per cent of the graduates become priests.

In the midst of a farming community the school has a wonderful chance to teach agriculture, but this has not as yet been undertaken. It is the chief English-speaking Catholic school in eastern Canada after St Francis Xavier.[11]

In 1923 MacLellan became parish priest of Tignish and was replaced as rector by D.P. Crocken, whose three-year tenure is remembered chiefly for the increased recreational facilities he sponsored. In 1926

10 See *Report of the Royal Commission on Higher Education for Prince Edward Island*, 20 Jan. 1965, 9.
11 William S. Learned and Kenneth C.M. Sills, *Education in the Maritime Provinces of Canada*, New York: The Carnegie Foundation, 1922, 27–8

J.A. Murphy, who had for six and a half years been a member of the staff, began his seventeen-year term as rector, the longest of any St Dunstan's rector or president to date. His rectorship divides naturally into two phases: 1926–41, when the college was still an affiliate of Laval; and 1941–3, the final years before his retirement to a parish during which the college began to function as an independent university.

The first and longer phase of Murphy's rectorship coincided with the marking of the seventy-fifth anniversary, a moment of hope, and with the coming of the great depression, a period of deep disappointment. These years saw four important kinds of development. First was Murphy's building programme. Immediately upon taking office he replaced the college rink. In 1927 he added a storage plant. During 1928 he had classroom and academic facilities remodelled, and in the same year, still mindful of criticism in the Sills-Learned Report, he had a chemistry laboratory installed. From 1929 and throughout the thirties he could undertake no building, for obvious reasons. But in 1939–40 he had a new and modern science building erected opposite the main building, filling a serious academic gap and giving the campus something of its modern contours.

The second area of development was the training of staff, made possible in the first instance, ironically enough, by the discouraging decline of student enrolment. In 1929 there were approximately 300 students and a staff of sixteen – eleven priests and five lay professors. During the worst years of depression the student body dropped to about one hundred. It was during this difficult period that Murphy introduced the more modern policy of having his staff seek higher academic qualifications in the secular sciences, a policy which has been maintained to the present day, and which has contributed to the increased prestige of the institution.

Thirdly, during the fall of 1934 an adult education programme was begun much along the lines of the earlier programme at St Francis Xavier, that is, was directed towards the untrained and uneducated people of the island, whose means of livelihood required modernization and organization. The work, begun largely outside the college among farmers and fishermen, was integrated into an extension department where leadership courses could best be rooted. The work of the adult education programme was strongly supported and to some extent directed by Murphy with the full approval of the chancellor, Bishop J.A. O'Sullivan. As was the case in Antigonish, the programme utilized the relatively new potential of radio broadcasting and brought the work of the college closer to the consciousness of the population of the entire island, both Catholic and Protestant.

The final development to take place under Murphy during the twenties and thirties, one which resulted from the possession of an academically improved faculty, from the new and closer contact through social action with a wider group of islanders, and from the newly acquired facilities provided by the science building – was the courageous decision to activate the charter of 1917. The last Laval degrees were conferred at the May convocation in 1940. With this event closed both what was described above as the first phase of the Murphy regime and the forty-eight year period of affiliation with Laval University.

ST DUNSTAN'S UNIVERSITY, 1941

The second and briefer phase of the Murphy regime was the period 1940 to 1943 when the university really got under way. The first step was the granting of degrees under its own charter. In May 1941 the BA (SDU) was conferred on candidates by the chancellor of the university, Bishop O'Sullivan. This marked the coming of age of higher education in Prince Edward Island. From September 1942 women were admitted to lectures on campus and enrolled as regular students. Previously, only a few sisters had taken a BA degree from the college, and this was by way of exception.

Murphy's last chore as rector, or now as president, was to obtain recognition of the new university's degrees. In one sense this was not a new problem. Before 1941 the degrees carried the prestige of Laval; that is, they admitted their holders to the university faculties of Laval and entitled them to such recognition as was enjoyed by graduates from the Quebec classical colleges. This normally meant in the other provinces of Canada advanced standing in the faculty of arts and sciences and admission to certain other schools and faculties, depending upon the actual courses taken. It was now hoped that the new St Dunstan's degrees would be accepted in English-speaking Canada and in the United States as the equivalent of the bachelor's degree from Dalhousie, McGill, and Toronto. There was at first some confusion and considerable hesitancy about admitting SDU students *ad eundem gradum* and especially in accepting them into the first medical and first dental year in universities where pre-medical and pre-dental programmes were required. Murphy's problem was twofold: first to see to it that the proper science courses were actually available at St Dunstan's; secondly, to have them recognized by the major universities. In solving both these problems by 1943, when Dalhousie, Queen's, and McGill gave practical recognition to St Dunstan's courses, Murphy achieved his greatest contribution to his institution at the strictly educational and academic level. In August 1943, Murphy, now Monsignor Murphy, was appointed pastor of Kinkora parish and was succeeded as rector by R.V. MacKenzie, who had been vice-rector for the preceding six years.

There have been three presidents since Murphy's time: R.V. MacKenzie 1943–56, J.A. Sullivan 1956–63, and G.A. Macdonald 1963–69. These men followed a uniform policy of development by which, in courses, standards, buildings, and objectives, St Dunstan's came to conform rather closely to the policies of the English-speaking universities of Canada and assumed a full and active role as one of the long-established maritime institutions of learning.

The building programme after 1943 was extensive. Memorial Hall men's residence was opened in 1947, housing 80 students, 6 staff members, and, for a few years, the college library. A chapel, a dining hall, and a heating plant were opened in 1950; a gymnasium, in 1951. Marian College, a women's residence, opened in 1959; the Kelley Library, in 1963; and St Vincent's Hall, a residence adjacent to the university property, was acquired in 1964.

This building and expansion programme was made possible by a campaign conducted by MacKenzie in which $400,000 (nearly twice its objective) was raised; by the increased availability of funds during the post-war years and raised by the alumni association; by the per capita operating grants provided for university education since 1951 by the federal government; and by the capital grants fund of the Canada Council since 1957.

From the strictly academic point of view, the opening of the Kelley Library marked the most important single advance of these years. The Sills-Learned Report had commented on the lamentable condition of the library in 1921; during the forties a distinguished alumnus, Bishop Kelley of Oklahoma City and Tulsa and founder of the Catholic Church Extension Society of the United States, had set aside $20,000 against the day when a suitable library could be built, and in addition he bequeathed his personal library to the university. When the Kelley Memorial Library was opened in 1963, it was immediately recognized as a model for small university libraries and has constituted the finest single contribution thus far made to higher education in Prince Edward Island.

The academic programme was broadened after 1941. In 1947 a course in business administration was begun and bachelor of commerce degrees have been regularly conferred since 1951. Since 1954 the first three years of the engineering course have been available at St Dunstan's, as earlier at St Francis Xavier and St Mary's. The two final years and the engineering degree are provided by the Nova Scotia Technical College. In 1957 a teacher training programme was undertaken and since 1960 the degree of bachelor of education has been available.

The great St Dunstan's problem of the last few years has been its relation to Prince of Wales College, Charlottetown on the one hand and to the government of Prince Edward Island on the other. This issue became disturbingly real with the petition of Prince of Wales College to become Prince Edward Island's second university.

The background of the current situation is as follows. In 1802 land in Charlottetown was ceded to the government for a 'College.' A college was impractical in 1802, but during the next two decades a school – Breading's School or the National School – was operated on the property. In 1834 a Central Academy was established by an act of William IV. This academy functioned as a secondary school. Its name was changed to Prince of Wales College in 1860. In 1885 the Normal School – previously established by the government but now in difficulties – was annexed to Prince of Wales College. In 1932 the first two years of university training were added to its programme, and its students admitted to advanced standing in Dalhousie, McGill, and other universities. During 1964 the college requested a new act which would enable it to provide the four years of an undergraduate programme and confer its own degrees. The questions which thus arose were these: Should the government of PEI enter the field of university education? Have the historically prior rights of St Dunstan's in the field of university education to be considered? Is the population of the province large enough to maintain two universities? Identical answers to these questions were not at the moment forthcoming from Prince of Wales College, St Dunstan's University, or the government of Prince Edward Island.

In 1949 the dynamic Dr Frank MacKinnon became principal of Prince of Wales College. It has been no secret since that he wanted to release the schools of education and pedagogy from political domination by moving them into the faculty of arts and science. His book *The Politics of Education* made him a controversial figure in provincial politics and a puzzling one at St Dunstan's. There was fear that he had little respect for either St Dunstan's or Prince of Wales and that he had both of them in mind when he wrote in *The Politics of Education*: 'Institutions which are but glorified high schools and whose degrees are worth little more than matriculation certificates (there are several of them) should not be permitted to train teachers.'[12] MacKinnon was pleased when in 1964 the government of Premier Walter Shaw passed a new Prince of Wales College Act. In the history of Prince Edward Island this is an important act because it represented, if one disregards the act of 1917 incorporating St Dunstan's as a degree-conferring university, the province's first venture into university education. If the act was not actually the province's first venture, it was at least its first commitment. After passing the Prince of Wales Act, the government decided not to promulgate it immediately; the royal assent was withheld and a Royal Commission on Higher Education for Prince Edward Island appointed. The appointing of this commission provided an opportunity to re-assess the situation and even, one might legitimately suppose, to have second thoughts about the Prince of Wales Act.

The members of the Royal Commission were John Sutherland Bonnell (chairman), minister emeritus of the Fifth Avenue Presbyterian Church, New York City; Dr Norman A.M. MacKenzie, former president of the University of British Columbia; and Dr Joseph A. MacMillan, a practising surgeon of Charlottetown. The commission studied the question for four months and reported to Mr Shaw and his cabinet 20 January 1965. The report had two major sections: 'Recommendations and Observations,' 'Suggested Patterns.' The discussion in these sections is summarized in thirty recommendations, of which the following seem particularly pertinent to St Dunstan's: (1) that the Prince of Wales Act be immediately promulgated; (2) that the high school departments be removed from SDU and PWC; (3) that a basic inaugural grant be made to PWC; (4) that offerings be limited to courses leading to BA, BSC, BED, BCOMM, but that negotiations be made with hospitals to include nursing; (5) that there be a pooling of resources like the Piedmont Centre Plan in operation in North Carolina; (6) that the province make SDU and PWC per capita grants of $300 a student; (7) that the creation of a federated University of PEI be regarded as a distinct future possibility. A further section provided more specific details for the implementing of the last-mentioned recommendation. Of four possibilities – amalgamation, isolation, federation, co-operation – only co-operation with a view to federation appealed to the members of the royal commission.[13]

The report had weaknesses from the point of view of the administration of St Dunstan's. The commissioners called for the immediate

12 Frank MacKinnon, *The Politics of Education*, Toronto: University of Toronto Press, 1960, 165
13 *Report of the Royal Commission on Higher Education for Prince Edward Island*, Charlottetown, 1965, 57

promulgation of the Prince of Wales Act without apparent serious reconsideration of its background, regarding such reconsideration as outside their terms of reference: 'The task of our Commission has been greatly simplified by the fact that we have not been asked to decide whether or not the new university, known as Prince of Wales College, should be established. That decision has already been made by the Government and the Legislature.'[14] Such a setting aside of discussion of the act was interpreted as prejudging the nub of the basic question: Is the maintaining of two universities for a population of 120,000 islanders either economically or academically feasible? The commission's answer seemed to some people to be: It is feasible for now, so promulgate the act; but it will not be feasible for very long, so prepare for federation. For such, the government and the commission were, both individually and together, wanting in courage. The commission's reasoning was that one university was enough but that federation would be possible only if between two institutions of equal status, that is, both with university powers.

The report was, from the point of view of equity, generous towards both institutions, recommending on the one hand that Prince of Wales College be granted the powers it sought and be treated like a provincial university, and on the other that the unsympathetic precedents set in Ontario and the west on the matter of direct aid to church-supported colleges not be followed in the case of St Dunstan's: 'We are living in a new day and this calls for a revolutionary change of attitude. It is the opinion of this Commission that financial assistance should be given annually to St Dunstan's University for operating expenses on the basis of the number of students enrolled full time.'[15] But these and some of the other recommendations are of a secondary nature. They should only be subsequent to a frank and understanding evolution of the two institutions concerned as authentic twentieth-century universities. When all is said and done, the Bonnell commission's report called for a two-university solution in the near future. Everyone knew that the government could not afford to run two universities and would have sooner or later to settle for supporting only one of them – and this one would likely have to be the already public-supported Prince of Wales. MacDonald of St Dunstan's feared this and thought it unjust. MacKinnon counted on it, and looked at the report as a double victory.

Unpleasantness followed the issuing of the royal commission's report because it was thought to have produced a stalemate. During February

14 Ibid., 14
15 Ibid., 22

1965 a private report was issued by a 'group of ten' Protestant and Catholic citizens, including some St Dunstan professors and notably John Eldon Green. Their report called for a forthright one-university solution in which the names St Dunstan's and Prince of Wales would disappear and in which religious differences would be taken for granted.[16]

In June 1965 the Prince of Wales Act was promulgated, as the commission asked, but the report was not further implemented. Prince Edward Island's two universities lived from day to day, their respective boards more or less committed to their continuance. The next four years saw almost everyone grow weary of the unsolved 'university problem.'

In 1967 Premier Alex Campbell's government took a positive move towards further implementing the Bonnell report. It established a Universities Co-ordinating Council. The move worried both MacDonald and MacKinnon because it made clear that both institutions would have to curtail some of their public services and made real the possibility of their legal dissolution. The co-ordinating council actually held but two discussions and got nowhere. Rumours circulated that the premier was going to apply pressure, that there was likely going to be in Prince Edward Island one university and one college of applied arts and technology. Rumour became fact when Bill 57 was introduced early in 1968.

Bill 57 was not designed to create one university. It was designed to meet the very serious criticism that 'the only public financial aid available to Prince Edward Island university students is provided through the Canada Student Loans plan.'[17] Bill 57 proposed to establish a Prince Edward Island university grants commission of the kind presumed to exist by the Duff-Berdahl Report on University Government in Canada (1966) and specifically called for by the Bladen Report on Financing Higher Education in Canada (1965) and by subsequent statements made from the Association of Universities and Colleges of Canada. The new university grants commission was to plan all post-secondary development and to allocate government funds under conditions determined by the government, which conditions included primarily that there be only one university recipient, that is, that the two existing universities be merged.

The students of Prince of Wales demonstrated against the bill and MacKinnon decried the excessive control the government was taking over education. The uproar produced a 'white paper' read by the pre-

16 *The Globe and Mail*, Toronto, 27 Feb. 1965
17 See *University Affairs*, 9 Supplement (1968), 3

mier on 2 April 1968, in which he utterly rejected any duplication of university services in Prince Edward Island. He was willing to amend the bill or to replace it, but not to abandon his position. Following the 'white paper' MacKinnon resigned. Campbell replaced Bill 57 with Bill 72, which passed 25 April 1968. This bill set up a commission on post-secondary education headed by one full-time executive director and two part-time directors who had in effect the power to establish the University of Prince Edward Island, the only university the government would support, and in which there was to be no duplication of services. To implement Bill 72, planning committees were established and placed under the interim chairmanship of Edward F. Sheffield, professor of higher education, University of Toronto, with E.T. Jefferys of the department of education as secretary.

Premier Campbell was serious about having only one university. He accepted questions about his policy, answered them both in writing and orally at a public interview.[18] The premier claimed not to be interfering in education but to be intervening on the side of the provincial community in a controversy between that community (whose elected spokesman he was) and the universities of the province. He made clear that in any change effected, tenure and legitimate commitments would be respected, that justice and moderation would mark the period of transition, and that alternatives to the one-university policy, especially federation, had already been examined and dismissed.

The first move would be to find a president for the new university, who could hardly be either president G.A. MacDonald of St Dunstan's or interim principal T.M. Lothian, the successor of MacKinnon, of Prince of Wales. After considerable reflection and debate, the name of the first president-designate of the University of Prince Edward Island was released – Ronald J. Baker, head of the English department and director of academic planning from 1964 (a year before it opened) of Simon Fraser University, Burnaby, British Columbia.[19]

Baker visited Charlottetown in mid-February to meet the administration of St Dunstan's and Prince of Wales. He asked both parties to make

18 See the following documents: (1) summary of points listed by members of the University and College Planning Committees for clarification of the premier's 2 Apr. 'Policy Statement on Post-Secondary Education,' (appendix 2 to meeting of 5 Aug. 1968); (2) answers to points listed etc. (as above), presented 8 Aug. 1968; (3) transcript of questions and answers following presentation on 8 Aug. 1968, by the premier of PEI of written answers etc. (as above).

19 Ronald J. Baker first came to Canada under the Commonwealth Air Training Plan. After the war he studied at the University of British Columbia. He was named professor of English and director of academic planning at Simon Fraser University in 1964, a year before it opened. He subsequently became head of the English department.

no new staff appointments, to realize that they would find the new budget tighter than the old ones, and to phase out their academic operations by the end of 1969. The new university, he said, would have a department of religious studies, but would not provide denominational theologies.

St Dunstan's held its last convocation during May 1969. One hundred and seventy-five graduates, the largest graduating class in its history, received their degrees. The total enrolment for this final year, 1968–9, was 1100 students. For the most part, staff and students were pleased with the proposed change and hoped that the era beginning would be as important for Church and Canada as the long span of years back to Angus MacDonald, first rector of St Dunstan's, and beyond him to Edward Walsh, the Irish rector of St Andrew's.

St Mary's University

HALIFAX, NS

1838 (1802, 1818)

St Mary's University is located on the Gorsebrook property, a thirty-acre estate at Robie and Inglis Streets near downtown Halifax. It is housed in a complex of modern structures: an immense all-service main building, a faculty residence, student residences (Tower building), an enlarged science wing, and a library. It offers regular university programmes leading to degrees in arts, science, commerce, and theology. It also provides the first three years of engineering for admission to Nova Scotia Technical College, a diploma course in journalism, and master's programmes in education and (by special arrangement with the Maritime School) social work. Its property is held for the archdiocese by a university board. Its academic and administrative policies, established by the Jesuits of Upper Canada, are carried on by a combined Jesuit and lay faculty.

PRELIMINARY: 1802–38

St Mary's has a pre-history from about 1802[1] when the Reverend Edmund Burke, whom Bishop Denaut of Quebec had transferred from the Ontario missions to Halifax in 1801, as vicar general of Nova Scotia, had a two-storey building erected on Barrington Street at Spring Garden Road to serve the Irish of Halifax as a college or seminary which he planned to link up with the Séminaire de Québec or the Sulpician college in Montreal. The college did not open because the lieutenant-governor, Sir John Wentworth, provoked possibly by the violence of one of Burke's pastorals,[2] refused to relax the legal restric-

1 Cornelius O'Brien, *Memoirs of Rt. Rev. Edmund Burke*, Ottawa: Thoburn, 1894, esp. chap. XIII; John L. Quinan, 'History of St Mary's,' *The Gazette*, Halifax, 24 June 1926, and 'Historic Barrington Street's St Mary's,' *The Mail-Star*, Halifax, 13 Sept. 1904, 61; John C. Macmillan, *The Early History of The Catholic Church in Prince Edward Island*, Quebec: Evénement, 1905

2 See letter of Bishop O'Donnell, vicar apostolic of Newfoundland, 2 July 1804 to Bishop Plessis, quoted in *Mémoire sur les missions de la Nouvelle-Ecosse au Cap Breton, et de l'Ile du Prince Edouard de 1760 à 1820*, Quebec: Darveau, 1895, 267. This is a long rejoinder to O'Brien's *Memoirs of Rt. Rev. Edmund Burke* by an unnamed author who took exception to the impressions left by O'Brien that the bishops of Quebec had neglected the missions to the Maritimes, even to the Acadians living there. It is well documented, if bitter in tone.

tions on Catholic schools,[3] and because, when in 1805 it appeared that such restrictions might be overlooked, professors could not be found. Burke sought priest-teachers from the Irish bishops, from the Propaganda in Rome, and from the Jesuits in Russia, England, and Baltimore. Two Jesuits, Fidelis Grivel and Felix Syglinski, were actually named for Halifax, but negotiations to bring them, involving several bishops, the superior general, Propaganda, and others, and carried on between 1805 and 1808, ultimately broke down. The building, erected to serve as a college, was put to other uses. About the time Burke became vicar apostolic of Nova Scotia in 1818, he opened a school for small boys in the original building which had become both a glebe house and his own residence. He also brought some seminarians into his house to read theology for ordination. Two of them taught for him in the boys' school. These seminarians, numbering at least the five known to have been ordained in 1819 and 1820, can be regarded as a partial fulfilment of the bishop's earlier dream of a college in Halifax.[4] Instruction at the higher level seems not to have continued after Burke's death, which took place towards the end of 1820.

First Period: 1838–68

The real story of St Mary's College or seminary begins in 1838, the year in which it became evident that the Nova Scotia legislature was prepared to support higher education on a denominational basis. While negotiations were in progress to open Dalhousie College, Queen's College (later Acadia), and the Methodist Schools of Halifax (later Mount Allison, NB), Michael Tobin and a group of Halifax Catholics, without consulting Bishop Fraser, who lived by preference with his Gaelic parishioners in Antigonish, laid plans for St Mary's. They asked for and were promised teachers from the archbishop of Dublin; they raised money to pay for the passage of these teachers and for school furnishings; and they prepared a memorial to be presented to the government asking for degree-conferring powers and for an operational grant. The progress of their preparations is twice noted during the fall of 1839 in

3 From an early statute book: 'If any popish recusant, papist or person professing the popish religion, shall be so presumptive as to set up any school within this province, and be detected therein, such offender shall for every such offense, suffer three months' imprisonment without bail or mainprise, and shall pay a fine to the King of ten pounds.' Cited by R.V. Bannon, 'St Francis Xavier University' in P.F. Martin, ed., Catholic Diocesan Directory of Nova Scotia, Halifax, 1936, 110–11.
4 A.A. Johnston, A History of the Catholic Church in Eastern Nova Scotia, Antigonish: St Francis Xavier, 1960, 404. See also pp.413 ff. for plans drawn up with Angus B. MacEachen (later Bishop MacEachen) for a regional seminary at Arisaig. Burke's death in Halifax, 29 Nov. 1820 and the long interregnum put an end to these plans.

Joseph Howe's *Novascotian*: two priests, R.B. O'Brien and Lawrence J. Dease, arrived by ship from Ireland (19 September); and there arrived from abroad 'philosophical instruments to furnish the Physic Hall of the new Catholic Seminary in this town' (21 November). Classes began in the seminary in January 1840, and the school was properly described as having been in operation for more than a year in the petition of the memorialists presented to the assembly on 20 February 1841.

The first president of St Mary's was R.B. O'Brien, and his staff consisted of W. Iver, Michael Hannon (later archbishop), and E.J. Gleason. The college got off to a good start at a new location on Grafton Street. The original staff of four (or five if Dease was teaching) compares favourably with Dalhousie's three. Indeed, since there seems to have been some emphasis on French, Spanish, and Italian at St Mary's, its course is said to have proven more attractive to local students, mindful of commerce, than Dalhousie's.[5] On 29 March 1841, there passed 'An Act for Incorporating the Trustees of the St Mary's College at Halifax.'[6] This act granted general degree-conferring powers, specifically stating that St Mary's, described in one part of the act as a college and in another as a seminary, being limited to eleven years; it was made permanent by further legislation on 18 April 1852.

The first problems seemed not to have been in academics but in ecclesiastical politics. On 15 February 1842 the vicariate apostolic of Nova Scotia became the diocese of Halifax. Bishop Fraser remained in Antigonish but was provided with a coadjutor, the Irish-born William Walsh, to look after Halifax.

At this stage Fraser seems not to have respected the new college, probably because it was not designed to meet the needs of theological students. Writing to Archbishop Signay of Quebec, 13 September 1842, on behalf of two young men whom he wished to place in a seminary, he said 'They were for a year or two in the so-called College of Halifax. They got disgusted with the proceedings there, and not without reason.' And on 13 October of the same year, in a letter of recommendation for still another candidate, he wrote: 'I could easily get him admitted into the so-called College of Halifax, but that establishment is not yet on such a footing as to justify me in sending there any ecclesiastical candidates, till a radical change be effected in discipline and some other essentials. I have two young lads there now; this, however, is more owing to necessity on their part and mine than any predilection or confidence

5 D.C. Harvey, *An Introduction to the History of Dalhousie University*, Halifax, 1938, 61
6 Statutes of Nova Scotia, Anno quarto Victoriae Reginae, cap. xxxix

in this institution at Halifax.' It is clear from the context that Fraser is specifically concerned with 'education for the priesthood.'[7]

In 1844 the diocese was divided, with Fraser becoming, by his own choice, bishop of Arichat, Walsh, apostolic administrator (later bishop) of Halifax. These changes were accompanied by discord and the forming of factions with the result that by 1844 the Irish priests of Halifax, including President O'Brien, had returned to their homeland. The vicar general, Thomas L. Connolly, seems himself to have taken charge of the college. At any rate Connolly was president in 1850, and no other name turns up as holder of that office between 1844 and 1850. Two years later, 1852, Connolly was named bishop of St John; he was to succeed to the see of Halifax in 1859. Between 1852 and 1868, when the first era of diocesan administration of the college came to an end, the following are described as president or principal of St Mary's: Michael Hannon 1854, Canon Patrick Power 1859–62, Robert Raftis 1862–3, Canon John B. Woods 1863–5, Thomas Butler 1865–6, Thomas V. Allen 1866–8.

Relatively little is known about the St Mary's of this period. The American Catholic directories and almanacs provide the names of some professors from 1859 on.[8] Directory data, however, is not always up to date. It is curious that there are so many presidents during the sixties. All of them, with the exception of Raftis,[9] are also listed as members of the cathedral staff. The directory entry for 1867 lists Allen as president, then adds curtly: 'Professors in the various departments, Christian Brothers.' This is a year before the Brothers of the Christian Schools (De La Salle Brothers) took over the direction of the college.

7 *Mémoires sur les missions*, 251–2.
8 *Dunigan's American Catholic Almanac*, edited and published by Edward Dunigan and Brother, New York, begins carrying Canadian data in 1858. The first Halifax entry is 1859. [For detailed information on American Catholic directories see Eugene P. Willging and Herta Hatzfield, *Catholic Serials of the Nineteenth Century in the United States*, Washington: Catholic University Press, second series: part fourteen in two volumes, Vol. 1, New York City, 1967, 6–7. Catholic directories have been appearing in the United States since 1822, and annually since 1833, except in the years 1862 and 1863. These directories have been published by Fielding Lucas, John Murphy of Baltimore, Edward Dunigan, D. and J. Sadleir, Hoffmanns, Wiltzius, and P.J. Kenedy of New York. In a few cases there is overlapping. Canadian data began to appear in 1858 and continued until 1964. For recent data on Canada see *Le Canada Ecclésiastique*.]
9 Robert Raftis, b. 1839 Ballyluskey, Ireland, student at Carlaw College, Ireland, emigrated to Montreal in 1860 and was sent to Halifax in 1861. He was ordained in Halifax in 1863. He is listed as president of St Mary's College during 1862–3, the year of his ordination at the age of 23. He seems to have been on St Mary's staff from 1861 to 1863. He was parish priest of Chezetcooke 1863–4, and of Minudie 1864–5. He died in the fall of 1865 at the age of 26. John T. Raftis, *The Raftis Family of County Kilkenny*, Colville, Wash., 1968, 'Legend of Father Robert Raftis, 98–106

The college seems during this whole first period, unlike Dalhousie which opened and closed three times between 1838 and 1863, to have followed an unbroken if unimpressive course. The small government grant was paid regularly, and it must have gone a long way towards meeting the expenses. The grant began in 1841 in the amount of £300. It was increased to £444 annually from 1842 through 1844. In 1845 St Mary's received only £250, the same amount and on the same basis as Acadia, to continue as long as the School Act of 1845 was in force. Although a new School Act was passed in 1850, the subsidy remained unchanged. During 1863 St Mary's received $1000, raised to $1400 in 1865 and to $1500 in 1876. All grants to the college were terminated in 1881.

Second Period: 1868–76

In 1868 Archbishop Connolly brought the De La Salle Brothers to Halifax. He was able to offer them one Catholic boys' school, St Patrick's, operating under Sir Charles Tupper's Free School Act. At the same time he arranged for them to reopen and administer St Mary's College. Brother Geoffrey was in charge of the college. Almost nothing is known about these eight years. With the coming of the Brothers, the college was moved to a new site at Belle Aire Terrace and Agricola St and a new 'Act Respecting St Mary's College' was passed 30 April 1873. This act is described as reviving that of 1841 'which Act has been allowed to expire through forfeiture.' This could mean that college work had been suspended for a time, but it could also merely mean that the vacancies arising on the board of trustees had not been filled by the lieutenant-governor and assembly as the original act required. At any rate the new act ignores the trustees in whom the original incorporation was vested and names the archbishop as the one who appoints the chancellor, thus providing a simpler and more ecclesiastically centralized method of continuing the board and officers of the institution.

During 1873 Brother Victorian replaced Brother Geoffrey as president and Father E.F. Murphy of the cathedral staff was designated chaplain. The staff was made up of three brothers: Bartholomew, Ulten Hugh, and Justin. This was the situation until the end of the academic year 1875–6.

Third Period: 1876–81

In 1876 the site of the college was moved back from Belle Aire Terrace to Grafton Street and the administration was again taken over by the diocese. This was the year in which the Nova Scotia government made its first move to bring a measure of co-operation into its university complex. By the University Act of 1876 it established the University of Halifax, an examining body patterned after the University of London. St Mary's was affiliated with the University of Halifax as were King's, Acadia, Dalhousie, Mount Allison, St Francis Xavier and, in 1877, Halifax Medical. The fellow and examiner representing St Mary's on the University of Halifax was Rev. Thomas J. Daly. Daly was not president. E.F. Murphy, the chaplain, took over as president and the brothers continued on the teaching staff for another year. The president in 1878 was Richard Kearns of the cathedral staff, and the teaching brothers were replaced by a layman, Professor J.B. Currie, M.A. of London, and by William Kearns and J. Purcell, candidates for the priesthood. The University of Halifax examined candidates for only three or four years and was then allowed quietly to expire. Shortly afterwards, that is in 1881, the government discontinued its policy of making university grants. St Mary's had at once to close and remained so until 1903.

The twenty-two years during which the operation of the college was suspended were not without events significant for its later history. One of these events was the death on 23 December 1881 of Patrick Power, wealthy Halifax merchant and long-time Canadian senator. Power's will contained a number of charitable bequests, one of them destined to play a long and troublesome role in the history of St Mary's. Under a clause in this will the revenue from a portion of the residue of Power's estate was left 'for the introduction and support of the Jesuit Fathers in the said City of Halifax.' Though not specific on the point, the clause seemed to provide for the operating of a college under Jesuit direction. The Jesuits were twice approached by Archbishop O'Brien between 1883 and 1889, and twice had to refuse his invitation to re-establish the college. Could the bequest be paid to some other religious order? Or could it be paid to the diocese for the operation of St Mary's? The archbishop felt that the bequest was intended for the college. The executors were uncertain and divided on the matter. A trial court upheld the archbishop's contention, as did the supreme court of Nova Scotia in 1903. These decisions, however, were reversed in 1903 by the Supreme Court of Canada. The problem of how to use the Power bequest has been part of the St Mary's problem ever since. It could have been solved easily had the Jesuits come to Halifax in the eighties. By 1889, however, the archbishop no longer wanted them and contended before the courts that payment of the bequest was therefore 'impracticable.' He approached the Benedictines twice during this same period and the Christian Brothers of Ireland once, but without success. In 1893 he approached Father Ange Le Doré of the Eudist Fathers about the possibility of their taking over and re-opening St Mary's. Father Le Doré proposed rather the opening of a combined Eudist and diocesan seminary, and to this Archbishop O'Brien ultimately agreed.[10] The reopening of St Mary's became by the turn of the century if not an obsession of O'Brien's, at least his dominating concern, and he frequently met bitter opposition from some of the well-to-do laity who were disposed to ridicule the notion of a Halifax education when better was available abroad. The bitterness of the disagreement caused the bishop much personal suffering.

Fourth Period: 1903–13

The reopening of St Mary's in 1903 was largely the work of Archbishop O'Brien who had, prior to his consecration, been president of St Dunstan's College, Charlottetown. Long resolved, especially in view of the Power will, to revive the college in Halifax, O'Brien left no stone unturned until the mission was accomplished. Temporarily stalled by the Supreme Court of Canada, which would not allow him the use of these extraordinary revenues, he conducted a drive for funds, placing all his personal capital into the project;[11] he set aside a portion of ten acres of land on Quinpool Road at Windsor Street which he had earlier acquired for the diocese, and he erected on this site a building designed to meet the needs of the moment. He had again, in 1902, offered the new college to the Irish Christian Brothers, and then for the second time to the Eudist Fathers, who had been conducting Holy Heart Seminary in Halifax since 1895. The Eudists did what they could: they promised to provide the college with a professor from their seminary, and it was thus that John Boyle O'Reilly joined the staff when the college reopened. The first president of the revived St Mary's was a priest of the archdiocese, Monsignor Edmund Kennedy, who held the office from 1903 to 1905. Kennedy's successor, Charles E. McManus, presided until 1913.

The St Mary's of 1903–13 had a flavour all its own. Its faculty in-

10 Eugène Lachance, *Construire pour le Christ: Paul Lecourtois; 1863–1951*, Halifax, 1953, 32–3

11 O'Brien used his own funds to purchase a strip of land not included in the original purchase. It was this strip of land which became the site of the college. For this period see 'St Mary's College, Windsor Street,' *The Catholic Diocesan Directory of Nova Scotia*, Halifax, 1936, 17–19.

cluded an abnormally large number of laymen for a Catholic institution of the period. These laymen formed a rather urbane and sophisticated group which succeeded in imparting a somewhat English atmosphere to what one would expect to be an Irish campus. There was Professor W.F.P. Stockley, regular teacher of English at St Mary's and guest lecturer at Dalhousie, bearded Irish convert to Catholicism and diligent disciple of Frédéric Ozanam, who became one of the more distinguished academic figures of the city. Stockley subsequently lectured at the University of New Brunswick, then completed his D PHIL under Skeat at Oxford and joined the faculty of University College, Cork, where he was a contemporary of Sir Bertram Windle, who was to move in the opposite direction and finish his academic career in Toronto. With Stockley at St Mary's was Professor Maxwell Drennan, likewise a distinguished beared convert who lectured in romance languages and classics. Drennan's subsequent and lively career took him to Belfast and Witwatersrand. Another layman at St Mary's was the mathematician Bernard Gavin from the Universities of London and Lille, who spent his later years with the Canadian Society of Engineers. Gavin was described by Frederic H. Sexton, principal of the Nova Scotia Technical College and graduate of the Massachusetts Institute of Technology, as the 'greatest mathematician in Nova Scotia.' Still another layman on St Mary's faculty was Professor John Cobb, also from England and a fine Greek scholar.

The records from this period on are fairly complete. The college reopened in 1903 with 24 students in two classes. Perhaps the most distinguished graduate of this period, and one who has played an important role in Canadian education, was Gerald B. Phelan, PH D, of Louvain, member of the Royal Society of Canada, one of the founders and the second president of the Pontifical Institute of Mediaeval Studies, Toronto.

Archbishop O'Brien's St Mary's was a bold experiment, but there were insufficient funds to maintain it on so ambitious a scale. The laymen could not be kept because they could not be paid, and with regrets on both sides they had to go elsewhere. When Charles McManus became president in 1905, the squeeze was beginning. To keep down the costs he had himself to provide lectures in commerce for which he prepared himself by enrolling simultaneously in an evening course given elsewhere in the city. By 1912 St Mary's had again seriously declined. The total registration for 1912–13 was only 53 students. It was literally saved by the Christian Brothers of Ireland, who accepted a new invita-

tion (this time from Archbishop Edward J. McCarthy who had succeeded O'Brien in 1906) to come to Halifax and take over St Mary's.

Fifth Period: 1913–40

It was in 1910 that Archbishop McCarthy began to make arrangements
with the superior general, Brother Calasanctius Whitty, for the coming
of the Christian Brothers of Ireland to Halifax.[12] The first agreement
was dated 24 April 1913, and the revised final contract was signed in
March 1914. Its terms were as follows: the St Mary's property on
Quinpool Road was leased to the brothers at a nominal rental of one
dollar a year; the time of the contract was sixty years, but the brothers
were free to withdraw at the end of each fifteen-year period; the revenues of the college, including fees, bequests, and burses, were to be
paid to the brothers; the brothers were to be responsible for rates,
taxes, repairs, insurance, and maintenance; advance payments which
the brothers might be called upon to make for whatever legitimate
reason, and operational deficits should be made good to the brothers
by the archdiocese. A further stipulation, insisted upon by Whitty, was
that the brothers be protected from all outside interferenc in the operation of the college.

The contract was recognized from the beginning as generous to the
brothers. Indeed, it was in view of the objections of one of the executors of the Power will, Mr Justice Meagher, that the first draught of the
agreement drawn up in 1913 was subsequently modified in 1914. But
generosity on the part of the archdiocese seemed to be called for in view
of the then almost moribund condition of the college and the rather fine
record of the brothers as administrators at St Bonaventure's College (St
John's, Newfoundland) and elsewhere. Moreover, the trustees of the
Power estate accepted the contract in its revised form, and passed the
following resolution: 'Be it resolved that the portion of the income from
the residue of the Estate which for some time past has been divided
between the Monastery of the Good Shepherd, the Orphanage of St
Joseph, and the House of the Guardian Angels, shall, until ordered by
the Trustees, be paid towards the support and maintenance of St
Mary's College Halifax, conducted by the Religious Order commonly
known as the Irish Christian Brothers.'[13]

12 'History of the Institute, Chapter LXXXIV: St Mary's College Halifax,' *The
Christian Brothers' Educational Record* (1941), 12–17; also Brother Jerome Lannon,
'A Survey of the History of St Mary's College, Halifax,' *The Christian Brothers'
Educational Record* (1952), 118–44
    13 Lannon, 'A Survey,' 125

The brothers' administration began with the opening of term, 8 September 1913. In that year the entire school, consisting of high school and college, numbered 55 students, 13 of whom were in residence. In 1914 there were 73 students, 22 of whom were in residence. In 1915, 94 studens, 32 in residence. When the brothers withdrew in 1940 the number of students registered was over 300, still including a sizeable high school. The growth of the institution, though constant, was slow, with the college division suffering severely from the presence of the high school, yet largely supported by it.

The reputation of St Mary's as a university college had never been distinguished. It had always been 'embedded in a high school' and had received little recognition from established universities. St Mary's was described as late as 1922 in the Sills-Learned report as at best a junior college;[14] and between 1922 and 1940, one of the major concerns of its presidents was how to add to the number of established institutions willing to admit St Mary's graduates into their professional schools. By 1940, when the brothers left Halifax, they had compiled a real if limited list of such universities.

The right of St Mary's to provide three years of pre-engineering and to send students to the Nova Scotia Technical College dated from 1907. The brothers' decision over 1915 and 1916 to make real use of this right was an important step forward. It provided for St Mary's, however, an unfortunate pattern by which other than engineering students transferred after one or two years to Dalhousie so as to be able to leave college with a fully recognized degree. Thus it was that even some years before the Carnegie Foundation began to interest itself actively in a maritime federation, negotiations for an affiliation of St Mary's with Dalhousie were 'in progress.'[15]

When the federation question came up in 1922, the two St Mary's presidents involved, brothers Cornelia and Stirling, were strongly in favour of it, and remained so even after the Sacred Roman Congregation, 24 October 1924, discouraged the project. Indeed, during 1924, the senate of St Mary's had its archbishop-chancellor submit on the occasion of his *ad limina* visit to Rome a petition to be allowed to enter a private affiliation with Dalhousie distinct from the plan for federation which the Holy See had discouraged. Discussions were held with Dalhousie representatives and terms of agreement proposed. St Mary's was to look after all the academic needs of its students during their first

14 K.C.M. Sills and W.S. Learned, *Education in the Maritime Provinces of Canada*, New York: The Carnegie Foundation, 1922, 26

15 Lannon, 'A Survey,' 128

two years, but to provide only philosophy, psychology, economics, pedagogy, history, and biology, during their last two years, when the students would be enrolled in Dalhousie. Roman approval of such a proposed affiliation did not come until 1927, but by that time Dalhousie's official thinking on the subject proved not to be that of her earlier spokesmen. By 1933, when Dalhousie had a new president, C.W. Stanley, and when there were many new faces on its board of governors, and when St Mary's had very strong encouragement from the apostolic delegate, Archbishop Cassulo, more hopeful discussions were held; but these too came to nothing because they were based on the assumption that the expenses to be incurred would be borne by the Carnegie Corporation, which turned out not to be the case.

This painful struggle for wider recognition of its work characterized the St Mary's of the entire period of the brothers' administration. Whether they would ultimately have attained their objectives will never be known. That they did not attain them before 1940 is in large part to be attributed to the distracting controversy over their contract with the archdiocese of Halifax, which dissipated so much of the brothers' energy and so completely frustrated their hopes for a great university college.

The contract between the Christian Brothers of Ireland and the archdiocese of Halifax, as has been seen, was generous to the brothers. Two factors, the assuring the brothers that there would be no outside interference in the operation of their college, and the directing of all revenues towards them with no specific provisions for reimbursing the diocese for sums paid to cover college deficits, or with no assigning of responsibility for physical expansion, were to prove quite troublesome. Besides, there was some flaunting of privileges: a freedom from interference clause was actually written into a new act of the provincial legislature in 1918. This new act was felt to be necessary lest legal forfeiture had occurred during the period 1881 to 1903 when the college was closed. The act served to confirm the charter and other university powers enjoyed by the institution. It also specifically named the archbishop as chancellor *ex officio*, whereas the act of 1878 had named the archbishop as the person whose duty it was to appoint the chancellor. Lest this specifying of the archbishop as chancellor be taken to give him internal rights in the operation of the college, the act, in referring to the agreement of 1914 between the bishop and the brothers, makes clear that the new act is not to be construed 'to authorize any interference with the teaching staff of the college or with its internal or domestic management which is in the hands of the said Order.'

So long as Archbishop McCarthy was in charge of the archdiocese there was no trouble. In 1929, however, the ailing McCarthy was given a coadjutor, Archbishop Thomas O'Donnell, a Toronto priest who had been bishop of Victoria since 1924. O'Donnell at once took the position that the archdiocese of Halifax was putting too much money into St Mary's for the return it was getting, and that the archbishop was being improperly deprived of his right to interfere in the affairs of a college which was ecclesiastical in its foundation and operation and whose buildings and properties, moreover, he owned.

The gathering storm broke during commencement exercises in the fall of 1929. The president, Brother Stirling, referred in his opening address to building plans. O'Donnell, speaking later on the programme, reminded the audience and Brother Stirling of a prior indebtedness of the college to the archdiocese in the amount of $37,000, an indebtedness incurred when the archdiocese had a few years back added to the original property leased by the brothers. He informed the president that he would begin immediately to hold back certain annual payments – from the Power estate – which came to the college through his hands in order to remove this indebtedness. There was, in other words, disagreement both as to the nature and the justice of the original contract. Indeed, the archbishop implied on a number of occasions that his predecessor had never been of sound enough mind to make so important a contract.

The issue was not faced calmly, nor the contract sensibly reviewed and revised, owing to intransigence by both parties concerned. O'Donnell referred the matter to the Roman congregation of religious. The congregation appointed Archbishop Villeneuve of Quebec as special visitor to the college, asking him to prepare a full report. The congregation's final decision of 21 December 1931, announced through Andrea Cassulo, the apostolic delegate, upheld the validity of the original contract and the legality of the position taken by the brothers. The archbishop never bowed to the decision which he attributed to the influence of the Irish Christian Brothers in Rome. He refused thenceforth to have any dealings with St Mary's 'except in so far as canon law requires.' He asked his priests to keep away from the college; and he informed the brothers that 'we no longer desire to be considered chancellor.'[16] The deadlock thus produced remained unchanged until O'Donnell's death in 1937.

When Archbishop John T. McNally came to Halifax during 1937, he was determined to settle the St Mary's question once and for all. He

16 Ibid., 135

immediately reopened the case in Rome, taking it not to the congregation of religious but to the congregation of seminaries and universities,
raising not the issue of the inviolability of the original contract but the
canonical right of a bishop to concern himself in the affairs of an ecclesiastical institution. This time the decision went against the brothers.
The archbishop was to have full and direct administration of his college
and to be free to name one of his priests to the presidency; he was to
maintain a minimum of three brothers on the college faculty, and was
to provide places for the others elsewhere at a lower educational level
and provide them with a religious house to live in. The superior general
of the Christian Brothers, J.P. Noonan, decided not to carry on under
these new conditions and announced the withdrawal of his men from
Halifax, effective in 1940, so as to give the archbishop a full year in
which to arrange for a new administration.

The year 1939–40 brought to a close the twenty-seven year administration of St Mary's by the Christian Brothers of Ireland. In Mc-
Carthy's day their experience had been in the main happy, although
what with World War 1 and the subsequent abortive efforts at a maritime university federation, they had not been able to develop the college academically as either they or their friends would have liked. Their
regime was an extraordinarily popular one with the Catholic citizens of
Halifax. Their suspending of classes, for example, for two months
following the Halifax explosion of 16 December 1917, so that the
building could be placed at the disposal of the United States Medical
Corps as a hospital, was everywhere regarded as an earnest of genuine
public spirit. So too were their countless financial concessions to penni-
less students

The brothers, however, had not found a way to prevent the college
from being a financial burden on the diocese, nor were they able to
bring to it great academic prestige; nor had they been able to recruit
vocations for the diocesan priesthood on what the bishops felt to be an
adequately large scale. Failures of this kind, which the brothers could do
little about, lay behind their differences with archbishops O'Donnell
and McNally. The general public was less disposed than the bishops to
think of these as failures. A strong popular expression of gratitude and
love marked the gala convocation held in the spring of 1940 just before
their departure. When the brothers left Halifax they were not dis-
persed, but sent as a group to New Rochelle, where they opened Iona
College, which has since become an important centre of their university
activity in America.

The presidential appointments during the years 1913 to 1940 were as follows: Brother Culhane 1913–19, Brother Cornelia 1919–22, Brother Culhane 1922–5, Brother Stirling 1925–31, Brother Cornelia 1931–7, Brother Lannon 1937–40.

Sixth Period: Since 1940

When Archbishop McNally received a favourable judgment in his case against the Christian Brothers of Ireland, his first thought was to name a president from among his own priests. He had in mind to recall Gerald B. Phelan, who had been loaned to St Michael's College, Toronto and who was at the time president of the Institute of Mediaeval Studies. Phelan was a graduate of St Mary's and had taught there as a priest under the brothers from 1917 to 1922. He was not himself in favour of the appointment, but was prepared to accept it out of deference to his ordinary. Other counsel happily prevailed, particularly that of John Quinan, who strongly urged that another attempt be made to bring the Jesuit Fathers to Halifax. McNally was hesitant at first. He was disposed to offer the Jesuits St Mary's on a trial basis for six years. He visited Winnipeg and mentioned his plan in conversations at Camp Morton with his friend Archbishop Sinnott. Sinnott made light of a cautionary measure not likely to encourage acceptance. His advice, based on six years' experience with the Jesuits in St Paul's, was that St Mary's be offered firmly and permanently to the Jesuits. McNally took the advice. This time the invitation was not refused and the fall term of 1940 opened with the college under the direction of the Jesuits of the Upper Canada Province. The Jesuits agreed to run the university if the board of governors and the diocese would assume the burdens of owning and financing it.

Since 1940 the issues have been rather different. With all his well-known extravagance and, indeed, magnificence in the older theological sense of the word, Archbishop McNally wanted a college, or rather, a university, of which the citizens of Halifax could be proud for the brilliance of its learning and the splendour of its home. The regime of the Jesuits in Halifax has been a courageous if halting and uncertain progress towards the fulfilment of such a dream.

Something both of the larger concept of university and of the unfortunate controversies of the thirties and earlier can be traced through the succession of parliamentary 'Acts respecting St Mary's' passed since the coming of the Jesuits. The first of these acts, that of 1949, authorized the episcopal corporation to enter an agreement with the Jesuits or any religious order permitting that order to conduct St Mary's free of control or supervision *of the senate*, protecting the archbishop's victory of 1939 yet not placing the teaching order under another academic body; and also enabling the Jesuits to use the name of St Mary's College to collect debts due them, assuring in other words that the Power estate would benefit the college. The act of 1952, the last during McNally's lifetime, was 'an Act Respecting St Mary's University as the name now reads' which spelt out clearly the earlier and less assuming 'college ... deemed and taken to be a University' of the original act of 1841. A subsequent recent act, that of 1962, set up a university corporation distinct from the episcopal; and although it left the institution under Archbishop J.G. Berry and his consultors, it did so in a capacity other than the strictly ecclesiastical, and created a reasonably autonomous board of governors and a university administration more in line with contemporary practice, and more in line, incidentally, with the original act of 1841.

In 1951 St Mary's was moved from Quinpool Street to the Collins estate at Gorsebrook, not far from the Dalhousie campus. Archbishop McNally's attention had been called to the availability of this splendid downtown property, in use at the time as a golf course, by Fathers Quinan and Phelan. He purchased it at once and himself personally supervised the erection of the present main building. The heavy debt incurred by this transaction has, since 1951, constituted a major problem both for the archdiocese and the university. Until it is solved, the development of the university must remain painfully cautious. The debt, however, has not been the only problem. There have not been up to the present enough Catholic students from Halifax to support two distinct and fully developed universities, one for men and one for women, although this situation could right itself in time.

The obvious suggestion that the two institutions unite their operations is not easily implemented. There was a stage back in 1948 when something might have been done. Mount St Vincent was in search of a new site. Archbishop McNally offered to sell the Sisters of Charity ten acres of the Gorsebrook estate for their new college. The sisters, especially Mother Berchmans, had misgivings but indicated their willingness to accept the offer. It was, however, ultimately withdrawn because the Jesuits thought the property too small for subdivision and because the provincialate was not at the time disposed to have women on the campus. Following the disastrous fire at the motherhouse in 1951, the Sisters of Charity built their present building at Rockingham at considerable expense to themselves. An additional factor in the perpetuating of the present situation is the importance of Mount St Vincent for the educating and qualifying as teachers of the Sisters of Charity, a convenience not easily continued in the event of Mount St Vincent's being taken over by St Mary's.

St. Mary's University has in recent years been of considerable service to the Jesuit houses of study elsewhere in Canada. In 1957, Ignatius College (the novitiate house in Guelph) and Regis College (the seminary in Toronto) effected an accrediting affiliation with St Mary's by which their students might qualify for civil degrees carrying general recognition. St Mary's also provides degrees in theology for Regis students.

Important for the development of St Mary's has been the discontinuing of the high school since 1963, and the subsequent interest in expanding into graduate studies: theology and education on their own campus, social work at the Maritime School, and other disciplines occasionally at Dalhousie. Such expansion into Dalhousie is pretty much an *ad hoc* arrangement and is not easily implemented, partly because it is costly, partly because Dalhousie has always been hesitant about collaboration, and especially at the graduate level. Late in 1966 the first purely academic post-graduate programme was announced by Bernard S. Sheehan, dean of arts and sciences, one leading to the MA in history of science – an interdisciplinary field in which scholars of widely separated interests could collaborate. History of science is still only beginning to be cultivated seriously in Canadian universities. Meanwhile, St Mary's continues to need more opportunities if it is to satisfy the scholarly ambitions of the staff.

Other recent developments have been the opening up of registration in all courses to women; and a re-evaluation in depth of the academic structure of the modern university. The decision to go co-educational followed years of discussion with the administration of Mount St Vincent and the archbishop, and after some experimenting in the evening and adult divisions. Mount St Vincent objected until the end on principle: that Catholic women's colleges are sociologically sound, that the presence of a nearby Catholic co-educational university could only be disruptive, and that historical circumstances had made the older situation a commitment. In December 1967 the board of governors, chaired by Archbishop Hayes, decided that St Mary's had to go co-educational for its own integrity as a contemporary university. The decision became effective during 1968–9. The impact of the move on the overall pattern of Catholic higher education in the Halifax area is not yet clear.

In a material way, there has also been important recent development made possible by the successful functioning of the Association of Atlantic Universities and the formation of a Nova Scotia grants committee. The government is now financing up to 90 per cent of certain types of new university building. Thus in 1968 and 1969, the Tower building for residence students was added to the complex; and in 1969, several storeys were added to the science wing.

Recent years have also begun to see at St Mary's experimentation in the strategies of teaching and learning paralleling similar revolutionary movements elsewhere. The first of these experiments was 'Project Parallel,' an attempt to exploit the principle of co-ordination in the giving of key courses – theology, history, literature – within the more traditional college structure. It was a professors' experiment: Patrick J. Kerans in theology, Roger Crowther in history, Robert J. Bollini in literature. Project Parallel led to the establishing within St. Mary's of an Institute for the Study of Values. Speaking for this institute in the fall and winter of 1968–9, Father Daniel Fogarty published a document in which he set forth in detail a proposal to establish at St Mary's an Inner College where selected students and professors would attempt to break loose from traditional admission norms, the lecture system, the fragmentation of learning into subjects and departments, and examinations by formally patterned competitive testing. The proposed Inner College was a sort of amalgam of current tendencies in the sociology of education: separation from the stirps, healing illnesses, establishing new community, achieving personalized excellence. Such an experiment, valid in these times, seeks to function creatively within the enclaves of knowledge.[17]

St Mary's has had a turbulent kind of history since 1940. The Jesuits accepted the challenge to build a modern university and have moved convincingly toward their objective: The provincial administration has sent a sequence of strong rectors and presidents to direct the project: Christopher Keating 1940–3, Francis Smith 1943–5, T.J. Mullaly 1945–50, F.J. Lynch 1950–6, Patrick G. Malone 1956–9, C.J. Fischer 1959–67, and Henry J. Labelle 1967–70. The presidents down to and including Fischer have also been religious superiors. In 1966, after Fischer's canonical term as president and religious superior had been completed, the offices were divided. Fischer remained president during 1966–7 but John Hochban became rector of the house. When Labelle became president in 1967, he did not take the rectorship.

Moving into the seventies St Mary's was still in the process of revolutionary change as the board sought new ways to remove the debt on

17 Daniel Fogarty, *A Proposed Inner College for Saint Mary's University*, Halifax: Institute for the Study of Values, St Mary's University, 1969

the archdiocese and to modernize the university's governance. A completely new St Mary's University Act was put through the Nova Scotia legislature during March and April 1970.[18] The act provided for the formation of a new board of governors constituted as follows: the archbishop and his vicar general ex officio, 3 members appointed by the archdiocese, 1 appointed by the Jesuits, 6 by the faculty, 4 by the students, 6 by the alumni, 5 (including 2 named by the governor-in-council) by the board itself.

The act also provided for the complete autonomy of the university from archdiocesan control, and for the making of a new agreement between the board and the episcopal corporation concerning the method of handling the existing debt. Perhaps archaic in the act is the provision for the archbishop and his vicar general to be chancellor and vice-chancellor respectively.

When the new act was in preparation, Labelle resigned the presidency in order to allow the proposed new board a free hand. A search committee for a president was appointed. One of the first pieces of business of the new board of governors was to announce in September 1970 the name of the new president, David Owen Carrigan, principal and dean of arts of King's College, London. Carrigan, a layman, was a young but experienced administrator who was now for the second time taking over the senior appointment in a Catholic institution from a clergyman. Carrigan's appointment was effective 1 July 1971. In the meantime St Mary's was left in the hands of an acting head, Edmund Morris, Vice-president in charge of finances and development. During 1970–1 the university functioned normally with the Jesuits maintaining teaching and administrative roles and their involvement in the future of St Mary's.

18 An Act to Amend and Consolidate the Acts Relating to St. Mary's University; Bill no. 102, House of Assembly, Nova Scotia, Session 1970; signed 31 July 1970.

St Francis Xavier University

ANTIGONISH, NS

1855

St Francis Xavier University is located between the Trans-Canada Highway and trunk road no. 4 at the west end of the small town of Antigonish near the straits separating the mainland of Nova Scotia from Cape
Breton Island. The campus covers an area of over one hundred acres
on which now stand 25 buildings with more on the draughting board[1]
and three extensive playing fields. Replacement value is in excess of
20 million dollars. The academic operation as of 1969 is as follows: a
faculty of arts providing unstructured concentrations in two related
subjects in 17 arts courses, departments including business administration, education, theology, and secretarial arts; a separate faculty of
science with 10 departments and including three years of engineering,
home economics, and nursing; an extension department and TV People's
School; the Coady International Institute. There is no formally erected
graduate division, but graduate work is carried on in some departments,
especially in chemistry, Celtic studies, education, social work, and
guidance.

The history of St Francis Xavier University properly begins with the
opening of a seminary at Arichat, 20 July 1853, when higher education
in eastern Nova Scotia can be said to detach itself from the grammar
schools.[2] The recurring names met in the surviving records of the earlier

1 Buildings on the St Francis Xavier campus from west to east: 1 MacIsaac Hall
(residence 1969); 2 The John R. MacDonald Building: Coady International Institute
(1961); 3 The Malcolm F. MacNeil Building; Coady International Institute (1969);
4 Music Building (former TV station acquired by university 1965); 5 Oland Centre
(gymnasiums, physical education, recreation 1967); 6 Academic Centre (classroom
complex, Nicholson Hall, and office tower 1969); 7 Memorial Rink (1922, renovated
1963); 8 Central Heating Plant and Laundry (1921, renovated 1959); 9 Maintenance Building (1960); 10 Old Gymnasium (1916, renovated as Studio Theatre
1969); 11 University Chapel and Auditorium (1947); 12 Plessis, Fraser, and Burke
Houses (three-house residential unit 1962); 13 MacKinnon Hall (1951); 14 Morrison Hall (1938, addition 1962); 15 Cameron Hall (1945); 16 Mockler Hall (1916);
17 Old Library (1916, renovated 1964 as temporary student union building, additional renovation 1969 to provide student lounge); 18 Xavier Hall (1880, with
several additions); 19 Physics and Chemistry Building (1957); 20 MacNeil
Engineering Hall (1910); 21 Angus L. Macdonald Library (1964); 22 Immaculata
Hall (1917); 23 Gilmora Hall (1938); 24 Camden Hall and Marguerite Hall (1963);
25 Lane Hall (1967)
2 A.A. Johnston, *A History of the Catholic Church in Eastern Nova Scotia,*

institutions reveal both the sequence of educational development in the eastern diocese and the true genesis of the Arichat Seminary. In 1824 Rev. William B. MacLeod and Mr Malcolm MacLellan, master, began to provide instruction for pre-seminarians, first privately at Grand Narrows, then formally at the East Bay School (locally described as 'the college'), with Colin Francis MacKinnon a member of the original class of nine students. In 1838 MacKinnon, by this time parish priest of St Andrew's, and MacLellan, headmaster, established the not undistinguished St Andrew's Grammar School where John Cameron was a student. In 1853, His Lordship, Colin Francis MacKinnon, second bishop of Arichat, named Dr John Schulte of Paderborn and Rome first rector of his advanced seminary and had Cameron studying at the Urban College of the Propaganda against the day when he would take over the rectorship of the seminary at Arichat.

A pastoral letter issued by Bishop MacKinnon on the day of his consecration in February 1852 announced his decision to found a seminary, a decision which he began to carry out within six months. He had hoped, but in vain, to be able to staff it with priests from Dublin. He was successful, however, in obtaining Schulte from Rome through the kindness of Cardinal Franzoni, prefect of the Sacred Congregation for the Propagation of the Faith. There was, indeed, much haste and makeshift about the new institution which opened its doors on 20 July 1853: it could at first offer no course in theology; it was housed in a rented building, possibly because the bishop intended from the beginning to move it to the more centrally located Antigonish; it attracted during the first year only fifteen students; and the rector, unused to pioneer conditions, seems not to have been suitable for the office. At any rate when in 1854 Dr Cameron returned from Rome, where he had been studying at the Urban College and where he had stayed on an extra three months as acting rector, he took over the rectorship. Schulte became director of studies.[3]

The move to Antigonish took place on 2 September 1855. The idea of an advanced seminary was not abandoned, but was greatly modified. The new institution was to be a 'college for the public' and it was to provide its constituency with teachers as well as priests. At Arichat the seminary had no official name. It was understood that it would, after its removal to Antigonish, be known as the Seminary of St. Ninian, in honour of the patron of the parish Church at Antigonish. It was given

Antigonish: St Francis Xavier University Press, 1960; Malcolm MacDonnell, 'The Early History of St Francis Xavier University,' Report of the Canadian Catholic Historical Association, 15(1947–8), 81–90

3 Schulte's subsequent record was disappointing. He went from Antigonish to Simcoe in Canada West and is known to have apostacized in 1861.

the name St Francis Xavier College by the rector either to acknowledge financial help from the Society for Foreign Missions or in honour of the tercentenary of St Francis Xavier celebrated some three years before.

St. Francis Xavier College opened in Antigonish with a staff of six, including the rector Dr Cameron, Dr Schulte, Father William Chisholm, Mr Rod MacDonald, and Mr Hugh Cameron, and with 49 students. The college was housed in a building in town erected for the purpose. In addition, Bishop Fraser's house (the 'Big House') on the site of the present campus was acquired as a residence. The academic programme of the new college is nowhere described in detail. But in view of the ecclesiastical background of the institution, and because graduates were in many cases to go to Laval Seminary, the course taken must have closely resembled that of the usual *collège*. In addition, at least within a few years after the opening, theology was being read under the direction of priest-professors by lay masters proceeding to orders.

The financing of the college was primarily the responsibility of the bishop and was a serious problem. The college had from the beginning, that is, from 1855 on, an annual grant of £250 from the Nova Scotia government. This grant became $1000 in 1863, $1400 in 1865, and $1500 in 1876.[4] Its discontinuance after 1881 was to cause considerable hardship. Some early gifts of a private nature are also recorded: one-half of a bequest of £5805 which came to the diocese shortly after the opening of the seminary at Arichat; a direct gift of 20,000 francs from the French Society for the Foreign Missions; and a library of 2000 books from a bequest of John Ryan of Halifax, who died while still a student at the Propaganda College in Rome.

The rectorship of the college at Antigonish was an episcopal appointment and was held by Dr John Cameron from 1854 (when the college was still at Arichat) until 1863. In that year Cameron was appointed parish priest of Arichat. Dr Cameron is always regarded as the first rector of St Francis Xavier since he held the office when the 'public college' was established at Antigonish. The identity of his successor is not at all clear. It is rather likely that Bishop MacKinnon made no appointment and himself assumed the duties of the rector.[5] The bishop had actually taken up residence in the college building back in 1858[6] and could well have taken on the duties of the office after 1863. If he

4 D.C. Harvey, *An Introduction to the History of Dalhousie University*, Halifax, 1938, 88, n.1

5 This statement is based on the carefully weighed opinion of Father A.A. Johnston, who has consulted all the known documents. Bishop MacKinnon, who was deeply attached to the college, was subject to fits of depression if not, indeed, of insanity.

6 A.A. Johnston, *The First Five Bishops of the Diocese of Antigonish* (pamphlet reprinted from *The Casket*, Antigonish, NS, 7, 14 July 1960), 9

did so, his intermittent mental illnesses which began about that time must have been a source of embarrassment to the staff. The next man described by the records as rector was Hugh Gillis, who is so listed in the college prospectus for 1878–9.[7] Gillis is also described as 'Rector of the College' during 1878 in the reminiscences of Bishop Alexander Mac-Donald.[8] How long he held the rectorship before 1878 cannot be determined, but he was long closely associated with the administration, being the first priest of the diocese trained and ordained right in Antigonish, and ever since that time a member of the college faculty.

Little is known of the history of the college during the years 1865 to 1877, but they must have been interesting enough years. Noteworthy during this period is that on 7 May 1866, the legislature of Nova Scotia passed the act which gave St Francis Xavier its university charter. At this time the college, or university, was still receiving the small annual provincial grant, the discontinuance of which in 1881 was to lead to the first of many appeals for endowment and to the creation of a board of governors. Also noteworthy is the following statement in the prospectus of 1878–9: 'In 1875 it [St Francis Xavier] was affiliated to the Halifax University.'

The University of Halifax was actually established by an act of the legislature in 1876. This act was the provincial government's reply to the sectarian requests made during 1875 for larger and fairer distribution of grants. The act increased the grants to sectarian institutions (St Francis Xavier was raised from $1400 to $1500), but also set up a new experimental University of Halifax, which, like the University of London, was to be an examining body only. The existing colleges did not lose their own degree-conferring powers but were invited to experiment in this new co-operative venture by sending candidates to Halifax for examination by a board of examiners chosen from all the universities. The universities were the more disposed to acquiesce in this arrangement in view of the fact that the University of Halifax was established by the same piece of legislation which assured them of their increased grants until 1881.

During Bishop MacKinnon's time St Francis Xavier sent no candidates to Halifax for examination. In 1877, however, Bishop MacKinnon resigned and was succeeded as bishop by Dr John Cameron, the same Dr Cameron who had been the second rector of the college. The univer-

7 'Prospectus for 1878–1879' located in the president's office of St Francis Xavier University
8 Rt Rev. Alexander MacDonald, DD, *A Bit of Autobiography*, Victoria, BC: Willows Press, 1920, section headed 'College.' The pages and chapters of this interesting little volume are unnumbered.

sity felt the change at once. Orders came from Arichat that the university was to participate in the government's plan for examining students in Halifax; a new rector, Dr Angus Cameron, was explicitly named to the office which may or may not have been formally held by Hugh Gillis; and a new building, which still survives as the east wing of Xavier Hall, was erected with costs borne by the bishop and clergy of the diocese.

Bishop Alexander MacDonald speaks dramatically and with feeling of the University of Halifax and its examinations:

It was an examining university, modelled on that of London. Mr Sumichrast, later of Harvard, was secretary, and the examiners were representative men from the various Colleges. The late Archbishop MacDonald, then the Rev. Ronald MacDonald, PP, Pictou, was examiner in logic and psychology. The thing is fresher in my memory that I took the BA examinations in the University in the summer of '79 and failed to pass. But hereby hangs a tale: ... During the month of February, if I remember rightly, the late Bishop Cameron, who then resided at Arichat, wrote to the faculty urging that some of the senior students should prepare to go up for the Halifax University BA examinations in the coming June. Four volunteered, but only two faced the exams – Angus Chisholm and myself. The enterprise was but a forlorn hope from the first, for the work of two years had to be crowded into twice as many months. We failed in chemistry, but had good marks in all the other subjects, and the superintendent of education wrote the bishop a congratulatory letter on the showing made by the college. There was question at the time of withdrawing the grant from denominational colleges, and the examinations of 1879 were meant to put their efficiency to the proof.[9]

Bishop MacDonald goes on to explain how he and Chisholm prepared themselves in Latin, Greek, and chemistry. They found Latin quite easy. Greek was more formidable but they got it sufficiently under control by June to pass creditably an examination covering grammar, a book of Homer, and a book of Xenophon. 'But,' writes the bishop, 'William's Inorganic Chemistry was too big a mouthful.'

The University of Halifax scheme was quietly shelved after the academic year 1880–1.[10] With its demise grants to the colleges came to an end, and St Francis Xavier, like the others, had to seek new means of

9 Ibid.
10 The act was still on the books in 1909. P.J. Nicholson of the class of 1890 wrote in *The Xaverian*, 13(1909), 27–30, an article entitled 'The University of Halifax – Should it be Revived?' The future president of St Francis Xavier gave as his opinion at this early date that the Halifax examining body ought to be revived.

survival. In 1881 was launched the first public appeal for funds, an endeavour which ultimately raised an endowment of some $21,000. In 1882 St Francis Xavier ceased legally to be a 'bishop's college' and all its property was transferred from the episcopal corporation to a board of governors created at the direction of the provincial government. In the same year the episcopal see was transferred from Arichat to Antigonish.

Another event of this period with great significance for the University was the opening in 1883 of the Young Ladies' Academy of the Convent of St Bernard. Though not at first intended for university students and not technically part of St Francis Xavier, it quickly established itself in the campus complex and was one day to house the women students of the university.

Angus Cameron was succeeded as rector by Dr Neil McNeil, who held the office from 1884 to 1891. McNeil's rectorship was in no way spectacular but it was a period of strength and steady advance. McNeil added the west wing of Xavier Hall and conducted a sound academic institution. The records from 1890 show that 106 students were registered, that the first MA degree was conferred upon A.J.G. MacEachan, and that the alumni then included two bishops, fifty-five priests, a judge, two senators, five members of parliament, nineteen lawyers, nineteen doctors, and many teachers. The university was now an influential factor in the life of Nova Scotia and Canada. The rector attracted little attention to himself while he held the office, but he was a genuine and able man, and was throughout his subsequent career to be instrumental in bringing St Francis Xavier's to the attention of Canadians. He became, as is well known, one of English-speaking Canada's leading ecclesiastical figures. He was named bishop of St George's, Newfoundland, in 1895, archbishop of Vancouver in 1910, and archbishop of Toronto in 1912. His knowledge of Canada, his continuing interest in education, and his close contact with events and people in Antigonish during the 1920s were to enhance greatly the national stature of the institution which during his rectorship in the 1880s and early 1890s was only beginning to move towards economic stability and academic maturity.[11]

Two more rectors, Dr Daniel A. Chisholm, who held the office from 1891 to 1898, and Dr Alexander MacDonald Thompson, from 1898 to 1906, guided the university through the closing years of its first half century. The significant events of their combined rectorships were these: the organizing in 1893 of the Alumni Association, which was destined to become far and away the most influential and successful of

11 George Boyle, *Pioneer in Purple: The Life and Work of Archbishop Neil McNeil*, Montreal: Palm, 1951

such bodies in Canadian Catholic institutions; the affiliation of St Bernard's Academy in 1894, giving St Francis Xavier the distinction of being 'the first Catholic university in America to provide for women courses leading to the bachelor's degree'; the founding and consolidating between 1895 and 1897 of the diocesan Sisters of St Martha for the providing of domestic facilities for the university, a community which was one day to direct the university's school of nursing; and the opening in 1899 of courses of instruction in civil and mechanical engineering, the first instance of such courses in Nova Scotia. In 1907 the Nova Scotia Technical College was set up with Acadia, Dalhousie, King's, Mount Allison, St Francis Xavier, and St Mary's willing to collaborate in a common programme. They agreed to provide in their own institutions a uniform two-year pre-engineering course preparatory to a final two years taken at the Nova Scotia Technical College in Halifax.

Dr Thompson's address, delivered in 1905 on the occasion of the celebration of the fiftieth anniversary of the founding, fittingly closes the formative period of the university's development by calling attention to the constant condition of material poverty in which it had always existed, the uncompromising dedication to diocese and Church which governed its objectives, and the warm humanity of the Scottish, Irish, and Acadian people of eastern Nova Scotia.

Dr Thompson's transfer from the rectorship of St Francis Xavier to the pastorate of St Anne's, Glace Bay, was the occasion for considerable criticism of his financial, academic, administrative, and disciplinary policies. He was, it was being said, not finding the funds for development and consequently not attracting scholars to Antigonish, not surrendering to the board of governors sufficient autonomy to permit it to function effectively to the advantage of the university, and was permitting the hitherto rigid discipline of student life to be wantonly relaxed in favour of the more relaxed and benign principles of St John Bosco, which he had come to appreciate while a student in Rome. Bishop Cameron rightly referred to the criticisms as 'persecution,' but they no doubt only reflected the tensions of the incipient expansion which was to mark the thirty-year rectorship of Dr Hugh (H.P.) MacPherson, who took office in November 1906.

MacPherson, rector from 1906 to 1936, in real if not always harmonious collaboration with the remarkable Father J. J. Tompkins and Dr M.M. Coady, brought the university through what is now felt to have been the distinctive and characterizing period of its development.[12] Ordained in 1892 before the completion of his course at Laval, and

12 W.X. Edwards, 'The MacPherson-Tompkins Era of St Francis Xavier University,' *Report of the Canadian Catholic Historical Association*, 20(1953), 49–65

honoured in 1906 by a doctoral degree conferred by his alma mater in view of his native talent and approaching appointment, he turned his tremendous energies to the making of a great modern university. The special achievements of his administration can be briefly outlined under three headings: financial support, academic awareness, social doctrine and action.

The finding of financial support is the constant bugbear of any rector or president. MacPherson's first step was taken at the local level, where he elicited enthusiastic if relatively limited support from parish units, the Knights of Columbus, and the diocesan clergy. He then had the governors turn seriously to endowment, and as early as 1907 they were at work on their first $100,000 objective. Gradually, benefactors outside the local community were found, particularly the Boston contractor Neil MacNeil and Dr John E. Somers of Cambridge, who were largely responsible for the building of MacNeil Engineering Hall (1911), the University Chapel (1912), the Mockler Hall residence (1916), and the Gymnasium (1916). By some standards of judgment these benefactions were modest enough, but they far outmeasure those received by any other Catholic institution in English-speaking Canada.

During these same years there was a broadening of academic awareness. New incentive certainly came with J.J. Tompkins, who joined the staff in 1902, and it became accentuated with his appointment as vice-president and director of studies in 1908. Tompkins was a vigorous advocate of a policy of sacrifice in favour of a trained and qualified staff. He also believed that dignity should attach to appointment. His influence is to be detected in the following: the establishing in 1907 of a chair of English, held by A.J.C. MacEachan, the university's first MA, and of the chair of Gaelic (1907), held by MacLean Sinclair; the sending of C.J. Connolly to Munich for biology, of D.J. MacDonald to Washington for English, of A.B. MacDonald and Myles N. Tompkins to Guelph for agriculture, and P.J. Nicholson to Baltimore for physics. Tompkins' efforts to raise the intellectual tone of the campus are further seen in the establishing at the end of World War 1 of two additional important chairs: one in Latin and Greek, donated by Dr J.E. Somers; one in French, established by the Carnegie Corporation in recognition of the university's obligations to its Acadian constituency. The university itself established a chair of education, and provided special scholarships for Acadian boys. Tompkins also took a keen interest in university associations. In 1912 he attended the meeting of the Association of British Universities held at University College, Oxford, where as will be seen he acquired his first clear insight into the work of university extension and where he learned that competent professors were sometimes disposed to accept offers from outside England. He was notably successful in 1913 in getting Professor W.H. Bucknell to come from Cambridge to Antigonish. Tompkins' achievements in the area of strictly academic awakening are too often forgotten, overshadowed as they are by his better-known work in the areas of Christian social doctrine and practice.

H.P. MacPherson's administration also saw the birth and growth of activity in social theory and action which has in more recent years been identified as the 'Antigonish Movement.'[13] Attention here is directed specifically to this movement as it concerns the university. The department of university extension of St Francis Xavier, formally established in 1929, has an interesting background which must here be traced at least in outline.

Between 1912 and 1914, Dr Hugh MacPherson of the university faculty (not to be confused with 'H.P.,' the rector) began to interest himself in the problems of local woolgrowers, first, by providing them with advice about the proper preparing of high grade wool, then by introducing them to the techniques of co-operative selling. The immediate success of his efforts led to his appointment in 1914 as agricultural representative of Antigonish county to the provincial government. Moreover, his little producers' co-operative assumed sufficient cohesion to become the basis of the Canadian Woolgrowers Association later established. During 1915 Hugh MacPherson actually gave a short course of lectures in agriculture.

Coincidental with MacPherson's communal interests came Father Tompkins' attending the British Universities Conference in 1912, where he heard Dr Barrett of Melbourne report on the extension programme under way at the University of Wisconsin. Tompkins was always to remember Barrett's remark: 'The University of Wisconsin bases itself on a tripod: research, instruction, and popularization.' It was not long until Tompkins and MacPherson were sharing interests and exchanging ideas. 'Father Tompkins,' writes Hugh MacPherson, 'was my first convert.' It was Father Tompkins who succeeded in arresting the attention of others, notably of Father Moses M. Coady, the first director of university extension in Antigonish, and of Angus B. MacDonald, the future secretary-general of the Co-op Union of Canada.

The next significant step towards the Antigonish Movement was

13 A.F. Laidlaw, *The Campus and the University*, Montreal: Harvest House, 1961; George Boyle, *Father Tompkins of Nova Scotia*, New York; P.J. Kenedy and Sons, 1953

Tompkins' decision to utilize the columns of *The Casket*. It was he who had encouraged Bishop Morrison to buy out Michael Donovan's controlling shares of this local newspaper, so it was only natural that he should make it a means of communication between gown and town. In January 1918 he supervised a new regular column, 'For the People,' a sort of professors' forum. The column's constant theme was that education must become a social apostolate and go to the people, and that people must be converted to education and go, even as adults, to school.

The identifiable influences bearing upon Tompkins and his colleagues (who included in addition to university personnel like Hugh MacPherson, C.J. Connolly, M.M. Coady, and others, Henry Somerville and Archbishop Neil McNeil of Toronto) were the following: the new state university outlook as exemplified in Wisconsin and Alberta; the experiences of the Workers' Educational Association founded in England in 1903; the success of Alphonse Desjardins' *caisse populaire* after its introduction into Canada in 1900; Bishop Grundtvig's Danish 'people's schools'; and Dr Warbasse's volume *Co-Operative Democracy*, to say nothing of Leo XIII's *Rerum Novarum* in 1891 and trends in current Christian social thought.

The classic statement of the position and objectives held by Father Tompkins appeared in 1920 in a pamphlet entitled *Knowledge for The People*. The pamphlet is almost a charter for extension work and adult education in Canada. It is essentially an appeal for popular education in social subjects by intelligent educators rather than leaving these areas to anarchists and charlatans; it proceeds from a haunting dread that the Canadian university is far too prone to exist in 'isolated eminence.' The doctrine set forth in *Knowledge for the People* was subsequently programmed in the People's School. Two sessions of this school were held in Antigonish, the first, between 17 January and 12 March 1921, the second during the following winter. Two more sessions of the People's School were held in Glace Bay in 1923 and 1924. These were noble experiments. They were not tried often nor were they much imitated because they tended to place the school outside the university, which was not to prove the enduring pattern of university extension, not at least until radio and television made the task more possible. In the meantime Tompkins himself left the universitly, an episode (as will shortly appear) in an entirely different story.

The final drive for a fully patterned university department of extension came from outside the university from a sequence of five clergy conferences held by the priests of Antigonish diocese (which included, of course, the priests of the university) between 1924 and 1928. These conferences were held to deal with social and economic problems in eastern Nova Scotia. They invariably called for a policy of adult education by the university, a position subsequently reinforced by the Alumni Association, the governors, and the Scottish Catholic Society of Canada. To a considerable extent the pressure behind all these bodies was from the same group of diocesan clergy and notably J.J. Tompkins, Michael Gillis, and John R. MacDonald – later Bishop MacDonald of Antigonish. The result was the formal establishment of a department of university extension under the direction of Dr M.M. Coady and closely aligned with and intended to serve the agricultural and industrial workers and the fishermen of Nova Scotia. The board of governors' resolution to establish this department was passed near the end of 1928, and the organization of the department around Dr Coady and Professor A.B. MacDonald completed in 1930.

The St Francis Xavier extension department, though not the oldest, became almost at once perhaps the most celebrated and most widely influential in Canada. The distinctive elements in the techniques it employed are these: emphasis upon informal, non-credit courses; heavy reliance upon local study clubs; the holding of annual rural and industrial conferences at the university; since 1933, there have been provided special short courses for the training of leaders; also since 1933 there has been published the *Extension Bulletin*, which became in 1939 *The Maritime Co-operator*. The financing of extension has been a constant strain on the resources of the university alleviated somewhat by Carnegie Corporation assistance after 1932 (over $85,000 in 10 years) and by subsidies from Canada's department of fisheries since 1937 ($37,000 a year, raised to $51,000 a few years later). Speaking on this subject in Montreal in 1940, D.J. MacDonald, president of the university, said: 'The annual cost of our extension department, apart from the fisheries grant during the past few years has been approximately $30,000 a year and the total cost to the university, apart from donations and grants, since 1930 is about $125,000.'[14]

A third aspect of H.P. MacPherson's regime calling for special discussion is university organization both internal and external. When MacPherson took office he was faced by two immediate problems: first, criticism of the overly autocratic administration provided by his predecessor; second, a suspicion that Tompkins, already installed as vice-rector and master of discipline, was not altogether suited to the combined functions. Accordingly, MacPherson moved to meet both

14 D.J. MacDonald, 'The Antigonish Movement,' *L'Académie Canadienne Saint-Thomas D'Aquin*, 10(1940), 38

problems by expanding the duties of the vice-rector and dividing them between two men, J.H. MacDonald whom he named vice-rector and prefect of discipline, and J.J. Tompkins whom he appointed vice-president and prefect of studies. This adjustment explains in part how Tompkins' interests were to be academic rather than ecclesiastical, and were sometimes after 1912 to diverge sharply from those of the chancellor, Bishop Morrison. It also accounts for the rather logical use of the title president-rector for MacPherson himself, an unusual piece of terminology which was written into the provincial act of 23 April 1909, and which only disappeared in 1944 when Dr P.J. Nicholson was officially designated president of the university.

The important external administrative decision of the MacPherson era came late in 1922 when the chancellor, the president, and the board determined to have nothing to do with the proposed federated University of the Maritime Provinces.

During the fall of 1921 the Carnegie Corporation, which had already shown interest in St Francis Xavier's Acadian constituency, began a systematic analysis of higher education in the Maritimes. Two experienced investigators, William S. Learned of the Corporation and Kenneth C.M. Sills, president of Bowdoin College, were sent to assess the situation. Their fifty-page report, published during 1922, *Education in the Maritime Provinces of Canada*, recommended the establishing of a federated university, embracing at least Dalhousie, King's, and Pine Hill of Halifax and St Francis Xavier, Mt Allison, and Acadia outside Halifax, under such conditions as these: the axis of the federation should be the Dalhousie campus, the federating institutions should preserve both their identity and their denominational character, professional faculties should be neither duplicated nor concentrated, there should be arts colleges on all six campuses but senior students only in the Maritime University in Halifax which alone should confer degrees although each constituent college should be identified on the diplomas of its own students, an honour course programme should be available for all students able to carry it. The corporation was prepared to subsidize the project heavily, possibly as high as three million dollars, and the government was urging co-operation.

The proposal was an adaptation of the Toronto plan to conditions prevailing in the Maritimes. It was, moreover, thought of as providing a pilot pattern for similar federations to be undertaken in the United States. The Sills-Learned Report provoked much discussion and controversy throughout 1922 and for some years after. St Francis Xavier was deeply involved in it through Tompkins, who was a strong supporter of the plan and something of an unofficial advisor to Dr Learned. The teaching faculty of the university unanimously approved the project in principle at a meeting held 30 January 1922 with the president in the chair and 14 other professors in attendance.

Bishop Morrison was at first non-committal on federation but grew constantly more hostile towards it during 1922. He named a committee to study the plan and to advise the faculty of St Francis Xavier about it.[15] A special meeting of the board of governors was held on 20 October 1922 to decide how the university ought to proceed. The governors were informed by the bishop that the hierarchy of Nova Scotia and Newfoundland had met in Halifax on the previous day and had passed a resolution against federation. The board decided, accordingly, that St Francis Xavier should not be represented at any subsequent Halifax conference devoted to the subject. That the bishop urged the decision is fairly clear. His position was shared by the non-university constituency. That the faculty in view of its resolution of 30 January, or indeed, many members of the board, can have agreed with the decision is doubtful. Tompkins, for one, did not; and Tompkins was within two months transferred from the university faculty to the parish of Canso.

During the spring of 1923, while the federation issue was still a real one in the rest of the Maritimes, it was becoming less and less so in Antigonish. Bishop Morrison referred what has been called 'a version of the matter' to the Holy See, asking whether colleges, Catholic and non-Catholic, could be federated into a single neutral university. The answer received was in the negative, unless it were a question of a state-supported university, in which case there would be no objection.[16]

The withdrawal of St Francis Xavier from the proposed federation was perhaps the crucial step in its ultimate abandonment. For St Francis Xavier itself, the decision was a firm commitment to become an autonomous, multifaculty university. The history of the university since the early twenties is in a sense the record of the progress of just such a commitment. Almost certainly the successful establishment of the extension department, already dealt with, is the first significant step to be entered in that record. The extension department dates from 1928–9. It dominates the history of not only the final years of the presidency of Dr MacPherson, that is up to 1936, but of the entire presidency of D.J. MacDonald, 1936–44. It also absorbed the interest and time of a high

15 J.L. MacDougall, *History of Inverness County, Nova Scotia*, no place of publication, 1922, 'Appendix: The College Merger of the Maritimes,' 622–83

16 Boyle, *Pioneer*, 118; the decision of the bishops of the Maritimes was confirmed by the Holy See in a pronouncement sent to Bishop McCarthy by the apostolic delegate 15 May 1923.

percentage of the best men of both the diocese and the university. The marriage of autonomy and the movement was not an easy one but the St Francis Xavier of today is its legitimate child.

D.J. MacDonald succeeded H.P. MacPherson as president-rector of St Francis Xavier in 1936. He stood firmly behind the university's two-fold commitment to the Antigonish Movement and to university autonomy. This position was not always easy because the two commit-ments were less than complementary. Men like Jimmie Tompkins and Michael Gillis favoured some form of federation, in part at least, be-cause they felt that it would release more university resources for extension work and would place responsibility for academic excellence elsewhere. MacDonald, who did not share their feelings, found that he had as president not only to make up extension deficits but to proceed with plans for the general development of the university. That he made headway on both fronts is more a credit to him than his failure to distinguish himself is to be blamed.

All have not looked kindly on D.J. MacDonald. Laidlaw's account of the Antigonish Movement does not so much as mention his name and one can sense a certain tension between MacDonald and Coady. A governors' report of 1938 describes the carrying of the extension de-partment as a 'burden,' refers to a university deficit of $24,461.25, and speaks of the danger of having to 'curtail the expenditure of the exten-sion department.'[17] This was just one year after the federal department of fisheries began providing an annual grant of $37,000. Yet with all this, MacDonald was personally friendly to the movement and delivered a paper on it in 1940 at the tenth annual meeting of L'Académie St Thomas D'Aquin held in Quebec City.[18]

When MacDonald assumed office in 1936, he undertook, with the aid of the university's bursar, H.J. Somers, to implement some of the plans of a development committee on which the two had served during the final years of the MacPherson regime. The key step was to engage, on the recommendation of American college planners, the services of the Dartmouth architect, Jens Frederick Larsen of Reynolds, North Carolina, for the building of Morrison Hall, which was to house the university dining hall, kitchen, and an administration wing. Morrison Hall, completed in 1938, was so attractively functional that Larsen became the university's continuing architect and is mainly responsible for both the general pattern of the present campus and the choice of Georgian colonial as its dominant style.

17 Laidlaw, *The Campus and the University*, 90
18 See note 12

MacDonald's successor, P.J. Nicholson, was president of St Francis Xavier from 1944 to 1954. He was personally a gentle man, a fine scholar with a doctorate in physics, and a distinguished Celticist. It was Nicholson who succeeded beyond all his predecessors in integrating St Francis Xavier into the university life of Canada as a whole. He was from the beginning an active member of the National Conference of Canadian Universities (NCCU), and was its president in 1950. He was also anxious to strengthen the academic and scholarly focus of the university. Like all post-World War II presidents, he held office during a period of unprecedented expansion, of rising costs, and of federal aid. He opened two new residences: Cameron Hall, a complex of four residential units, in 1945, and MacKinnon Hall, a combined residence and administration unit, in 1951. Also in 1951 he arranged for the establishment of Xavier Junior College in Sydney, appointing Malcolm A. MacLellan as its first principal. This has been St Francis Xavier's only academic venture off the Antigonish campus. Other university presidents, and especially Nicholson's close friend Sidney Smith of Toronto, were discussing the wisdom of opening junior colleges as a measure to cope with expanding enrolments. Nicholson moved quickly in this case not only because the policy seemed to him to provide a genuine service to the city of Sydney but also because it kept Sydney within the Antigonish orbit at a time when there were rumours that another maritime university had its eye on Cape Breton. It would have been unfortunate for Catholic higher education in Canada had the proportion of local students registered in St Francis Xavier been allowed to drop at that time.

Xavier Junior College, which provides its students with the first two years of the university programme, has been an important feeder for the higher years and for the increasing number of specialized programmes available at St Francis Xavier. When MacLellan opened the junior college in 1951 some 520 full-time and 120 part-time students enrolled. At the time of his transfer to Antigonish, the enrolment had risen to 300 full-time and 500 part-time students.

It was during 1953, towards the end of Nicholson's presidency, that St Francis Xavier celebrated its centenary. From the strictly university point of view, the highlight of the year was the holding of the Twenty-Ninth Conference of Canadian Universities on the Antigonish campus, 8–10 June. The invitation had been extended by Dr Nicholson in 1950 when he was president of the NCCU. The meeting, presided over by the retiring president of the association, Dr. W.A. Mackintosh of Queen's, was structured around three symposia. The subject of the first symposium, 'The University Department of Extension – Its Nature, Function, and Validity as Part of the University Programme,' was selected as a conscious tribute to the reputation established by St Francis Xavier in this field. Papers on extension work were read by Dr M.M. Coady of St Francis Xavier, Mr Donald Cameron of Alberta, and Dr C.H. Stearn of McMaster. Coady's paper brought out the special character of the Antigonish Movement: an awareness of 'the terrible urgency of bringing the people of the world within the sphere of university influence.' For him this was primarily the teaching of the techniques and benefits of co-operative group action in trade unionism, marketing, credit unions, consumers' co-operatives, social services, socialization or compulsory state action in certain activities. The university in a democratic society had the obligation, he felt, to carry positive social action to the people in a dynamic way.[19] He was less concerned than Stearn with credit courses or than Cameron with community art and fine art centres. He was in full agreement with Cameron, who would have the university 'get out among the people,' and do its job 'by the selection and training of lay leaders.' But he had less in common with Stearn for whom 'the Cinderella of the campuses does not exist primarily to teach skills.' This successful meeting of the NCCU was but one of a series of activities held in Antigonish to mark the centenary of the university. It gave evidence of the stature of both president and university in the academic life of Canada.

When D.J. MacDonald became president-rector of St Francis Xavier in 1936 he was ably advised and constantly assisted by the brilliant and personable bursar, Hugh J. Somers, who had been expropriated for administration from the university's history department. In 1944, when Nicholson succeeded MacDonald, Somers became vice-president of the university and secretary-treasurer of the board of governors. Between 1936 and 1954 he was party to all presidential plans and was in large part responsible for the university's successful dealing with one financial challenge after another as new buildings were erected and general deficits increased.

When Nicholson retired from the presidency in 1954, Somers was appointed in his place. Somers continued the Nicholson policy of increasingly heavy emphasis on academic development. He sought out qualified lay professors on a somewhat more lavish scale. He provided for the introduction of honour programmes into some of the university departments. He also began to place a heavier emphasis on science. Moreover, his first major piece of construction was the Physics and

19 M.M. Coady, 'Extra-Mural University Adult Education,' *Proceedings: The National Conference of Canadian Universities*, 29(1953), 17–22

Chemistry Building, opened in 1957; he also established a faculty of science distinct from the faculty of arts. In the new faculty he included, besides the general course and the honour course in science, the divisions of engineering, home economics, and nursing. By 1964, the end of Somers' presidency, 585 students were enrolled in this faculty, about one-third of a total enrolment of 1600 regular students.

With the new science building erected, and with the old Neil McNeil Engineering Hall completely renovated, facilities for scientific research were made available, an important milestone in the history of any university. Somers was able to assemble a small group of research scholars in physics and chemistry who not only made a first-class science programme a reality in the university, but who undertook in collaboration with scientists elsewhere and with the support of the National Research Council and other bodies fundamental research in electron physics, radiation-polymerization, energy transfer, and other projects.

An important event to take place during Somers' administration was the establishing of the Coady International Institute.[20] This project was announced by the president on 2 December 1959. It was in full operation when the first wing of its Bishop John R. MacDonald Building was opened at a convocation held 17 October 1961. The establishing of this Institute in St Francis Xavier was intended not only to memorialize Dr Coady but to consolidate his work by finding a valid and completely uncompromised arrangement for its continuance within the central structure of a great university.

There has always been some ambivalence about relations between the movement and the university. Born of social disorders particularly prevalent in Nova Scotia, the movement tended to impart a local non-academic character not only to the extension department (where such a character is not necessarily out of place) but in some degree to the university itself whose policies it strove, perhaps unreasonably, to direct. Pioneers in the movement and their immediate successors wanted to keep one foot firmly planted in the university; H.P. MacPherson, Hugh MacPherson, J.J. Tompkins, M.M. Coady, John R. MacDonald, M.J. MacKinnon, A.F. Laidlaw, and others wished to maintain the

20 R.M. McKeon, 'The Coady International Institute,' *Social Order*, 11(1961), 7–11. McKeon has written a number of articles on the Antigonish Movement and the Coady International Institute. These have been digested by Brian O'Connell and published by the *Antigonish Casket* for St Francis Xavier University in two pamphlets, *The Antigonish Movement* and *The Antigonish Movement Abroad*, 1961. See also 'The Quiet Revolution' and 'A Focus on the Antigonish Movement,' addresses by Dr Howard L. Trueman and Dr Alexander F. Laidlaw at St Francis Xavier University, 17 October 1961, also published by the *Casket* for the university.

university attachment. They succeeded in maintaining a stronger attachment than an extension department is quite able to bear.

By the 1950s, the movement had taken on an international character unenvisaged in 1929. In 1953, for example, the director of extension, M.J. MacKinnon, found himself a member of a mission studying fisheries in Ceylon. The sponsorship of a seven-week course offered during the same year was shared by the Canadian Colombo Plan and the United Nations. In 1957 A.F. Laidlaw was directing from an office in Kerala a five-year plan in co-operatives for the Indian central government. Examples of this kind of development abound. Meanwhile, all through the fifties, students of advanced qualifications, and even official delegations, were coming in increasing numbers from every quarter of the globe. Here was a development which called for its own place in the formal structure of the university not only because it belonged to what Coady had called 'the formula of human progress' but because it required study and research of a kind that only a university can provide for. The institute opened in 1961 was the right solution.

The idea of an institute was not new with Somers. It had, as R.M. McKeon puts it, 'long been in the mind of the late John R. MacDonald.' Somers, however, established it, sought out a competent director, Monsignor Frank J. Smyth, to conduct it, and made him a vice-president of the university, a position from which it became more possible to reassess the work to be done and to reorganize the scale on which its techniques were to be taught.

Somers' long contact with the problems of university financing, extending over a period of 31 years, made him acutely aware of the dependence of the modern university on the resources of industry and government. He found unprecedented financial support for his own university, and was, through his work on NCCU and other committees, instrumental in bringing the federal government to the support of Canadian universities and colleges generally. When his retirement from the presidency of St Francis Xavier was announced in 1964, he was immediately drafted into the position of full-time director of the Associated Atlantic Universities (AAU). The appointment of such a full-time director of the AAU had been a specific recommendation of the University Grants Committee to the governor-in-council of Nova Scotia.[21]

The AAU itself is an association of maritime universities formed to consider co-operation and co-ordination of facilities, personnel, and

21 *Higher Education in Nova Scotia: A Survey Report with Recommendations*, by the University Grants Committee, Halifax, NS, 1964. The members of the committee were: N.A.M. MacKenzie (chairman), A.L. Murphy, and E.L. Goodfellow.

academic standards among the institutions of higher learning in the
Atlantic provinces. Its formation preceded by a short interval the decision of the maritime governments to appoint a grants committee and to
begin once more to support their universities financially. The decision
of Colin Mackay, president of the University of New Brunswick and
chairman of the AAU, and of Henry Hicks, president of Dalhousie and
vice-chairman of the AAU, to force the appointment on Somers is evidence of his ability along these lines demonstrated over a period of
many years.

Dr Somers realized, on reluctantly accepting the AAU appointment,
that some analogy could be drawn between the present move for
co-ordination and that for federation back in 1922. He felt, however,
that methods and objectives were different now and that expectations
could be so too. No longer were the participating universities competing
institutions in the old sense; their relation with their respective constituencies had become more clearly defined; they had all grown considerably in academic stature; and they were prepared for a collaboration respectful of one another's internal autonomy.[22]

As Somers planned to leave the university, it was with the knowledge
that the long period of neglect by the provincial government had come
to an end, that provincial subsidies were already again a reality, and
that he was himself to be in a key position to serve the maritime universities in co-ordinating plans for a growth that seemed assured.

On 26 May 1964, the chancellor of St Francis Xavier University,
W.E. Power, bishop of Antigonish, announced that the new president
would be Malcolm MacLellan, principal and director of studies at
Xavier College, Sydney, for the past thirteen years. One of MacLellan's
first official functions was to arrange for the opening of the new Angus
L. MacDonald Memorial Library planned largely by his predecessor
and paying tribute by its name to a Nova Scotia premier, graduate of
St Francis Xavier, who dared to carry the cause urged upon him by the
university presidents into the political arena.

President MacLellan continued the policies of his predecessor but
managed also to meet the many changes called for in university education by the times. No president of St Francis Xavier had comparable
revenue at his disposal especially since the province of Nova Scotia
began seriously, encouraged by its grants committee and the AAU, to
support all its universities to the limit of its resources. Between 1966
and 1970 St Francis Xavier received in excess of a million dollars from

22 'President's Report,' a lecture given by H.J. Somers to convocation on 13 May
1964, 4ff.

combined government sources, and this aid was reflected in improved facilities and enlarged competent staff. In line with revenue, there was also increased enrolment – which in 1965 passed 2000 for the first time and in 1969 reached almost 3000. Much of the increased enrolment was from Nova Scotia, an encouraging sign, considering the depressed economy in the eastern end of the province.

The MacLellan years were marked by special developments: the appearance of a small art department, and the engaging of a resident artist, Angus MacGillivray, who acquired a considerable reputation in sculpture painting; the growth of graduate programmes in guidance, conducted by the departments of psychology and sociology; the establishment of a computer centre servicing various sections of the university and providing courses in computer science and programming; the forming of a campus planning body to guide and regulate the rapid material growth which was so real during the sixties and which included six major campus additions since 1967.

Along with these changes, attention continued to focus on the faculty of science and the Coady Institute. The latter maintained an enrolment of over 80 students annually, representing some 83 countries, over its first ten years of operation and constituting a valuable arm of the Canadian Aid Office and other agencies interested in the developing nations.

St Francis Xavier had the distinction, among the Catholic post-secondary institutions of English-speaking Canada, of maintaining during the sixties the most complete university programme, possessing the most extensive facilities, and enjoying the most solid support from its provincial government. Its enrolment was second only to Loyola's. St Francis Xavier continued to be blessed with Canada's best alumni association, and with a strong forward-looking board of governors on which representatives of the staff had long served, and which after 1968 included students as well.

The university was not, in spite of these advantages, without problems. Large revenues in an operation which cannot by its nature meet its expenses – which is the case of all good universities – meant that even larger additional funds had to be found elsewhere.

The corollary of this situation was that the accepting of funds for a full university programme carried with it the obligation of maintaining such a programme. This obligation was MacLellan's great worry. Should he and his board concern themselves only with areas of special competence, and make these the goals of St Francis Xavier? Or should they simply parallel the structures and achievements of other universities over the broad field? Should, for example, theology, sociology, Celtic studies, and education be highly developed, even at the highest level, until such time as St Francis Xavier might lead the field? Or should the operation remain general and, though solid, relatively ordinary? The issues of 1922 had not by MacLellan's time been entirely removed, though the solutions were seen to be very different.

When MacLellan's term of office came to an end in 1970, the board invited Malcolm MacDonnell to accept the presidency. MacDonnell, priest of Antigonish and Gaelic-speaking Nova Scotian, professor of history and director of the alumni association, took over during the summer of 1970.

Mount St Vincent University

HALIFAX, NS

(1872 [1914])

Mount St Vincent University is located on the property of the mother house of the Sisters of Charity, in Rockingham, Halifax, Nova Scotia, overlooking the Bedford Basin. The university is housed separately from the motherhouse in three beautiful modern buildings: Evaristus Hall, the main building put up after the fire of 1951; Assisi Hall, a 12-storey residence, 1966; and Rosaria Hall, a student union building. Land and buildings are evaluated at about $9,000,000. Mount St Vincent was recognized as a normal school in 1895, as a junior college of Dalhousie University in 1914, as a chartered college in 1925, and as a chartered university in 1966. It gives courses leading to the BA in arts and business, to the BSC in science, home economics, and nursing, and to the BED in education. It also provides a number of diploma courses in business and of diploma and graduate courses in education.

The American Sisters of Charity, who are said to have laid the foundation of the American parochial school system,[1] were founded by Elizabeth Bayley Seton in Maryland in 1809. The order established a house in Halifax, 11 May 1849, coming from New York.[2] Two weeks later they opened St Mary's Girls' School with a mass celebrated by Bishop Walsh. In 1855 St Mary's Convent became an independent motherhouse of the Sisters of Charity. During May 1857, the sisters began teaching in their second Halifax school, St Patrick's, opened in the basement of St Patrick's Church; in September they opened their convent on Lockman Street. When Sir Charles Tupper's Free School Act of 1864 was passed, St Mary's and St Patrick's became free schools. The foresight shown in and the needs created by this participation in the school system of Nova Scotia from its beginning and on a constantly growing scale ever since, eventually called into existence Mount St Vincent as a higher school for women and as a training centre for teachers and especially for those sisters destined to teach in the schools.

In 1872 the sisters moved their motherhouse to Rockingham, calling

---

1 A.M. Melville, *Elizabeth Bayley Seton, 1774–1821*, New York, 1960; J.J. Dirvin, *Mrs Seton: Foundress of the American Sisters of Charity*, New York, 1962
2 Sister Maura, *The Sisters of Charity, Halifax*, Toronto: The Ryerson Press, 1956, 2. See also P.F. Martin, ed., *The Catholic Diocesan Directory of Nova Scotia*, Halifax, 1936, 55–61.

it Mount St Vincent. The following year they opened a private academy at Rockingham in order to prepare their novices and young sisters for a career of teaching in both New England and Nova Scotia. Girls from the city attended from the beginning. The Mount's reputation grew during the eighties and nineties and it became a favourite school for the girls of Halifax. Its programme also expanded somewhat beyond the usual high school course as special courses in education were added for prospective teachers in grade XII. By 1895 these courses came to be recognized as satisfying normal school requirements, thus qualifying those who took them as teachers.[3] The academy was from the beginning a rival of the Sacred Heart Academy, also an exclusive girls' school. There has always been in Halifax, even in the free schools, a strong tradition favouring separate schools for girls.

Mount St Vincent began to offer an arts programme in 1914 when an arrangement of affiliation was made with Dalhousie University.[4] The reason for seeking the affiliation was just what one would expect – to qualify sisters for principalships and other offices where the bachelor's degree was becoming essential. Classes in the first two years of the arts course were given by the Mount's own teachers; classes in the third and fourth year were provided by professors from Dalhousie. The girls who took the course – not all in the school did – were graduates of Dalhousie. The arrangement was highly successful, so much so that although Mount St Vincent received a college charter from the Nova Scotia legislature, May 1925, it actually continued to use the Dalhousie affiliation up until 1941 when it was amicably terminated at the sisters' request.

The college was conducted in the academy building at Rockingham from 1941 to 1951. In 1951 a disastrous fire completely destroyed the school and college building.

Developments at Mount St Vincent prior to 1951 are important for understanding the present situation of the college. The university is literally owned by the order, which built it almost without assistance from industry, diocese, or provincial government. The college was called into existence by the demands of the order's particular teaching apostolate. The Mount of today has no founder in the usual sense; it is nevertheless largely the brain-child of Mother Berchmans Walsh, general of the order 1901–26, who believed in the concept of the indepen-

---

3 Sister Maura, *The Sisters of Charity*, 54.
4 Ibid., 77–8: 'At the conference held in 1914, Mr Stanley MacKenzie the president, Professor Howard Murray of beloved memory, Professor Murray MacNeil for many years registrar, and Professor Archibald MacMechan, distinguished head of the department of English, represented Dalhousie; Mother Berchmans, Sister de Chantal, Sister Evaristus, and one of the young sisters represented the Mount. ... By this step, Mount Saint Vincent attained, with ecclesiastical approbation, the status of a junior college.'

dent and totally committed women's college, who brought in the Dalhousie professors to teach, and who was largely responsible for acquiring the first or college charter in 1925. Mother Berchmans Walsh, who was general, did not become the first president, but Mother Evaristus Moran, who did, shared her ideals. It has been shared ideals which account for the order's investing nine million dollars in the project in such a way that the college itself has never really had a debt. The college is the order's investment in the training of its personnel and its active university apostolate. No order in Canada has invested so much in a public enterprise.

Interest in the science of education is in part the inheritance of the Sisters of Charity from Elizabeth Seton. In Canada, this interest was given its own character when the sisters came to be so completely involved in implementing Tupper's free school act. Later, as the government placed normal schools and schools of education under a minister and a council of public instruction, the sisters' normal school was not excluded from their consideration. Thus when Henry D. Hicks, in June 1954, shortly after Angus L. MacDonald's death and just before becoming premier himself, announced a new plan of teacher training, Mount St Vincent was one of the five universities to house a training school. This factor must be remembered in assessing Mount St Vincent.

The training of teachers, however, is only a part of the picture. The Mount also developed before 1951 an active programme in nursing education. Students in the earlier years began their nursing education at the Mount, then transferred to an infirmary, then returned to the Mount for the finishing touches and their B SC N. The Mount was never fully satisfied with this arrangement – the hospital floor had too much time, the college too little, in the making of the woman. But the Mount felt it was doing something for woman and society.

In arts and science, up to 1951, Mount St Vincent acquired the reputation of providing quality education: maintaining a large staff (about one instructor for seven students), a high proportion of whom (35 per cent) held their doctorate. Archetype of the woman the Mount most likes to produce is its own sister Maura Geoffrey: Halifax-born, Mount-educated, Dalhousie MA, Notre Dame PHD; author of some dozen books and numerous articles on criticism, poetry, drama, history; head of the Mount's English department after 1925; member of the Canadian Authors' Association and the Canadian Poetry Society; visiting professor at Notre Dame, Boston College, Dalhousie, Fordham; truly distinguished Canadian and saintly woman.[5]

5 Sister Maura Geoffrey, 1881–1957. Among her writings are: *Shakespeare's Catholicism*, Cambridge, Mass., 1924; *Breath of the Spirit*, Toronto, 1937; *Rhythm*

When the fire wiped out the building which housed the mother-house, the academy, and the college, the task of replacement was gigantic. Whether the college would be rebuilt at Rockingham was at first in doubt. There had been some feeling in the forties that the college should work more closely with St Mary's. The sisters made one important gesture: they tried to purchase ten acres of the Collins estate (the Gorsebrook campus on which St Mary's is located) from Archbishop McNally. The archbishop was disposed to sell to the sisters until word came to him from the Jesuit provincialate that in their opinion the property was too small to divide this way and that the province did not care to become involved in co-education.

With this background, the new Mount St Vincent College was built in 1952 in Rockingham. It is here, of course, where most of the present debt, taken over by the order, was incurred. Thus far the investment has been worthwhile as the college has prospered in every way. Enrolment in 1952 was 191; it rose steadily to 452 in 1962, and 627 in 1967 – a healthy, manageable increase.

During 1963 and 1964 pressure began to be brought on the Mount to amalgamate with St Mary's. The archbishop and his advisors felt that the annual payment of $250,000 a year on the St Mary's debt (which would have to be continued until 1975 when the entire indebtedness would be re-financed at $1,000,000) was more than the Church of Halifax could carry. At the same time, all this heavy annual expenditure in no way aided the necessary development programme at St Mary's. Any real expansion had to mean increased annual payments.

A meeting of some of the administrators of the Catholic colleges and universities of Halifax was held on 7 February 1963, to look into the matter of effective collaboration between St Mary's and Mount St Vincent to see if the cost of local university education could be reduced and necessary development made possible. Following this meeting, the president of St Mary's, C.J. Fischer, prepared an exploratory 'Proposal for the Unification of Catholic Higher Education in the Archdiocese of Halifax.'[6] Fischer's proposal was directed to the objective university situation. In effect, it invited the Mount to federate with St Mary's, to hold its degree-conferring powers (except in secretarial studies, nursing, and home economics) in abeyance, to move to the St Mary's campus where places would be provided for the students and teaching

Poems, Toronto, 1944; A Sheaf of Songs, Lower Granville, NS, n.d.; The Sisters of Charity, Halifax, Toronto, 1956. Related to her teaching are her genre writings: Via Vitae (a morality), Christus Vincit (a miracle), The Angelus (a mystery), The Rosary in Terza Rima (poetics).

6 Fischer to Sister Francis d'Assisi (and to Gerald Berry, Mother Maria Gertrude, Gordon F. George), 18 Feb. 1963, Archives of the Archdiocese of Halifax

posts for the sisters and other staff, and to operate women's residences on the Gorsebrook property. Sister Francis d'Assisi McCarthy, president of the Mount, and Mother Maria Gertrude, general of the Sisters of Charity, were not disposed to accept the proposal, which they feared was tantamount to absorption of the Mount by St Mary's. They did not regard the solution proposed as a federation of academic equals. The sisters sent the archbishop two briefs: one prepared by the board of governors, the other by the staff of the Mount.[7] The board's brief expressed the unsympathetic attitude of the president and the mother general; the faculty brief was also unsympathetic; it pointed out that Fischer did not seem to grasp the nature of the Mount's commitment to the education of women. The sisters invited the archbishop to express his own opinions on the subject.

During September 1963, Archbishop Berry formed a committee to study the possibility of co-operation between St Mary's and Mount St Vincent. The committee began meetings on 5 November 1963. During the spring of 1964 the archbishop invited L.K. Shook of Toronto to visit Halifax in order to prepare an analysis of the situation in Catholic higher education and to suggest ways and means of coping with it. Shook spent some time in Halifax during June and submitted his report to Archbishop Berry at the end of the month.[8]

Shook recommended as possibly effective (and unlikely to be accepted) the formation of a new University of Halifax into which all four Catholic institutions (St Mary's, Mount St Vincent, Sacred Heart Convent, Holy Heart Seminary) would be federated. He thought the government might help with the preliminary costs of setting up such an institution. He also recommended a series of *ad hoc* co-operative measures: common concentration and honour courses, exchange of professors, full co-ordination of extension and summer courses, a common approach to Dalhousie's graduate school on behalf of distinguished professors in the Catholic institutions who should be offering graduate seminars, controlled admission of women to St Mary's, increased offerings in theology, attendance of seminarians at university lectures, re-

7 The board's brief was entitled 'A Proposal for Further Consideration of the Problem of Unification of Catholic Higher Education in the Archdiocese of Halifax'; the staff brief was called 'Comments on the Proposal for the Unification of Catholic Higher Education in the Archdiocese of Halifax.' Both are attached to a letter: Mother Maria Gertrude to J. Gerald Berry, 5 June 1963, Archives of the Archdiocese of Halifax

8 'Report on Catholic Higher Education in the City of Halifax having in mind Ways and Means of Encouraging fuller Co-operation among Existing Institutions.' This report was attached to a letter, Shook to Berry, 29 June 1964, Archives of the Archdiocese of Halifax.

duced duplication of library acquisitions, and extensive use of shuttle services to transport books, students, and professors. The controversy was not resolved.

Presidents of the Mount since 1925 when it became an independent college have been as follows: Sister Evaristus Moran 1925–44, Sister Maria Rosaria Gorman 1944–54, Sister Francis d'Assisi McCarthy 1954–65, Sister Alice Michael (Catherine Wallace)[9] since 1965. All four presidents adhered to their order's original objective: the providing of a distinctive education for women in the liberal and related arts. All four feared that amalgamation would entail the rejection of the principle of subsidiarity because it would mean the loss to the general public of a special competence which the large institution could never have.

President Catherine Wallace and her board of governors erected, after 1965, two more buildings on the Rockingham campus: a 12-storey residence for 142 students, Assisi Hall; and a 2-storey students union, Rosaria Hall. Between 1965 and 1969 they also experimented with changes in the academic programmes: they took advantage of the introduction into the college programme in 1962 of major subjects of concentration in arts and science to discontinue specialties which no longer seemed to appeal to scholarly university women; that is, B sc programmes in secretarial studies, radiologic technology, elementary education, and journalism. They also encouraged students to contact these areas by studying in depth such disciplines as economics, physics, and the traditional arts subjects. The study of music was moved largely into the liberal arts; nursing was in large part withdrawn from the hospital floor into college life; and architecture was given a new cultural emphasis during three years of preliminary study before students intending to become architects transfer to the Nova Scotia Technical College. The library's great centennial project was to acquire a huge special collection of books relating to women and their history.

Along with these emphases, felt to be in direct line with the feminine mystique, attention was also given to general changes taking place in the university world, and particularly in university government. Mount St Vincent got its complete university charter from the Nova Scotia legislature 6 April 1966. Ownership of the university remained vested in a corporation of six Sisters of Charity. These six officers were also members of the board of governors which included in addition two members named by the governor-in-council, two elected by the alum-

---

9 The Sisters of Charity may now, if they so wish, resume their maiden names. Most members of the faculty of Mount St Vincent have done so.

nae, two students (one named by the board, one by the student body), and 13 members continued or named by the board itself. There was also a senate, largely made up of staff, but with the addition of student senators projected.

On 1 September 1969, 'Mount St Vincent University' and 'the governors of Dalhousie College and University' entered into a formal agreement committing both parties to a policy of co-operation for a period of five years. By this agreement the Mount was to be considered a multi-faculty college with its own teaching staff, students, programme, and facilities; a women's college extending the use of its facilities to men; a Catholic college with no tests or restrictions based on religion; a small college, but a separate corporate entity with its own board and senate. Convinced that co-operation is possible, but that it can only evolve slowly, the two institutions undertook to work together to improve their educational programmes, to prevent unnecessary duplication of academic and administrative effort, to exchange students, faculties, and administrative staff, and to provide free access to each other's facilities.

With the turn into the seventies, Mount St Vincent was providing the bachelor's degree in arts, science, education, and business. It was still giving graduate courses in education but conferring no graduate degrees. Professional courses in home economics were centralized at the Mount, professional courses in nursing at Dalhousie. The Mount was also admitting applicants from grade xi (Dalhousie admitted only from xii) and was registering its grade xii and equivalent students jointly in the Mount and Dalhousie.

This joint registration of the Mount's students was the most radical aspect of the 1969 agreement. It established between the two universities a form of association by which the Mount conferred its own degrees on its own students but did so in Dalhousie's name as well as its own – a maritime refinement on federation unknown in the rest of Canada.

Holy Heart Seminary

HALIFAX, NS

1895

Holy Heart Seminary is an interdiocesan major seminary, located on a five-acre property at 55 Quinpool Street, Halifax, NS, under the direction of the Congregation of Jesus and Mary (Eudists). It offers a four-year course in theology for diocesan seminarians. It has a limited civil charter from the province of Nova Scotia and an affiliation with Laval for pontifical accreditation.

Holy Heart Seminary was opened in 1895 by the Eudist Fathers of France. The same religious order had opened a classical college, Collège Ste Anne, at Church Point, Baie Ste Anne, in 1890. Archbishop Cornelius O'Brien of Halifax met the superior general of the Eudists, Ange LeDoré, when he was visiting Ste Anne's in 1893. The two discussed the opening of a seminary of philosophy and theology in Halifax, and formally signed an agreement authorizing the Eudists to erect a seminary and public chapel in Halifax. The Eudists were to provide staff and buildings, the archbishop was to provide the land and to use his influence to encourage the maritime bishops to send students to the seminary, which would also accept Eudists.[1]

O'Brien acquired a property on Quinpool Street and turned it over to the Eudists, who began the construction of a building in the spring of 1894 and completed it during the summer of 1895. Funds to pay for this first unit came from LeDoré with the help of a substantial gift provided by two Eudists, Jean and Ange de Saint-Jouan, from a family inheritance.

On 9 August 1895, three Eudist priests, Pierre-Marie Cochet, Paul Lecourtois, Prosper Lebastard, one lay brother, Frère Henri and a domestic staff of three religious sisters from Paramé moved into the seminary. On 19 September, classes began for a total of ten students – five in philosophy and five in theology – most but not all were Eudists from France and Canada.[2] O'Brien did not find it easy to convince his episco-

---

1 Eugène Lachance, *Construire pour le Christ: Paul Lecourtois, eudiste, 1863–1951*, Halifax, 1953. For a selection from the agreement see p.33, n.1.

2 Halifax priests from this first class were James Charles MacKinnon and Désiré Comeau. See *Holy Heart Seminary 1895–1945: An Album Commemorating the Fiftieth Anniversary of Holy Heart Seminary*, Halifax, 1946, 20.

pal colleagues to transfer students from Quebec and Montreal seminaries to Halifax. The Halifax seminary was a gamble, whereas the
others were established and proven, and they were all, for the time
being, equally French in language, character, and tradition. And the
Halifax seminary was a religious scholasticate more than a diocesan
seminary, a disadvantage in the minds of some bishops. In addition,
some burses had been established in the older seminaries for use of
students from the Maritimes.[3]

The staff of three divided their professional duties as follows: Cochet, the rector, taught moral theology; Lecourtois (who was also bursar) taught dogmatic theology, canon law, and sacred scripture; Lebastard taught philosophy, church history, and liturgy.

Cochet died after only eight months in office. He was succeeded in
1896 by Jean Levallois, who was sent out from France to take over the
combined responsibilities of superior and professor of moral theology.
A fourth priest was now added to the staff – Father Rabasté, who took
over church history and liturgy and some philosophy from Lebastard.

During the first year of Levallois' rectorship, Holy Heart was incorporated by the province of Nova Scotia. The act included an unusual
clause, one granting the seminary the right to confer civil degrees in
philosophy and theology. Until 1966 no degrees were conferred on the
strength of this civil charter, but it did permit the seminary to collect
federal grants when these were introduced in 1951.

Levallois was succeeded in 1899 by Paul Lecourtois, one of Canada's
most outstanding seminary professors, who headed Holy Heart from
1899 to 1908 and again from 1911 to 1921. During the interval between
Lecourtois' two terms, that is, between 1908 and 1911, Charles Lebrun
was rector. The two men gave Holy Heart its lasting scholarly character
and made a genuine contribution to seminary education in Canada.

Paul Lecourtois was sent out from France to Ste Anne's for the year
preceding the opening of Holy Heart, but obviously to prepare himself
for the seminary post. He held two doctorates – in theology and canon
law – from the Gregorian University, Rome; and he had taught in
seminaries for five years before coming out to Canada: one year at the
Collège Saint-Jean de Béthune at Versailles, and four years at Roche du
Theil near Redon in the Parish of Bains-sur-Oust, where the Eudists
had their scholasticate.

Lecourtois knew no English when he arrived in Canada. While still
at Ste Anne's, however, one of his charming and imaginative exercises
was to translate Longfellow's *Evangeline* into French prose and verse.

3 Lachance, *Construire pour le Christ*, 44

In 1896, at Cochet's month's mind, he delivered the funeral eulogy in English. When he became superior himself in 1899 he made a remarkably successful effort to make Holy Heart, until then staffed largely with French-speaking professors and serving mainly French-speaking students, acceptable to the English-speaking Catholics of Halifax.

This, of course, was one of the new seminary's problems – to satisfy the two main language constituencies in these maritime dioceses. Lecourtois was insistent that the English-speaking and French-speaking students teach one another. As a result he and his staff are responsible for a generation of bilingual priests. A striking example was Gerald B. Phelan, student of theology at Holy Heart from 1911 to 1914. There he learned to converse in French with such facility that when he went to Louvain for higher studies in philosophy and psychology he could give full time to his research with none of the language handicaps faced by so many English-speaking students. He probably owed his *agrégé* to the language facility acquired in the seminary.

Lecourtois and Lebrun each added to the original building. Lecourtois added the beautiful chapel in 1906–7, and the north wing in 1920. Lebrun joined the main wing and the chapel in 1910 with an addition which housed the permanent library.

Lebrun was not at Holy Heart long, but he gave it the pleasure and honour of the service of a truly productive scholar. Before leaving France for Canada he edited, with Joseph Dauphin, the definitive 12-volume French edition of the works of St John Eudes which came out in Paris between 1905 and 1909.[4] Lebrun wrote all the prefaces, including the 'Préface général.'[5] Subsequently, that is, after leaving Halifax, he wrote eight monographs on various aspects of the life, work, and spirituality of St John Eudes, some of which have been translated into English.[6] Lebrun was the leader of several Eudists who worked seriously on the saint and founder of the order prior to his beatification in 1909 and his canonization, 31 May 1925. Other Holy Heart professors, two of them rectors, who published in this context are John O'Reilly in 1909, Patrick A. Bray in 1925, and Patrick J. Skinner during the thirties.[7] The library built at the chapel end of the seminary by Lebrun

4 Charles Lebrun and Joseph Dauphin, eds., *Oeuvres complètes du vénérable Jean Eudes*, Paris: Beauchesne, 12 vols, 1905–11

5 See his statement in the preface of his *La spiritualité de Saint Jean Eudes*, Paris: Letheilleux, 1933

6 See Charles Lebrun, *The Spiritual Teaching of St John Eudes*, tr. by Basil Whelan, London, Sands, 1934

7 John O'Reilly, *Blessed John Eudes*, Halifax, 1909; D.A. Bray, *Saint John Eudes*, Halifax, 1925; W.E. Myatt and P.J. Skinner, *Selected Works*, 6 vols, New York, 1946–8

houses appropriately one of English-speaking Canada's finer collections of theology and spiritual writings.

During Lecourtois' first term, that is, during 1905, Archbishop O'Brien pressed the Eudists to take over the direction of St Mary's College, although they did not yield to the pressure because they were convinced that any diversion of their interest could only, since they were so few, injure the seminary. However, after Charles E. McManus accepted the presidency of St Mary's in 1905, the Eudists arranged for John O'Reilly to commute to the college for a regular course.

In 1914 the Eudist students were withdrawn from Holy Heart and sent to the congregation's own scholasticate at Bathurst, NB. The move was probably a good one for Holy Heart: it made it an exclusively diocesan seminary, a better situation for the various bishops and dioceses concerned in that it gave the seminary a certain homogeneity and made the bishops more personally responsible for its staff and curriculum. Holy Heart has remained exclusively interdiocesan since 1914.

The Halifax seminary not only came to mean more to the dioceses of the Maritimes at this time, but it drew quite close to the citizens of the city of Halifax: with them it suffered seriously from the explosion of 6 December 1917, when the Mont Blanc and the Imo collided in the Bedford Basin and the city was devastated; with them it made a deliberate effort to create beautiful gardens, and the seminary flower garden and arbour, tended knowledgeably by Lecourtois himself, rivalled the beautiful public gardens on nearby Spring Garden Road; even the campaign conducted to build the new wing in 1920, and the formation of the active Friends of the Seminary, confirmed the bonds of mutual understanding and affection between Holy Heart and the Halifax citizenry.

Lecourtois gave up his rectorship of the seminary during 1921, moving to the scholasticate in Bathurst the following year. His successors in office have been as follows: Francis Tressel, 1921–30; Patrick A. Bray, 1930–46; Patrick J. Skinner, 1946–9; Albert D'Amours, 1949–52; Charles Louis Aucoin, 1952–8; Patrick McCluskey, 1958–64; Léger Comeau 1964–70.

From the twenties to the sixties Holy Heart continued to enjoy a fine reputation among the Catholics of Canada for its curriculum and discipline. Indeed, in McCluskey's time, the discipline was sometimes thought to be excessive. The academic curriculum in theology, until very recently, varied little. It was built around what *Deus Scientiarum Dominus* calls the principal subjects: theology (fundamental, dogmatic, moral), sacred scripture, history (including patristics), canon law; and a long list of auxiliary subjects: ascetic and pastoral theology, liturgy and sacred music, sacred eloquence, catechetics, Greek and Hebrew. These subjects constituted the four-year seminary course: a fundamental year taken by all first-year theologians and three years given in a cycle, that is, taken by all students in the second, third, and fourth years. Only the principal subjects were taught in all four years.

From the opening of the seminary in 1895 until the end of the 1935–6 year, the seminary also offered two years of philosophy, the usual requirement for admission to theology. These years were for students who had not taken their two years of philosophy in a classical college, or their equivalent in a university. The two years were obligatory for students entering the seminary after a four- or five-year matriculation from a Canadian high school.

During the thirties, seminaries everywhere had to examine their consciences on the justice of insisting upon philosophy unless the students received academic accreditation transferable to civil universities should the boys decide at some stage not to continue with their studies for the priesthood. In London and Toronto, the seminaries had their philosophy division turned into an accrediting college through civil affiliation. In Halifax, philosophy was, in 1937, dropped from the seminary's programme. Students would henceforth have to take philosophy in a college or university before entering the seminary.

Holy Heart could have followed a different policy: it could have invoked and used its civil charter obtained in 1897. The decision – a fairly mature and courageous one for the thirties – was no longer to admit students who had not already taken their philosophy. As so often happens in the case of such decisions, the meeting one problem only created another. The first year of theology became somewhat nondescript and difficult to teach properly because of the wide variety of preparation in the students coming to the seminary from different institutions. An attempt was made to deal with this problem by introducing in 1938 a propaedeutic or preparatory year.

There were two strategies behind the propaedeutic year: one was remedial, to cope with the inadequacy of preliminary training; the other was scholarly, to make theology a five-year programme as recommended for pontifical faculties of theology by *Deus Scientiarum Dominus*. The additional year was maintained until 1943, then dropped, probably because too demanding by comparison with what other seminaries in America were doing.

The many rectors from the thirties to the fifties made it their responsibility to maintain the curriculum with vigour and to turn out holy and learned priests. Two of these rectors, Bray and Skinner, became bishops. One of them, D'Amours, left much of the responsibility for the seminarians to his prefect, Aucoin. Most of them, but especially Mc-Cluskey, were regarded as disciplinarians. With the professional staff behind them, and usually the bishops, they established a fine tradition and have deeply influenced the Church in the Maritimes.

After 1965, during the rectorship of Léger Comeau, Holy Heart Seminary experienced the same malaise that affected other seminaries following Vatican II, and like most of them took positive steps to cope with it. These were four: the acquiring of pontifical accreditation; the activating of the civil charter; ecumenical collaboration and modification or suppression of traditional rules and attitudes.

Pontifical accreditation was sought through Laval University. Laval affiliated Holy Heart on 25 November 1965, and the affiliation was approved by the Congregation of Seminaries and Universities, 25 December 1965. Holy Heart then began to grant the STB to properly qualified students after four years of theology; and the DD to those who completed the same work but on lower admission or performance standards. When these degrees were given through Laval, corresponding civil degrees were conferred by the seminary on its own civil charter.

In 1969 Holy Heart Seminary, Pine Hill Divinity Hall, and the University of King's College inaugurated a formal exchange of professors. It worked in two ways: some professors giving their courses in more than one institution; some students attending courses given only in another institution. This paralleled similar experiments in Montreal, Toronto, Boston, Chicago, Berkeley, and elsewhere.

Modifications within the seminary, affecting discipline, liturgy, orientation of mind became in Halifax as elsewhere largely exploratory. Courses were reduced in number, lectures became increasingly informal, St Thomas was not insisted upon so rigorously, and many of the traditional rules were relaxed or removed. Holy Heart had not to contend with the problem of geographical isolation, yet neither had its history been one of close association with St Mary's or Dalhousie. Modification of seminary discipline grew out of demands and expedience, and seemed irresistible in the context of modern society and the decline of vocations. During 1952–3, Holy Heart enrolled 96 students in a seminary built to house 80. In one year the registration reached 117. After 1965 numbers declined steadily from 65 students in that year to 23 in 1969. Both Aucoin and Hayes recognized that the education of candidates for the priesthood might well have to be totally integrated into the large universities, and as a possible step in that direction closed the seminary at the end of the 1969–70 year.

The history of Holy Heart has been an edifying and a noble one. It has served the Church in the Maritimes with dignity and in a learned and holy tradition. Its closing does not necessarily preclude its reopening but it is one of the many signs of the passing of sectarian and Tridentine christianity. *Nisi granum ... mortuum fuerit.*[8]

8 John 12: 24. 'Unless the grain of wheat ... dies.'

Convent of the Sacred Heart

HALIFAX, NS

(1849–1905)

The Convent of the Sacred Heart is a junior liberal arts college located in a four-storey red brick building on Spring Garden Road, Halifax, opposite the Public Gardens. It is a private academy for girls conducted by the nuns of the Society of the Sacred Heart and provides a modern equivalent of the 13-class programme of studies characteristic of the Society's many schools for young women. For many years students of Sacred Heart could, on the successful completion of the programme, be admitted to advanced undergraduate standing in Dalhousie University. During 1969 the post-secondary part of the programme was transferred to St Mary's University.

The Society of the Sacred Heart was organized in Paris in 1800 by Joseph Varin d'Ainville and others around Madeleine-Sophie Barat and three companions, who formed the nucleus of a religious society dedicated to the restoration of faith and the education of women. They adopted many of the educational ideals and patterns put into practice earlier by the Society of Jesus. Varin himself wanted to be a Jesuit, and was in Paris in 1800 in an attempt to restore and reorganize the society.[1]

Mother Madeleine-Sophie Barat became superior general of the Society of the Sacred Heart in 1806 and was responsible for its spread throughout Europe. In 1818 the society was brought to America by Philippine Duchesne.[2] The Halifax foundation was established from New York in May 1849 when Archbishop Walsh arranged the coming of the first group of nuns to the city: Mothers Mary Ann Aloysia Hardey and Mary Frances Peacock (superior), Mothers Donnelly and Dussart, sisters Anna Smith and Henrietta Obold

Within a week of the arrival of the nuns in Halifax, the new academy was opened in Brookside, a dwelling owned by the Dwyer family, and put at the temporary disposal of the sisters. In May 1849, 13 girls enrolled; by the end of the year the number had reached 40. In 1851 the

1 Louise Callan, *The Society of the Sacred Heart in North America*, New York: Longmans Green, 1937. The Halifax foundation is dealt with pp. 418–26. A bibliography is supplied, pp. 784–94.

2 Louise Callan, *Philippine Duchesne*, Westminster, Md., Newman, 1965

academy was moved to a new frame building erected by Mother Peacock on the present site. Major additions were made to this building in 1876, 1890, and 1909.

Two features distinguished the Halifax convent school from the society's other foundations: the presence of a government school for boys and girls attached in 1864 on the passing of the Free School Act; and the development of a larger day school than boarding school. The programme offered, however, was traditional and was given without reference to either departmental credits or university degrees. Students were accepted into the programme as little girls and remained until their formal education was presumably complete.

The first change, significant in the context of post-secondary education today, came on 27 June 1905. During the convent school's graduation exercises Walter C. Murray, professor of philosophy at Dalhousie University (later first president of the University of Saskatchewan) announced in the name of President Forrest that Dalhousie would henceforth admit Sacred Heart graduates to advanced standing in the university. This meant in practice that Dalhousie was willing to equate the work of the last two years of the convent's 'class' programme with the first two years of the four-year general arts course – an important concession to a school whose students did not write their grade XI (matriculation) examinations or who were not preparing for university entrance. The arrangement made in 1905 continued without major modification until 1926, when it was revised in the direction of curriculum conformity.

The staff of Sacred Heart has never been well known in Canadian university circles. Two sisters have perhaps received more public notice than the others. Mother Clare Murphy was one of the girls who graduated from Sacred Heart in 1905 and was present at the ceremonies on the occasion of Murray's announcement. She subsequently went to Dalhousie, took her university degree, and entered the Society of the Sacred Heart. From the time of her appointment to the convent school's faculty she watched over internal academic standards and external university relations. She was twice superior of the Halifax convent. On her retirement in the early sixties she continued teaching in the convent school in Vancouver. Mother Mary Reid, a colleague of Mother Murphy's, also achieved public stature. She was one of the architects of the junior college affiliation and carried her experience into wider context when in 1911 she was elected superior-vicar (provincial) of the southern houses of the society in the United States. She put her Halifax experience to good use when she succeeded in incorporating Maryville College – largely her own creation – into the structure of the University of St Louis.

The Sacred Heart-Dalhousie agreement has been the cause of occasional local tension: it was felt by the administration of Mount St Vincent to aid and abet the registration of Catholic women in Halifax's non-denominational university; and it was interpreted as giving tacit approval to co-education at Dalhousie during the years when co-education was explicitly forbidden at St Mary's. The tension never became acute because of the restricted size and exclusive character of the Sacred Heart enrolment.

Sacred Heart Convent has never had university pretensions. When the Sills-Learned report on education in the Maritimes was published in 1922 it did not take the convent school into consideration, not even listing it among 'schools of not more than junior college grade.' Nor has Sacred Heart been given any post-secondary status by the AUCC.[3] It has remained what it was intended to be from the beginning: a school preparing girls and young women for the Christian life. On 1 July 1969, after Archbishop Hayes had invited the Catholic colleges of Halifax to collaborate more effectively, Sacred Heart moved the more advanced part of its programme and the staff concerned to St Mary's University.[4]

Consideration of Sacred Heart's programme belongs in the context of the present volume because it provides a unique example of a valid kind of education to which contemporary systems stand in some debt and which may well be lost to the North American continent.

3 Sacred Heart is not listed in *Universities and Colleges of Canada* (1969), the annual handbook of the AUCC.

4 *A Commitment to Higher Education in Canada. A Report of a Commission of Inquiry on Forty Catholic Church-Related Colleges and Universities.* Ottawa: National Education Office, Feb. 1970, 14

St Thomas University

FREDERICTON, NB

1910

St Thomas University opened as a high school and arts college in Chatham, NB, in 1910. It received its charter in 1934 and its full university status in 1960. The university is located on King's Road on the main campus of the University of New Brunswick, Fredericton. Its relatively small property is leased from the provincial university and on it have been erected three red brick, Georgian buildings: an arts and education building, an administration and classroom building, and a residence building for men and women. The buildings were completed in 1964 at a cost of $2,000,000. St Thomas University is federated with the University of New Brunswick under an agreement drawn up in 1964 whereby St Thomas confers its own degrees in arts and education, but shares the university's other academic programmes, its library, and its social and recreational facilities which are furnished by the provincial government.

THE BASILIANS AT CHATHAM

In 1860 James Rogers, the first bishop of Chatham, Miramichi, NB, established a school for ecclesiastical students and academy for boys, St Michael's Male Academy, in his own residence. The bishop took personal charge of the institution and staffed it with his own priests and candidates for the priesthood. Among those who taught in St Michael's were fathers Thomas F. Barry, L. Gagnon, and William Varilly. In 1867 Rogers brought the Christian Brothers of Halifax to Chatham where they conducted a high school until 1880. From 1880 to 1910 there was no Catholic institution at Chatham beyond the elementary grades. Towards the end of 1909, or right at the beginning of 1910, Bishop Thomas Francis Barry wrote to the Basilian Fathers in Toronto inviting them to send a few men to Chatham to open and operate a classical college for the diocese. Barry's letter was read at a meeting of the provincial council of the Basilians on 14 January 1910 and laid over.

The provincial, Jean-Pierre Grand, and his council could not see their way clear to staff another college; they doubted that there would be enough students in Chatham to support it; and they were not sure that the superior general, Noël Durand, and his council would be in favour of taking on a college owned by the bishop and only operated by the community. The provincial council met again on 25 January and decided to send Father Michael V. Kelly to Chatham to discuss the project personally with the bishop. The two reached an agreement the exact terms of which nobody afterwards seemed to know, but which Kelly subsequently reconstructed as follows: the bishop was to fix up St Michael's Church, his pro-cathedral, for use as a college building; the Basilians were to send four priests to operate a classical college; the bishop assured them that there would be enough money to run it by guaranteeing an overall registration of 125 students or to pay $20 (a day student's tuition) for each student short of this total; the property was to be turned over to the Basilians if they made a success of the school and the agreement was to be reviewed after five years.

There were some points not clear about this agreement. It was taken for granted by both parties that the four priests were to receive their room and board and their personal 'salary' of $80 a year, but nothing seems to have been said about recompensing the community for its four priests. It was not clear either whether Grand, the provincial, really had permission from the superior general to open the college; however, he accepted the bishop's invitation on 21 February 1910. The general council, at its meeting of 23 April 1910 deferred approval until after the forthcoming chapter, which was to be held in the summer at Geneva.

The college opened in the fall of 1910 with Nicholas Roche as superior and J.T. Finnegan as treasurer. There were two other priests on the staff and a few laymen. Not much is known about this first year at St Thomas. The boarders paid $150 a year for their room, board, and tuition; the day students paid $20 for tuition only. There were probably about 75 students in all, estimating from the number enrolled the next year when there were 81 (33 boarders and 48 day scholars). What grades were involved is unknown, but the college aimed at offering what we would today call a high school course and two years of arts. Since there were lay teachers, there must have been some advanced students, because lay teachers in such schools were usually senior students who received their keep plus a Basilian priest's salary of $80 a year for teaching and disciplinary work.

Roche remained principal and superior for only one year, at the end of which he was called upon to take over the post of provincial, replacing Daniel Cushing, Grand's successor. At the same time, that is, during July 1911, authorization to open the college came from Father Joseph Schwarz of the Sacred Congregation of Seminaries and Universities.

The second superior of St Thomas College, William J. Roach, took over in the summer of 1911, and remained in office until the summer of 1919. The pioneering of St Thomas is usually associated with him. Roach brought experience and academic prestige to the young institution. He had graduated from the University of Toronto in 1896 with a distinguished class that includes Arthur Meighen, Sir Thomas White, J.S. McLean, and Malcolm Wallace. Roach was close to all these men and to Mackenzie King, who graduated a year before him. In the fall of 1906, Roach went to the Basilian novitiate. He was ordained in 1901, and spent two years (1902–4) in graduate study at Catholic University of America. By 1911 he was an experienced college teacher and his appointment to St Thomas College was evidence that the Basilians did not take the college lightly.

Roach became an influential public figure. He ran an excellent school, was respected by diocesan priests and the people of Chatham, and went out on the hustings to give memorable recruitment talks during the trying war years. Under him St Thomas became a college of great promise both locally and for the Church at large. Two of Roach's protégés became bishops – Francis P. Carroll and James M. Hill – and many others became diocesan priests; a good number went to Toronto to join the Basilians.

Roach was anxious to place the college in the people's affection by providing public services. His rink was such a service. In 1913 he undertook to buid a community rink, borrowing $1000 from the bishop at six per cent to be repaid in tuition. The college showed an operating loss of $1301.17 this year. The rink was an interesting experiment quite in line with Roach's enthusiasm for school sports. It was primarily for the townsfolk but it brought town and college together, providing both support and revenue for the college. The priests themselves and the boys looked after the flooding, cleaning, and supervision of the rink and the hiring of bands. This unique college venture was the occasion for an interesting exchange in 1917 between Roach and his provincial, Father Francis Forster. Roach wrote Forster in November expressing his distress at losing from his staff Paul Costello, who was being released for chaplain services in the armed forces. Roach understandably wanted a replacement at once. To emphasize the extent of his need he added: 'After Christmas we shall have the rink on our hands.'[1] Forster's reply was characteristic. 'With regard to the skating rink, we

---

1 Roach to Forster, 15 Nov. 1917. Archives of the Basilian Fathers, Toronto. Much of the material on the early history comes from personal letters and other data preserved in these files.

don't know all the circumstances; Father Player gave his impressions. Now I can't see where community men should be caretakers of a rink for the benefit of town Catholics even if it does add something to the revenues of the college. A farm might do the same thing, or a billiard parlour downtown ... It is unreasonable to expect a priest to do that work, or see that it is done by boys, or to expect that the province will supply a man with that idea in view.'

Roach was not easily daunted. His next letter argued the eminent reasonableness of the college maintaining a rink. It is no surprise that in these years Chatham should begin to produce great hockey teams, and even that some of them should be coached by college priests like Sylvester Nicholson and Jack Spratt. Roach, the college, town athletics, combined to give Chatham a national awareness. Add to this the fact that there was considerable exchange not only of staff but of students between the St Thomas campus and that of the renowned University of Toronto and the importance of the college socially and in human values becomes evident.

Roach's great problem was shortage of funds for running a proper college. Bishop Barry and the Community of St Basil had differing views of the sense of their agreement. The community received no revenue for its four priests in Chatham during the first five years they were there. Little was expected at first. But when there was no return of any kind year after year, not even the railway fare for moving staff to and from Toronto, something had to be done. The provincial complained to the bishop and reminded him of his agreement. But nobody could or would produce a copy of the agreement. Forster had to rely on M.V. Kelly's recollection of what took place in his evening of negotiations in the bishop's residence. The college priests, of course, had their room and board and were entitled to draw on the college treasury $80 a year for their personal expenses. The bishop felt that this was adequate, especially as he regarded the bursar, Terence Finnegan, as inexperienced and uneconomical in the handling of accounts – a harsh enough judgment on a dignified and sophisticated gentleman who taught, bought, accounted, collected fees, and who had in his best years as bursar a gross revenue of less than $16,000 on which to demonstrate his skills as an economist. When the five-year period of trial was over, the Basilians were on the point of withdrawing. Roach pleaded with the provincial council to retain the college and the bishop guaranteed the community $500 a year for the next five years for each priest sent to Chatham.

A constant worry of the Basilians in Chatham was the wretched state
of their college building. It was originally a long rectangular building
with a dividing wall near the middle separating the nave of the pro-
cathedral from the bishop's residence. It was the residential area of this
building, four storeys high, that had been remodelled for the college in
1910. A few years later the entire building was given over to college
use. It was a long wood and plaster structure, set on a stone foundation,
housing priests, boys, and classrooms. Emil J. Plourde, Finnegan's successor as treasurer, described it as a draughty building difficult to heat.
Worse, it was a real fire-trap. Plourde, writing on 28 July 1917, said
that its preservation from fire was 'a continual miracle.' Roach wrote a
similar letter, also mentioning the fire hazard. It was not, however, an
unpleasant building to live in and had apparently a lovely college
chapel. The terse telegram which came to Toronto on 12 March 1919,
could not be called surprising: 'College burned down last night. Everyone saved, Father Pageau injured but not seriously.' There was strong
suspicion that the fire, which started inside the main door in a stairwell,
might have been deliberately set; but it could also have been caused by
defective heating equipment. The fire trapped Father John Ernest
Pageau in his room and he broke his hip in dropping from the ledge
outside his top-storey window. The students were never in danger, but
the building was totally destroyed. The college was able to carry on as
a day school for the rest of the year in the Knights of Columbus hall;
the staff moved into the bishop's residence. Classes were not held
during 1919–20, while the building was being replaced.[2]

There was no question of discontinuing the college. A drive for
funds was undertaken immediately after the fire. The money raised,
along with insurance amounting to $25,000, made possible the erection
of a fine new building on a new site just east of the old at a cost of
$93,000. The new college was ready for occupancy during the summer
of 1920 and was formally blessed in September by Bishop Louis J.
O'Leary of Charlottetown, who had been auxiliary bishop of Chatham
from 1914 to 1920.

The period between the fire and the opening of the new building saw
much discussion and many changes. The provincial, Father Forster,
who favoured withdrawing the Basilians from Chatham, carried on a
heavy correspondence with both Bishop Barry and his auxiliary Bishop

2 See *St Thomas College Year Book*, I, 1922 which provides a useful survey of
life in the college between 1910 and 1922. A copy is preserved in the archives of
St Michael's College, Toronto.

O'Leary. A working arrangement was eventually reached whereby the Basilians agreed to stay on at the college, while the diocese and the college were jointly to reimburse the community in the neighbourhood of $1200 a man each year. Forster was adamant on this point. He was being pressed for staff by both Assumption and St Michael's, who were now paying $2000 a year for extern teachers, and he wanted to help them. He was, moreover, convinced that the Basilians should not accept foundations like Chatham, which were not operated at the community's own risk. 'We should never,' he wrote on 22 March 1919, 'undertake to conduct a school for a bishop.' At Chatham he was dealing with two bishops, both of them personally friendly and helpful, but neither understanding what a real college should be. Forster felt himself party to something approaching academic malfeasance. 'Four priests,' he wrote a few years later, 'cannot conduct a boarding school satisfactorily. Academically, the school year by year is disappointing' (24 July 1922.

On 19 January 1920, that is, a few months after Forster recommitted the community to Chatham, Bishop Barry died. On 20 January the auxiliary Bishop O'Leary was transferred to Charlottetown. On 9 September Patrick Chiasson was named bishop of Chatham, and when he was consecrated in December, the new college was already open. By then there had also been a change of superiors. Father Roach received a new appointment as superior of the community's scholasticate in Toronto. The new superior of St Thomas College was Father F. Daniel Meader, whose term began with the academic year 1920–1. Meader went to Chatham during the summer, was there when the building was opened in September, and welcomed Bishop Chiasson in December. Meader remained at the head of St Thomas College from 1920 to 1923, its last Basilian superior. He was an able and a scholarly man. He was the first, so far as is known, who seriously thought of making a university of St Thomas College. On this subject he wrote as follows to Forster on 17 February 1921: 'We are drawing up at present a private bill to have passed at the coming session of the New Brunswick legislature granting to the college powers to confer university degrees.' On 22 February, Meader forwarded to Toronto a copy of a bill proposing to incorporate the University of St Thomas. It contained 13 clauses, chief among which were those that would set up a board of governors and a senate and would provide for the bachelor's and master's degrees in arts and science.

Forster sent Meader his reaction to the text of the proposed act on 1

March. He felt that the wording contained many flaws and that the bill did not go far enough. 'It is better to wait till a later session of the legislature if you can thereby secure a completer charter.' Meader seems to have withdrawn the bill. He did not, however, forget it. On 30 April of the following year he expressed regrets that the college had no charter, but he had prepared a fine college calendar outlining a full college course in arts and science projected for 1922–3. He spoke of there being seven boys in first-year arts in 1922 with the prospect of five of them advancing to second year in 1923. He also thought that the matriculation class would yield them a first arts class of seven or eight boys in 1922–3.

These plans of Meader's describe in prospect the history of St Thomas College during the next eleven years: the story of a developing high school carrying on through two years of liberal arts and sending its boys elsewhere for their final college years and professional training. Even while Meader was writing about the prospects for next year he knew that the Basilians would not be in Chatham much longer because Chiasson and Forster, the bishop and the provincial, were not facing each other's problems. Chiasson had written Forster on 30 July 1921, saying that the diocese could not take on the burden of a salary subsidy. He offered either to rent the college to the Basilians at a nominal rental or to give it to them for as long as they remained in Chatham. To Forster these alternatives were no more viable than the present arrangement. He did nothing further for a year. On 24 July 1922, he wrote Chiasson to inform him that the provincial council had decided to give up the college and served notice of the withdrawal of the priests twelve months hence.

At the close of the academic year 1922–3 the four Basilians, F.D. Meader, J.J. Sullivan, J.S. Nicholson, and M.J. Pickett returned to Toronto. This was not as Meader wanted it nor, indeed, as any priest who had ever served in the college wanted it. Forster, however, continued to think the foundation a mistake and was confirmed in his judgment by consistently unfavourable reports pressed on him by Kelly and Player. Kelly was particularly opposed to staying in Chatham, possibly because it was he who made the original recommendation that the Basilians go there and he felt a certain responsibility for the decision. He visited the college again shortly after the priests had been withdrawn and could, he said, detect no local regrets over their going. His report is not corroborated by the bishop's written comments, by statements of succeeding rectors, or by evidence of a continuing stream of vocations to the Toronto novitiate throughout the next few years. Eight candidates for the Basilians went to Toronto the year the Basilians withdrew.

THE DIOCESAN COLLEGE

After the departure of the Basilians, Raymond Hawkes, priest of Chatham diocese, became rector of St Thomas College, holding the post until 1927. The college continued much as before, that is, maintained commercial and high school departments, and two years of arts. It was now, of course, staffed by local priests, advanced students, and laymen. In 1927, James M. Hill replaced Hawkes and held the rectorship until 1945.

Hill's rectorship was marked by a number of changes, notably by a shift in the ecclesiastical geography of New Brunswick, and by the obtaining of a charter in 1934.

The charter was applied for in January 1934 over the signatures of Hill and his staff, and was granted in March of the same year. The charter established a board of governors and gave the college power to establish faculties and to confer the bachelor's, master's, and doctoral degrees. The institution continued to be known as St Thomas College, continued to give commercial and high school work, but added the two final years of the college course.

In 1934 there were still only two ecclesiastical dioceses in New Brunswick – St John and Chatham. The English-speaking Catholics of St John were in general more closely associated with St Joseph University, the bilingual university at Memramcook. The English-speaking people of Chatham strongly supported St Thomas. On 22 February 1936, the archdiocese of Moncton was established and St Joseph's University fell within its territorial limits rather than those of St John. It had become clear that the French-speaking population of New Brunswick was increasing more rapidly than the English, and that the French had been somewhat overlooked in the original distribution of dioceses. On 15 May 1938, the diocese erected in Chatham in 1860 was transferred to Bathurst. The newly-arranged diocese had two small universities: Sacré-Cœur for French-speaking, St Thomas for English-speaking students. Hill felt the need to become more expansionary in his thinking and in 1941 acquired from the diocese a large stone residence, no longer needed in Chatham, and converted it into a university residence. Shortly after, 1945, Hill gave up the rectorship. In 1946 he became bishop of Victoria, British Columbia.

Hill was succeeded as rector of St Thomas by Charles V. O'Hanley, who held office from 1945 to 1948, and then by Andrew McFadden, who guided the college through what are now seen to have been very important years, 1948 to 1961. The McFadden years were expansionary and revolutionary: in 1955 McFadden was successful in getting Lord Beaverbrook to give St Thomas a large modern arena and other recreational facilities. This marked a gain. On the other hand, the church of Chatham was not at ease in the diocese of Bathurst, with the result that in 1959 the section of Northumberland county in which Chatham is located was transferred to the diocese of St John. Whether this was a gain for St Thomas remained to be seen. Would Chatham's college become also St John's? And if it did, would it remain in Chatham? At any rate, McFadden made every effort to develop the college. In 1960 he erected the J. Arthur Scott Memorial building, considerably expanding the university's facilities. At the same time he designated the house earlier acquired from the diocese by Hill as a Women's Residence, although women were not yet actually in residence. Also in 1960 he had the legislature amend the act of incorporation, changing the name of the college to St Thomas University. In 1961 he had all high school courses removed from St Thomas and placed in the new regional high school buildings. This same year, in view of other coming developments, McFadden accepted the post of vice-chancellor, and turned over the presidency of the university to Donald C. Duffie, chaplain and professor at Mount St Vincent College, Halifax.

At McFadden's last convocation of 1961, 19 students received their BA, 10 their B ED, one the B SC in nursing; and there were three honorary degrees. Full-time students in the regular session of 1962–3 totalled 277 (90 per cent from NB) exclusive of evening and summer sessions.[3] The operation which McFadden turned over in 1961 can be fairly described as a lively, respectable if small, Catholic liberal arts college with a university charter and expanding university aspirations.

When Duffie came to St Thomas in 1961, it was with full knowledge that St Thomas University would almost certainly be moved to the campus of the University of New Brunswick at Fredericton. This move was not in line with McFadden's thinking nor Chatham's vested interests, but it was on the advice of the royal commission established by the province in 1961 under the chairmanship of John Deutsch.

New Brunswick had in 1960 and 1961 three English-speaking universities – the University of New Brunswick at Fredericton, Mount Allison at Sackville, and St Thomas at Chatham; and it had three French-language colleges, St Joseph at Memramcook, Sacré-Cœur at

3 *Calendar of St Thomas University*, 1963–64, Chatham, NB

Bathurst, and St Louis at Edmundston. After months of serious investigation the commission reported in June 1962 to the following effect:

1 that New Brunswick should have henceforth three universities, one (English-speaking) at Fredericton, one (French-speaking) at Moncton, and a limited-enrolment university (Mount Allison) at Sackville

2 that St Thomas should become a university federated with the University of New Brunswick, moving to Fredericton where a new campus should be made available for it without charge

3 that St Thomas should continue to be responsible for its own administration and financing

4 that duplication of offerings and especially facilities, should, wherever possible, be discontinued

5 that St Thomas should continue to control the academic content and administration of courses to its BA and B ED degrees, both of which, however, it would continue to grant

6 that all other academic programmes be left to the University of New Brunswick to develop.[4]

It is noteworthy that the commission did not try to dictate the terms of confederation. The respective institutions were left to seek the advice of others and to arrive at terms suitable to all concerned.

The change-over was not made without causing hard feelings in Chatham, the only constituency to suffer through the new policy. The people of Chatham hoped, in view of the history of the college since 1910, to keep some college work on the local scene. It was particularly trying to see provision made in the commission's report for a branch of the new university, and even a branch of St Thomas College in St John and no similar provision for Chatham. The change meant both loss of municipal prestige and loss of revenue to the city. It was, they felt, carried out without the courtesy of genuine consultation. They felt that they had been presented with a *fait accompli* in a way the French constituencies and Mount Allison had not. Feelings ran very high for a period of three to four years.

St Thomas University acquired a fine property on the university campus where three buildings were erected. Following the suggestions of the Deutsch Report, it made a compact with the university in 1964 by which it now gives its own degrees in arts and education but holds its other university powers in abeyance. Wherever possible it shares the university's facilities and avoids unnecessary duplication. Of special significance also is that it can arrange to have its own professors give university courses, both undergraduate and graduate. Where called for, especially where enrolment is light as in advanced Latin, resources are pooled even in arts and education.

In 1964 the English province of the Holy Cross Fathers in Canada agreed to maintain a residence on campus for its own students attending university and for such staff men as it could provide for St Thomas University. This arrangement considerably simplified the finding of suitable and competent staff. Prospects for the immediate future are promising.

4 John J. Deutsch, *Report of the Royal Commission on Higher Education*, Fredericton, NB, June 1962; esp. 98–100

St Bride's College

ST JOHN'S, NEWFOUNDLAND

1884 (1952)

St Bride's College at Littledale, or Kilbride, in St John's, Newfoundland, is a residential teacher-training institution affiliated with Memorial University of Newfoundland and under the direction of the Sisters of Mercy. The college serves mainly young women from outside St John's and the young members of Newfoundland's two teaching sisterhoods, the Sisters of Mercy and the Presentation Sisters. Students of St Bride's take their first two years – one of arts and one of teacher-training – at Littledale, and their last two years at the university. Curriculum and examinations throughout the course are those of the university. The joint degree in arts and education is conferred by the university at the end of the fourth year, or of the fifth in the case of transfer students. St Bride's building, of modern construction, was erected in 1965 and is located a mile or two from the university campus.

St Bride's Academy was established as a girls' boarding school in 1884 by the Sisters of Mercy in the homestead of Judge Little (after whom it has been called Littledale) on Waterford Bridge Road. The property was acquired 13 November 1883 and the school formally opened 20 August 1884.

The Sisters of Mercy were founded to perform the works of mercy among the poor, the sick, and the ignorant of Dublin by Elizabeth McAuley in 1830. The community grew very rapidly and opened a house on Military Road in St John's Newfoundland, in 1842, the first of their many foundations in America. In 1859 they opened St Michael's Orphange in Belvedere, St John's, then in 1884 St Bride's Academy. By this time, sisters of the order were teaching in many parts of Newfoundland and had received into their novitiate a good number of Newfoundland girls. From the moment of opening the academy the Sisters of Mercy had in mind a special mission to educate Catholic girls from the outports, which explains why St Bride's was in the beginning and has remained ever since an almost totally residential operation.

The foundation at Littledale did not start auspiciously. Registration on opening day totalled four, and it rose to only thirteen during the first year. The academy, however, once under way, grew steadily and additions to the original house and replacements were made from time to time: the Talbot wing in 1901, an extension in 1909, the five-storey west wing in 1912, a science laboratory in 1927, and the present college building in 1965.

A secondary school programme was maintained from the beginning; and during the nineties a pupil-teacher course was introduced which prepared high school girls for teaching in Newfoundland schools, particularly in the outports. St Bride's has always been teacher-oriented.

By 1917 the school was providing a full academic course to the end of grade xi, and during that year commercial and domestic science departments were added. The name of the academy was stepped up to St Bride's College.

In September 1918 came the first major academic expansion: courses were provided, for girls who had completed grade xi, in apologetics, ethics, and sociology, and in the philosophy, psychology, and history of education, with a view to Christian catechetics and general pedagogy. At the same time practice teaching was introduced.

A few years later, all the academic subjects of grade xii were put on the curriculum so that students could take the certificate of the Common Examining Board of the Maritime Provinces and Newfoundland, and so that St. Bride's College could became a University of London associate. The school's reputation grew as its girls, especially its industrious sisters, began to go elsewhere to teach and study. By the thirties some Littledale girls were being admitted to the second of the four-year arts course in the maritime universities.

St Bride's College, during the forties featured its teacher-training programme and co-operated with Memorial University College to the extent that even before 1943 some Memorial professors went regularly to Littledale to give lectures and in some cases whole courses. By 1945 it was possible to speak of a loose, informal kind of affiliation between the two institutions, an affiliation that was fully formalized in 1952.

The fifties were good years at St Bride's, with a large enrolment of prospective teachers. By 1958, the high school department was moved to Holy Heart, a regional high school staffed conjointly by the Sisters of Mercy and the Presentation Sisters. Meanwhile the teacher-training enrolment passed 400.

In 1965, a large new building was erected at Littledale which is the present home of the college. The course now provided consists of the first two years of a four-year programme to a joint arts and education degree. The first year is the general arts year prescribed for all students of Memorial. The second year is a professional year. The curriculum for both these years is set by the university, as are the examinations. The last two years (three years in the case of transfer students) of the programme are taken at the university. There has always been at least one of the sisters attached to the Memorial staff to teach in these final years: Sister Mary Edward Roche in educational psychology, or Sister Nolasco Mulcahy in philosophy of education. A third, Sister Chrysostom McCarthy, has been assistant librarian.

The superiors of St Bride's since formal affiliation in 1952 have been: Sister Basil McCormack, Sister Teresino Bruce, Sister Hildegarde Dunphy, and Sister Nolasco Mulcahy, the present superior and professor of the philosophy of education.

There has been some controversy over the wisdom of building the new college at Littledale in 1965. The Sisters, however, were absorbing the full cost, and the decision was ultimately theirs. Many hoped that the sisters would locate their building on the Memorial campus both as a material contribution to the university and as a Catholic voice on the secular campus. The minister of education, the Hon. G.A. Frecker, strongly recommended this course. The grounds for the decision to rebuild at Littledale were largely pastoral: it was felt that girls coming into St John's from the outports would find the transition easier to make if they had two years in the convent atmosphere. This arrangement, which preserved the Littledale tradition unbroken, is said to have had the support of Archbishop Patrick Skinner. Differences on the matter ran deep. When from 11 to 13 September 1968, the Catholic high school students of St John's staged a strike over the introduction of shift classes in the Catholic high schools, their spokesmen publicly questioned the spending of this money on the new St Bride's. This, however, does not mean that they felt the college should have been built on the campus, because they also criticized the subsequent building of St. John's. They probably regarded the very idea of a separate Catholic teacher-training institution as reactionary and as an extravagant use of funds that might have gone into an additional high school.

The sisters, as has been mentioned, are on the Memorial campus in their capacity of professors of education. There is also, since 1968, a Catholic residence and centre on the campus, St John's College, under the direction of John Lynch, a Jesuit priest who is also a university professor of engineering. Meanwhile, St Bride's College functions satisfactorily off the campus, under favourable terms and circumstances, as an effective teacher-training college for Catholic young women of the province.

III
CENTRAL CANADA

CHAPTER ELEVEN

The University of St Michael's College

TORONTO

1852

The University of St Michael's College, which is federated with the University of Toronto, holding its degree-conferring powers in abeyance except in theology, is a chartered university comprising a faculty of arts (St Michael's College), a faculty of theology (with two streams: a professional course to the STB, and a graduate academic course to the MTH and DTH, both in collaboration with the inter-denominational Toronto School of Theology), a graduate Institute of Christian Thought leading to the MA and PHD, and an autonomous and pontifical Institute of Mediaeval Studies. The faculty of arts (St Michael's College) includes St Joseph's College and Loretto College and is the federated arts college in the University of Toronto. St Michael's was founded by Bishop de Charbonnel in 1852 and placed under the direction of the Basilian Fathers. Its small campus of about five acres is located in downtown Toronto along St Joseph Street between Clover Hill and Queen's Park, and along the eastern extremity of Toronto's St George campus. Near the centre of St Michael's campus stands St Basil's Church and clustered around it are some 22 miscellaneous academic and residential units: Cloverhill, Brennan (student-faculty centre), Loretto, Elmsley (including Charbonnel), the heating plant, the institute, More, Fisher, Teefy, Carr, the library, St Joseph's, Maryhall, Fontbonne, St Basil's College (the seminary), and eight old homes on Elmsley Place. The university is presided over by a president, a collegium, and a senate.

JEAN-MARIE SOULERIN, SUPERIOR, 1852–65

The history of St Michael's College, Toronto, begins with the opening of St Mary's Little Seminary, 67 Queen Street East, opposite the site of the present Metropolitan Church, by Bishop de Charbonnel and the Basilian Fathers on 15 September 1852. This seminary was one of two educational projects undertaken simultaneously by the diocese. The other was a boys' college, St Michael's College, which was opened in the episcopal palace, also in September 1852, under the direction of the Brothers of the Christian Schools. The two institutions became one some six months later; they were continued in the palace as St Michael's

College and were staffed by the Basilian Fathers. The story of these beginnings can be simply told.[1]

The first bishop of Toronto, Michael Power, died of the plague in 1847. His successor, who was not appointed until the beginning of 1850, was Armand-François-Marie, Comte de Charbonnel, French nobleman and Sulpician who had taught some years in the Grand Seminary of Montreal. De Charbonnel had returned to France after a serious illness, and it was there that he received news of his appointment as bishop of Toronto. He was embarrassed by his lack of fluency in English and asked Pierre Tourvieille, the superior general of the Priests of St Basil, who had been his teachers when he was a student at their college in Annonay, to permit Father Patrick Molony, professor of English in the college, to accompany him to Toronto. When de Charbonnel sailed from Southampton for New York, Molony was one of the small band of eight recruits whom the bishop had been able to gather together in France to help him with his work in Toronto.

Aboard ship, and afterwards in the cathedral rectory where Molony lived with the bishop for a period of two years before any project in higher education was undertaken, the two talked over the possibility of establishing a college in Toronto. The bishop's idea was to open two institutions, a minor seminary and a classical college, and to attach them to a parish or parishes, hiring religious priests to run them for him. It was his impression that it would be more economical to proceed this way than to turn over the project to a religious order. Revenue, he surmised, would accrue to the diocese from both the parish and the educational institution. His plan was perhaps not realistic, but it grew out of his desperate awareness of the very large dimensions of his diocesan debt (some $70,000 was owing on his cathedral alone when he arrived in Toronto) and of the many new obligations he would soon have to assume if he were to try to do all the work that needed to be done.

De Charbonnel approached the Jesuits and the Oblates with his plan. Both orders preferred to build their own church and college and to operate them at their own risk. The Jesuits in any event had no men available for an English-language college in Toronto although they had already received an offer of property for a college from Captain John Elmsley, the prominent Toronto convert. The bishop eventually reached an agreement with the Community of the Priests of St Basil to staff a

1 See L.K. Shook 'St Michael's College: The Formative Years, 1850–1853,' *Report of the Canadian Catholic Historical Association*, 17(1950), 37–52. Also, Candide Causse, *Evêque d'or, crosse de bois, vie de monseigneur de Charbonnel, évêque de Toronto*, Paris: Société S. Francoise d'Assise, 1931.

minor seminary for him, and with the Brothers of the Christian Schools to staff a college, both institutions to be operated at his risk. There was a tentative and even a desperate quality about both these agreements. The Basilians were not an experienced religious community and had never before worked outside the Vivarais, where they had been organized under the local bishop. Besides, they were not an English-speaking community. The brothers had already come to Toronto but with the intention of working in the field of primary education. Two separate educational institutions thus came into being at the same time: St Mary's Little Seminary, taken on by the Basilians and called St Mary's because it would later be attached to St Mary's parish, then under construction at Adelaide and Bathurst Streets, and St Michael's College, opened by the brothers in the bishop's own cathedral rectory or palace. The real significance of the founding of two institutions is that the bishop envisaged them as functioning at two different levels, presumably secondary and post-secondary.

By early 1852 de Charbonnel and Molony had prevailed upon Tourvieille to promise to send four additional men to Toronto. These were: Jean-Mathieu Soulerin, Joseph Malbos, Charles Vincent, and William Flannery. Soulerin, the superior-elect of the new foundation in Toronto, and a distinguished man within his tiny community, had very nearly been elected superior general during the general chapter of 1848, and was actually to become superior general in 1865. Malbos, a personally difficult man, perhaps even a malcontent, but highly competent, was named bursar or treasurer. Vincent and Flannery were still unordained: Vincent had received minor orders, Flannery was a tonsured cleric. Molony, who had been in Toronto since 1850, was named assistant to Soulerin. The new members arrived at the cathedral rectory in August 1852.

Classes in St Mary's Little Seminary began on 15 September 1852 in temporary quarters on Queen Street with nine students in attendance. By December this number had increased to twenty-one, of whom nine were boarders. The seminary was much better off than the college, which attracted only eight students, none of them boarders. Since a high proportion of the two student bodies could not afford to pay fees, and since the rent on the Queen Street property had to be paid monthly, the two schools failed to produce enough revenue to meet ordinary expenses. It is not surprising that by the beginning of 1853 the bishop was wondering whether the operations should not be merged.

The precise difference of curriculum between the two institutions is not clear. The seminary no doubt provided more advanced work than the college, but even so it had a number of young students who were only beginning their secondary education. Soulerin, writing to Tourvieille on 1 October 1852, referred briefly to the programme: 'Mr Flannery has charge of the six youngest who have not yet learned *rosa*. Fathers Malbos and Molony are sharing the rest of the teaching. Mr Vincent is on discipline and is studying English and theology.'[2] The cathedral college was advertised in the *Toronto Mirror*, 20 August 1852, as about to provide 'solid instruction preparatory to commerce and the arts.' It is likely that the seminary's programme reached down and included most of what was being offered in the college. There was apparently no reason why the two institutions could not be merged other than the feeling on the part of the Basilians, and voiced by Tourvieille, that a seminary was not simply a college but a way of life for aspirants to the priesthood and that it filled a very different need in the Church. Moreover, the Basilians felt that their successful experience at Ste Barbe and Ste Claire in the Vivarais qualified them for the precise task they had undertaken in Toronto; they were not sure that they were competent or prepared to take on the additional and different burden of directing a secular college.[3] Gradually, the bishop convinced Soulerin that a single institution combining a secular college and an ecclesiastical seminary was the only practical solution to the Toronto problem; Soulerin brought Tourvieille around to the same conclusion.

The decision to merge the two institutions created two new problems: what to do about the two brothers teaching in the college; and what to do about the new building going up in St Mary's parish for a religious house and seminary. The brothers were, after some unpleasantness, relocated in two elementary schools, leaving behind for their successors such equipment as had been mustered for the college staff and students. Soulerin thought they had been treated unfairly: 'It takes more than four or five months to judge the success or failure of an enterprise.'[4] The idea of placing the Basilians in charge of the new St Mary's parish was abandoned, and the building being prepared for the Little Seminary was placed at the service of the Sisters of Loretto.[5] Moreover, it was now patent that the palace could only be a temporary location for the expanded institution. The college would have to go ultimately to Power Street where the diocese had some land, or to the Elmsley property if its owner was still willing to provide for a college. Soulerin and his colleagues were coming more and more to the mind of the Jesuits and

2 Shook, 'St Michael's College,' 60
3 Tourvieille to de Charbonnel, 15 Mar. 1854, *Letter Book*, 58
4 Soulerin to Tourvieille, 21 Feb. 1853, *Letter Book*, 2
5 Shook, 'St Michael's College,' 49

Oblates that religious were wiser to run their own school than to hire out to a bishop. The bishop too was learning about the cost of education the hard way. In the diocesan retreat of August 1853, de Charbonnel had to tell his clergy that he would require as much as one-tenth of their parish revenues and two annual parish collections to provide for the education of priests even if he were successful in getting the government to provide him with a small subsidy.

On 14 February 1853, the minor seminary was transferred to the palace, where it took over the college students and itself became known as St Michael's College. Results justified the move. The new St Michael's grew steadily as a combined college and seminary and by November had an enrolment of 47 students, 30 of them boarders. Almost all years of the college and seminary programmes were now being provided. Soulerin wrote to Tourvieille, 21 November 1853, that there were five students taking philosophy and two theology. Additional teachers, Mr Rooney and Mr Keleher, had to be taken on to supplement the Basilians.

The Basilians experienced from the beginning great difficulty in keeping their non-teaching commitments within reasonable bounds. They assisted with the ministerial duties of the cathedral, served as chaplains to the two convents and to the brothers, and tended a mission in Weston, north-west of the city. The bishop was prodding them to take on more, including even the entire pastoral care of two parishes, St Paul's and St Mary's. They had reason to fear that their religious life would suffer and their teaching work become a secondary preoccupation. The record of their resistance is strong evidence that Soulerin was an excellent college head and that his policy of keeping the emphasis on teaching was sustained by Tourvieille. Indeed, Tourvieille's directives on this matter were more rigid than the priests could observe.[6]

After the move to the palace, plans were afoot to find a permanent location. By April the land previously offered the Jesuits by John Elmsley was offered to the bishop and the Basilians. When Elmsley had made the original offer to the Jesuits, it was on the condition that they erect a college. When he renewed the offer to de Charbonnel and Soulerin, it was on the condition that they build a parish church. During April 1853, Elmsley deeded over to the college four building lots on his Clover Hill estate. Shortly after, the French Basilians sent out to Toronto the sum of 30,000 francs (roughly $6000): 10,000 for incidental expenses of the priests, 20,000 for the purchase from Elmsley of four additional lots immediately north of the donated lots, thus assur-

6 Charles Roume, *Origines et Formation de la Communauté des Prêtres de Saint-Basile*, Privas, 1965, 338

ing not only a property adequate for the kind of college they hoped to build, but a measurable stake by the community itself in the project. It was 1855 before the construction of a building on the property was begun and September 1856 before St Basil's Church and the new St Michael's College were opened on Clover Hill. In the meantime, three other matters occupied the college community.

First was the making of a treaty or concordat between the Community of St Basil and the bishop.[7] In the concordat, dated 1 November 1855, the bishop arranged for such aid as the diocese could afford the college: fees for seminarians stationed in the college; half the government subsidy paid the diocese for educational purposes; half the seminary collection taken up in the parishes. He also promised that his theological students would teach in the college for three years after their ordination and that the Basilians could seek vocations in his diocese. The Basilians undertook to help with parish missions under the direction of their superior and to provide certain other diocesan services. Most important for the history of the institution, the Basilians took over full responsibility for the foundation with its risks and perils. Though this meant assuming a large building debt over and above the property purchase, it also meant that the college was in large part their own project. So far as they were concerned, it could and should be given priority to every other local consideration – a priority which no bishop could at that time concede to an educational institution directly under his own control. Bishop de Charbonnel visited Ottawa late in 1855 and spoke with some satisfaction to Bishop Guigues about these arrangements. Bishop Guigues cited what the Basilians had undertaken as an example for Mgr de Mazenod to follow in Ottawa.[8]

The second issue to appear during this period was the relation between St Michael's College and the University of Toronto. The bishop thought of St Michael's as functioning at the university level and doing for Catholics what the University of Toronto neither succeeded in doing nor wanted to do for them. 'In the University of Toronto,' de Charbonnel wrote somewhat inaccurately to Cardinal Franzoni, prefect of the Propagation of the Faith, 30 May 1853 'degrees are granted to Catholics

7 R.J. Scollard, 'Notes on the History of the Congregation of St Basil,' II, 8–14. These unpublished volumes are available in the library of the University of St Michael's College. See also, for some appendices to the Concordat, 'Tourvieille to Soulerin' August 1857, Letter Book, 146.

8 Bishop de Charbonnel visited Bishop Guigues in Ottawa late in 1855. Guigues, writing to de Mazenod, superior general of the Oblates, cited what the Basilians had undertaken as an example to be followed in Ottawa. Charbonnel to Guigues, 28 Dec. 1852, cited in Gaston Carrière, 'Le Collège de Bytown,' Revue de l'Université d'Ottawa, 26(1956), 73.

if they reject their faith ... Catholics are excluded from burses ... they follow courses determined by the state and are instructed in history and philosophy by Protestants ... nine-tenths of the students and nineteen-twentieths of the professors are Protestants.'[9] St Michael's College was in his mind to be a university institution, and it was to look after Catholics. He did not mean by this that it was to have nothing to do with the University of Toronto. When de Charbonnel and Molony arrived in Toronto during 1850, the Baldwin Act (1849) establishing the non-sectarian University of Toronto had just been passed. Some of the Protestant churches had opposed this change; de Charbonnel at the time favoured it. He stated, according to the *Toronto Mirror*, Friday, 17 January 1851, that 'in his opinion they [the University Acts] are fully calculated to meet the wishes and expectations of the whole community of Upper Canada; and announcing his intention on behalf of his people, to become affiliated with the university, charging himself with their religious instruction.'[10] The bitter comment to Franzoni two years later deals with actualities and reveals a less sympathetic attitude. De Charbonnel and Soulerin continued, largely for financial reasons, to seek the affiliation of St Michael's with what the Protestants were describing as the 'Godless university.' On 12 June 1855, Soulerin wrote to the senate of the university asking for affiliation.[11] Soulerin was referring to this letter on 5 July 1855, when he wrote to Tourvieille, the superior general, as follows: 'We have also asked to be affiliated with the University of Toronto, which is so richly endowed. If the conditions attached to the affiliation are suitable, we shall be in line for help from the government just as are the Protestant colleges. This is what we are asking for in our petition. The secretary of the university has so far replied only to the effect that our request would be sent on to the senate of the university as soon as possible.'[12] The letter was twice read in the senate, 18 and 21 December 1855. The senate was evasive: 'The registrar was directed to inform the authorities of that College, that, by a general statute of the University, students are admitted to degrees without reference to the educational institutions in which they receive their education.'[13] The request was rejected no doubt for several reasons, but chiefly, it seems, because the college was now actually eligible

---

9 Francis J. Boland, 'An Analysis of the Problems and Difficulties of the Basilian Fathers in Toronto, 1850–1860,' unpublished dissertation, University of Ottawa, 58

10 This item in the *Mirror* is taken from a letter of P.B. de Blaquière, chancellor of the university, to Bishop Strachan. See J.G. Hodgins, *Documentary History of Education in Upper Canada*, Toronto, 1904, XI, 54.

11 Ibid., 276, 278

12 Soulerin to Tourvieille, 5 July 1855: Archives of the Basilian Fathers, Toronto

13 Hodgins, *Documentary History*, XI, 278

for grants subsequent to its incorporation in 1855, and because the affiliation of perhaps the smallest and least influential institution in Toronto was more likely to weaken than strengthen the position of the university in its Toronto constituency.

The third matter to arise in these years prior to the actual move to Clover Hill was the legal incorporation of the college. This went through the legislature during the fall of 1854 and the spring of 1855 and received royal assent 19 May 1855.[14] The act was a public one and normal in every way, though resisted by George Brown, reform member from Lambton county and editor of the *Globe*, and Joseph Hartman, member from the north riding of York, both as a whole and in that clause which granted St Michael's the right to hold real estate and to derive revenue from it. The bishop of Toronto petitioned for the bill and was named a member of the corporation, which also included the superior, the professors, and other members of the college. There was no mention of the college having any university status.

This act of incorporation was part of the general preparations made for moving the college from the cathedral rectory to its new site at Clover Hill. The building erected there during 1855–6 was but the central portion of a larger plan drawn by the Toronto architect, William Hay. The cornerstone of the new building was laid 15 September 1855; the parish Church, St Basil's, was opened 14 September 1856; and on 15 September classes began in the new St Michael's. The classical college programme continued to be followed during the succeeding years with theology added for some of the masters who were seeking ordination. Soulerin continued as superior until 1865 when he was recalled to France to become the superior general of the Congregation of St Basil. His years on Clover Hill were hectic ones. The financing of the school was always precarious, and doubly so after his bursar, Father Malbos, offended Bishop de Charbonnel by arranging, in 1857, to leave St Michael's and become superior of the new Assumption College.[15] At the request of Pierre-Adolphe Pinsonneault, bishop of the new diocese of London, Malbos took over the Sandwich school from the Jesuit pastor of Assumption parish Pierre Point, and for a year, made a rather clumsy effort at directing it. The bishop of Toronto was so annoyed by what he took to be an act of desertion that he modified the concordat with the Basilians by removing from it all reference to any supplemen-

14 Ibid., 132–3
15 L.K. Shook, 'The Coming of the Basilians to Assumption College: Early Expansion of St Michael's College,' *Report of the Canadian Catholic Historical Association*, 18(1951), 59–73

tary gift of funds from himself. Soulerin weathered this storm personally and never broke with the bishop. The episode, however, created a coolness in some quarters towards the Basilians which was still observable when Bishop Lynch succeeded de Charbonnel in 1860.

Father Soulerin's term as superior of St Michael's lasted until 1865. He was a quiet, holy, strong, and intelligent man, loved and admired by his subjects, though sometimes criticized as inattentive to public relations. He was always extremely busy; he was on two occasions, once for two years, administrator for Bishop de Charbonnel and afterwards vicar general of Bishop Lynch, and also of the bishop of London; he was religious superior in the house and deeply involved in structural changes affecting the Basilian community as a whole; he was the academic head of the college and, at various times, professor of logic, natural philosophy, and chemistry. He instituted no academic changes of great significance, but merely adapted the college system he knew in France to the situation he met in Toronto. The college continued throughout his headship to be largely a high school with a commercial programme for boys preparing for business and an advanced programme of philosophy and theology for the older boys and young men who were considering orders, many of whom were teaching assistants in the college, and some of whom actually went on to professional schools. He seems not to have continued to look toward the University of Toronto academically, though he is known to have maintained warm personal relations with its president, Dr McCaul, who is said to have had respect for Soulerin's theological insight and to have regretted that he 'had not a more progressive religion.'[16]

Soulerin had from the beginning assumed responsibility for the construction of the college building. In 1862 he undertook to finance and supervise an addition to the college wing, which involved him again in dealing with contractors and the collecting of funds in parishes of central and western Ontario. This first addition, eastward, was a simple extension of the original wing and was completed in 1865. When Father Actorie, the superior general, died suddenly in 1865, it became fairly obvious that Soulerin would have to return to France to replace him. He had almost been brought back in 1859 when Tourvieille, the preceding superior general, had died, but it was generally felt at that time that Soulerin's departure from Toronto might have led to the closing of St Michael's and Bishop de Charbonnel was strongly opposed to his leaving. The situation was easier by the summer of 1865. Soulerin returned

16 Scollard, 'Notes,' III, 91–2

to France and his office in Toronto was taken over by Charles Vincent who had, while still an unordained cleric, accompanied Soulerin to Toronto in 1852 when the original Little Seminary was opened.

1865–1906: VINCENT, CUSHING, TEEFY

Charles Vincent, Superior, 1865–86

Charles Vincent was superior of St Michael's from 1865 to 1886, a period of serious trials and genuine progress. Vincent had come from France with the founding fathers in 1852. He was ordained in Toronto in May of the following year and taught constantly and successfully on the college staff right through to 1865. Although not a particularly distinguished man, he was devoted to Soulerin's policies and attitudes and was his logical successor.

Vincent's first ten years as superior were difficult enough: he had financial worries of a pressing nature to contend with, and he lost for a time the support of the bishop. Fees during those years were very low: $100 a year for room, board, tuition (usually paid in monthly instalments) in 1868; $125 a year in 1869. The government subsidy of $3000 was discontinued after 1868. Soulerin's addition (1865) to the old wing was still being paid for. The number of students was too small to carry an ambitious operation: 92 students in 1866, 191 in 1877, 140 in 1881, 115 in 1885. Vincent had also to add the northerly part of the east wing between 1871 and 1873. There were several moments when for financial reasons alone there was real danger of the college being closed.

There was also a fairly serious falling out between the bishop and the college authorities over a whole complex of situations. In the first place, Bishop Lynch did not regard the academic programme as fully successful. It served the needs of the younger boys and of older students going on for the priesthood, but it was not geared to the university patterns taking form throughout Canada. Boys who really wished to attend university in the full sense had either to break the sequence of the college programme and prepare to take the university's matriculation examination or they had to enter philosophy with the intention of transferring later to an American college or professional school. A letter of Father Denis O'Connor to Robert Brady (later, McBrady), a student whose family, like his own, was from Pickering, Ontario, and who had entered the Basilian novitiate, reveals the situation: six of Brady's classmates, the letter says, are still at school; they are in Father Ferguson's class, and their names are Cassidy, Quinlan, Brennan, Cushin, Post, and Horgan. One of these boys, Quinlan, is preparing for his matriculation examinations because he intends to go to the university next year. Another boy, McCarthy of Pickering, senior to Brady, has now taken his first-class certificate before the County Board of Ontario; he too will try to go to the university next year. Four older boys, whom Brady will remember, took part in last Trinity's ordinations: two (McEntee and Harris) received tonsure, two others (Cassidy and Kilkullen) were made subdeacons.[17] Filling out the letter, it could be added that the college would be able to look after the advanced studies of Brady's five remaining classmates without handicapping them provided they went on for the Church, but at some risk if they had other plans. A situation of this kind was not one to inspire the fullest support from either the Catholic constituency or the bishop. It was quite unimpressive beside the situation of Victoria University at Cobourg, of Trinity in Toronto, or of Catholic colleges in the United States. The bishop was particularly aware of this last contrast since he had himself in 1856 founded the Seminary of the Holy Angels in Niagara Falls, NY, and he now saw his seminary moving ahead towards university status, which, in fact, it attained in 1883 when it became Niagara University. It is not surprising that Lynch grew cool toward St Michael's and thought that some other order like the Jesuits or the Oblates, or his own Lazarists (Vincentians) might do a better job.

There were other problems too. Vocations to the priesthood were coming all too slowly. The Basilians were over-expanding, opening a mission in Owen Sound in 1863, a college in Louisville, Ohio, in 1866, and were from 1868 on negotiating to reopen Assumption College in Sandwich. All this expansion entailed a reduced operation in Toronto. This at any rate is what O'Connor thought: 'It is the opinion of most of the confreres here that the community takes too many colleges and does not pay sufficient attention to the mental formation of its members.'[18] Add to this that a number of priests on the college staff asked to be allowed to withdraw from teaching in favour of parish work, that there were one or two regrettable cases of irregularity, and that the Fenian raids had created pro- and anti-Irish tensions between the bishop and members of the college staff, and the rift in relations which resulted becomes quite understandable.

The following excerpts from letters written between 1870 and 1875 to the superior general in France give a good idea from the college point of view of the situation in which Vincent found himself.

1 Vincent to Soulerin, 3 November 1869: 'Mgr de Toronto a pris le mer Samedi dernier. Je le quittai en New York le vendredi, m'y étant rendu

17 Ibid., VII, 170–1   18 Ibid., VIII, 98

pour l'ordination de Mr. McEvoy ... Mgr Lynch fit toutes les ordinations et fut d'une humeur charmante. Faites lui un peu fite.'[19] 2 O'Connor to Soulerin (from Sandwich), 24 January 1871: 'Poor Archbishop Lynch was never remarkable for his good sense, but since his return from Rome, he seems to have parted company with it completely. He has run counter to nearly everybody, and at last the storm has burst upon St Michael's. They are much annoyed there, as they scarcely know what he finds fault with.'[20] 3 O'Connor to Soulerin, 7 April 1873: 'I shall endeavour to mind exactly your advices as to the conduct we are to hold concerning the Toronto troubles ... Lately again during Father Vincent's visit to Louisville, His Grace summoned some of the boys before him, repeated to them his complaints against the college, and against the students, etc. The boys denied all his charges, and on their return home told all the other boys, who appointed six of their number, three Canadians and three Americans, to draw up a protest against such charges. Of course, Father Vincent on his return would not allow the protest to be presented ... It has been supposed here that the archbishop would ask you to remove Father Vincent and to put Father Molony in his place ... we trust you will make no change as all are of opinion that Father Vincent is the only man amongst us who has coolness and judgement enough to come safely through these difficulties.'[21] 4 Vincent to Soulerin, 2 April 1873: 'Je n'ai pas eu et ne puis pas avoir de communications avec l'archevêque. Vous comprenez que je ne puis me dédire et me faire ce que je ne suis pas, pour à Dieu. Cela ne se pardonne pas.'[22] 5 Soulerin to the Sacred Congregation of Religious, 1874 (re Art. 2, Discipline et Administration temporelle) : 'J'aborde cet article sous la pénible impression des milles reproches de Mgr Lynch. Sa Grace se plaint en général que nous ne valons pas les Jésuites, les Oblats de Marie, etc. Hélas! ... Relativement au temporel, nous prenons toujours garde de ne pas dépenser au delà de nos moyens ... notre établissement de Toronto peut seul nous donner d'inquiétude, à cause du capital considérable que nous avons employé là, et du circonstance pénible où nous nous trouvons avec Mgr l'Archevêque.'[23] 6 Vincent to Soulerin, 3 February 1875: 'L'Archevêque nous a fait une visite lundi soir. Il a été bon et affable. Puisse cela durer.' 7 O'Connor to Soulerin, 13 July 1875: 'Archbishop Lynch seems to be converted. God grant the grace may last.'[24]

The petulance of the bishop came from something more personal. One of Vincent's priest-professors, Michael J. Ferguson, undertook at the request of his friend Sir John A. Macdonald, to soften the anti-

19 Ibid., 2   20 Ibid., 50   21 Ibid., 190–3
22 Ibid., 189   23 Ibid., IX, 9   24 Ibid., VIII, 127, 148

English attitude of pro-Irish clergy in Toronto over the Fenian raids. The bishop took offence at Ferguson's action, and the two were in personal but public controversy over the issue. Ferguson was transferred to Assumption College in 1872.[25]

Lest Vincent's trials, which were real, be allowed too much significance, it is important to point out that his years, especially the seventies, may well have been for students in residence the most delightful and the richest in memories in all the school's history. Boys who attended the college in his time turned out well; and the best and most moving memoir ever produced by a former student was that of the distinguished John Talbot Smith, who has left a stirring description of student life during that decade.[26]

The trials of Father Vincent during the first half of his superiorship were more than compensated for by consolations during the last half. The very academic situation which annoyed the bishop became the occasion of working out an entirely new and ingenious arrangement with the University of Toronto which has since become a mark of the structure of higher education in all parts of Canada.

Since 1853, when the Hincks-Morin government reduced the University of Toronto to a mere examining body and established University College as the teaching body in the university, the legal machinery was available for affiliating denominational colleges with the university, but no Church college chose to avail itself of it. The breakthrough came during the later years of Vincent's superiorship through the efforts of John Read Teefy.

Teefy had never been a St Michael's student. He went to high school in Richmond Hill and graduated from the University of Toronto in 1871 as silver medalist in mathematics. He taught high school in Port Rowan, Beamsville, and Hamilton. A sermon preached on vocations by Bishop Farrell of Hamilton was the occasion of Teefy's going to the Grand Seminary in Montreal to study theology. In 1877 he transferred to the Basilian novitiate. He was ordained 20 June 1878 and appointed to St Michael's during the following summer. Teefy began at once to investigate the possibility of reopening the matter of affiliation. He initiated conversations with Sir William Mulock, who was at that time vice-chancellor of the University.[27]

The matter first came up in the senate of the University of Toronto on

25 R.J. Scollard, *Dictionary of Basilian Biography*, Toronto: Basilian Press, 1969, 53–4

26 John Talbot Smith, 'St Michael's College Forty Years Ago,' *St Michael's College Year Book*, Toronto, 1916, 38–44

27 Henry Carr, 'The Very Rev. J.R. Teefy, CSB, LLD,' *Report of the Canadian Catholic Historical Association*, 7(1939–40), 85–95; also Alfred Baker, 'Rev. John Read Teefy, MA, LLD,' *The University Monthly*, 11(1911), 397–402

28 January 1881, when a letter from St Michael's respecting affiliation was read and a committee named to consider the request and report on it. On 28 February and 4 March, the committee was enlarged, and on 9 March it reported back to senate recommending the affiliation of St Michael's according to the following scheme:

1 St Michael's College is to be a college in affiliation with the University of Toronto; 2 In the Sub-Department of History (Mediaeval and Modern) no authors are to be specified in the University Curriculum. The periods of history embraced in the University Curriculum are to be the subjects of examination without necessary reference to any particular authors, and examiners are to be instructed by the Senate to so conduct examinations as to carry out the spirit of this memorandum. 3 In the Department of Mental and Moral Science and Civil Polity no authors are to be specified in the University Curriculum. The questions will have no necessary reference to any one author or school of authors. In matters of opinion answers will be judged according to their accuracy of thought and expression.[28]

This report was signed by J.J. Cassidy, MD, a former student of St Michael's and a graduate of the Toronto medical school, J.R. Teefy, and D.A. O'Sullivan, MA, LL D. The acceptance of the report was moved by the vice-chancellor and seconded by Principal Caven. A statute was read for the first time on 11 March. It was read a second time and passed on 14 March. Teefy attended this meeting. After the vote was taken, he addressed the senate.[29] On 26 May 1881, a letter from Father Vincent was read informing the senate that he (Vincent) had been appointed by the faculty of St Michael's to be its representative on the senate.

Teefy was not fully convinced that the affiliation of 1881 was either the only or the best alternative. Alfred Baker's account of Teefy in The University Monthly, July 1911, records as follows: 'At a university dinner shortly after the affiliation of St Michael's, which took place in 1881, Professor Teefy frankly said that the arrangement did not realize the ideals of his Church, declaring that he would have liked to see created a great Catholic university bearing the same relation to modern times that the University of Salamanca did to medieval; but he declared the arrangement was satisfactory as being the best attainable' (399–400).

28 Scollard, 'Notes,' II, 200–5
29 See remarks of Sir William Mulock in A Record of the Proceedings at the Centenary of the University of Toronto, Toronto, University of Toronto Press, 1927, 5.

The affiliation agreement of 1881 was an important event in the history of both St Michael's and the University of Toronto. For St Michael's it marked the first major step towards university status; for the University of Toronto, it was the beginning of the end of a long period of isolation from a large part of its constituency.

A letter of 23 July 1881, from Archbishop Lynch stated that affiliation under the conditions provided had the approval of the bishops of Ontario. The college calendar for 1881–2 is an interesting document. The new arrangement, it says, is deemed advantageous for those studying for the liberal professions.' Affiliation has been 'effected upon a basis similar to that of the affiliation of many of the Catholic colleges of England and Ireland with the London University.' Again, 'students are considered as matriculated upon passing the matriculation examination before the University Examiners. At the end of the first and the third year of the University pass course, certificates from the College are received in lieu of the University examinations. At the end of the second and fourth year the University Board examines.' The classical course is outlined as a five-year course, the fifth year resembling honour matriculation, and is followed by a section headed 'Higher Course.' The prescription for this course is: mental philosophy (Sanseverino), selected questions from St Thomas, moral philosophy (Jouin), elements of natural philosophy, chemistry, inorganic chemistry. 'This course is adapted to two years. ... Special lectures are delivered in the subjects of the Department of Mental and Moral Science, and the sub-department of History, as prescribed by the Senate of Toronto University.' The content of the course is not appreciably different from philosophy as previously provided.

Although affiliation was announced with considerable enthusiasm, most advanced students continued to follow the old programme not leading to a degree. Between 1881 and 1910 only about nine students availed themselves of the advantages provided by the combined action of the senate and the bishops, and communications with the university were minimal. The example set by St Michael's in affiliating in 1881 was followed by Knox College and Wycliffe College in 1885.

The middle eighties saw a movement afoot to affiliate and even federate every denominational college in Ontario with the University of Toronto. The Ontario legislature passed its first act embodying a scheme of federation in 1887. The act of 1887 made possible the federating of existing theological colleges into the legal structure of the university. The act provided for the resumption of teaching by the university of subjects not taught in University College; it made free instruction in these 'university subjects' available to students of the federated colleges; it gave a federated arts college (Victoria) the right to provide its own instruction in courses taught by University College, thus establishing for Victoria College the status of an instructional arts college within the University of Toronto, which was something far more meaningful than St Michael's status as a federated theological college. It is true that St Michael's could teach history and philosophy, and to this extent was something more than a federated theological college,[30] but St Michael's students who wanted a university degree in arts had to enroll as students of University College and, in effect if not in theory, dissociate themselves from St Michael's. The act of 1887 solved nothing for St Michael's and very little for the university. Its more serious weakness as a piece of legislation was that it failed to provide adequately either funds for the university to operate or an administration geared to an ambitious project like university federation. Under the terms of the act, however, St Michael's became in 1890 a legally federated theological college.

Under affiliation as achieved in 1881 and federation in 1887, academic relations between St Michael's and the university, though friendly were not close. Two kinds of student were involved: the student who by previous registration belonged to St Michael's but who, on electing to take his BA, enrolled in University College for all subjects other than philosophy and history; and the Catholic student initially registered in University College who was permitted to go over to St Michael's for his philosophy, and possibly also (although this is neither verifiable nor likely) for his history. In either case the student was enrolled in University College. In this circumstance, it is understandable that the normal procedure for the St Michael's student was to remain in the classical college pattern, to retain his identification with St Michael's and not to proceed to a university degree.

The teaching of history during these years seems to have introduced a special problem. Pressure was apparently necessary to convince Catholic students in the university that they should take their philosophy and history at St Michael's. Such must be the explanation of the following letter from Archbishop Lynch to Vincent, 6 October 1884:

We learn with sorrow and dismay that the lectures on metaphysics given at present in University College are highly tinged with scepticism. When Baine is taken as a basis for the nature of the soul, and Kant is given in the study

30 W.J. Alexander, ed., *The University of Toronto and its Colleges, 1827–1906*, Toronto, 1906, 192

of thought – while the standard of morals is the general good, we deem such metaphysics as calculated to undermine and eventually destroy the principles of Christianity itself.

We also learn from undoubted authority that history, which should be only a true unbiassed statement of facts, is in the very basis upon which it is nowadays placed, used to belittle the work of the Catholic Church and to insinuate the fatality of events, which will be calculated to utterly destroy free will.

We consider therefore that we would be completely derelict in our duty, as chief pastor of souls, and accountable before God, if we not only did not exhort our Catholic students, but if we did not also forbid them to expose their eternal salvation by attending lectures upon the subjects of logic, metaphysics and history in any non-Catholic College.

There is ample provision made in St Michael's College, under the tutorship of the learned Reverend Father Teefy, for students to obtain a full and accurate knowledge upon the subjects without at all entrenching upon their holy faith.

As the teaching upon the above mentioned studies in non-Catholic Colleges is dangerous to Catholic young men, we only gave our consent to the affiliation of St Michael's College with the University upon the express condition, generously accepted by the University, that these studies should be specially exempted. The examinations were to be held upon the instructions as given in St Michael's College, which would entitle the successful candidates to the same rank and honors as students of University College.

The Catholic views of philosophy and history as taught in St Michael's College have an equal value with those upon the same subjects taught at University College.

We write to you, as you know the Catholic students, trusting to your zeal to make known to them the contents of this letter.[31]

The same problem seems still to have been present eleven years later in an incident 'of a not very agreeable nature' recalled by Rev. T.F. Battle in a statement sent somewhat reluctantly and long after the event to Father M.J.Oliver, 6 November 1929:

In the late Summer of 1895, having completed my class of rhetoric at St Mary's College, in Montreal, I interviewed the late James Loudon, then president of the University of Toronto, about my being admitted *ad eumdem gradum*, third or fourth year, University College. After procuring from St Mary's College and submitting to President Loudon a certified statement of

31 Lynch to Vincent, 6 Oct. 1884. This letter survives only in a copy attributed to M.V. Kelly.

the studies I had completed at St Mary's, President Loudon said he would admit me to the third year pass course University College, at the same time explaining that certain subjects such as logic, psychology, moral philosophy, would be taken by me at St Michael's College and in addition advising me to take my history at St Michael's College. For some reason I did not take my history at St Michael's College but attended lectures by Professor G.M. Wrong at the University College. Later on, as mentioned to you, I submitted a criticism of Professor Wrong's history lectures to the Reverend J.R. Teefy, who at that time was rector of St Michael's College and a member of the University Senate. As a result this matter came before the University Senate and subsequently Professor Loudon sent for me to come to his office in University College. President Loudon then said to me with what appeared to be a little annoyance, 'I thought I told you to take your history at St Michael's College.' I agreed that he had so told me but that I had not done so but had attended Professor Wrong's lectures. This is about all the incident amounted to, although I have a memory that Professor Loudon went on to say it would have been better had I done as he told me to do.[32]

Cushing and Teefy, 1886–1906

In 1886 Father Vincent, who was also vicar general of the archdiocese and provincial of the Basilians in America, asked to be relieved of the superiorship of the college. He was replaced by Father Daniel Cushing, who held office for two short terms: 1886 to 1889 and 1904 to 1906. Cushing was already college head when the act of 1887 was negotiated and passed. He was pre-eminently an Assumption man. He made his academic course in Sandwich, taught there before his appointment to St Michael's, and returned there for a long and successful term as superior on leaving St Michael's in 1889.

John Read Teefy, who had played a key role in the original affiliation of St Michael's with the university, became superior of St Michael's in 1889 and held the office until 1904. It is perhaps ironical that the promise of 1881 and 1887 should be so little apparent during his administration and that federation should only flower subsequent to his leaving the college. One advance made under Teefy was the gaining of complete control by the college over its examinations in philosophy (mental and moral science). At first the college certified its students in the second and third years while in the fourth year they wrote the common university examination. Since this examination in philosophy was set alternatively by a University College and a St Michael's professor, and

32 Battle to Oliver, 6 Nov. 1929, from the copy preserved in the archives of St Michael's

since different text books were followed in the two courses, the St Michael's text usually being in Latin, there was considerable confusion among students taking this examination, and especially after one examination set by Father Sylvester Dowdall. The matter was raised in senate by University College with the result that on 22 November 1889, the following statute was enacted: 'In the honor department of mental and moral philosophy in the fourth year the senate shall institute two distinct examinations on the two systems of philosophy taught in the confederating arts colleges.'[33]

During the last decade of the century St Michael's paid great attention to its classical course but very little to the university, maintaining only a 'Varsity Course' (a matriculation course) for the few boys who might like to apply for admission to the university, at best a gesture towards the needs of the local constituency. Moreover, Teefy lost much of his earlier interest in the university. He became a prominent public personality, an eminent preacher, and a speaker much in demand. He published the jubilee volume for the archdiocese in 1892, and became editor of a diocesan paper. He also became personally involved in French-English tensions within the religious community, and increasingly concerned in non-college affairs. His vice-superior or vice-president, as he was then coming to be called,[34] Albert Pierre Dumouchel, took over many of the academic responsibilities. In 1902 Dumouchel announced an ingenious plan to correlate the college academic programme with the programmes of the provincial department of education and the university. The calendar of 1902-3 announced that the seven-year classical course hitherto followed (Latin I, II, III, belles lettres, rhetoric, philosophy I, II) would be divided into two distinct sections: a four-year course paralleling the Ontario high school curriculum and a four-year arts course paralleling the pass course in the university. Dumouchel appears not to have had in mind that students in part I of his revised programme should write Ontario matriculation examinations or that those in part II should take their degree. He simply wanted to provide St Michael's curricula with a more recognizably modern coverage. His plan as announced appeared grandiose, but it cannot have been supported because it seems not to have been introduced into the college in spite of the announcement in the calendar.

The Dumouchel plan was in line with a climate of thinking rapidly

33 See *Catalogue of St Michael's College, 1900–1901*, 9 Records of the senate prior to the fire in University College, 1890, are not available.

34 A college brochure of 1876 describes Charles Vincent as 'president of the college' and the term is thereafter sometimes used in public documents; however, the term 'superior' was always the more common, especially within the college.

becoming more general, that Catholic institutions would have to adapt their curricula to the needs of the times. The initiative in this area seems to have been taken by those responsible for high schools for Catholic girls. The following letter of Mother Margarita of Loretto Abbey records some interesting history on this subject:

As early as 1874, Fr Michael Stafford set up a convent school in Lindsay in order to have a Catholic high school after the pattern of the public high school. He invited Loretto nuns from Toronto to staff it. Here girls followed the regular high school program and presented themselves for the university and departmental examinations.

When our nuns withdrew from Lindsay in 1890, the convent school was taken over by the Sisters of St Joseph from Peterborough. My impression is that the same program continued.

Two of our nuns who had taught in Lindsay were appointed to Loretto Academy, Hamilton, where they inaugurated certificate and matriculation, Junior and Senior Leaving classes, for those girls who wished to follow them. The older academic program continued in general.

By 1900 this was also the state of affairs at Loretto Academy, Guelph, and at Loretto Abbey, Toronto, the number taking the departmental courses being in greater proportion each year. By 1906 the older academic program, even at the Abbey, had given way entirely to the university and education department curricula.

The Sisters were in the meantime obtaining degrees at Queen's University, Kingston, by correspondence courses. It was 1910 when we began at Toronto. It seems to me that St Joseph's Convent, Toronto, must have been doing certificate work soon after 1900 or perhaps before.[35]

The year in which Dumouchel announced his plan, two important events took place: the opening of the new high school wing at St Michael's, and the marking of the golden jubilee of the founding of the college.

The golden jubilee was held on 28 and 29 April 1903. It should have taken place in 1902 but had to be delayed a year until the completion of the new wing. Mass was celebrated by Donatus Sbarretti, titular archbishop of Ephesus and apostolic delegate to Canada. The sermon was preached by Richard A. O'Connor, bishop of Peterborough, the only survivor of the nine boys present on the first day of class, 15 September 1852. Some 400 guests attended dinner at the college, including a goodly number of university personnel. A poem, 'Vestigia Retrorsum,' was composed by Thomas O'Hagan to mark the occasion.

35 Mother M. Margarita to L.K. Shook, 9 Apr. 1964

The real event, however, was not the marking of the day but the opening of the wing at the south-east end of the college building. The new wing was executed in a more modern but less pleasing style than the old collegiate-gothic building. But it revolutionized college life. It contained science laboratories, classrooms, dormitories, and a huge study hall. It made possible for the first time some separation between younger and more advanced students, a factor which no doubt stimulated Dumouchel to propose the somewhat abortive curriculum which was in the wind until swept away by the far more revolutionary plans of Henry Carr.

1906–12: ROCHE AND POWELL

The University of Toronto Act, 1906

Henry Carr came from Assumption College to Toronto to be ordained subdeacon on the feast of St Thomas, 21 December 1904.[36] His ideas about the kind of changes needed at St Michael's were positive: he would commit the college to the adoption of the high school curriculum prescribed by the Ontario department of education; and he would integrate the higher years, from belles lettres through philosophy, into the structure of the University of Toronto. He was not satisfied that the so-called 'Varsity Class' was anything more than an appendage to the regular college programme, a mere gesture towards the growing constituency whose sons it ought to be putting into university in larger numbers.

As the youngest member of the staff he was diffident about pushing his revolutionary ideas too boldly. M.V. Kelly, pastor of St Basil's and somewhat of a rebel in his own right, egged Carr on to sharing his opinions with Cushing, who had just replaced Teefy as superior of St Michael's. Dumouchel, director of studies, yielded to the accumulated pressure and allowed Carr to take charge of second academic (that is, second classical or the second year of high school) with a view to transforming it into a junior matriculation class. This was in January 1905. Doing all the teaching himself, Carr looked after the class until it wrote the junior matriculation examinations in early July 1906. This meant that St Michael's had ready for belles lettres 1906–7 a class which was also for the most part eligible for admission to the first year of the general course in the university.

The class did not, as it might have done, enrol in the University of

---

36 Carr to Scollard, 21 Mar. 1963. See also, Henry Carr, 'St Joseph's College,' *St Joseph Lilies*, 40(1951), 156–61; and E.J. McCorkell, *Henry Carr: Revolutionary*, Toronto: Griffin House, 1969.

Toronto (University College) but remained at St Michael's to prepare itself for the senior matriculation examinations the following spring.[37] Meanwhile the next academic class, carrying on the same experiment, wrote junior matriculation in July 1907. Thus did it come about that at the beginning of 1907–8, St Michael's had two regular classes, most of whose students were eligible for admission to the University of Toronto, one to first-year general, the other to second-year honour philosophy.[38] For these classes, entering Toronto would have meant leaving St Michael's. They did not leave St Michael's. The younger or matriculation class went, like its predecessor, into the senior matriculation class. The older group entered second-year honour philosophy, taking it in St Michael's, but registering by special arrangement in University College. This class would graduate in 1910 – a St Michael's class graduating from the university through University College. The next class would graduate in 1911 from the university through St Michael's College. The arrangement, which was a happy one, can only be understood in the context of what had been happening in the university itself as well as in St Michael's.

Several obstacles had for some years, indeed ever since 1887, continued to separate St Michael's, in spite of its status as a federated theological college, from the university. There was the 'little seminary' complex of some of the faculty and some of the Catholic constituency who regarded the providing of priests for the diocese as the first obligation of the college. There was the real risk of losing American students who neither required the Toronto degree nor were disposed to meet its requirements: such a loss could have meant financial disaster. Finally there was the somewhat discriminating legal factor that St Michael's had no university charter and could not have an arts course in a sense identical or parallel with the existing federated denominational arts colleges, Victoria and Trinity.

The time, however, was ripe for the maturing of Carr's project, and indeed was already provided for in the University of Toronto Act, 1906, again in part by Carr's visionary action. University federation was in 1906 in process of completing another of its many periods of reassessment. The University of Trinity College had been admitted to federation in 1903 (formalized by an amendment to the University Act, 3–4 George v, ch.74; 26 April 1904). Two years later Trinity was still

37 This class wrote the special senior matriculation papers prepared for students of Albert College which were written in June rather than May. The later date was more convenient in the traditional college schedule.

38 Senior matriculants were admissible to either second-year general or second-year honour philosophy.

experiencing difficulty in making its admission effective and its predicament was perhaps the crucial testing of the University Act of 1887. When the new provincial government of Sir James Whitney came into power in 1905, a commission was appointed to investigate and recommend on the university situation.[39] This commission reported on 4 April 1906.

It is curious, indeed, what little interest was shown around St Michael's in the urgent and important business of the commission. Throughout the text of the report, St Michael's is dealt with as a theological college along with Knox and Wycliffe. Never once in the report itself is St Michael's mentioned as a prospective arts college in the new university. This omission is the more surprising in that the brief to the commission from the University Council specifically recommended that St Michael's now be included among the arts colleges.[40] Nor is it because the administration of St Michael's was unaware of the existence of the commission. Indeed, a brief, dated 5 December 1905, and signed by Daniel Cushing and Michael V. Kelly had been submitted to it. This brief regretted the university's failure to win the confidence of Catholics, to provide for religious influence in its organization, and to make endowment available for federated colleges. The brief asked for the encouragement of federated colleges, the discouragement of extramural students, and the entrusting of the proposed new residences to the supervision of the colleges.[41] There was no mention of the possibility

39 The members appointed by Whitney to this commission were J.W. Flavelle (chairman), Goldwin Smith, W.R. Meredith, B.E. Walker, H.J. Cody, D. Bruce Macdonald, A.H.U. Colquhoun (secretary).

40 See *Report of the Royal Commission on the University of Toronto*, Toronto, 1906: '*Faculties and Council* 1 That a Faculty of Arts be Formed to consist of the Professors and Associate-Professors of the Arts Professoriate of the University and of University College, Victoria College, Trinity College and St Michael's College, with the permanent lecturers as assessors without a vote,' Appendices, 92.

41 See *Report*, 121: 'From St Michael's College. Secretary University Commission, we would ask the members of the University Commission to kindly give their attention to the following: –

1 That, notwithstanding, the federation of St Michael's College for a quarter of a century, the University of Toronto has not succeeded in gaining the confidence of the Catholic population of Ontario, as is evidenced by the small number of students aspiring to a degree in the University, and the ever increasing numbers attending five Catholic Colleges in the Province.

2 That the only explanation of the above is the want of sufficient provision for religious influence in the organization, administration, and general life of the University.

3 That the Provincial Government, in equipping University College, and excluding the Federated Colleges from a share in the endowment and subsidies to education, would seem disposed to assist students who object to religious surroundings, and to deny her assistance to students who feel convinced that religious and moral influence should not be separated from training in secular studies.

4 That, believing as we do, that the intimate association of students with one

of St Michael's becoming an arts college of the university. This was certainly a missed opportunity and looked like the victory of anti-university forces both in and outside of St Michael's.

The draft bill proposed by the commission in the appendix to its report made no mention of St Michael's save in section 4, number 7 where St Michael's was still listed among the federated theological colleges. Between 4 April 1906 when the report was submitted, and 16 May 1906, when the new act was passed, a number of amendments were introduced by the committee of the house, the most significant for St Michael's being the addition of the entirely new section 145 somewhat enigmatically providing for the setting up by the board of governors as a 'college of the University' a 'college federated with the University' which has established or hereafter establishes a faculty of arts.'[42] How this amendment came about is not quite clear. Carr says that he had Kelly and Cushing re-approach the commission but too late to catch the report, which had already been completed, perhaps even submitted. Some kind of gentleman's agreement arranging to have the vital section 145 added to the act was reached before it was passed by the House. Even as passed, the act still did not declare St Michael's a federated arts college but it provided simple machinery – a statute to be passed by the board – for its becoming one. A generous offer from University College to register St Michael's students and to provide them

another, and with their teachers contributes as much to true education as do the lecture room and library, we regret that the University has not made greater efforts to bring about conditions of such intimate associations, and especially do we view with regret the present tendency to facilitate the obtaining of degrees by extra-mural students.

5 That since the project of the University residences is in contemplation, and since such residences can be effectively disciplined only by a system which will place the conduct of the student body under the immediate supervision of their teachers, we would recommend that the administration of these residences be handed over to the several college faculties, viz.: – The faculties of University College and of the colleges in federation with the University.

Respectfully yours,
D. Cushing
M.V. Kelly

December 5, 1905

42 'If and when a college now or hereafter federated with the University shall establish a faculty of Arts in which instruction in the subjects of the course of study in Arts, not being University subjects, shall be provided, and a statute of the Board shall be passed declaring that it has so done, such college, so long as it maintains such faculty to the satisfaction of the Board, shall be known as and may be called a College of the University, and the teaching staff in such faculty shall have the same representation in the Council of the faculty of Arts as is by section 74 of this Act given to the teaching staffs of the federated universities, and the regular matriculated students of such college, who are enrolled therein and enter their names with the Registrar of the University, shall be entitled to the privileges which are by section 132 conferred upon the students mentioned therein. 'University of Toronto Act, 1906,' Section 145.

with any necessary instruction while leaving them also members of their own college was formally accepted by St Michael's on 14 November 1907. This arrangement made possible the establishment of the kind of faculty of arts prescribed by the act of 1906. On 8 December 1910 St Michael's became an arts college in the University of Toronto; the arrangement was not formally written into an act of the Ontario legislature until 1913.

Thus the class of 1910, consisting of B.D. Doyle, J.J. Greenway, M.J. Oliver, C.C. McNeil, and J.M. O'Connor, was the first St Michael's class to receive degrees from the University of Toronto. They were technically graduates through University College. The class of 1911, consisting of H.S. Bellisle, C.E. Coughlin, R.H. Dignan, B.P. Fitzpatrick, E.J. McCorkell, and T.M. Mulligan, was the first to graduate directly through St Michael's.

Competitive Sports

The period of federation, 1904 to 1911, was one in which St Michael's drew closer to the more university-minded of its constituency. The university degree, however, was not the only operative force. These years also marked the beginning of the only too successful search for athletic championships. The year 1909 was a particularly lively and successful one when college teams won two Canadian championships: the Allan cup in senior hockey and the junior rugby football title. The same year a college team won the handball championship of Toronto.

Sports have turned out to be an important aspect of college life, and a rich one too, especially intramurally. They have also served to carry the name of the college to people and places where it otherwise might never have penetrated. But competitive sports have also been a continual source of distraction, annoyance, and frustration. From 1908 onwards the desire became strong to be admitted to intercollegiate and preparatory school leagues, those great symbols of establishment among people of British connections. Games in such circles St Michael's was always able to arrange; the leagues proved harder to crash. In 1909 it was hoped that a St Michael's team would be admitted to senior intercollegiate, a hope which has periodically recurred and never been realized. Some years later a college team became part of the prestigious 'prep school' league with teams from Upper Canada College, St Andrews, and University of Toronto Schools. But St Michael's was inclined to try too hard and too successfully to win and was more prone than others, perhaps from a latent ghetto complex, to become a victim of athleticism. The latest appearance of this malady came with the development of the renowned Junior A s, which several times won the Memorial Cup, emblematic of Canadian junior hockey championship. What has perhaps most characterized the school's athletic programmes has been the appearance of a sequence of beloved and incredibly competent priest-coaches: Henry Carr, Jack Spratt, Joseph McGahey, Con Sheehan, Dave Bauer, Ted Flanagan. Whether this has been for good or ill is beside the point; but these coaches invariably got more out of their players than the boys were naturally equipped to give. Thus the history of competitive athletics at St Michael's has always been marred by too many wins, too much miscalculated professionalism, and a sporting image that only too often obscured the genuine intellectualism and scholarship which the college came gradually to acquire.

Superiors During the Federation Years

During these federation years, 1904 to 1912, public attention focussed upon Carr and the university movement rather than on the incumbents of the office of superior. The superiors, however, at least two of the three, were the right men for the times, which were rather troublesome inside the religious community, in that things were not going well in France, where the general administration was constantly beleaguered by an unsympathetic government and was disposed to be jealous and suspicious of what they imagined to be taking place in America. Cushing and Roche, in a way the short-tempered Teefy could not, allowed attention to shift from internal community tensions to external educational strategy, and this was a blessing.

When Carr set to work on the curriculum in 1905, Daniel Cushing was still superior of St Michael's. Cushing was an intelligent man but neither aggressive by nature nor in good health. He trusted Carr, however, gave him his head, and protected him from criticism. Without Cushing it is doubtful that Carr could have carried the day.

Cushing was replaced in 1906 by Nicholas E. Roche, who was local superior of St Michael's until 1910. Roche was a hard-working, deeply spiritual, and reasonably diplomatic if trying administrator. He had joined the Basilians in 1893, been ordained in 1897, and had, as a young priest, been sent to Texas where he founded St Thomas College in Houston. He was named superior of St Michael's in 1906 and was firmly in charge during the crucial years when Carr was working out university federation. Roche was not a university man. The development which he was encouraging was one almost certain to leave him behind. He welcomed the opportunity which came in 1910 to go to New Brunswick to open St Thomas College in Chatham. It is doubtful that St Michael's could have been better served by a superior during these years than it was by Roche – a point later made eminently clear by Carr with gratitude and respect.[43]

Roche was succeeded as superior by Francis Gerald Powell, who held office from 1910 to 1911. Powell's was an unhappy appointment. He was a scholarly man and a philosopher well trained in the limited systematic tradition of his day. He was sceptical about Carr as a classics man turned philosopher. He doubted that Carr knew Sanseverino; and he suspected that he might even be an eclectic. Thus there was increased tension within the college during these years, the more so in that Powell was not so devoted to his post as his predecessors, the gentle Cushing and the ascetic Roche, had been. Powell's leaving office in 1911 was a relief to all. He was replaced in 1912 by the brilliant classical scholar, Robert McBrady, who had divided his time between Assumption and St Michael's, and who was at 64 a somewhat older man than was usually placed in charge of St Michael's. Like Roche, he gave Carr his head, which meant that the period of Carr influence, which can be said to have begun in 1905, was to continue almost unbroken to 1925.

1912–25: MC BRADY AND CARR

The Higher Education of Women

During 1911 arrangements were first made to enrol women in the new arts course of St Michael's College. The arrangements were in full operation in 1912 when there was one woman enrolled in third year (Agnes Murphy, later Sister Mary Agnes, who had transferred the year before from University College) and seven enrolled in each of the second and first years. The event was, on the local scene, quite as revolutionary as federation itself. Some background of the development is essential for an understanding of the fact.

Loretto Abbey on Wellington Street was the motherhouse of the Institute of the Blessed Virgin Mary (Loretto sisters) in Canada. The institute itself was founded in 1609 by Mary Ward to provide a girls' boarding school for English-Catholic refugees at St Omer, Flanders. Attached was a free day school. The institute spread throughout Europe. The Micklegate Bar Convent was opened in York in 1686 by Frances Bedingfeld; from there Frances Ball opened a Dublin house in 1821; and from Dublin at the invitation of Bishop Michael Power a group of five sisters, including Teresa Dease, who was to be Canadian

43 Henry Carr's sermon preached at the funeral of Nicholas Roche in St Mary's Church, Owen Sound, 18 May 1932. See Scollard, 'Notes,' XIII, 149–59.

superior general of the Loretto nuns from 1851–89, began the first
North American foundation in Toronto in 1847. The sisters first lived
in a tiny convent on Duke Street and went out to teach. The convent
was moved in 1849 to Simcoe Street, in 1852 to Bathurst Street, in 1862
to Bond Street, and finally in 1867 to the abbey on Wellington Street
where their well-known school for young ladies remained until removed
to the present site at Armour Heights in 1930. The abbey was long a
private grammar and finishing school following a pattern distinctive of
the Loretto tradition. When the convent school in Lindsay was established in 1874, it was staffed by sisters from the abbey, but at the will
of the founder, Father Michael Stafford, followed the instructional pattern of the public high schools. From the convent school in Lindsay,
then, students began sometime in the seventies to present themselves
for departmental and university entrance examinations. Other Loretto
schools at Hamilton, Guelph, and the abbey in Toronto began to prepare some of their girls for junior matriculation and senior leaving examinations. By 1906 the older academic programme had given way
entirely before the departmental and university entrance curricula.
Some sisters in the meantime began to obtain degrees by correspondence courses from Queen's, and in 1900 also from Toronto.[44] Loretto
Abbey, though not convenient to the university campus, was definitely
interested in the recent developments taking place at St Michael's.

The Sisters of St Joseph who came to Toronto in 1851 belonged to a
congregation with a long history of charitable works in France. The
congregation was founded during the years 1650–1 in Le Puy. Its
houses were confiscated in 1793. The congregation was gradually restored after 1807 with a motherhouse established at Lyons with Mother
St John Fontbonne the first general and the second foundress. In 1836
a hospital was established in Carondolet near St Louis, Mo., and from
there works were undertaken in many parts of America; an orphanage
was opened on Nelson Street in Toronto in 1851, at the invitation of
Bishop de Charbonnel. The Toronto foundation expanded immediately
into teaching in the parochial schools. When the Sisters of St Joseph
opened their Toronto motherhouse, the 'White House' on Power Street
in 1854, they included a private girls' school. In 1863 the motherhouse
and school was moved to St Alban's Street on John Elmsley's Clover
Hill estate, one block south of the site on which St Michael's had relo-

44 Margarita to Shook, 9 Apr. 1964. See also *Life and Letters of Rev. Mother
Teresa Dease*, edited by a 'Member of the Community,' Toronto: McClelland,
Goodchild and Stewart, 1916, for the early history of Loretto College. For further
information on the old abbey building see B.W. Connolly, 'After 100 Years – A
Jesuit Seminary,' *Loretto Rainbow*, 52(1946), 138–45.

cated in 1854–5. From the girls' school developed St Joseph's Academy (the present high school on Wellesley Street) and St Joseph's College and residence, one of the two women's divisions of St Michael's College.

The sisters' private high school began preparing some students for the departmental examination during the nineties, and by 1906 the high school programme was that of the Ontario department of education. Before 1907 a few girls living in St Joseph's were registered in university courses as regular students of University College. There was also initiated during these years a private tutorial programme in order to help girls, and especially some of the sisters, prepare for university examinations as extramural students. Behind this was a change of admission requirements to the Normal schools. To cope with new demands, Sister Perpetua Whalen, Sister Austin Warnock, and others registered in University College. Sister Perpetua Whalen was to receive her degree in English and history in 1911, Sister Austin in modern languages and history in 1912. Like the Sisters of Loretto, those of St Joseph's were also intensely interested in St Michael's progress to the status of an arts college in the University of Toronto.

The realization that they would have to admit women students to their arts course came at first as a shock to the administration of St Michael's. The task of integrating women into the college was begun in 1911 but not fully resolved into full co-education until the forties and fifties. The beginning came about as follows. Carr began to teach Greek philosophy during 1910–11. In about the third week of his lectures (at his seventh lecture to be exact), five girls from University College turned up at his lecture. These were probably all Catholic girls, residents of Toronto or boarders in St Joseph's or Loretto. So far as is known this was the first time women ever appeared in a regular class at St Michael's. The girls had begun the course in Greek philosophy at University College and decided to exercise their right to take the course at St Michael's. Carr was surprised, even embarassed, by their presence but allowed them to remain until the lecture was over. For the rest of the year he took the five girls twice a week in a special group in the priests' community room.

Shortly after this episode Mother Irene and Sister Perpetua of St Joseph's approached Sir Robert Falconer, president of the university, requesting that their institution be allowed like St Michael's to participate in university federation. Falconer gave as his opinion that the two women's colleges were not likely to be admitted to the university as additional distinct arts colleges. He suggested as an alternative that St

Michael's be asked to enrol women students and to add the sisters to the college staff, an arrangement quite possible under the terms of the act. Falconer's suggestion was followed and in October 1911 an agreement was completed between St Michael's and the women's colleges: all girls proceeding to a degree in the faculty of arts should be enrolled in St Michael's; lectures in college subjects were to be given in both St Joseph's and Loretto as they were in St Michael's; lecturers in religious knowledge, ethics, logic, and psychology were to be supplied by St Michael's; university subjects were to be taken at the university proper as was the case with the men; degrees should be conferred by the university through St Michael's.

During 1910–11 one woman, and in 1912 fifteen women, as already stated, enrolled in St Michael's creating the need, since co-education had not been introduced, for staffs in the women's colleges to handle college subjects. Loretto's first staff consisted of Mother Estelle Nolan (dean), Mother Lucilla Breen, Mother Gertrude Gumpricht, and Mother Margarita O'Connor. Margarita became dean in 1913 and held that post until 1932.[45] The first staff at St Joseph's consisted of Sister Perpetua Whalen and Sister Austin Warnock. They were joined in 1914 by Sister Mary Agnes Murphy.

From one student in 1910–11, the enrolment of women steadily increased. Their presence in St Michael's had an immediate effect on the pattern of course enrolment. The original assumption had been that all or most St Michael's students would take honour philosophy. The women were not interested in this course nor were they wanted in it. There was still present an assumption that the arts course led primarily

45 Loretto College has, since 1912, been located as follows: 1911–18 at the abbey, 403 Wellington St; 1918–37 at 387 Brunswick Ave; 1937–59 at 86 St George St; and since 1959 at 70 St Mary Street. In charge of the college and holding the office of dean have been: Mother Estelle Nolan, 1912–13; Mother Margarita O'Connor, 1913–32; Mother St Margaret Kelly, 1932–45; Mother Aloysius Kerr, 1945–7; Mother St Margaret Kelly, 1947–9; Mother Boniface Hopkins, 1949–55; Mother Angela McKeown, 1955–9; Mother Bernadette Culnan, 1959–65; Mother Philomena Cassin, 1965–6; Sister Maria Lanthier, since 1967. St Joseph's College has since 1911 been located as follows: 1911–26 at St Joseph's Academy on Breadalbane St, with the first college girls' residence distinct from the academy located for a few years in two houses on Breadalbane; 1926 to the present at 29 Queen's Park to which two separate buildings on Wellesley St were added in 1954 and 1956. Deans at St Joseph's have been: Sister Perpetua Whalen, 1911–14; Sister Austin Warnock 1914–16; Sister Perpetua Whalen, 1916–29; Sister St John O'Malley, 1929–33; Sister Mary Augusta Murphy, 1933–5; Sister Bernard Tuffy, 1935–41; Sister St John O'Malley, 1941–8; Sister Blandina Hitchen, 1948–53; Sister Geraldine Thompson, 1953–60; Sister St Stephen O'Connor, 1960–8; Sister Janet Fraser, daughter of St Joseph's first graduate, Madeleine Burns, since 1968. For an account of the early history of the Sisters of St Joseph in Toronto see Sister Mary Agnes, *The Congregation of the Sisters of St Joseph: Le Puy, Lyons, St Louis, Toronto,* Toronto, 1951.

to the seminary. The first woman student, who transferred into second year, when it became possible for her to do so in 1911, was in modern languages. The next year it was discovered that most women wanted to take either the general course or an honour course other than philosophy. It was apparent at once that this discovery opened a new horizon to the college administration. Articles written by Daniel Meader and Henry Carr in 1914 both reveal this new outlook. 'The course in philosophy is only one of the twenty courses which St Michael's offers to Catholic young men,' wrote Meader. 'In the faculty of arts,' wrote Carr, 'there is the general course, and for students who wish to give thorough special study, twenty special courses. ... St Michael's College in the coming year will be in a position to throw open all of these courses to Catholic students.'[46] Although Carr's statement was an extravagant one in that St Michael's was not in a position to give any of these courses without help from the other colleges, it was at least a declaration of policy. St Michael's was not, once it had admitted women, to remain a one-course college.

The registration of women in St Michael's came relatively late so far as the Canadian scene was concerned. Mount Allison, Sackville NB, admitted women to classes in 1858 and in 1875 graduated Grace Annie Lockhart as the first woman in the British Empire to receive a university degree, the B SC. Toronto was declared a co-educational institution in 1884, mainly for economic reasons: it was cheaper to be co-educational than to support separate women's colleges. Toronto's first dean of women, or 'Lady Superintendent,' was on government salary in the university until 1906. The first degrees to women in Toronto were conferred in 1885. Victoria in Cobourg graduated a woman the year before. The MacDonald Institute in household science at Guelph was opened in 1903. In 1883 a Toronto Women's Medical College was opened; it merged with the University of Toronto Medical College only in 1905.[47] St Michael's was no pioneer. It did not, however, unreasonably resist the registration of women; in fact the merger or affiliation of 1911 is evidence to the contrary. Its real tardiness appeared when it came to implementing co-education, as will be seen. But the responsibility here must be divided. The women's colleges were, over the next twenty-five years, quite as jealous of their relative autonomy and their vested interests as St Michael's was hostile to admitting women to classes. The fact remains that every time a major concession was made towards the

46 *St Michael's College Year Book*, Toronto, 1914, 50–1
47 Marion Mann and Janet Berton, 'The Canadian Co-Ed,' *The Chronicle*, 40(1867–1968), 41–3

fuller integration of women into the college, a distinct advance in academic excellence followed.

The Department of Philosophy

The role of philosophy in the nineteenth-century *collège* was central, linking the classical or academic with the professional. The classical without philosophy was not complete, the professional without philosophy had not yet begun. As far as the priesthood was concerned the code of canon law had frozen this structure. The old St Michael's knew little else than this tradition; and the newly- federated St Michael's was not disposed to reject it. Indeed with the new order of things, the prime importance of philosophy became even more accentuated. Father Meader in a brief description of the new programme pointed out the increased hours (the college was now providing 37 hours of instruction a week in philosophy where it had formerly provided only 12) and praised the 'more intense application' called for in the new programme, which he compared with the post-graduate programmes of Louvain's Institute and Rome's Angelicum.[48]

Philosophy, then, in the spirit of almost immemorial tradition was much in favour in the new degree-course at St Michael's. There were other considerations too. Philosophy was proving a useful discipline, both in Canada and the United States, for students contemplating law, a profession almost as popular with St Michael's men as the priesthood. Honour philosophy offered other practical and administrational advantages: a student who had completed either first-year general or senior matriculation could be admitted to second-year honour philosophy, not first-year as in the case of most other honour courses – a consideration for sons of the poor. Finally, because St Michael's had the right by the act of 1881 to teach its own philosophy, and also by the decision of the senate in 1889 to conduct its own examinations in philosophy, and because these conditions obtained also after the passing of the act of 1906, and because the courses other than philosophy taken in this honour course could all be college subjects, that is, taught in the college and examined by the joint departments, the college enjoyed relative autonomy in the conduct of this course and had less to fear from irreligious forces within the university and from critics of such forces outside the university.

Between 1907 and 1911, when the new arts course was being fashioned, the college had a relatively good supply of professors of philo-

48 F.D. Meader, 'Philosophy at St Michael's College,' *St Michael's College Year Book*, 1914, 50

sophy, although they were of uneven competence: Dumouchel, Roche, Cushing, Purcell, Powell, Meader, Vaschalde. Most of these men crossed areas: Dumouchel was in French and ethics, Meader was in mathematics and cosmology, Vaschalde in oriental languages and psychology, and so on. Only a few were restricted to one discipline: Hurley to literature, McBrady and Carr to classics.

Carr's, of course, is an interesting case. His control of Greek and German gave him a certain advantage in Greek philosophy; and when the need arose he took over the course in the history of Greek philosophy, extending it to cover the mediaeval and modern periods as well. When he came to do the mediaeval period he was filled with all the enthusiasm of a man who has discovered a new world. He was determined that St Michael's should share in the flowering of scholasticism that had followed Leo xiii's *Aeterni patris*, and that St Michael's should assume a role comparable with Louvain's. His appointment as superior of St Michael's in 1915 placed him in an advantageous position to promote such a policy. When he heard at the end of 1918 that Maurice DeWulf was accepting visiting lectureships outside Louvain, he brought him from Poitiers to Toronto pressing him in 1919 to join St Michael's staff in philosophy.

DeWulf was professor of the history of mediaeval philosophy at Louvain's Institute of Philosophy and editor since 1894 of the Institute's *Revue néo-scholastique*. He arrived in Toronto in January 1919 and gave a regular course in the history of mediaeval philosophy to St Michael's students, a special series of eight lectures to university people on the invitation of Sir Robert Falconer, entitled 'Civilization and Philosophy in the Heart of the Middle Ages,' and, on 11 March, a public lecture in Convocation Hall on Cardinal Mercier. DeWulf returned to Belgium in April but remained on the college staff, coming out to Toronto to give regular courses over the next three or four years.

The same year, 1919, Carr was able to attract to Toronto Sir Bertram Windle, distinguished professor of astronomy and anthropology, recently resigned principal of University College, Cork. Windle's coming to Toronto in December 1919 as a permanent member of St Michael's staff made quite clear that Carr was in process of developing philosophy along the widest possible lines and that St Michael's was indeed willing and ready to assume a kind of leadership in one corner of the scholarly world. Windle's coming was followed in 1925 by the appointment of Gerald B. Phelan, priest of the archdiocese of Halifax and recent agrégé of Louvain, as professor of psychology.

Carr's superiorship ended in the summer of 1925. He remained at St

Michael's as head of the department of philosophy continuing the positive programme of the past ten years. So we find him bringing out Léon Noël from Louvain as visiting professor in the fall of 1926 and Etienne Gilson in the winter of 1927. Carr's first monument had been the creation of a faculty of arts in St Michael's and federating it into the university; his second was the creation within that faculty of what must fairly be described as Canada's most vitally dynamic department of philosophy, a position it maintained for a generation.

The culmination of this particular activity, the creating of a department of philosophy, was the attracting into graduate work of a substantial group of post-graduate students. The kind of interest that creates a graduate department was evident from 1922 onwards with the formation of the Philosophical Society, a truly university activity, comprising students, faculty, and scholarly alumni. Here was established a certain scholarly camaraderie and a spirit of research that simply could not be held to the undergraduate level. Papers given over three years, 1922 to 1925, by Oliver, Carr, Bellisle, Windle, Brett, Roach, McCorkell, Sullivan, DeWulf, Milner, Bott, Moore, Robinson, Tracy, and Stock, were of high calibre and provoked inter-university discussion, which was remembered long afterward and which was instrumental in making Toronto a major centre for philosophical studies in America whether in the graduate school of the university, in St Michael's or, subsequently, in the Pontifical Institute.

During 1926–7 a cluster of at least 13 such students pursued higher Toronto degrees within what can be called the Carr-Phelan orbit. The names of these students were: J.F. Flaherty, R.J. Dobell, J.A. Mahon, J. Riordan, F.E. Neylon, V.I. McIntyre, J.A. Ford, J.H. Whelan, M.S. Lynch, Paul J. Martin, J.B. Ryan, V.A. Dermody, A.J. Denomy, E.J. Lajeunesse, J.W. Dore, H.P. Coughlin, J.E. McGahey. Philosophy pursued relentlessly and knowledgeably, even though some students were drawn into it who might better have cultivated other disciplines, created an atmosphere of study and excitement which in the conjunction of events of 1929 gave existence to the autonomous research centre now known as the Pontifical Institute of Mediaeval Studies. This development, one of St Michael's most far-reaching achievements, is dealt with elsewhere in this work.[49]

The department of philosophy's unique position in the college was to level off somewhat during the thirties and forties as other disciplines developed in a comparable manner. Philosophy, however, never ceased to be strong and directive. Within its own domain it maintained its

49 See below, 210–33

increasingly historical and textual orientation as contrasting with the older methodological and textbook phase. Since the fifties and sixties philosophy has tended to lose the functional and ancillary role which once related it to the various professions; it now tends to be cultivated in itself as a terminal profession, maintaining something of its Thomistic tradition, but fragmenting also into the more fashionable modes of linguistic analysis, existentialism, and even process theology.

The Terauley Street Extension

During his superiority Carr had other problems than the creating of a philosophy department to contend with. He had to give time, thought, and action to the very continuance of the college on its Clover Hill site.

The four lots donated by John Elmsley in 1853 for a college and the four lots subsequently bought from the Elmsleys by the French Basilians with the addition of two or three neighboring lots acquired during the nineteenth century still constituted the college 'estate' in 1912. The Basilians of the college also owned a 50-acre farm, purchased for $7500 by Father Brennan in 1881, in Deer Park or, as the area is better known today, on the Spadina extension north of St Clair Avenue. On the basic property, the 50 St Joseph Street property, stood the college and church building, erected in 1854–5, with the various extensions made to it in 1865 (48 feet eastward), 1871–3 (the east wing), 1877 (the church sanctuary), 1886 (the church vestibule and tower), 1902 (the high school or Clover Hill wing). The property was a small one contained by St Joseph Street on the south, Chapel lane on the east, St Mary Street on the north, and the lane or right-of-way from St Joseph Street to St Mary Street, passing by the west wall of St Basil's Church, on the west.

The setting of the college was at first rural, then suburban and residential, and by 1912 beginning to be busily urban as the life of the city expanded around and beyond it. The city was also in the first years of the twentieth century beginning to feel the need for a new traffic artery from downtown Bay Street, up Terauley and St Vincent Streets, through the college grounds and northwards along North Street to Davenport Road. It was during the academic year 1911–12 that the terrifying expression 'the Terauley Street extension' began to be heard. The planners were said to want 86 feet off the east end of the college property so that the thoroughfare could be built under the very windows of the high school and the east wing, and across the east end of the playing field. The property wanted by the city was about one-third of the whole parcel of land.

In January 1914 the city's board of control approved the Terauley

Street extension. Property owners, including the trustees of the college property, were notified that the city had expropriated and now owned the lands required for the extension. These particular expropriation laws (nos. 6884 and 6927) were repealed on 14 May 1917 because the war made proceeding with the work impossible for the time being. The college, knowing that the matter would be revived, purchased from the Elmsleys for $85,000 the house known as Barnstable and two acres of property at the north end of Elmsley Place and west of the lane bordering the college land. This was bought primarily for a new arts building.

Following the war, in the fall of 1920, the city issued new expropriation by-laws (nos. 8509, 8566, and 8583). For a short time following the expropriation Carr negotiated by letter with the city, first in an attempt to have the new street diverted around to the east of the college property, and when that failed, by agreement made, as he thought, on the basis of replacement. The city was in a hurry and planned entering the property without an agreement. At this stage, 21 July 1921, the college sought and secured an injunction on the ground that the city could not expropriate the lands of a federated college. The next few months were spent reaching an agreement so that the action could be discontinued and the city given entry, both of which occurred during November 1921.

The college was of the opinion that the discontinuance and entry were granted on the following guarantees: that the lane on the west end of the property would be closed; that Elmsley Place would also be closed when the college acquired all the property on it; that recompense would be paid covering the cost of the land taken, the cost of replacing the kitchen, servant quarters, and sacristy which had to be demolished in order to extend the playing field westward on to the newly acquired Elmsley property; that compensation would cover also the cost of buying the houses on Elmsley Place so that the new arts college could be built there; and that the actual amount of compensation should be determined by arbitration.

When the arbiters attempted to determine costs they found that the city and the college differed over the nature of the settlement, the college holding that it was on the basis of replacement, the city that there was no agreement beyond the decision of the board of control. The city also contended that the immunity from expropriation (which it did not concede in any event) had been waived in that Carr had not raised the point earlier. So there were two issues: whether St Michael's was exempt from expropriation, and how much compensation the arbiters should assign. The case was before the trial judge Mr Justice Riddell

in June 1924; before First Appelate Division of the Supreme Court of
Ontario in 1925; and before the Supreme Court of Canada in 1926. No
judgments were identical but the final outcome was as follows: St
Michael's College was declared legally protected from expropriation;
the lane and street were to be closed; compensation to the college was
to be based on replacement, that is, on the value of the land taken, plus
diminution of the value to the college of its remaining property, plus
loss incurred in demolishing, removing, remodelling of buildings necessary in view of the city's having taken the property, plus accrued interest on the city's indebtedness in this regard from 11 November 1921.
The board of arbitration, composed of Frank Arnoldi, Judge Fredrick
Morson, and Sir Thomas White assessed the compensation at $345,000
($280,000 plus accrued interest), a large sum for the time but less than
the college claimed. Time, however, has shown that the college received
unexpected and unforeseen compensation in being driven westward
toward the university.[50]

Carr's superiorship has been superbly and succintly described in a
'Resolution Respecting the late Reverend Henry Carr CSB' by the
senate of the University of Toronto: 'He was appointed Superior of St
Michael's in 1915 and retained that office for the succeeding ten years.
He continued to expand the department of philosophy of which he was
a member and to a great extent gave it its character; it was Christian in
its background, international in its involvements, scholarly and re-
search-conscious in its methods and orientations.'[51]

1925–40: MC CORKELL AND BELLISLE

Plans for the Future

Edmund J. McCorkell, for some time registrar of the college under Carr,
familiar with Carr's policies, and sharing his confidence in the University of Toronto, took over as superior of St Michael's in the summer of
1925. Replacement of superiors had in the past come at irregular intervals as judged necessary or advisable. But the new code of canon law
of 1918 to which the Basilian Fathers had conformed in 1922, when the
American and French provinces separated, provided for the appoint-

50 The text of the judgment of the Supreme Court of Canada is recorded in
S.C.R. for 1926, 318–37. Much of the discussions of the case can be read in *Appeal
Case in the Supreme Court of Canada between St Michael's College and the
Corporation of the City of Toronto*, Wm. J. George Co., 1926.

51 Resolution of the senate moved by Rev. J.M. Kelly, CSB, seconded by
W.S. Martin, QC, 10 Jan. 1964. See also McCorkell, *Henry Carr: Revolutionary*

ment of superiors not *ad nutum* but for a three-year term, renewable once. Carr's second term was calculated to end in 1925. His presidency of St Michael's was accordingly terminated during the summer and he was succeeded by McCorkell.

McCorkell followed Carr's general policies. He worked very closely with the university; continued to bring in distinguished professors: Phelan in 1925, Noël in 1927, Gilson in 1927; and he supervised the founding of the Institute of Mediaeval Studies in 1929. He also went on acquiring, with a view to erecting an arts college, properties on Elmsley Place and private residences standing on university land on the east side of Queen's Park Crescent north of St Joseph Street. The board of governors of the University of Toronto had given St Michael's to understand that when the college acquired all the houses from 49 to 63 Queen's Park Crescent it could lease the land at a nominal rental for as long as it was required for college purposes.[52]

McCorkell's interest in the curriculum of the college was broader than Carr's and he gave more time than Carr to the development both of the general course and of the honour courses other than philosophy. Moreover, McCorkell was more disposed to emphasize the material plant. Realizing that the seventy-fifth jubilee of the college was to take place during his tenure of office, he planned to use the occasion to launch both a building programme and a public campaign for funds.

The seventy-fifth anniversary ceremonies took place in May 1927. The first day of the ceremonies was given to the university world, an indication of how far St Michael's had advanced on the international scene. The opening session, held in Convocation Hall on 11 May, heard addresses by Monsignor Baudrillart, rector of the Institut Catholique of Paris, by Sir William Mulock, chancellor of the University of Toronto, and by Neil McNeil, archbishop of Toronto. At dinner in Hart House that evening, with the Honourable Mr Justice H.T. Kelly as toast-master, speakers included Thomas Mulvey, graduate of St Michael's and undersecretary of state, Sir Robert Falconer, Canon H.J. Cody, Warden J.B. Bickersteth, the Honourable Howard Ferguson, minister of education, Father Francis P. Duffy, and Sir Bertram Windle. With overflowing audiences of alumni, educationists, churchmen, and others, the occasion resembled the installation of a president or an especially important convocation at one of the great established universities.

The second day of festivities was in the tradition more familiar to the spirit of the college consisting of pontifical mass at which Thomas

52 On the history of this land see Scollard, 'Notes,' II, 90–2.

O'Donnell an alumnus and bishop of Victoria, preached, and of alumni meetings under Judge Kelly, Thomas Mulvey, and Michael Oliver. One of the issues probed on this day was whether the alumni or some broader public group should conduct a campaign to raise funds.

Ever since Bishop de Charbonnel turned St Michael's over to the Basilians to be operated at their own risk, the Basilians had assumed responsibility for operating the college and financing the necessary expansion. The soliciting of contributions through the parishes of Ontario was authorized in the case of the original building in 1855 and 1856. Contributions were reported weekly in the Catholic press. After that time the college administration relied on its own normal revenues (tuition, board, Sunday work income of priests). The alumni was consistently friendly and loyal but it was not a wealthy constituency nor was it ever effectively organized for fund-raising.

The first recorded alumni association was organized on the occasion of Father Vincent's jubilee in 1878. A serious attempt to re-organize it with a view to assisting with extraordinary college expenses was made in 1900 when J.R. Teefy, J.P. Treacy, J.J. Foy, J.J. Cassidy, H.T. Kelly, Thomas Mulvey, and J. Amyot constituted themselves the nucleus of a formal alumni or old boys' group. They solicited supplementary aid for the new high school wing, largely the gift of Eugene O'Keefe, and they held an alumni meeting on 28 April 1903, which over 300 attended. The association, however, did not remain effectively or continuously active.

In 1909 there appeared a rather special group known as 'Old Belles Lettres.' This was really the belles lettres class of 1906, the last such class in St Michael's. Old Belles Lettres had 21 original members from among whom came the graduates of the first university class of 1910 and also a group of non-university men. The rather famous class met for a number of years in the St Charles Cafe under Joseph L. Seitz, president, and Michael J. Oliver, secretary, and it provided over these years a scholarship for a St Michael's student.[53] It also provided the spirit which made Seitz a life-long benefactor of the college and Oliver the man who was in 1923 to revive the alumni association and who organized the meeting of 12 May 1927 with Judge Kelly – also a life-long benefactor – in the chair.

The alumni undertook to support and work for the projected drive; it also adopted as its own Archbishop Neil McNeil's suggestion that a public board be created to handle funds collected and that an appeal be

53 For the first association see Scollard, 'Notes,' I, 57. An interesting booklet of 14 pages entitled *Olde Belles Lettres: SMC '10*, Toronto, 1912, lists the members of the society, and recounts its activities. This booklet is in the St Michael's College archives.

made to a wide public. Both the alumni and the Basilians of St Michael's agreed that it would not be adequate to contact only former students, so many of whom were priests (reflecting the college's early history), but that the campaign when it came should reflect rather the new role which the college was already playing in the life of Canadian Catholics.

Following the jubilee, St Michael's entered a period of intense planning. First and basic were the building plans which were announced in 1928. These provided for a series of buildings around the perimeter of the combined college property and college-designated university land. These buildings were: a new arts building along the Queen's Park frontage; a library on St Joseph Street near the park; east of the library a church and faculty residence; a field house along Bay Street; and an enlarged playing field on the south side of St Mary Street west of Bay. Within the property were to be erected several residences and a refectory which in juxtaposition with the perimeter buildings were to complete a total of three quadrangles. The high school was to be moved to the south side of St Joseph Street.

These were good plans, architecturally speaking, but too confining. They were made to fill the needs of a college of 1000 men, half of whom were resident students, and they were so complete and self-containing as to be unsuitable for the kind of expansion the college had ultimately to accept. It was not altogether a misfortune that, as matters turned out, they could not be implemented.

A campaign to raise $3,000,000 for this development and for substantial endowment was announced in April 1929 with the Toronto lawyer and alderman John Boland as chairman and Father M.J. Oliver as general manager. The campaign was launched with a gift by Frank P. O'Connor in the mount of $125,000 pledged over ten years. The campaign was nicely under way when the economic depression which struck America in the fall of 1929 removed all possibility of reaching the announced objective. Enough was raised, however, to proceed some six years later with a modified building programme and to carry the institute through its first ten years. McCorkell's appointment as superior and president ran out in 1931 and he was succeeded by his assistant superior.

Time for Experiment

Between 1931 and 1934, Henry S. Bellisle was superior and president of St Michael's. He had worked closely with both Carr and McCorkell in various capacities: assistant superior, principal of the high school, registrar, professor of philosophy. He had little time for appeasement or compromise, was aggressive and determined by temperament, but the kindest of men in human relations. He was without fear and would tackle anything, which was manifested during the three short years of his presidency when he introduced new militant sports policies, expanded the high school concept, and successfully solved a perplexing problem affecting American students.

McCorkell's presidency had been one of prudent thoughtful planning, a kind of planning that ultimately worked but only after almost everything that could possibly go wrong had gone wrong. Bellisle's presidency was marked by quick and often reckless experiment. His sports policy is illustrative. St Michael's had long hoped and was still hoping, when Bellisle became president, to be allowed to field a senior team in intercollegiate rugby football competition. The league, however, was not yet ready for St Michael's, and Bellisle would not wait for the league. McCorkell had, before 1932, allowed the athletic directorate of the college to operate a team in the senior Ontario Rugby Football Union, but he would not countenance any extraordinary promotion of the team. Bellisle, however, as of the summer of 1932, authorized the directorate not only to enter a senior team in the ORFU but to promote and develop it as well. This meant playing against Balmy Beach, the Sarnia Imperials, and the Hamilton Cubs, on their own rugged and near-professional terms. The policy once opened up this way, produced in 1932–3 a spate of major teams: a senior team in the Ontario Hockey Association and a team in the junior OHA's Big Six group, the strongest group in age-limit hockey. The policy was aggressive and ambitious and made exciting news in sports circles. It also called for the importing of players so that the necessary level of competition could be maintained. The policy of having senior teams was short-lived – the three years of Bellisle's presidency. When McCorkell returned as president in 1934 the senior players on hand were integrated into the major Varsity squads. Junior hockey of championship calibre was continued, but rather as a high school than college activity. When the time came in 1950 to move the high school, the junior A hockey team moved to St Clair Avenue with it.

Another of Bellisle's impulsive experiments was the opening of auxiliary junior high schools in the east and west ends of Toronto. The Catholic high school situation was worsening in Toronto during the thirties, partly because depression conditions made private schools too costly for most people, partly because the population was shifting to the suburbs, and the trip downtown every day was too much for many boys. Bellisle, however, fervently believed in Catholic high schools and moved to make them less costly and more accessible. As soon as he became aware of the problems and found himself in a position to act, he made the extraordinary move of reducing all fees, then of taking over a Bell Telephone exchange on Lee Avenue in the east end, and a house belonging to the Separate School Board near St Joan of Arc Church on Dundas Street in the west end. First-year classes were established in these schools in 1932 and second- and third-year classes in subsequent years. Students were expected to transfer to the downtown high school for the work of the higher forms.

Excellent teachers were assigned to the junior schools and they were during the first few years of operation highly satisfactory; but as the buildings were old to begin with and not designed for school use they deteriorated rapidly; growth was also too slow to justify Bellisle's hope that they would one day be replaced by modern junior high schools. Their failure was not, if one can judge by the subsequent development of junior high schools in many cities, in Bellisle's vision, which was noble and progressive, but in the impetuous manner in which they were undertaken. In 1935 the experiment was discontinued.

Bellisle's third experiment, the creation of a 'Western' or freshman course for Americans, has proven to be of tremendous importance for holding American students in St Michael's and for developing the genuinely international character of its arts course.

This experiment had a twofold background. The first is the story of Bellisle's generosity where the welfare of the community as a whole was concerned. In 1931 Assumption College, operated by the Basilians in Windsor, was in crisis. The superior, Daniel Dillon, found himself unable to meet obligations incurred a few years earlier when a new high school had been erected. By 1931 no bills had been paid for telephone, electricity, and coal for over two years. Dillon's health broke and his assistant T.A. MacDonald had gradually to take over. MacDonald at Dillon's request telephoned Bellisle telling him he urgently needed $15,000 to pay off bills so that ordinary services could be continued at Assumption. Without demur, Bellisle sent a cheque for $15,000 in the next mail with a note saying that no interest would be charged and that the debt would not fall due until Assumption could pay it.

The second background to the Western course was in the decision of Ontario's department of education to make grade XIII rather than grade XII the normal admission requirement for university. Behind the change was the financial saving in expenditures for both the government and for parents. It was also claimed that grade XIII would be a better preparation for most honour courses than was first-year arts. All educators did not think so, and the event has shown that adding a year to high school was to prove to be an unfortunate attempt to retain too many boys and girls in an adolescent milieu at an age when every fibre of their being was summoning them to maturity. Toronto was one of the universities willing to conform to the department's new admission requirement.

For St Michael's the proposal was shattering. As the smallest of the university's arts colleges, the loss in a single year of over thirty per cent of its student body was a crippling prospect. But the loss was likely to be higher in that since 1927 St Michael's had revived its contingent of American students. Father McCorkell had encouraged the return of Americans during his first term. Indeed by 1927 enough Americans had come to St Michael's to stimulate the founding of an American Club. That same year the American students held a banquet of their own in Hart House with Emil Sauer, the local consul general, present. By 1931, when Bellisle took over, the American students were numerically powerful and economically essential because they were in these depression years almost the only students still paying tuition. The new requirements were certain to freeze them out: few American high school graduates were likely to come to St Michael's if they had first to spend a year and possibly two years taking grade XIII in a Canadian high school.

Father Bellisle was on the point of accepting what struck him as a disappointingly harsh blow from the establishment. He was urged by his registrar, Basil F. Sullivan, to approach Assumption in the interest of the American students already pre-enrolled for the coming year. Bellisle telephoned T.A. MacDonald asking him to enrol his Americans in Assumption as extramural students or, if this were impossible, to arrange for their transfer. These boys would still be admissible to Assumption, which was not going to conform to the new admission proposal. MacDonald, with Dillon's approval, because both were still mindful of the recent favour, agreed to take steps to enrol them extramurally in Assumption. There remained the matter of approval of such an arrangement not only by the University of Toronto but also by the University of Western Ontario, with which Assumption was affiliated. It is this last circumstance that lies behind the expression 'Western course' which students of St Michael's have now for over 25 years given to the programme followed by Americans during their freshman year. Since no one, either in Toronto or London, and least of all Alfred T. De Lury, the acting president, and A.B. Fennell, university registrar, wanted to see St Michael's seriously hurt by the change of admission requirements, and since saving the American students was some consolation to the small college for the loss of one entire year of Canadian students, the complex and somewhat bizarre arrangement went through. Two stipulations were made the next year: that St Michael's not admit Canadian students to the Western course, this at the request of Dr H.J. Cody, the new president; and that women not be admitted, at the request of the Ursuline sisters, who did not want competition from Toronto for prospective students from the United States. No other action of Bellisle has so deeply affected the history of St Michael's as this arrangement. It continued without change until 1953 when Assumption obtained its own charter and terminated the affiliation with Western, at which time the senate of the University of Toronto allowed St Michael's to take full responsibility for teaching, examining and accrediting its freshman course for non-Ontario students. After this time (1953) the course was open to both men and women. The Western course, which Bellisle initiated, was to impart a distinctive international character to the student body of St Michael's.

Bellisle's policies were immediately felt and they affected relations for both good and ill. One of his undertakings which was to have a stormy career at St Michael's, and which was less his own idea than Carr's, who was by now superior general of the Basilians, was the purchase of the college farms.[54] The slow progress of the campaign through the thirties and the hopeless state of investments led Carr to accept the advice of friends of the college and look to land purchases as the best means of acquiring future endowment. Bellisle accepted Carr's advice, liquidated a large part of the college investments, and purchased a number of farms in the area of Aurora, Gormley, and Richmond Hill. The policy of buying and operating farms was criticized by many of Bellisle's colleagues because it diverted not only money but the attention of the academic community away from books and the advancement of education.

The investment in land in the thirties was not in itself a bad one. In the hands of administrators who could share the patience of Job and the daring of Bellisle, it might well have provided the college with the endowment Oliver and McCorkell had dreamed about. As things turned out, the lands were disposed of at a small profit in the late forties.

Towards the end of his three-year term, Bellisle's health began to fail him. This was not the first time. He had suffered bad health in 1927 when he had taken sabbatical leave and gone to Louvain for further study; now in 1934 he had his first heart attack. This along with under-

54 Scollard, 'Notes,' v, 9

standable disagreement over policies led the general council of the order not to renew his appointment when it expired in 1934. McCorkell returned to the presidency of the college; Bellisle taught for a year at St Basil's Seminary, then went to Assumption College in Windsor where he taught philosophy until his death 28 December 1938.

Time to Rebuild

Father McCorkell returned as president of St Michael's in the summer of 1934, holding the post until 1940. He conducted the college along lines similar to those followed during his earlier term of office, that is, with the academic focus on the university at large, and with internal business conducted on a highly personal basis.

The measurable achievement of these years was the erection of new buildings. The Queen's Park building (comprising Teefy Hall, Fisher House, More House, the Institute) was the first erected. The cornerstone was laid on 27 August 1935, and the building was opened 15 September 1936, in a splendid ceremony presided over by James Charles McGuigan, the recently appointed archbishop of Toronto. The new heating plant was completed the same year. Brennan Hall, containing refectories, kitchens, common rooms, and guest rooms was opened in 1939. All these buildings were beautifully conceived and economically constructed in Indiana limestone. The plans actually adopted were considerably modified from those proposed in 1928, being more open to varied development, less costly, and less similar in exterior design to the Victoria College residences which had been put up in the meantime.

McCorkell was the last president to resist the fuller integration of women into the life of St Michael's College. There was, of course, even in his time some general relaxation of attitude. Men had gone to St Joseph's for instruction from sisters as early as 1921. In the late thirties, some co-education was being tolerated in honour courses to avoid costly duplication and uneconomical use of competent professors. But the feeling that the students enrolled in St Michael's belonged to three separate colleges endured, and no facilities were provided for women in the new buildings. Consequently both St Joseph's and Loretto consolidated their positions. St Joseph's had acquired the lovely Christie house at 29 Queen's Park in 1926 and planned on constructing a complete college complex. Loretto moved from Brunswick Avenue to 86 St George Street in 1937 and also planned a complete college.

The college registrar over many of these years, Father Basil Sullivan, was careful not to concede that the women's colleges had status in the university save through St Michael's. The appointment of 'registrars' in St Joseph's and Loretto sometimes complicated his work, especially when the 'registrars' dealt directly with the university. Indeed the increasing importance of the women students enrolled through St Michael's was a contributing factor to the very significant development of the office of college registrar in St Michael's between 1925–40. Other factors contributing to this development were the superior's mounting involvement in expansion programmes and his increasing responsibilities for a structure which ranged from a preparatory class (up to 1938) at one end of the spectrum to the Institute of Mediaeval Studies at the other; also, in Bellisle's case, a certain impatience with university procedures. In any event during the Sullivan years it was the registrar who became the college's most knowledgable academic official, the man whom students, faculty, and university officers alike approached on almost every conceivable subject pertaining to life in St Michael's.

Carr, Bellisle, and McCorkell constitute an important trio of college presidents. Under their supervision, St Michael's experienced growth on all fronts and integration not only into the life of the University of Toronto but into the broader society of international scholars. Under them, too, crystallized that classical image of the federated Catholic college now characteristic of Canadian university structure.

1940–52: THE WAR AND ITS AFTERMATH

The Presidency of T.P. McLaughlin

During the summer of 1940 Terence P. McLaughlin was appointed superior and president of St Michael's to succeed McCorkell. The war had already broken out but was still in what the American press was describing as the 'phoney' stage. Thus far St Michael's had not been affected seriously but was soon to be.

McLaughlin's appointment was itself a sort of incident. He was professor of mediaeval law at the Institute of Mediaeval Studies, which had only in 1939 received its pontifical recognition. He was also one of the most distinguished and best trained mediaevalists in his field in America. His appointment to an administrative post in St Michael's shocked the Institute's president, Gerald B. Phelan, who not only objected to the appointment but questioned the right of the general council of the Basilians to make it. McLaughlin's pontifical appointment to the Institute, Phelan maintained, removed him from the jurisdiction of his religious superiors so far as a change of appointment of this kind was concerned. It is unlikely that Phelan's contention was correct, but McLaughlin, being the student of law he was, cut the Gordian knot by electing to accept the appointment of his religious superiors and to retain at the same time his professorship in law at the institute, the annoyance of the president notwithstanding.

The episode explains in part why in 1942, at the chapter of the order which took place early in McLaughlin's regime, the institute was set up as a *domus formata* distinct from the college. The other contributing factor to this particular development was the spirit of uneasiness created within St Michael's by the disparity of working conditions as between high school teachers with 35 hours teaching a week, university professors with 10 or 12, and research scholars with 2 or 3 hours. Establishing the priests of the institute as a separate Basilian house solved several problems.

The impact made by the war on student life and on college registration is poignantly told by McLaughlin himself in an account written for the year-book in 1946 and attached to the two (incomplete) lists of young men whose courses had been interrupted by the war, the one list containing the names of 34 boys killed in action, the other of 31 recipients of military awards and citations.[55]

Those years, 1939 to 1945, were marked by uncertainty as to just how an arts college really stood in relation to the government and the general public during wartime. At first it looked as though teaching in arts might have to be abandoned. Later it became apparent that the wiser policy for all concerned was to keep the college open, at first for all who successfully passed their examinations, eventually for those only who ranked in the upper half of their class. Registration of Canadian men, what with enlistments at the end of high school, voluntary in-course enlistments, and the drafting of the less successful, declined steadily. The United States draft took away most of the American students: of the 160 Americans in the college in 1940-1, only one remained in 1944-5. The registration of women, clerics, and religious remained constant, but whereas 55 laymen graduated in 1940, only 16 graduated in 1945. Arts students in the men's residences totalled forty.

There were compensations. The number of professional and high school students in residence rose sharply. And although interest and participation in athletics declined, dramatics, music, student societies, and studies themselves flourished. Women also now became deeply involved in what were before strictly St Michael's (as distinguished from Loretto and St Joseph's) activities, and their importance for the life and development of the college was recognized and appreciated as never before. As McLaughlin remarked in the article already cited: 'We

55 'The War in the Queen's Park-Bay Street Sector,' *St Michael's College Year Book*, Toronto, 1946, 14

are not anxious to repeat the experience ... but these years did enable us to prove that even a small college has its place in the field of education.'[56]

The chronicle of these years includes a number of significant and memorable issues. First of all there was total collaboration with the wartime government not only in co-operation with its policies affecting students as, for example, the restricting of enrolment to satisfactory students or the establishing of military training in both the college and high school, but also in such *ad hoc* matters as the housing of British children in the Queen's Park residences until homes could be found for them with Canadian families, and in sending students, as happened in October 1942, to the Saskatoon area to bring in the badly needed and threatened wheat harvest. There was also the more or less routine implementation of policies established in more prosperous days: the buying, for example, of Bishop Fleming's property at 2 Elmsley Place, the last remaining private property between Bay Street and Queen's Park, so that the dislocation caused by the Terauley Street extension in 1922 could at last be fully rectified; the attending to the college farms; the more concentrated attention to the high school against the day when it would be moved to its own site, attention which included the buying of the Sacred Heart Orphanage on Bathurst Street and the launching of a distinct and subsequently highly effective Old Boys' Association. Indeed, the Bay Street high school became in McLaughlin's time, under the principalship of Viator I. McIntyre, one of Ontario's largest and best-staffed high schools. Teachers in those years included men like Norbert J. Ruth, Donald T. Faught, J. Francis Boland, Joseph B. Dorsey, Hugh V. Mallon, Robert E. Lamb, and others, who have since become distinguished deans, professors, and administrators on university campuses.

There were also the devices of competition and experiment by which active academic programmes were maintained when so many regular students were gone: the acceptance, for example, of a group of Benedictine clerics into a campus residence so that their own monastic building in New Hampshire could be released for the duration of the war to the American government; the canvassing everywhere for students so that the college doors might be kept open and ordinary services maintained; the sending of staff as full-time or part-time chaplains and instructors into the training schools, enlistment centres, and convalescent hospitals of the various branches of the armed forces; and the opening of a Summer School of Catholic Thought at the end of 1944–5.

General policy during the McLaughlin period was as abnormally over-cautious as the times themselves. McLaughlin, like his registrar

56 Ibid., 14

Basil F. Sullivan and most of the priests on his staff, was inclined to envisage the St Michael's of the future as an academically strong but otherwise severely circumscribed operation: its high school would be moved and the balance of its economy thereby upset; its arts division, which in conjunction with the institute was all that would be left, would like all liberal arts institutions develop more slowly than professional faculties; moreover, with increasing urbanization, residential facilities would be less in demand.

This may explain why McLaughlin showed no special interest in properties held by the college on the north side of St Mary Street and on the south side of St Joseph Street. The former were sold off, the latter he proposed to put up for sale but was overruled by the general council. Neither was he in favour of holding the farms longer than necessary to recover the investment.[57] He showed no possessive concern for the St Clair Avenue property other than to designate it for high school development, releasing it eventually in 1944 for that purpose without first settling its ownership, an embarrassing oversight as time was to show. The St Clair farm had been bought in 1881 by Father Laurence Brennan for future development. No one was ever quite sure whether the property actually belonged to the Basilians or to the college. For many years it made little difference since the two were virtually the same and since the priests of the college held most of the Toronto property in their own names in trust for the college. Legally, the Toronto Basilians were the corporation of St Michael's College. Community and college had, since 1925, when Francis Forster, the superior general, bought 21 St Mary Street and placed the curia in it, attained separate identities. It would have been prudent to have settled ownership before releasing all or part of the land for the projected high school, because this action which created a separate high school created thereby a third claimant.

McLaughlin's term of office was over before the high school project was under way. He was, however, vitally involved in the preparatory stages. During 1944 he informed the superior general that the local council had agreed to discontinue the present high school, to give the new school its 'property at the novitiate,' to contribute approximately $225,000 in cash, to turn over to the high school various pieces of equipment and bursaries, clearly belonging to it, to share the Sunday work places and convent assignments, and to provide at regular rates board and accommodation of high school students 'for a short period.'[58]

---

57 Minutes of the Local Council, St Michael's College, 5 Feb. 1945
58 McLaughlin to McCorkell, 27 Feb. 1944; copy of this letter is incorporated into the Minutes of the Local Council of St Michael's College.

McLaughlin was also party to the purchase, by the Committee in Charge of the New High School, of the Richmond Hill Infirmary from the Sisters of St Joseph. He authorized the contribution of over $40,000 to cover purchase cost and repairs.[59] He also approved of the purchase of the Sacred Heart Orphanage from the Sisters of St Joseph at $235,000 so that the southern portion of the St Clair Avenue property could be made adequate for the school project.

In these negotiations, McLaughlin left the detail of the purchases in the hands of the superior general, Father McCorkell, who with a committee co-ordinated the various transactions involved, that is, the buying of the orphanage, the selling of the old novitiate, and the purchasing of the new. During all this McLaughlin displayed an uncharacteristic acquiescence, patiently enduring a paternalistic procedure, evidence perhaps of a total willingness on his part to support and promote the high school project.

During 1945 hostilities ceased on the European front, and in March 1946 the first veterans were received. The college staff collaborated with the university in providing an accelerated arts programme so that returned veterans with grade XII standing could graduate in 26 months. In many ways this proved to be one of the most profound experiences in the history of St Michael's. The veterans were students of mature age and experience and they dominated the life of the college through their numbers and prestige. Veteran students of 1946 were hungering for higher education. They loved lectures and seminars, and were not reluctant to admit it, and they introduced a new rugged practical intellectuality which endeared them to their professors. They were also the first students at St Michael's who had as a group enough money to be independent. They were mature persons who had already accepted personal responsibility with air force squadrons over Germany, on escort duty on the Atlantic, in active front line regiments. They were a far cry from the boys who lined up for admission to the Little Seminary on Queen Street in 1852.

The veterans were the first students of St Michael's for whom the traditional regulations – lights out at 11, report to the house prefect when returning from the city, no visiting of taverns, no liquor in their rooms – were utterly without meaning. This does not mean that they were difficult students, because they were not. It is possible that no group in the college's past matched their essential docility, their enthusiasm, their sobriety, even their devoutness. But these qualities, in the

59 McLaughlin to McCorkell, 5 Feb. 1945, also in the Minutes of the Local Council of St Michael's College.

degree the veterans possessed them, did not proceed from either respect for regulations or fear of authority. If college life was a wanted and unforgettable experience for them, they were for college life itself an experience which was to modify its character forever.

The veterans came just before McLaughlin completed his term of office. He was the hard, honest, knowledgable kind of man whom they could resist and respect; and they were (although he tried to hide it) men after his own heart. Their coming made it possible for him, on relinquishing office in the summer of 1946, to return to his research in mediaeval law with a sense of both personal and institutional fulfilment.

The Presidency of L.J. Bondy

Louis J. Bondy became superior and president of St Michael's during the summer of 1946. He was a distinguished academic who in the opinion of many ought not to have been wasted in administration. He came from one of Windsor's oldest French families; was a graduate of the University of Toronto, University of Chicago, and Johns Hopkins University of Baltimore; and was head and backbone of the college department of French. He was also widely known to priests and sisters across Canada for his retreats; and he was respected within the Basilian community as the creator of a vigorous seminary which was by this time graduating priests and scholars in gratifying numbers.

When Bondy came into office the growth and development of the post-war years had already begun and it became his task to carry through a number of urgent and important adjustments: the separation of the college and the high school; the courageous resetting of the directional course of two seminaries; and the planning of the centennial celebration which marked the emergence of St Michael's into the family of Canadian universities.

Separation of College and High School

During 1946–7 the college enrolment passed the 500 mark and that of the high school approached 900. It was evident to Bondy that the construction of the new high school had to be given priority. His first major move after taking over was to release the necessary funds. This he did by revising the policy of Bellisle and Carr, converting all but one of the college farms into cash. The first Richmond Hill farm was sold during 1946, the Dufferin Street farm during 1947–8, and the remainder (with the exception of the 95-acre pig farm at Gormley) by 1951. At the time, the sale of the farms was both gratifying to the community and necessary. Subsequent criticism is not usually mindful that without the revenue from them the high school could not have been built, and that the operation of the farms with incompetent help was in a fair way to destroying both the academic and the religious life of too many Basilians.

Since the purchase of the orphanage made in McLaughlin's time had provided suitable land for a school building, there now only remained, before proceeding with the project, the laying of a storm sewer in the bed of the creek north from St Clair Avenue, and the filling in of the valley, necessary prerequisites to providing a playing field. The sewer was begun 26 September 1946 when Bondy and his council undertook to spend $100,000 on a storm sewer. From then on, action was constant and rapid. The new high school site was blessed by Cardinal McGuigan 8 December 1948, the cornerstone laid 31 August 1949; the school opened 10 September 1950.[60]

The high school was set up as an independent religious house under Father H. Basil Regan, who had been assistant to Bondy and principal of the high school department from the time of V.I. McIntyre. When the apostolates were separated, the high school property on St Clair Avenue was left in the name of St Michael's College in the hope that the college's exemption from expropriation, upheld by the Supreme Court of Canada, might protect the school from a second seizure like the Terauley Street extension. The college turned over to the new school, besides the land required for the school building and its playing field, the $300,000 spent on enlarging and developing its property. The college also loaned the school an additional $300,000 without interest and not to be repaid if the projected centennial campaign scheduled for 1952 reached a total of $500,000. The new school was also given $500,000 by the archdiocese from its high school drive. When the separation took place both institutions had fine properties; the high school had a new building with an indebtedness of $600,000 and no endowment; the college was debt-free but virtually without funds or endowment and faced with an extensive and imminent building programme. Bondy's handling of the delicate problem of division of assets and redistribution of liabilities at the time of the separation of the two houses was a masterly exercise of generosity and justice.[61]

During the academic year following the separation, that is, during 1950–1, a small high school was maintained on Bay Street partly to look after those students from the east end of Toronto for whom transportation to the new school was inconvenient, and to provide accommodation

60 Minutes of the Local Council of St Michael's College, *passim*
61 For further details see Bondy to McCorkell, 3 Jan. 1950.

for the high school boarders who could not yet be accommodated on St Clair Avenue. In 1951 all high school work, both academic and residential, was removed to the new school.

The change effected in St Michael's by the separation of college and school was revolutionary, ranking in significance with university federation itself. It was more than a redistribution of material resources and liabilities: it was a profound altering of personal and institutional directions and commitments. The academic advantages require no elaboration, nor do the potentialities for service to Canadian Catholics. But at the purely human level both parties suffered a severe wrench. The high school Basilians lost the practical, disillusioning but comforting contact with college professors and research scholars. The college priests saw slip away much of the old warm personal way of life with their own students which had long brushed off on them from their high school colleagues. Now, without high school priests to help with the college residences and without the rivalries that made high school and college men subject themselves to periodic self-examination, there resulted on both sides a decline in awareness of the continuity between the boy and the man, a decline that has become endemic to contemporary education. With all the advantages and disadvantages entailed, St Michael's moved with this division, belatedly to be sure, into the bewildering mixture of competence and confusion which marks the twentieth century.

Bondy and the Seminaries

While the high school separation was in progress, Bondy was called upon to cope with two major changes affecting the college in its relations with the Basilian and diocesan seminaries.

Chronologically if not in importance the problem of the Basilian seminary same first. The older Basilian tradition was to train seminarians (or scholastics as they were more properly called until recently) within their colleges. Young men were taken directly from the novitiate into the religious family and put to work and to school at the same time, looking after boys and teaching for much of the day and night, and attending classes in philosophy and theology if and when there was time for it. A more formal scholasticate was opened in Toronto about 1918 when scholastics and their master were put together in a house but left with their work and school outside that house. In 1926, some four years after the community adopted the new code of canon law, the superior general, Father Francis Forster, opened a scholasticate strictly so-called at 21 St Mary St, placing Father Henry Carr in charge of it. In

1928 Bondy succeeded Carr as master of scholastics and undertook to create at the edge of the St Michael's campus a scholasticate or seminary along canonical lines. Bondy's scholasticate was a strict one. He encouraged his men to immerse themselves in the academic life of the university but not any more than absolutely necessary in its extracurricular life. Although this principle has since been contested, it was, judging by results, reasonably successful as applied during the 1930s. In literally creating a Basilian scholasticate, Bondy became an acknowledged authority on this kind of institution. When in 1934 he completed his six years as master, he moved to St Michael's as professor of French and head of the department. He also served as moderator for scholastics assigned to live in St Michael's, a post he held uninterruptedly for twelve years, that is, until he became president of the college.

With this background, it is understandable that the whole area of college-seminary relations should be very real for him in his new post. The scholasticate building at 21 St Mary was, when taken over in 1926, with the exception of the east wing, an old and rundown building. By 1946 it was almost unusable. The general council was anxious to replace it. Considerable pressure was brought to bear on the superior general, particularly by the master of scholastics, E.J. Lajeunesse, to move it to a quiet place, preferably outside the city. Bondy was opposed to this move. A seminary, he said, needed the atmosphere of the university campus; and a seminary had too much to give a college campus to be allowed to get away. Always a shrewd fighter, he settled the question by offering to turn over to the general council for a new seminary the houses owned by the college on the south side of St Joseph Street right in the heart of the college campus, and $50,000 to boot, in exchange for the old scholasticate on St Mary Street.[62] The deal was accepted; and the new St Basil's Seminary was ready for occupancy in the autumn of 1951. In its own way, this action of Bondy's has, especially since the development of a civil faculty of theology at St Michael's, been almost as important for the college as the removal of the high school.

A second seminary development, this time affecting relations between the college and the diocesan seminary, also took place during Bondy's presidency. The background here is a little more complex than the preceding but it is important.

From 1852 to 1913 St Michael's had served the diocesan needs in so far as a little seminary was concerned. Candidates for the priesthood could transfer from St Michael's to a grand seminary at the end of their

62 Minutes of the Local Council of St Michael's College, 3 Jan. 1950. The address of the scholasticate was always given as 68 St Nicholas Street, the side door of the St Mary Street building which the scholastics always used. The 21 St Mary address was reserved for the curial house located in the same building.

philosophy. Some, indeed, even read their theology at St Michael's, doing so privately under one or more of the college priests and paying their way by teaching in the academy or high school. In the background was always the realization that when the pioneer period was over Toronto would have either a diocesan or perhaps even a regional seminary.

From 1890 on, there began to be talk of a new seminary. Archbishop McEvay was particularly set on the idea. After the turn of the century, Eugene O'Keefe expressed a willingness to finance the project as he had, in part, the new high school wing at St Michael's. As the college moved into full federation into the university and was preparing to emphasize the needs of other than candidates for the priesthood, the diocese prepared to open its own seminary of philosophy and theology, which it did when St Augustine's Seminary came into existence, 28 August 1913.[63] From 1913 to 1938 the college and the diocesan seminary, although maintaining cordial relations, pursued their different ways.

During 1937–8 the rector of St Augustine's, Monsignor Edward M. Brennan, requested that seminarians in philosophy who were properly qualified be enrolled as university students through St Michael's. They would remain at the seminary and continue to be instructed by seminary professors. In making this request the rector and the seminary administration had in mind the strengthening of the seminary's academic programme by giving both students and professors recognized university status; they also felt the need of competing with St Peter's Seminary of London which had become a federated division of the University of Western Ontario. Brennan's request was a crack in the protective armour of the isolated Tridentine seminary. After negotiations with Dr Cody, president of the University of Toronto, and the university senate, an agreement was reached whereby, beginning in the fall of 1938, the seminary professors were placed on the St Michael's staff and qualified seminarians were enrolled in pass arts through St Michael's.

The arrangement of 1938 functioned smoothly and to the satsifaction of all concerned until 1949 when the university's plan to replace the old pass course by a new general course, in which a university subject (mathematics or science) became mandatory for all students, jeopardized the seminary-college agreement. Seminarians would henceforth have to appear on campus at least twice a week during their first year.

Bondy took the matter up with the new rector of the seminary, Monsignor John H. Ingoldsby, and with Cardinal McGuigan. Bondy suggested placing the seminarians on the campus during their first year. McGuigan took him up but went him one better by insisting that his seminarians remain on the campus for the full three years of their general course. This was the final solution. It created for the seminary the regrettable necessity of separating university from non-university seminarians, but it anticipated what has become widespread policy since Vatican II, the restoration of the diocesan seminarian to the university campus.

When the St Augustine seminarians came to St Michael's in the fall of 1950 they were housed on the Irish flat. The following year they were moved to what were to be temporary quarters – the old recently-vacated Basilian seminary on St Mary Street. Father Walter Kerr became rector of the St Augustine's University Residence. The St Mary Street building continued to be used as the seminary's university residence until 1962, when the seminarians were moved back into the old high school wing at 50 St Joseph Street, where they remained until the opening of St Augustine's College in 1964.[64] In the meantime there was carried on, on the Toronto campus, perhaps the liveliest and most forward-looking experiment in seminary education that English-speaking Canada had thus far known.

Federal Aid, Co-education, Centenary Plans

In the wake of these changes affecting the structure of St Michael's came an important fiscal change which considerably widened the potential of the college – the decision of the federal government to aid Canadian universities and colleges regardless of the source of their normal operating funds. St Michael's had been without direct aid from government at any level since 1868. Late in the 1940s came the first change when the Department of Veterans' Affairs made supplementary grants towards the cost of facilities provided for veteran students. By 1951, however, these grants were drying up as veterans graduated. Rather than provoke a crisis, and recognizing that changing conditions in Canada called for a new generosity to colleges and universities, the federal government instituted its university grant policy.

The federal government could not, for valid political reasons, distinguish between one citizen and another, nor could it, for the same reasons, exclude certified colleges merely because their normal operating expenses did not come from a provincial government. This meant that sectarian institutions became as eligible as the government-supported for whatever aid was to be made available.

When the grants were first announced during the fall of 1951, the University of Toronto urged its federated colleges to share their new

64 See below, 231–2

revenues as they had shared the DVA grants, on the basis of instruction given, that is, allocating three-fifths of the federal grant to the university. The colleges were also urged to receive their cheques through the university. Although the Toronto colleges yielded on both points, they were not permitted in the final instance to receive their federal aid indirectly.

The payment of federal grants began in February 1952 when St Michael's received from Ottawa a cheque in the amount of $81,605.62 on behalf of a total of 646 students, 526 of them Toronto undergraduates, 60 in the 'Western' course. Of this sum, $39,888.01 was turned over to the university as three-fifths of the grant made on behalf of the 526 St Michael's students registered in the University of Toronto.

The 60–40 division on the basis of instruction was arrived at without taking into consideration the situation at St Michael's, where philosophy was also a college subject. Bondy preferred to accept the inequity rather than resort to special pleading. When the first cheque arrived from Ottawa, he sent his three-fifths for his Toronto undergraduates to President Sidney Smith personally by the next mail, avoiding the understandable temptation to delay and negotiate.

St Michael's had also an internal problem related to its federal grant. Should the forty per cent allocated to the college be shared by its affiliates St Joseph's and Loretto since both were still doing much of their own teaching? Bondy's decision was that the grant should not be further subdivided but that St Michael's should assume responsibility for all teaching whether of men or women. Thus did the federal grant become the catalyst that completed the process of co-education.

The grant was not the only factor in determining that St Michael's should become completely co-educational. The process which had begun during McCorkell's presidency in the thirties and had been accelerated by the war was proving satisfactory and could be pleaded in its own right. Now, however, in 1951–2 there were plans under consideration to mark the centenary coming in 1952 with a new academic building which would house administration, student activities, lecture rooms, and an interim library. The feeling was strong that the building should be planned with a co-educational institution in mind. The reorganization of St Michael's along these lines was first broached in what must always be regarded as an epoch-making document – Bondy's letter of January 1952 to the deans of the two women's colleges.

As you have doubtless heard, we plan to erect a new building on the corner of St Joseph Street and the Park. The building will house the co-op, students' common room, administration, library and classrooms. It is intended for both women and men students.

It seems to me that this is the proper time to re-organize our rather complex institution in order to achieve a more effective and less wasteful use of our academic resources. Next year will furnish an additional reason for this since the second year of the new general course will require additional courses in practically all departments.

I think we should also consider some plan for more equitable distribution of the financial load. In this connection we would propose, beginning with September 1952, that all tuition fees be collected by the Bursar of St Michael's and that we try to devise some scheme whereby both you and St Joseph's [you and Loretto], would receive a fair remuneration based on the number of students and the amount of teaching done by your Sisters.

Beyond this we have no detailed plan to suggest just now. Such a plan can only be the result of honest and cordial discussion with nothing in view but the good of our institution and of our students, both men and women. I am writing to you now so that you may have ample time to discuss this matter with your staff and your community before we come together to reach a solution.[65]

Following the discussions which arose from this communication there came the financial arrangements spelt out in what is perhaps the final act of Bondy's presidency:

The problem of a fair remuneration to your Community is very complex. You will notice that there are about as many Sisters on our teaching staff as there are priests. In the undergraduate student-body last year there were 173 women students (including Western) and 413 men. It therefore seems impossible to arrive at a satisfactory salary schedule under the present circumstances. We would like to submit the following proposals to be tried out *for one year*. Perhaps the year's experience will give us a clearer view of the problem.

1 St Michael's will pay the salaries of all lay teachers.
2 Will furnish chaplain services free of charge throughout the year.
3 Will be responsible for all scholarships, bursaries, and awards, making proper provision for women students.
4 Will honour commitments already made to women students by Loretto [St Joseph's].
5 Will pay a basic sum of $5000.00 plus an additional sum of $50.00 for each

65 Bondy to Mother Marcia; Bondy to Sister Bernard; 18 Jan. 1952; in SMC Archives

paying student affiliated with Loretto [St Joseph's]. If a student receives a bursary or partial scholarship, this amount will be scaled down in proportion. Would you please give some thought to these proposals so that we can discuss them and, if possible, arrive at a definite agreement around July 1st.[66]

Although the arrangements were made for only one year, they remained in effect almost unchanged until 1959 when they were completely revised on a direct salary basis.

Concurrent with the preceding financial and co-educational developments, were the not unelaborate plans which Bondy produced through a committee for the celebration of the centenary. His committee consisted of Charles J. Lavery, Hugh V. Mallon, Robert J. Scollard, Matthew T. Mulcahy, and Laurence K. Shook, and it arranged a year-long sequence of centennial events as follows:

(1) 25 January 1952, the students' centennial 'At Home' held in Brennan Hall, which featured the unveiling of the centennial mural designed by Patricia Lippert and executed with the help of other college students;

(2) 16 March 1952, the centennial arts banquet held in the Royal York Hotel at which Mr Paul Forestell was toastmaster and Louis St Laurent, prime minister of Canada, guest of honour;

(3) 14 May 1952, the special convocation called by the University of Toronto and held in Convocation Hall to mark the centenaries of the University of Trinity College and St Michael's College, and at which the LL.D. was conferred for St Michael's on T. D'Arcy Leonard, Paul Martin, C.P. McTague, Michael C. O'Neil, and Gerald B. Phelan;

(4) 27, 28, 29 September 1952, a sequence of public celebrations: an open house and dance at St Michael's College School with Leo Sullivan as chairman; the opening of the academic year with an academic procession to St Basil's Church for pontifical mass celebrated by Bishop Benjamin Webster with Laurence K. Shook preaching; a 'Grand Reception' in Brennan Hall convened by Mrs C. E. Knowlton; a pontifical mass of thanksgiving celebrated in St Michael's Cathedral by James Charles Cardinal McGuigan, archbishop of Toronto, before Edward Cardinal Mooney, archbishop of Detroit and Idebrando Antoniutti, apostolic delegate to Canada; a centennial state dinner held in the King Edward Hotel with Arthur Kelly as chairman.

(5) October-December 1952, a series of four centennial lectures delivered in Convocation Hall by Etienne Gilson, Hugh Taylor, Jacques Maritain, and Georges H. Levesque.

66 Bondy to Mother Marcia; Bondy to Sister Bernard; 19 June 1952

These events were heralded by a formal announcement issued 7 March 1952. The announcement, like the mural, featured a five-coloured reproduction of the Arms of St Michael's newly-prepared by Alexander Scott Carter and formally described as follows: 'Arms – Quarterly argent and azure. 1 a cross moline of the second. 2 an open book proper edged and clasps or 3 a laurel wreath or 4 an oak tree erased and fructed proper. Crest – a sword erect between two wings addorsed or.' The text of the announcement read:

The Superior of St Michael's College in the University of Toronto and The Superior of St Michael's College School with their Councils, Boards of Trustees and Teaching Staffs announce to their alumni and alumnae throughout the world, to friends and members of their academic families, and to all who seek to advance the cause of true education that the fifteenth day of September in the year of Our Lord, one thousand nine hundred and fifty-two marks the centenary of the founding of St Michael's College in the City and Archdiocese of Toronto, Canada.

Almighty God, in His Goodness, has given this College the privilege of serving Holy Mother the Church under the distinguished patronage of Bishop Armand Francis Mary, the Count de Charbonnel, of Bishop, and later Archbishop John Joseph Lynch, of Archbishops John Walsh, Denis O'Connor, Fergus Patrick McEvay and Neil McNeil, and of His Eminence James Charles Cardinal McGuigan, the present Archbishop of Toronto.

It has been His Will, too, that this College should grow in size from the Little Seminary that could be temporarily housed in restricted quarters at Queen and Church Streets, and that could be placed as a Classical College in a wing of the Cathedral Palace, into the flourishing institution of learning which today lies spread between the crest of Clover Hill and Queen's Park Crescent.

May God be thanked for one hundred years of faithful and unbroken service, and above all, for four events which have so deeply and vitally enriched this institution that they cannot be passed over in silence:

First, the federation of St Michael's into the Provincial University of Toronto, an event long foreshadowed by a request for affiliation made, with the approval of the Bishop of Toronto, in 1855, realized in part by agreement with the University in 1881, consolidated into full confederation by Acts of Parliament in 1887 and 1906, and exercised as an academic right and privilege from 1910 to the present day.

Secondly, the admission of women to undergraduate status by receiving, in 1912, the Colleges of St Joseph and Loretto into the collegiate family.

Thirdly, the founding of the Institute of Mediaeval Studies in 1929 as a separate school of research at the graduate level and its elevation to the dignity of a Pontifical Institute in 1939 at the unanimous request of the Bishops of Canada to the Holy See.

Fourthly, the setting up in 1950, one hundred years almost to the day after the arrival of the first Basilian priest in Canada, of an autonomous College School, with its own administration, thereby apportioning the labours of the Basilian Fathers during their second century in Toronto between two distinct but sister institutions.

These and other memorable events will be duly and solemnly commemorated on the Feast of St Michael, the twenty-ninth day of September, 1952.

The document was signed by H.B. Regan for the college school and by L.J. Bondy for the college.

Bondy's presidency came to an end on 30 June 1952 while the centenary was still in progress. Before leaving office he succeeded in getting C.P. McTague to accept the chairmanship of a centennial campaign to raise $750,000 from business, friends, and alumni to put a new building on the St Michael's campus. Bondy also engaged as chief architect of the centennial building Ernest Cormier of Montreal and as resident architect Frank Brennan.

When his six years of presidency expired considerable pressure was exerted on him and on the superior general, especially by McTague, to extend the period of his appointment until the centenary celebrations and the campaign were over. Bondy would hear nothing of such proposals and relinquished his office to Laurence K. Shook who had been a scholastic under him in the late twenties and early thirties and who had been his assistant throughout most of his presidency.

SINCE 1952: SHOOK AND KELLY

The Presidency of L.K. Shook

Continuing Action

During July of 1952 the presidency of St Michael's was taken up by Laurence K. Shook, professor and head of the college department of English. Shook had been at St Michael's continuously since completing his graduate studies at Harvard in 1940. As Bondy's assistant for five years, as chairman of the centennial committee, and possibly also as a Torontonian, he was not a surprising choice for the immediate task of continuing the operations which Bondy had set in motion: the public centennial functions scheduled for September, the erecting of the projected administration and library building, the implementing of the fund-raising campaign, and the carrying out of the final step in the slowly maturing process of co-education.[67]

The times were right for these undertakings not only because college enrolment was growing but because public relations were healthy. The high school constituency was still close to the college, and the public at large was aware that the downtown motherhouse was confronted with a serious problem of material rehabilitation. The campaign for funds, of course, was crucial. The general chairmanship was competently held by the Honourable Charles P. McTague; and Hugh V. Mallon of the college staff became his full-time manager. With Charles J. Lavery on special gifts and with a large and willing team of citizens and alumni sharing the burdens of collecting, a total of $853,000 ($100,000 above the objective) was raised – more than enough to build and furnish Carr Hall at Queen's Park and St Joseph Street.

Full co-education and academic integration also came easily. Bondy's letter written in June to the deans of the women's colleges was received with understanding and trust. When the term opened in September all lecture courses, including the general course, became fully integrated and the college library on Elmsley Place, as well as most student organizations, were opened to women. The integration was not intended nor was it allowed to reduce the women's colleges to residences; it was intended to bring the women, both students and faculty, into the fullest possible participation in the life of the college; it was intended also to strengthen the college academically and financially.

One problem immediately solved by the academic integration of women was the complexity of hiring lay professors. Strictly speaking, each of the three colleges had been responsible for supplying its own staff, which came for the most part from the three religious orders concerned. But there was usually some lay staff which was hired jointly, as when the three colleges engaged Victoria Mueller in 1931, or when all three contributed to the salary of Frederick Nims in the early forties and of Marshall McLuhan in 1946. The women's colleges had not contributed to the salaries of professors of philosophy; but neither were women really welcome in strictly philosophical courses. Anomalies like these were now easily removed and the building of a strong lay faculty if not yet really under way was at least structurally provided for.

Perhaps most essentially valuable of the effects of the new integration was the encouragement imparted to the sisters by the new sense of belonging to an academic community. Now really for the first time, with

67 See *The Basilian Annals*, 2(1951–9), 75–8

their offering graduate courses, with their clearly acknowledged eligibility for faculty fellowships, and with more incentive to undertake scholarly publication, they could be said to have become professional scholars. Certainly with the resolving of the three-college structural problem the scholarship of St Michael's women was brought to public attention as never before.

Building Development

The six years of Shook's presidency were marked by the opening of four major St Michael's buildings and the start of construction on a fifth. The contract for Carr Hall was signed in February 1953 and the building formally opened on 24 October 1954, with a symbolic presentation of its key by the general chairman of the campaign to his friend and teacher, Henry Carr, then of St Mark's College, Vancouver, in whose honour the building was named. Carr Hall, completed and furnished just before the giant inflation in construction prices, cost a total of $750,000.

In 1956, St Joseph's, encouraged by its new status in St Michael's, and confronted with increasing demands for residence both by Canadian girls and by Americans now eligible for the 'Western' course, opened Maryhall, a combined residence and refectory costing $900,000. Two years later, realizing that the rate of development had been underestimated, St Joseph's also opened Fontbonne Hall, a combined residence and chapel which cost $1,500,000. These buildings are monuments to the foresight and courage of Mother St Bridget (Penelope Gillen), the mother general, and Sister Bernard, dean of women at St Joseph's.

During 1956 and 1957, the new St Michael's residence, Elmsley Hall, was erected at a cost of $1,300,000. Elmsley Hall was built on the site of Barnstable, one of the old family houses of the Elmsley's acquired by St Michael's back in 1920. Since this property opened on to St Mary Street and had the character of a second front door, the Loretto sisters who had long been looking for a new college site, decided to build on the north side of St Mary Street. They sold their St George Street property to the board of governors of the University of Toronto. The board dealt generously with the sisters allowing them the use of their old buildings for two years after the sale and expropriating for them in St Michael's name the properties they required on St Mary Street. The expropriation and the many-purpose building were more costly than the community could afford. The total outlay of $1,800,000 would have been impossible had not St Michael's made available $400,000 from the funds set aside for its own expansion by the Canada Council when it was established in 1957. It is unlikely that Loretto would have come to the St Michael's campus had not co-education and academic integration become a practical working reality. Their move to St Mary Street in 1959, the combined policy of Mother Constance, the general council, Mother St Margaret, and others, imparted a geographical unity to the greater St Michael's, assembling within the St Mary-Bay-Wellesley-Queen's Park circumference an impressive if not yet fully consolidated congeries of university buildings.

Re-structuring St Michael's

It is likely that Shook's most characteristic and possibly most lasting influence on St Michael's proceeded from his sense of order. Possibly no institution in Canada has been so chaotically put together and its chaos so persistently maintained as St Michael's. It is true that in the first instance, a concordat was arranged between Bishop de Charbonnel and the Basilians and that a civil act of incorporation was obtained, both of these in 1855. But these were not really orderly documents. The concordat merely put the college irremediably and effectively into the hands of the Basilians at their own risk. No other party, civil or ecclesiastical, had since 1855 assumed serious financial responsibility for its welfare; the clauses in the original document pertinent to fees for seminarians, equity in seminary collections, sharing of government grants with the diocese, neither could be nor were ever honoured. The civil act gave the bishop and all members of the faculty membership in the corporation: so unacceptable was this to the Basilians that no property acquired by them subsequent to 1855 was ever placed in the corporation itself but was held in trust for the college by selected individuals. The awkwardness of such an anomalous procedure was particularly embarrassing at the time of the Terauley Street extension when various private trustees of the properties had to prove that they were holding them not for themselves but for the college. Government of the college was in practice vested in the local council of the religious house, and this council, although appointed by the general council of the Basilian Fathers, was while in office in complete control of the operation. St Michael's never acquired a board of governors, never diversified responsibility beyond its little local council of three. In compensation it neither expected nor received interference from Basilians, governments, or the diocese. Had there ever been such interference it could in the material order only have affected the original four-lot gift of John Elmsley and the four-lot purchase of the French Basilians. The civil incorporation was not the only structural matter calling for attention: there were academic complexities, especially the 'Western' course; and there were financial anachronisms waiting to be removed.

The first structural anomaly which Shook tackled was the Western course. This course was operated on the St Michael's campus; its students were registered in the University of Western Ontario but through Assumption College as an affiliated intermediary. How it came about in the time of Henry Bellisle has already been dealt with. Trying to explain it to students, their parents, even to the administrations of the University of Toronto and of the University of Western Ontario when changes of personnel took place in these institutions was almost impossible. The first real crisis to arise over it came with the introduction of federal grants.

When in January 1952 Bondy submitted the number of students registered in St Michael's to D.C. Abbot, the minister of finance, he claimed on behalf of 60 students in the Western course, explaining the status of these students, having first obtained authorization from Assumption to claim for them. This first year the government acknowledged their eligibility. The following year, however, when Shook claimed for them, the deputy minister, K.W. Taylor, sought legal opinion and was advised that these students could not be claimed for by St Michael's, Assumption, or Western: not by St Michael's because they were not enrolled there, nor by the University of Western Ontario because they were not in personal attendance there, nor by Assumption because they were neither enrolled nor in personal attendance there.[68] Although the decision was protested, it remained official policy.

The second crisis affecting the Western course came during 1953 when Assumption terminated its affiliation with Western and acquired independent university status. At this time Shook negotiated at first privately with Sidney Smith, president of the University of Toronto, then in public with the university senate, and succeeded in having the Western course recognized as an independent admissions programme acceptable to the University of Toronto for non-Ontario students. The faculty of medicine and other faculties supported the programme because the now long-standing grade XIII admission clause was preventing the university from admitting even the most gifted non-Ontario students; it was beginning to give the student body of those faculties an excessively parochial character. They welcomed a little flexibility in the hidebound admissions policy observed by the university since 1931. With this decision, St Michael's could henceforth enrol its own non-

68 Taylor to Shook, 5 Feb. 1953; SMC Archives

Ontario students, examine them (subject to senate supervision) and present them directly to the registrar of the University of Toronto for admission to any faculty. An attempt was made to drop the name 'Western' in favour of 'Freshman' but the students never gave up the usage. The Western students even under this new arrangement did not become eligible for grants, because by this time no grade XIII students or their equivalent in any Ontario university were regarded as eligible.

Shook's second assault on structure came at almost the same time. This had to do with the St Michael's College Foundation. The Foundation had been set up following the campaign of 1929 when funds donated to St Michael's were held by a small group of trustees in order to assure supervised disposal of campaign funds. By the time Brennan Hall was built there was only an H.T. Kelly trust in the foundation, and by 1953 even this had become inaccessible through the death and dispersal of the trustees.

On 21 October 1953 a meeting of the foundation was arranged at Gordon Taylor's home in Oak Ridges. The foundation was declared to have fulfilled its objectives and the Kelly trust turned over to St Michael's College Foundation (1953) with bylaws which would assure the possibility of a permanent quorum and leave the funds readily accessible for student aid. Funds were placed in it from the centennial campaign, from a number of recent bequests, and from certain college sources. This was the beginning of the active, growing, and only effective dollar endowment the college ever possessed.

A more important adjustment to the legal structure of St Michael's was made in 1954. The original Act of Incorporation of 1855 was, as has been indicated, unsatisfactory from the beginning: it was not an academic charter and it had never been amended to make it one. Thus when St Michael's entered university federation in 1910 its legal status was inferior to that of Trinity and Victoria, which were universities in their own right. The university statutes, for example, did not give identical recognition to instruction given in a federated college like St Michael's and instruction given by the college of a federated university whose degree-conferring power was held in abeyance.[69] This distinction was trivial enough, and in practice meaningless for the undergraduate arts college. But the general incorporated status of St Michael's in the larger sense entailed two limitations: such a college could not give theological degrees, nor had it university status to fall back on should federation ever be terminated.

The first of these limitations was dealt with in 1954 when the Ontario legislature passed an amendment to the original St Michael's Col-

69 See sections 113, 114 of the University of Toronto Act, 1947.

lege Act providing for the civil establishment of a faculty of theology. St Michael's had never had a faculty of theology, and never felt the need of one until it found, following the institution of federal grants, that it was the only federated college on the campus not claiming on behalf of theological students. Yet in St Basil's Seminary and in St Augustine's Seminary there were students who had their BA and who would be eligible for grants if, like the students of Knox, Trinity, Emmanuel, they were proceeding to a civil degree. Catholic colleges in English-speaking Canada had not thus far given civil degrees in theology. Shook consulted with Cardinal McGuigan, then had the legislature amend the act of 1855. On the feast of St Michael 1954 St Michael's held its first convocation when Bishop Francis V. Allen, acting for St Michael's first chancellor, Cardinal McGuigan, conferred the STB on 21 Basilians and 10 diocesan seminarians. The STB was only made available as a second degree, that is, restricted to theologians who already had a BA. Once the programme was established, seminarians proceeding to the degree were eligible for federal grants. It was not until after Shook's time that theology was expanded from the strictly professional to the academic, but the basis for such a development was laid.

The amendment to the St Michael's College Act naturally raised the question of whether St Michael's should not also have a university charter. The example of Assumption was a spur. Shook consulted Sidney Smith on the propriety of such a move, asking him whether the college might not one day need a charter should federation become unworkable. Smith gave as his opinion that not to seek a charter and not to bring St Michael's into a position of legal parity with the other federated colleges would, in the uncertain future facing Canada's universities, be tantamount to abdication from duty. With this encouragement Shook sought the aid of Arthur Kelly, the college solicitor and a member of the board of governors of the University of Toronto. Between them they drew up a totally new civil act providing for the establishment of a degree-conferring University of St Michael's College with its degree-granting powers held in abeyance except in theology. This university was given an incorporated governing body known as the collegium (so called so as to prevent confusion with other local boards of governors and regents), and a senate. The collegium and senate were empowered to establish appropriate subsidiary university divisions.

Two matters of significance came up in the course of preparing the act: the ownership of the college was to be vested in the collegium with neither the superior general of the Basilians nor the archbishop of Toronto as *ex-officio* members, so as to make clear the autonomy of the new university in relation both to its property and its scholarship; the power of expropriation was to be sought, in spite of the objections of the city solicitor, so that there would be no distinction in law between the new university and the other federated universities. The University of St Michael's College Act was introduced into the Ontario legislature 20 February 1958, and came into force on 1 July, shortly before the termination of Shook's term as president.

A final organizational change recommended by Shook towards the end of his term was the separation of the offices of superior and president. In one sense the new act called for this kind of division in that it was a move away from a college run by a local religious council towards one operated by a public board, a college whose faculty was likely to become increasingly lay and non-Basilian. The reasons for separating the two offices were scarcely debatable: the workload entailed by the duplication had become too heavy; the two-term or six-year canonical maximum for superiors did not always serve properly the needs of the college; the qualifications for the two offices were not identical; laymen could no longer be left ineligible for the top administrative posts in the college they served; religious were coming to feel that their university apostolate was not identifiable with campus administration but could be as well and sometimes better served by a religious house located on a non-religious or even secular campus. In line with Shook's recommendation, the official Basilian appointments for 1958–9 named John F. Madden as superior of St Michael's and John M. Kelly as president.

The Presidency of J.M. Kelly

Separation of Offices

John Michael Kelly and John Francis Madden took over as president of St Michael's and superior respectively, on 1 July 1958. In selecting them for these offices the general council of the Basilians kept in mind the experimental character of the new administrative structure and chose personable and highly competent men. Madden had his doctorate in English from Harvard, Kelly in philosophy from Toronto. Both were vigorous and aggressive by temperament; both were Irish-Americans; both commanded the confidence and respect of their colleagues.

The distribution of responsibilities under the new arrangement were to be as follows: the superior was to head the religious house; he was to preside at meetings of the local council and at religious exercises; he was to represent the religious house at public religious functions; give permissions and non-curricular assignments to Basilians; he was to supervise the parish staff, and assume responsibility for the pastoral side of campus life. He was to be followed and obeyed by Basilians in case of a jurisdictional dispute. The president, on the other hand, was to be the academic head of St Michael's, but in charge also of college government and administration; he was to be head of the St Michael's College Foundation, chairman of the collegium, and in charge of the university's funds and properties. The superior was appointed for three years, renewable once; the president's appointment was indeterminate.

Madden remained superior from 1958 until November 1961 when he abruptly resigned. During just over three years in office he undertook to deal with a number of new and important movements. He did what his predecessor could not do: introduce the *aggiornamento* into the religious life of the local community. This process involved the initiating of a policy to remove stereotyped rules and devotions, experimenting for a while and then replacing the old with new forms. He made a true contribution to the religious life on the campus and brought Basilians into the twentieth-century renewal at a relatively early date. Madden also, and with typical enthusiasm, promoted liturgical participation by the student body. Although *Sacrosanctum concilium* (Vatican II's 'Constitution on the Sacred Liturgy') was not promulgated until 4 December 1963, he kept close to the work of the preparatory commission and brought the priests and students of the college abreast of the new awakening, giving them the sense that they were fashioning it rather than watching it come.

In line with the directive from the general council that the superior's responsibilities were primarily pastoral, Madden paid particular attention to the care of souls both in St Basil's parish and among the student population. His parochial concern was not fully appreciated by the staff of St Basil's, nor was it really recognized by the chancery office which, history notwithstanding, preferred to deal in all matters with the parish priest. Madden felt that the superior of St Michael's was the responsible pastor and that the local parish clergy were his vicars. This was clearly the case during the days of Soulerin and Vincent, who were in fact and name parish priests of St Basil's when the parish was properly felt to belong to the college. After Vincent's time the parish priests were inclined more and more to think of themselves as vicars of the archbishop rather than of the college superior. Madden, of course, did his best not to interfere unfairly, but he found the delicacy of his situation trying and the exercise of self-restraint in the circumstances suffocating.

The student pastorate he took very seriously. It was a threefold pastorate: to resident men; to day students, men and women; to the New-man Club parish. The first two of these went smoothly enough; the third, the Newman Club, was a different matter.[70] For many years the Newman Club was not closely associated with St Michael's. During 1957, however, direction of the club was transferred to St Michael's and a chaplain, Thomas A. MacDonald, appointed by the general council. Like most Newman Clubs in America, the Toronto club worked against serious difficulties: an undefined clientele, a non-academic atmosphere, restricted revenue, domination by alumni. Madden regarded the club as offering a special challenge and hoped to make it a kind of experimental base. But he could get no response from the superior general, and squirmed with impatience at what he felt was a reactionary force on the campus. Again he found the pastoral impulse the occasion of frustration. It was largely this pastoral factor, accentuated by the slowness of certain priests in the college to respond effusively to his innovations, and neither incompatibility with the president nor rejection of the principle of dividing the offices, that led to his resignation in November 1961.

From November 1961 until June 1962, Kelly had himself to fill both offices. The situation was rather salutary. Kelly now fully realized how impossible it had become to wear the two hats. Moreover, the priests of the house realized how much they needed a full-time religious superior, and what the presence of one had begun to mean to them. Experience was confirming the wisdom of the policy of division. During the interim Kelly tried a little *aggiornamento* of his own, particularly in the context of consulting men in the ranks. He turned most local council meetings into executive committee meetings of the collegium, admitting observers and giving them a voice in local council decisions. The idea made good theory but in practice turned out to be rather artificial. It was not continued in this form when Donald J. McNeil became superior in the summer of 1962.

McNeil was a professor of Latin. He was highly regarded by his colleagues for the spirit of work and artistic sensitivity demonstrated over creditable years as college sacristan. He continued Madden's policy of updating liturgy and the common life, with two distinct advantages:

70 Newman Club was established in 1913 by the Paulist Fathers to provide pastoral service to University of Toronto students, especially those not enrolled in St Michael's. The club was opened on St Joseph St in 1913 by Thomas F. Burke. It was moved to St George St by the second rector John E. Burke. Other Paulist rectors were Austin Malone, Francis McNab, Joseph McMahon, and J.E. McGarrity. The club was served by diocesan directors from 1936 to 1957: A.E. McQuillen 1936–40, J.E. McHenry 1940–55, M.T. Griffin 1955–7. Basilian rectors have been T.A. MacDonald, F.M. Quealey, P.E. Sheehan.

he had the moral support of Vatican II which opened during his first year of office; and he had informed encouragement from George B. Flahiff, the former superior general of the Basilians, who had become a member of the conciliar commission on the religious life.

Like Madden, however, McNeil did not complete his canonical six years, although the circumstances of his leaving office were different. McNeil had a new worry: he had to cope with the unrest that developed among priests and students as the work of renewal progressed. This new worry he shared with religious superiors everywhere during this period of unprecedented change. He had, however, to cope with it in an accentuated form. The appearance of a faculty of theology on the campus had brought with it the conscious use of activist strategies. Some Basilians were quick to exploit these strategies, notably the Munich-trained Stanley Kutz, secretary of the faculty of theology, and Michael Quealey, a promising young historian. McNeil was sympathetic with the objectives of these more violent innovators but puzzled by their apparent rejection of the common life. His solution, and that of the superior general and of President Kelly, was to locate first Quealey, and then, along with him his disciple Kutz, in Newman Club, where they might be freer to experiment without being upset by misunderstanding colleagues – a daring solution that might have worked if the incumbents of Newman Club, T.A. MacDonald and Francis Mallon, had been removed so as to avoid an extravagant concentration of four priests (there were only 22 in St Michael's) of such divergent outlooks. The strategies of Quealey and Kutz, however, included personal, public diatribes against the hierarchy and the apparent espousal of the 'new morality.' The result was an unprecedented deluge of hostile criticism, not from the hierarchy, but from low-income, unsophisticated, working-class Catholics. The major criticism fell not on Quealey and Kutz but on Joseph C. Wey (the superior general), Kelly, and McNeil, who found themselves jockeyed into the position of public enemies and abdicators from responsibility. When the Basilians of St Michael's were brought together in the spring of 1967 to express by ballot their preference for superior during the following year, the vote indicated that their confidence in McNeil was shaken. The response of the general council was to terminate McNeil's superiorship, much to his satisfaction, after the completion of five of the six canonical years of his appointment.

A lesser man might have been broken, an ambitious man might have fought back and retained his appointment for the remaining year; an impatient religious would probably, as Kutz ultimately decided to do, have followed 'la voie courte,' left the community and taken a wife. McNeil continued with increased vigour the teaching career he had never allowed his superiorship to interrupt.

In July 1967, the present superior of St Michael's, Robert J. Madden, a younger brother of John Madden, came into office. He was the first superior to be virtually named by his subjects. Young, personable, and zealous, he was inclined to espouse the causes of the aggressive and innovating, to be kindly and friendly towards the old guard. His first years were a mixture of joys and disappointments. His principal joy was the almost universal support of his priests both liberal and conservative, his sorrow the defection of several of the colleagues who campaigned to elect him.

It would be futile to claim that the division of jurisdiction between president and superior was entirely without anomaly and strain. Clash is inevitable between a superior who must give priority to the theology of mission and to the spiritual and corporal health of his men, and the president whose sights are fixed on scholarship and the teaching commitment. Yet there was already at St Michael's a consensus that the principle of the division of offices was valid and that the details were and would always remain negotiable. There was also a consensus that St Michael's would hardly have survived the renewal without the legal division of authority and responsibility.

University Government: The Collegium

Kelly's major inherited task was the implementing of the University of St Michael's College Act, that is, providing St Michael's with a new government. The official date of his taking office was 28 August 1958. This meant that Shook was, technically, the first president under the new act; and it was Shook who presided over the inaugural meeting of the collegium, 2 July 1958. The two significant items of this first meeting of the collegium were the formal statement of the collegium's objectives,' and the announcement that the Basilian Fathers had appointed a new president and registrar.

The objectives have an interest of their own: 'To establish St Michael's as a university in its own right; to preserve as long as possible the principle of university federation; to provide St Michael's with satisfactory machinery for holding property, for carrying on all necessary business in a legal, expeditious manner; to accomplish these objectives within the spirit and the letter of the constitutions of the priests of St Basil and of canon law.'[71]

The second meeting of the collegium, 22 September 1958, met with

71 Minutes of the Collegium, meeting of 2 July 1958

Kelly in the chair; with H.V. Mallon, J.F. Madden, E.J. McCorkell, and J.S. Kelly the *ex officio* members; and with J.W. Dore, L.K. Shook, and M.P. Sheedy as the elected members. At this session Kelly began the long hard work of implementing the act, announcing as a beginning that a senate would shortly be established.

The record of the meetings of the collegium from 1958 to 1970 is the most impressive accumulative document in the long history of St Michael's. It contains the detail of the material and structural development of the university: the opening of the new Loretto; the accompanying contract between St Michael's and the Sisters of Loretto designed to assure that the portion of the Canada Council capital grant made in their favour should never cease to serve the new university; the establishing of lay professors' salaries at the going campus levels; the placing of all sisters and non-Basilian priests serving on the college staff on a firm contractual if still 'contributed-service' basis; the floating of a $700,000 loan to pay off the outstanding indebtedness on Elmsley Hall and the more recent additions to the heating plant; the demolition of 21 St Mary Street and the sale of that property in 1963 for private housing; the decision in 1966 to make a major addition to Brennan Hall providing for enlarged kitchens and the creation of a large student-faculty centre; the purchase of 113 St Joseph Street (the monastery of the Sisters of the Precious Blood) in 1967; the arrangements for the ultimate acquiring of the use of the old Ontario Research Foundation buildings; and, the culmination of a long dream, the engaging of an architect and the signing of a contract for a three-and-a-half-million-dollar library complex.

Two of these items merit special comment as revealing the spirit of Kelly's policy: the procuring of the vacated Ontario Research property, and the building of the new library.

The property long accupied by the Ontario Research Foundation lay along the east side of Queen's Park Crescent between St Joseph Street and St Joseph's College on Wellesley Street. When the Foundation removed to Sheridan in 1967, the property was on the way to being placed on the open market. By any standards it was a desirable property but especially to St Michael's, which completely surrounded it. Kelly presented the college interests to the prime minister and was largely responsible for the government's decision not to sell to private investors but to turn the property back to the University of Toronto.[72] Kelly is also responsible for the further decision of the board of governors to

72 This Queen's Park property was part of the original grant to the University of Toronto: the university had allowed it to pass into private ownership during the nineteenth century.

lease the property to St Michael's, after a few years of emergency use, on terms similar to those of the lease covering the property on Queen's Park north of St Joseph Street. This is the most encouraging property development at St Michael's since the twenties.

The second item involving Kelly and the collegium (and the senate too, as will become apparent) was the decision to build a new and adequate university library on the site vacated by the Sisters of the Precious Blood. This was a similarly encouraging project if frighteningly costly. It marked the coming of age of the University of St Michael's College. A new library concept took on new proportions, becoming a true 'university' library within the terms of the act, a supra-college, supra-theology, supra-Institute undertaking. The library's realization became the dominant fashioning force behind Kelly's many (too many, according to some of his colleagues) financial, organizational, and academic undertakings.

Some of these undertakings with the library-focussed pattern ultimately in mind were the following: he designated the residue of the Canada Council's capital grant (previously drawn on for Loretto and the student-faculty centre)[73] as being held for this purpose; he reopened with the general council and the high school the undetermined matter of the true ownership of the lands north of the high school property on St Clair Avenue and not used for the high school itself or its endowment, and he succeeded in obtaining an agreement that when this property is sold, 20 per cent of it will go to the Basilian Fathers, 60 per cent to the University of St Michael's College, and 20 per cent towards the endowment of the Institute, allocating such benefits as thereby accrue to St Michael's to the library account; he stepped up the capital of the Foundation by adding to it funds held over since the 1952 campaign, as well as all major bequests since that time, and by introducing a more modern investment policy, increasing the number of foundation directors to twelve, adding to the board William J. Lyons, David Roche, John H. Coleman, Stephen B. Roman, William F. James, Harry T. Carmichael, Joseph T. Crothers, T. D'Arcy Leonard, George T. Smith, and Harold J. Murphy, men whose advice could assure an informed investment policy. Still with the university library in mind, Kelly worked indefatigably to encourage the Ontario government to abandon its static anti-ecclesiastical fiscal policy in matters purely educational and to help him with the education of those citizens whom personal convic-

73 This grant, made in 1957, provided St Michael's with a total of $978,203; $400,000 for Loretto, $504,253 for the student-faculty centre, and $73,951 for the library.

tion has located in St Michael's. Similarly, within his own university, he encouraged St Basil's Seminary and the Pontifical Institute to collaborate with his library plans. The seminary turned its collection over to the new library without conditions. The Institute retained ownership over its holdings and, without dispersing them in any way, gratefully relocated its collection on the fourth storey of the new library building.

The announcement from Kelly and the collegium, made in 1967, that St Michael's would proceed with a four-storey library complex was epoch-making both for its magnificence and its vision. The building went up on the old Precious Blood Monastery property at 113 St Joseph Street and was designed by the Toronto architect John J. Farrugia working in consultation with a committee of the faculty spearheaded by a group of librarians including Bernard Black, Harold Gardner, Margaret McGrath, and Donald Finlay. It received the following collections: the undergraduate library of 65,000 volumes; a theological library of 22,000 volumes transferred from the Basilian seminary; and the specialized holdings, 40,000 volumes, of the Pontifical Institute of Mediaeval Studies.

The decision to build the library was part of the overall plan to develop St Michael's within the vision of the new act. The act set up the collegium. The collegium, in turn, directly took responsibility for the faculty of arts, the St Michael's College Foundation, the residence halls, the chancellorship, the library, and, indirectly, the high school, the seminary, and the Institute of Mediaeval Studies. The launching of a university library strictly so-called implements the function of the collegium in one of its most significant areas.

University Government: The Senate

Kelly committed himself at the second meeting of the collegium to establish the new senate called for by the act. He gave great care to the choosing of its first members with a view to representing every academic interest touched by the University of St Michael's College, including both the alumni and that wide general constituency served by the university. The new senate held its inaugural meeting on 2 December 1960, and took over the following functions: the granting of degrees in theology, the establishing of faculties and councils, the admitting and examining of students, the establishing of fellowships and scholarships, and the convening of convocation. In one sense these were limited functions in that under the terms of federation, many powers had been handed over to the University of Toronto; neverthe-

less, considerable scope remained for the St Michael's senate even in
these areas.

The senate acquired another function quite as important in its way as
the above: communication and information. It became the senate's task
to keep the entire college constituency aware of what was going on not
only in St Michael's itself but in education generally, especially at the
municipal, provincial, and federal levels. The establishment of the
senate placed St Michael's on the way to becoming a more effective
public institution. It began at once to deal with many highly significant
items, chief among them the establishing of a graduate school of
theology.

The senate undertook early in its career to carry out for St Michael's
the major piece of self-analysis called for by the Deutsch Report, the
first major report of the presidents of Ontario's provincially-supported
universities published in 1962. The import of the report was brought
to the attention of the constituency of the college, a non-provincially-
supported university, by a senate committee under the chairmanship of
Professor D.F. Theall. The Theall Report is one of the finest documents
to appear on the aims of a Catholic university and on the relations that
ought to obtain between a federated college and the parent university.
Its 25 recommendations provided a kind of contemporary record of
the paths being followed by St Michael's in higher education in Canada.

Other matters dealt with through busy committees and reported in
significant documents were the development of the library programme
(Black Report, 1963) and the material and academic development of St
Michael's itself (Dunphy Report, 1966). The senate's activity gave St
Michael's a new concept of confrontation and discussion on a wider
basis than the college had ever experienced before.

Dominant among all the Kelly policies as reflected in the deliberations
and acts of the senate was the development of a strong graduate faculty
of theology. There was some background to this development. There
was, as already dealt with, the teaching of theology to aspirants for the
priesthood within the college itself, or in St Basil's and St Augustine's
seminaries. This was professional theology at the primary level serving
the needs of the Church's ministers. On a few occasions in McLaughlin's
time and in Bondy's, informal summer courses in theology or religion
had been provided for a general public, but there had been no continuously organized programme of theology for either regular or extension students.

The revision of the college's incorporation in 1954 provided for civil
credit, that is, the awarding of civil degrees in theology, to St Michael's

graduates from the two professional seminaries associated with the college. This revision involved no reorganization of theology itself, but only academic recognition for the work already being done in these seminaries.

Academic recognition, however, along with the appointment of deans in theology – Walter H. Principe for St Basil's, Vincent Keating for St Augustine's – had salutary effects on students and professors alike. Dean Principe and Eugene Malley, rector of St Basil's, were especially keen to give balance and spread to their teaching faculty and, with this in mind, added to the seminary's staff, in the summer of 1959, Gregory Baum, recently arrived from doctoral studies in Freiburg. A year later Kelly gave Baum a further appointment, to the religious knowledge department at St Michael's. With men like Principe, Baum, Häring, Eschmann, Malley, and Crooker already on campus, and with Kutz, Belyea, Elmer, and Maloney studying theology abroad, Kelly began to think seriously about establishing a graduate department of theology. Setting up a senate and introducing graduate theology to the campus were closely associated in his thinking.

The first meeting of the senate, 2 December 1960, made clear how close this association was. The two seminaries were given representation in the senate and Principe was named dean of the incipient faculty. At Kelly's request, Principe went to work immediately on plans for a graduate faculty of theology, formally introducing it at the meeting of 27 April 1962, the same meeting at which the senate's statutes were passed. In the summer of 1962 Stanley Kutz joined the staff and in the fall offered a graduate course in moral theology. This same year the two-year programme to the master of arts in theology got under way with eight students registered in the second year of the new programme and five in the first. The MA in theology was awarded for the first time in the fall of 1963.

In the summer of 1963 Edgar Bruns joined the graduate theology staff as professor of sacred scripture, and in the fall of the same year the programme for the PHD in theology was announced. In 1968 the first PHDS from St Michael's were awarded to Joanne Dewart and James A. Finnegan.

In the fall of 1964 there was begun a regular extension programme in theology under the direction of Lawrence Elmer. From the beginning this course was successful, attributable no doubt to the renewed interest in theology aroused by Vatican II and to the thoughtful attention which Elmer gave to it. In 1965, the senate decided to transform this extension course in theology into adult or continuing education. The decisive factor in this decision was the willingness of the Metropolitan Separate School Board to recognize the programme as satisfying its requirements for the continuing education of its teachers. In 1965, three courses were offered in the summer session and four for the night sessions during the fall and winter. In the spring of 1966, the extension department granted its first certificate in continuing or adult education. The senate was careful to point out that the certificate was in continuing education, not in theology; but the certificate was significant all the same in that it was indicative that religious studies outside the seminary were part of pedagogical as well as educational strategy.

To return to graduate theology. At the end of the year 1963–4, Principe resigned as dean and chairman of the faculty of theology in order to give himself unreservedly to teaching and to the publication of his mammoth study of the hypostatic union in the writings of mediaeval scholars like William of Auxerre, Alexander of Hales, Hugh of St Cler, and Philip the Chancellor. He was succeeded by Edgar Bruns.

Under Bruns, theology continued to develop. More scholars joined the school: Timothy Suttor in 1964, Arthur Gibson in 1966, and Joseph O'Connell and Herbert Richardson in 1968, competent authorities in ecclesiastical history, patristics and contemporary atheism, the spirituality and sociology of India, and modern American theology, respectively. The growing department effected in 1966 an affiliation with the Toronto Graduate School of Theological Studies (TGSTS), reorganizing the advanced degree programme in conjunction with the non-Catholic faculties of Emmanuel, Knox, Wycliffe, and Trinity colleges. In line with this ecumenical development, and not unrelated to it, was the addition to the staff in 1967 of Leslie Dewart, controversial process theologian and author of *The Future of Belief*, who transferred into theology from the department of philosophy.

Early in the academic year 1968–9 a TGSTS committee was set up through the assistance of the American Association of Theological Schools, to recommend a structure for full or nearly full collaboration in theology on the Toronto campus as a whole. The committee recommended a single school granting its own degrees in theology on behalf of the constituent theological schools and faculties. The schools and faculties compromised with the recommendation. They agreed to phase out TGSTS and establish a Toronto School of Theology (TST); they agreed to give the degrees MTH and DTH to their candidates; but they decided to confer the normalized degrees individually by their own separate charters as they had been doing all along.

This development looked after theological students proceeding to the ministry, not academic and research students seeking the MA and PHD in the area of theological disciplines. Thus Bruns in 1969 led his faculty in still another direction by transforming the academic part of it into an Institute of Christian Thought (ICT) with a view partly to academic and research degrees and partly to future collaboration with a proposed school of religious studies within the graduate school of the University of Toronto itself.

The senate also set up a council of the faculty, through which the staff voice began to be heard in a new way. The primary concern of this council was curriculum and instruction in the arts subjects, including religious knowledge. Since the council dealt with matters directly affecting students, it became the body in which student-staff liaison was discussed and encouraged. When the contemporary demand for some student role in government came to the campus, it was to the council that a contingent of student representatives was first admitted, although student representation was not restricted to this body. Pressures brought to bear on Kelly during 1968–9 led to his forming a presidential committee to study the government of St Michael's. The appointment of such a committee was typical of Kelly's constant and close attention to the development of the governmental bodies of St Michael's and his openness on the whole matter of the governance of universities.

Faculty Development: Financial Problems

St Michael's changed greatly during the Kelly years, more than can be adequately stated, by reason of the strengthened collective stature and depth of the academic staff, and especially of its non-Basilians. Academically speaking, the teaching faculty ceased to be predominantly Basilian. This was startlingly reflected in the appointment of non-Basilians as departmental heads: classics – James J. Sheridan, priest of the archdiocese of Toronto, formerly of the staff of St Augustine's Seminary; English – Richard J. Schoeck, layman from Cornell and Notre Dame, associate editor of the Yale St Thomas More and the Toronto Erasmus series; French – Richard B. Donovan, Basilian, authority on liturgical drama; German – Victoria Mueller-Carson, laywoman from the former Loretto faculty; philosophy – Lawrence E.M. Lynch, layman, Toronto graduate, graduate school administrator; religious studies – Arthur G. Gibson, priest of the archdiocese of Winnipeg. These heads were all scholars of recognized distinction, and all, with the exception of Dr Carson, named to their headship by Kelly himself. Behind them in 1969 were departments of considerable depth comprising 38 Basilians, 15 sisters, 18 non-Basilian priests, 93 laymen –

a large staff, indeed, even allowing for some inflation of the number of laymen by the inclusion of teaching fellows, and considering that university federation made necessary the maintaining of only six college departments. The large lay group included, exclusive of the faculty of the Pontifical Institute, international scholars like Marshall McLuhan, David Dooley, Leslie Dewart, Herbert Richardson, August Rakus, Robert O'Driscoll, and William Dunphy.

Maintaining this large, competent, highly specialized, and predominantly lay staff required a large annual outlay, accentuated in that the increased student body, screened and intelligent, had to be supported with fellowships, scholarships, and bursaries on a scale never contemplated before. Although contributed services by Basilians, non-Basilian priests, and sisters remained considerable, the general financial condition worsened as the gap between normal operating expenses and normal revenues widened.

It was to this area of normal revenues that Kelly gave much of his attention. It was his assumption that if he matched the state-supported colleges and universities in measurable excellence and facilities, regular subsidies would be forthcoming from the provincial government. The assumption proved invalid. The Ontario government's denominational squeeze caught him at almost every turn. A student enrolled in his college in 1969 was worth less in government-support dollars not only than one enrolled in Toronto, York, Carleton, or Windsor, but less than one enrolled in Trinity and Victoria on the same campus. A student enrolled in the Pontifical Institute of Mediaeval Studies, which Kelly had in large part to support, was in 1969 worth one formula-financing unit to the college; the same student would (had he been enrolled in the University of Toronto and taken there the same courses from the same professors) have been worth from three to five units to the University of Toronto, without having had to suffer the personal indignity of being excluded as ineligible from $2000-a-year personal assistance through a Province of Ontario Graduate Scholarship. The fiscal situation of St Michael's under Kelly was seriously dangerous.

The financial picture from 1960 to 1970, however, was not one of unrelieved gloom. Normal revenues did increase; donations and bequests began to come in on a larger scale than ever before; good advice enlarged the capital of the Foundation; and the post of treasurer was expertly served by its Basilian incumbent, Norman M. Iversen. Of significance, too, for the college was the success of the University of Toronto's National Fund and its successor the Varsity Fund.

Toronto's National Fund, co-chaired by M. Wallace McCutcheon and

Neil J. McKinnon, and completed in 1960, raised a grand total of nearly $16,000,000. St Michael's participated fully in this campaign and received $1,000,000 as its share of the revenue. The National Fund was continued by the Varsity Fund – an alumni programme of annual giving – which brought St Michael's unprecedented annual alumni revenues from $7000 in 1961 to over $24,000 in 1969. These special revenues, plus the sale of some of the St Clair Avenue property and houses on St Mary Street looked after much of the capital costs incurred by the building of the student-faculty centre and the new library.

The University of St Michael's College under Kelly was not without other than financial problems. Looming up largely at the end of the sixties were two vital issues: whether religious orders should or would step out of their time-honoured role as missionary proprietors; and whether the university ought, in view of the temper of the times, to become fully or at least partially secularized. The answer to these problems had come to some institutions before the turn into the seventies; it had not come to St Michael's.

The Pontifical Institute of Mediaeval Studies

TORONTO

(1929)

The Pontifical Institute of Mediaeval Studies, Toronto, is an autonomous teaching and research institute, at the graduate and post-doctoral levels, specializing in the thought and culture of the middle ages as recoverable and as bearing on man in subsequent times including the present. The Institute is located at 59 Queen's Park Crescent, East, Toronto 5, in accommodations provided by the University of St Michael's College. The Institute was founded in 1929; received a charter from the Holy See in 1939; is supported by St Michael's College, the Basilian Fathers, and its own fellows; offers courses leading to the licentiate and doctorate in mediaeval studies; provides a specialized research library for scholars generally; and publishes materials relating to its specialization. It is governed by a president and a council of faculty and fellows according to statutes drawn up by itself and approved by the Holy See.

THE FOUNDING OF THE INSTITUTE

A number of Canadian Catholic colleges and universities have with the passing of the years entered in a relatively modest way the fields of graduate and research study. St Francis Xavier of Antigonish generated a co-operative movement and crowned it with the Coady International Institute; St Patrick's of Ottawa established an important School of Social Welfare; and St Michael's of Toronto directed large resources in men and money to the development of a professional and scholarly Institute of Mediaeval Studies. The history of these projects[1] shows how well and under what difficulties Catholic post-secondary education functions at the post-graduate and research levels. For the purposes of the present study, the Institute of Mediaeval Studies can serve as the paradigm.

The Pontifical Institute was the product of three distinct movements: the extraordinary flowering of scholastic philosophy in the late nineteenth and early twentieth centuries; the bold and progressive experimentation in the federating of provincial and sectarian colleges in

1 For the Coady International Institute, see above, 91–2; for St Patrick's School of Social Welfare, see below, 255

Canada; and a sudden maturing of American universities which made them attractive even to the best European scholars.

The first of these movements, the unprecedented revival of mediaeval scholasticism, received special encouragement when Pope Leo XIII in his *Aeterni Patris* of 1879 invited scholars to study philosophy 'according to the mind of St Thomas.' There was great activity in academic centres like Munich, Louvain, and Paris for many years following the appearance of this encyclical. By 1914 when World War I broke out, these new studies were taking two directions: one of these was more committedly scientific, the other perhaps more historical. Grabmann's researches into scholastic method[2] and Mercier's attempt to systematize mediaeval thought[3] reflect the first, Mandonnet's discovery of Averroism in Siger of Brabant the second.[4] The new study of mediaeval thought was already moving in diverging lines. Both of these trends were to appear in Toronto, but since it was the Paris trend which was to be more influential there, it should be looked at more closely.

In 1920, the war well past, appeared the first edition of Etienne Gilson's *Le Thomisme*. Shortly afterwards, in 1921, came the *Bulletin du Cange*; then, in 1924, *Bulletin Thomiste* and in 1926 the *Archives d'histoire doctrinale et littéraire du moyen âge*. The excitement of Paris was felt in America and scholars were wondering how to become part of the movement. The same excitement, felt in Toronto because it struck another chord, made men wonder whether the movement itself could not be brought there. It seemed to offer a solution to a quite unrelated problem.

This brings up the second movement. Since 1906, the University of Toronto had been functioning satisfactorily as a federated university. Three religious colleges were working in collaboration with a non-sectarian university college as the four constituents of a common faculty of arts. Collaboration in arts and science at the undergraduate level, with sharing of programmes and facilities, was producing with economy a basically state-supported university which nevertheless gave indirect aid to religious institutions, and at the same time seemed to be producing a university of considerable academic prestige. The system had advantages and disadvantages for the religious college. The great academic advantage offered was the opportunity to provide prestigious

2 Martin Grabmann, *Thomas von Aquin: Eine Einführung in seine Persönlichkeit und Gedankenwelt*, Kempten, Munich, 1912

3 L. De Raeymaeker, *Le Cardinal Mercier et L'Institut Supérieur de Philosophie de Louvain*, Louvain: Publications Universitaires, 1952

4 Pierre Feliz Mandonnet, *Siger de Brabant et l'averroisme latin au XIIIme siècle*, Fribourg, Suisse, 1899

honours courses in fields congenial to the ethos of a given college – in the case of St Michael's, the Catholic college, in philosophy, and especially in scholastic philosophy. The great disadvantage, however, was that the colleges were cut off at the graduate level. No outlet was provided for the more profound interests of staff or students either in graduate study or in independent research. Thus the same system of federation which made it economically possible for St Michael's to undertake honours work made it very difficult for it to provide the academic atmosphere proper to a staff capable of teaching that work.

Several means of coping with this limitation were tried at St Michael's. Thus Henry Carr, the superior, instituted a policy of bringing distinguished scholars to St Michael's for lectures, for one-semester appointments, and occasionally as full-time members of the staff. In April 1919 Maurice de Wulf of Louvain, disciple of the great Mercier, gave a course of eight lectures in Convocation Hall on the themes 'Civilization and Philosophy in the Heart of the Middle Ages.' For some time de Wulf came annually to Toronto and a few calendars of the twenties list him among the members of the permanent staff as professor of the history of mediaeval philosophy. In December 1919, Sir Bertram C.A. Windle came to St Michael's as a permanent member of the staff with an appointment in anthropology. In 1925 Gerald B. Phelan, recent agrégé of Louvain, was given a full-time appointment in psychology. Hilaire Belloc gave some lectures at the college in history in 1923; Professor Léon Noël spent the fall of 1926 at St Michael's and was to return in 1930 for the Institute's first and only summer course. Etienne Gilson gave his first series of lectures in Toronto in January and February 1927, returning for a second series in 1928. The Canadian Franciscan, Ephrem Longpré, palaeographer and textual scholar from Quaracchi, lectured on Thomas of York during the spring of 1928. This policy was one answer to the academic limitations of university federation. A second attempt to induce deeper scholarship can be seen in the establishing during the early twenties of a highly successful Philosophical Society. This society had a remarkable career at St Michael's. Nearly all the scholars named above were at some time active speakers and participants as were all the professors of philosophy both at St Michael's and in the University of Toronto. Many of the papers read at the meetings of the society dealt in a serious way with mediaeval philosophy. There was a good deal of interest in the Middle Ages shown around St Michael's before the Institute was thought of.[5]

5 The foregoing material has been assembled from the St Michael's College yearbooks between 1919 and 1930. These books can be found in the archives of the undergraduate library of St Michael's College.

It is only fair to point out that interest in the Middle ages in the twenties was by no means peculiar to St Michael's. Many American scholars were genuine mediaevalists and there were mediaevalists in Canada too. James F. Willard's bulletins, *Progress of Medieval Studies in the United States of America* list a total of 60 mediaevalists for 1923 and 328 for 1926. Neither figure is complete. What was unique at St Michael's in so far as the American continent was concerned, was the intense interest in the specifically philosophical thought of the Middle Ages from both the scientific and the historical points of view. Further, it was a desire to carry on research in mediaeval thought in the wider context of the entire civilization of the period that produced the Institute of Mediaeval Studies in 1929. The actual founding came about as follows.

During September 1926, the Sixth International Congress of Philosophy was held at Harvard. Dr Léon Noël and Professor Etienne Gilson attended as the delegates of their respective universities, Louvain and Paris. Following the congress, Noël spent the fall at St Michael's, Gilson at Harvard. Gilson visited Montreal and Toronto from Harvard. He came to Toronto for the first time in January 1927. He already had in mind a project for trying to make intelligible to modern times the nearly fifteen centuries of civilization which had been largely suppressed and rather generally divorced from its own philosophical and theological thought. This project was a research institute in mediaeval studies, and he had raised the matter privately in Paris and more openly at Harvard. When he raised the matter in Toronto, as he did in February 1927,[6] it was immediately taken up as the adequate solution to some of the problems created by university federation in that it was work at an advanced level, yet not work intruding upon the preserves of graduate education as then understood. Moreover, it was a solution in line with the special interests which had been developing in Toronto for at least a decade. Gilson returned to St Michael's during the next academic year, 1927–8, and accepted a permanent post on the staff of St Michael's 'in order to cooperate in the organization of the Institute of Mediaeval Studies and to direct the work of this department.'[7]

The Basilian Fathers held a regular general chapter during the summer of 1928. The question of founding the institute was referred to it because the life-long commitment of Basilian personnel was involved.

6 Etienne Gilson, 'Why Not?,' *The Year Book 1927: St Michael's College,* Toronto, 32–3. See also his unsigned article 'The University Will Lead the Way,' in *University of Toronto Monthly,* 27 (Mar. 1927), 253–4, and his signed article 'St Michael's Establishes Institute of Mediaeval Studies,' *University of Toronto Monthly,* 28 (Dec. 1927), 119–21.

7 G.B. Phelan, 'Our New Professor,' *The Year Book 1928: St Michael's College,* Toronto, 26

The case for the institute was presented by McCorkell and Carr, superiors of St Michael's College and St Basil's Seminary, and was given a good hearing both by Francis Forster, the superior general of the Basilians, and by the chapter as a whole. The project was approved.[8] A year later, 29 September 1929, the Institute of Mediaeval Studies was formally opened in a ceremony held in St Basil's Church, Archbishop Neil McNeil presiding. Henry Carr was named first president, Etienne Gilson, director of studies, Gerald B. Phelan, librarian, and Henry S. Bellisle, secretary. E.J. McCorkell, superior of St Michael's College, was an officer and a founder *ex officio*; in 1929 he launched a public appeal for funds to develop both college and institute. This campaign was led by John F. Boland, KC. The most spectacular and important gift was that of Frank P. O'Connor, in the amount of $125,000 to be paid at the rate of $12,500 a year for ten years to provide books and photostats for the Institute Library.

Thus does one record the institute's founding. In setting down or in reading the facts, however, it is well to recall that the essential vision was of an instructional and research project at the graduate level which would take scholars into all branches of mediaeval studies but in such a way that they would not be unmindful of the central position of theology and philosophy.

FIRST PHASE 1929–35: HENRY CARR, PRESIDENT

In his keynote address to the regional convention of the American Catholic Philosophical Association meeting 7 June 1933 in San Francisco, Thomas Gorman, first bishop of Reno, spoke of America's need for scholarship at small expense and cited the Toronto institute and its buildings as a prime example: 'The interesting new Medieval Institute at St Michael's College in the University of Toronto uses an old two-storey dwelling house for its work, yet Gilson and Maritain passed over tempting offers in numerous American universities, Catholic and secular, to go there this year to teach. It isn't the building that counts; it's the library and the staff, men and books, not brick and stone.'[9] The founders of the institute certainly adhered to this principle. They had two sources of special revenue during the early thirties: $32,000 over six years from the Carnegie Corporation of New York and the $125,000 over ten years from Senator Frank P. O'Connor. The first of these

8 Henry S. Bellisle, *The Institute of Mediaeval Studies*, Toronto: St Michael's College Pamphlets, 1933. See Basilian Archives. See also H.S. Bellisle, 'Address Given at the Loretto Abbey College Re-Union, August 1933,' *Loretto Rainbow*, 40 (1933), 77–85.

9 *The Monitor* of San Francisco, 10 June 1933, 12

revenues went into the training of six young professors released for mediaeval studies by the Basilian Fathers, the second into purchasing materials for what is possibly the finest research library in mediaeval studies on the American continent.

Yet the founders would have been unwilling to speak disparagingly of their material setting. When the institute was opened in 1929, it was assigned quarters of its own (and this was an important consideration) in the former residence of Sir John Willison, Toronto financier, at 10 Elmsley Place. The house was not large and was not intended to be the permanent home of the Institute, but it was eminently suitable in that the artist who built the house and from whom Sir John acquired it, had provided not only the amenities of a pleasant home but the special convenience of a spacious studio designed for his own use with a large northern light and with its private family entrance from the second storey leading past a cozy den, over a narrow balcony, and down into the working area by way of a handsome if miniature spiral staircase. Willison's studio served as library and special lecture room for the Institute from 1929 to 1936. It imparted a subtle charm and dignity to the project which served it well both then and in subsequent years. When the present Institute was opened at 59 Queen's Park Crescent in 1936 in the north wing of a long stone collegiate-Gothic building, its lovely reading and reference room recalled the original studio by retaining a northern light and a staircase spiralling down from a narrow balcony.

The original faculty of the institute consisted of the following: Etienne Gilson, founder and professor of the history of mediaeval philosophy; Henry Carr, founder and professor of Greek and patristic backgrounds; Edmund J. McCorkell, founder, professor of English and president of St Michael's College; Gerald B. Phelan, founder, librarian, and professor of the philosophy of St Thomas Aquinas; Henry S. Bellisle, secretary and professor of the history of patristic thought; and Joseph T. Muckle, professor of mediaeval Latin. The associated faculty included professors in St Michael's College, especially J.B. O'Reilly and B.F. Sullivan, and professors in the graduate school of the University of Toronto, notably dean George S. Brett. Each year new men and new courses became available. A summer course was offered in July 1930 with regular courses by Carr, Bellisle, and Phelan and a special course by Léon Noël of Louvain. Martin Grabmann of Munich was also to have given a special course; but he had, for reasons of health, to withdraw at the last moment. The offering of a summer programme was not successful. It drew many students but was too demanding upon a staff involved in research and too ambitious for part-time students whose graduate work, at least in those years, could at best be auxiliary or peripheral. During the academic year 1930–1, palaeography was given for the first time by Father Muckle; also given for the first time in 1931 was mediaeval theology by M.D. Chenu, director of the Saulchoir's *Bulletin Thomiste*. Chenu had come to Canada partly to lecture at this institute and partly to organize mediaeval studies, especially Thomistic studies, at the Institut Saint Thomas d'Aquin organized by the Canadian Dominicans in 1930 at their Ottawa convent on Empress Avenue. This institute was later moved to Montreal.

The original programme of the Toronto institute comprised from the beginning in 1929 both introductory and advanced courses in mediaeval studies. It offered, too, an unaccredited licentiate diploma of its own for three years of successful work. Most students of the Institute were enrolled in the graduate school of the University of Toronto and were candidates for an accredited MA or PHD degree through that institution. Such an arrangement though informal was open and understood. Dean Brett regarded all Institute courses as approved courses given by professors of his own graduate school. The college authorities regarded their providing and subsidizing of these courses as an academic and financial contribution to the life of the university. The further question as to whether this kind of arrangement was technically covered by the University of Toronto Act, which did not provide for graduate work in the colleges except in theology, was not officially raised. The Institute, as institute, was private, autonomous, and without civil or ecclesiastical academic status. The university accepted the institute's existence as desirable and useful, affording it full benefit of its facilities, experience, and prestige. Officially and formally the university neither approved nor disapproved of the institute; practically and personally it welcomed it warmly and affectionately into its campus complex.

Two further matters were of major concern to Carr and the institute's administration during the early thirties: the training of a specialized staff, and the obtaining of ecclesiastical recognition. The first of these desiderata was achieved by the willingness of the general council of the Basilian Fathers to assign at first five, and subsequently other young priests to the work of the institute and of the Carnegie Corporation to contribute financially towards their preparation. Thus Alexander J. Denomy went to Harvard to work in old French under J.D.M. Ford; George B. Flahiff went to Strasbourg and Paris for historico-methodological training under Marcel Aubert, Léon Levillain, and the Ecole des Chartes; Terence P. McLaughlin studied the civil and canon laws first at Strasbourg then at Paris under Gabriel Le Bras; Vincent L. Kennedy worked on liturgy and archaeology with Michel Andrieu at Strasbourg and later with Conrad Kirch and Cunibert Mohlberg in Rome. J. Reginald O'Donnell trained in palaeography under Aleksander Birkenmajer in Cracow and under Edmund Faral, Josef Koch, and others in Paris. These men returned to Toronto in 1935 and, under Gilson, Phelan, and the original staff, which now included H.P. Coughlin in theology, initiated what has become the characteristic pattern of mediaeval studies and research in Toronto. Other Basilians who were sent off for mediaeval studies later in the thirties were Wilfrid J. Dwyer in philosophy, T. Vernon Kennedy in theology, and Laurence K. Shook in vernacular literature.

The matter of ecclesiastical accreditation was perhaps less urgent, but it was important for different reasons than the preceding and was much more delicate because it involved approaching Rome for approval of a new kind of academic body not really provided for by the apostolic constitution *Deus scientiarum dominus* of 1931, and which was to be in effect a pontifical academy of advanced studies outside the city of Rome. The obtaining of a pontifical charter was much discussed in Toronto between 1929 and 1934. The administration considered asking the Sacred Congregation of Seminaries and Universities for a faculty of philosophy or possibly of philosophy and theology. The Roman Congregation had not considered the possibility of anyone asking for a charter covering advanced study and research in mediaeval studies. Carr went to Rome in March 1934 where, joined by Gilson, he approached Monsignor Ernesto Ruffini and Cardinal Bisleti, secretary and prefect respectively of the Congregation, for a charter for the institute. It was Ruffini who advised Carr and Gilson to ask for what they wanted, a charter covering mediaeval studies, and not for something they did not want, like a faculty of philosophy. Ruffini also urged them to have their statutes prepared for submission immediately. Carr went to Paris and worked with T.P. McLaughlin on the first draft of the statutes; they finished the task in Rome where they worked in collaboration with V.L. Kennedy and Father Riccione, secretary to Ruffini. The first version of the statutes was ready for submission to the Congregation 28 June 1934. At one stage Carr thought that the charter might be put through at once, especially in view of the sympathy of Pius XI for the institute as expressed during a private audience on 8 May. When, however, the statutes were deposited and the request for a charter could be said to be under formal consideration, there was nothing else to do but to wait for the wheels of the official machinery to grind out the matter slowly and cautiously. Ever since 1931 when *Deus scientiarum dominus* appeared, all existing charters had been under review by the Congregation. It was expecting too much to think that the institute's application and statutes could be afforded special priority. Indeed, they were not. The preparing of the statutes, however, and the presenting of an application for a charter was almost the last of Carr's presidential activities. He told Gilson in Europe that Phelan would be the next president.[10]

The period of Carr's presidency was an experimental and a pioneer one. It was partly a holding operation until the return of the newly prepared professors in 1935, but by no means entirely so. Carr, Gilson, and Phelan commanded increasingly important prestige in university circles. The three of them almost surpassed themselves when they succeeded in bringing Jacues Maritain to the institute during 1932–3. This event made it quite clear that the Institute was an international project of primary importance. Maritain lectured annually at the Institute from 1932 to 1938. He lectured regularly during the war years of the forties and on special occasions since that time. He has maintained close and warm associations with Toronto during all the years. Carr's resignation in 1935 meant that Gerald B. Phelan, who became associate director in 1932 when Robert J. Scollard replaced him as librarian, would take over as president.

PONTIFICAL INSTITUTE: GERALD B. PHELAN, PRESIDENT

Gerald B. Phelan succeeded Henry Carr, becoming acting president of the Institute of Mediaeval Studies in 1935. The syllabus for 1935–6 offered a considerably expanded programme for that year with new courses in theology, law, liturgy, art and archaeology and history. The programme was still organized around the Toronto MA and PHD but called for more courses than were prescribed by the university for these degrees. The statutes submitted to the sacred congregation in 1934 were returned during 1936 for revision in the light of the congregation's recommendation. Thus the statutes could now be put into effect *ad experimentum*. The archbishop of Toronto, James Charles McGuigan, became chancellor in 1936 and formally nominated Gerald B. Phelan to the congregation for his appointment as president, which was ratified in 1937. At the same time the institute's Council of the Faculty became a reality and it immediately initiated the statutory academic programme. The new programme, effective in 1937–8, was organized around three

10 This material is sympathetically related in E.J. McCorkell, *Henry Carr: Revolutionary*, Toronto: Griffin House, 1969, ch.9, 74–106, and esp. 8off.

years of courses for a *diploma licentiae* and two additional years for a *diploma laureae*. It was still assumed that the Toronto degrees would be taken, but the academic programme was no longer organized around them. With the adopting of a statutory programme in 1937, it became essential that the institute obtain a charter empowering it to grant the degrees around which its programme was organized. Supported by his new chancellor, Phelan drew up a petition to the Holy See asking that the charter be granted. The signatures of all Canada's 48 bishops were attached to the petition. It was presented to Pope Pius xii by Cardinal Villeneuve of Quebec in the spring of 1939. The pontifical charter was promulgated on 19 October 1939.

During the years in which the programme was established and the charter obtained, there was also initiated an active publications policy. The first major item published from the institute was the mediaeval Latin translation, *Algazel's Metaphysics*, edited by J.T. Muckle in 1933. The following year three items were published including the important doctoral dissertation of Anton C. Pegis, *St Thomas and the Problem of the Soul in the Thirteenth Century*. Four more items were published during 1938 and 1939: two monographs by Emmanuel Chapman and Bernard Müller-Thym, and two translations by G.B. Phelan and Ralph MacDonald. Of great significance was the appearance in 1939 of the first volume of the institute's learned journal *Mediaeval Studies*. This annual, published at first at great financial loss and with very little circulation, but called for by the almost inherent right of research to publication, has become one of Canada's most distinguished publications and is to be found in all the world's leading library collections. *Mediaeval Studies* has appeared regularly since 1939. Its distinguishing policies include the printing of unpublished or unavailable texts (the first volume contained the *Summa de officiis Ecclesiae* of Guy d'Orchelles, the *Exigit ordo executionis* of Nicholas of Autrecourt, and four old French poems dealing with the life of St Barbara) and a decision not to publish book reviews or items of ephemeral interest. The result of now 31 years of publication is a collection of research materials indispensable wherever advanced study of the Middle Ages is carried on.

With the charter of 1939, Phelan began his term as first official and canonically appointed president of the Pontifical Institute of Mediaeval Studies. The period of his presidency of the pontifical body extended from 1939 to 1946. During this period of the forties the institute staff was substantially developed. T. Vernon Kennedy had been added in theology prior to the charter, that is, in 1937. During the charter year, 1939–40, Gerhart Ladner began to lecture in early Christian and mediaeval art and architecture; during 1942–3, Ignatius T. Eschmann, authority on the writings of St Thomas and professor in Rome (the Angelicum) and in Cologne before his forced emigration to Canada, began to deliver lectures on the theology and philosophy of St Thomas Aquinas; and during 1944–5, Anton C. Pegis, distinguished institute graduate of the early thirties and an institute fellow since 1933,[11] came from Fordham University as professor of philosophy in the Pontifical Institute.

Development of programme, publications, and library continued. But there were problems in these years too. The war, for example, hampered graduate activity, kept Gilson in Paris, interfered with research. There was also disagreement between Phelan and the general council of the Basilians over the proper exercise of the right of the order to appoint or to assign duties to Basilian professors holding an ordinary or extraordinary professorship from the Holy See. The matter came up in a variety of crises: when the general council wished to have institute professors provide courses in the seminary; when the superior general was disposed to appoint G.B. Flahiff to a military chaplaincy; when the general council actually appointed T.P. McLaughlin as superior and president of St Michael's College in 1940; and when the general council set up a community for Basilians of the institute under their own local superior. There was enough friction in these and other cases to raise doubts about whether Phelan could continue as president after his first term ended in 1946. The chancellor consulted the council of the institute, the superior general of the Basilians, and Phelan himself. Following these consultations he recommended to the sacred congregation that it name Anton C. Pegis to succeeded Phelan as president. Concurrently with these negotiations, Phelan accepted an offer from Notre Dame University to open a mediaeval institute in South Bend. This was only one of several offers received by him at this time. Phelan's decision to continue pioneering in this field was in line with Etienne Gilson's prediction sixteen years before that there would be many mediaeval research institutes in the years to come.[12] It was also in line with what has happened in the sixties when some twenty institutes and centres of mediaeval studies have been opened in America, England, and the continent.

11 The naming of fellows by the Institute Council was to have become regular practice. It provided an excellent method of recognizing a student's work prior to the obtaining of the charter. Only Pegis was ever named a fellow in this sense. The institute will revive the practice of naming fellows but on a different principle.

12 Letter of Etienne Gilson to Henry Carr, 17 June 1934, a copy of which is to be found in the institute's archives. See also L.K. Shook, 'University Centers and Institutes of Medieval Studies,' *Journal of Higher Education*, 38 (1967), 484–92.

Phelan directed the Notre Dame Institute until 1952, when he returned to Toronto to his professorships in St Michael's and the Pontifical Institute. Phelan was by training and temperament a profound metaphysician and a brilliant psychologist. His decision in the twenties to engage these talents in the forming of the Toronto institute was important not only for its academic identity in Canada and elsewhere but for the intense scholarly direction it was to take. Working closely with Gilson, who was director of studies, and with the scholars whose services he attracted to the project, he successfully and competently saw the venture through its crucial formative years.[13]

POST-WAR DEVELOPMENTS: ANTON C. PEGIS, PRESIDENT

Anton C. Pegis took over the presidency of the Pontifical Institute during the critical post-war years when graduate studies in America were experiencing unprecedented growth. His own specialty, the philosophy of man, his experience, and competence in both graduate education and the publishing world made him a particularly acceptable president. That he was a layman was also important in that it made perfectly clear that the institute was not ecclesiastical in any limited sense of the word. The Council's major achievements under his leadership between 1946 and 1954 were in academic organization, in expansion of PHD work, especially in philosophy, and in a wise and broad expansion of the faculty into areas other than philosophy.

Pegis was a good organizer – particularly of academic programmes whether of the institute as a whole or of individual students. He saw to it that there were directors for the theses undertaken and that students completed their doctoral studies. He gave himself very largely to this work. In one year every doctoral candidate presented to the school and senate of the University by the department of philosophy was an institute student.[14] At one time seven active doctoral candidates were under Pegis's personal direction.

Consolidation of study programmes was accompanied by a staff consolidation as well. Nicholas Häring (theology) joined the permanent staff in 1948; Armand A. Maurer (philosophy) in 1949; Joseph C. Wey

13 Phelan died in Toronto in 1965. See Anton C. Pegis, 'Gerald Bernard Phelan, 1892–1965,' *Mediaeval Studies*, 27 (1965), i–v; J.R. O'Donnell, 'Gerald Bernard Phelan, 1892–1965,' *Proceedings of the Royal Society of Canada*, 1965, 155–9; Arthur G. Kirn, ed., *G.B. Phelan: Selected Papers*, Toronto: Pontifical Institute of Mediaeval Studies, 1967.

14 In 1948 five institute students received their PHD in philosophy in the University of Toronto: Ignatius Brady, Alfred Caird, Peter Nash, Linus Thro, Thomas Fagin. See 'Chronique' in *Culture*, 9 (1948), 80. During 1950 nine doctoral candidates were institute students, in each of 1953 and 1954 the number was eight.

(Latin palaeography) in 1950; J. Joseph Ryan (history) and Joseph Owens (philosophy) in 1955. Also during this period, Pegis and the council brought a considerable number of distinguished teaching scholars to the institute for one semester or more: Henry Pouillon, 1948, and Fernand Van Steenberghen, 1950, from Louvain; Astrik Gabriel, 1947, from Budapest; Bernard Lonergan, 1946, from the Jesuit Seminary in Toronto; and Louis M. Regis, from Montreal; and Daniel Callus, 1949, from Oxford. The period of the late forties and early fifties was one of tangible results attributable in part to post-war expansion and the re-opening of scholarly communications with the rest of the world and in part to twenty years of sure, knowledgeable, demanding policy-making and of visionary objectives, but partly also to the efficiency, contacts, and drive of the Institute's first lay president.

Gratifying to the institute and its friends was the receipt on 30 May 1947 of a 'Letter of Praise' from Pius XII by the chancellor, Cardinal McGuigan. The pope wrote in part: 'From the very beginning of our pontificate, We have taken on Ourselves the Institute of Toronto, conferring upon it favour and authority ... We now gladly add an exhortation to encourage the professors and students of the Institute that they hold fast to their noble purpose, and that with industry and zeal on the part of the bishops, especially of Canada, it may flourish as time goes on.'

In 1952 Pegis was reappointed president of the Pontifical Institute for a second term of six years. In accepting the reappointment he informed the council that he hoped in the future to make a contribution towards the creating of a healthier atmosphere in the Catholic textbook situation. There was, he said, a real possibility of his resigning the office and withdrawing temporarily to the Catholic Textbook Division of Doubleday and Company, New York. This is what actually happened. He left the presidency in 1954, moved to New York, but returned each year for a series of lectures on subjects within his special competence and interest, thus never actually severing his relations with the institute. He returned to his full-time professorship in 1961. His resignation in 1954 made necessary a new presidential appointment which went on the advice of council to Edmund J. McCorkell, one of the founders of the institute, who had just completed two terms as superior general of the Basilian Fathers.

BASILIAN PRESIDENTS: EDMUND J. MCCORKELL, LAURENCE K. SHOOK

Edmund J. McCorkell was president of the Pontifical Institute from 1954 to 1961. He was succeeded in office by Laurence K. Shook. The years of their administration, 1954 to 1970, can be said to represent the contemporary phase and are less susceptible of historical analysis. McCorkell had a new type of problem to contend with: an enrolment falling by reason of the appearance of new graduate schools offering work in Christian philosophy; a decline of interest in Thomism especially among the graduates of Catholic colleges; stiff competition through generous scholarship policies for the best students in the country. The appearance of these problems called for an increased emphasis by the Pontifical Institute on mediaeval studies of a non-philosophical character, an even more pronounced interest in the historical approach to mediaeval studies; and finally, an accelerated public-relations and fund-raising programme.

McCorkell's first labours were presentations to foundations and private persons for much-needed funds. He initiated the Sloane and Michaelmas scholarships and set in motion a number of approaches which have since borne fruit in the helpful Dooley bequest and the donations of Mrs Harry Hatch and William J. Bennett. Above all McCorkell found new endowments for publications. This helped council to initiate its new series of *Studies and Texts*. This series began in 1955 with J.R. O'Donnell's edition of *Nine Mediaeval Thinkers*, a remarkable collection of texts edited for the first time from projects carried out in institute seminars. Between 1955 and 1970 nineteen volumes of *Studies and Texts* have appeared, containing much of the fine scholarly research carried on in recent years by the students and faculty of the Pontifical Institute.

The faculty itself continued to expand under McCorkell's directions with the adding of Ambrose J. Raftis in history (1954) and Edward Synan in philosophy (1959). There have also been unfortunate losses: A.J. Denomy was taken by death in 1957, G.B. Flahiff became superior general, 1954 and archbishop of Winnipeg in 1961 and a cardinal of the Church in 1969. Joseph C. Wey was also taken out of active institute work when he became superior general of the Basilians in 1961.

In 1961 Laurence K. Shook took over the presidency from McCorkell. Developments and changes during the period between 1961 and 1970 are difficult to assess but they were real and perhaps deep. There took place in 1961 and 1962 a revision or better, perhaps, a renewal of the entire programme. It became increasingly possible to give more attention to the integrity of the institute's programme as it became increasingly disengaged from the university's. The programme is closer today in structure to that of the late thirties than was the programme of the fifties. In 1962 the statutes of the Pontifical Institute were revised by a committee of council in order to remove anachronisms, to give academic recognition to the librarian, and to incorporate where possible the experience of the institute itself and of other graduate schools in recent times.

In 1962 the University of Toronto announced that it was about to initiate a Medieval Centre. The institute encouraged this move from the beginning as expanding campus-coverage of the increasing mediaeval fields and as enabling the institute itself to concentrate more intensely on its own more strictly professional post-doctoral and research projects. The institute placed its facilities at the use of the centre, succeeded in eliminating double registration in the institute and the university, and worked out a new way of collaboration by which at the end of his licentiate programme an institute student could elect to proceed to his doctorate in either the university or the institute. There is every indication that the new trend in collaboration will go further: that the university's centre will offer the institute's licentiate programme as one of its streams to the PHD in mediaeval studies and that it will administer and accredit it civilly under the senate; and that the institute will further develop its resources and facilities, placing them not only at the service of the centre but of all established and continuing post-doctoral scholars.

During the sixties there also took place some decentralizing and possibly some strengthening of peripheral, that is, non-academic yet vital, activities. Scholarships, once financed by the institute itself, were detached from the main operation and funded in an independent chancellor's fund set up in 1963 with a gift of one hundred thousand dollars by the chancellor, Archbishop Philip F. Pocock. Publications were made a financially distinct operation, but with policies coming as formerly from the council. This arrangement began under McCorkell when J.A. Raftis, as director of publications, set up machinery designed to streamline the operation which even by then had become too large and too demanding to be handled by academics in their spare time. In 1964 James Morro became director of publication and carried on the operation with editorial and advisory assistance from the faculty council. In both cases, however, that is, of the chancellor's fund and the department of publications, control remained in the council of the institute.

Professorial appointments during Shook's presidency were as follows: Michael M. Sheehan, who lectured in art and architecture from 1953 and in mediaeval history from 1961, was in 1964 appointed professor ordinarius in mediaeval history; in the same year, Walter H. Principe, on the staff since 1962, became ordinarius in theology; Leonard E. Boyle began in 1961 to come to the institute annually as visiting professor in palaeography and diplomatics, and was named ordinarius in these disciplines in 1966; Richard J. Schoeck, professor of English in

St Michael's since 1961 and of vernacular literature in the institute since 1964, and James A. Weisheipl, visiting professor in the history of science since 1963, were appointed ordinarii in 1967 and 1968 respectively; Brian Stock was taken on in mediaeval Latin, John Quinn in philosophy in 1966; James K. McConica in history in 1967, and Robert W. Crooker in law in 1968; Peter Brieger became visiting professor of mediaeval art in 1968, and in 1969 Michael Gough became professor of Christian archaeology and Edmund Colledge, professor in vernacular literature. During the same period there were losses: Vincent L. Kennedy and Hubert Coughlin retired from active teaching; and Gerald B. Phelan, Joseph T. Muckle, Ignatius Eschmann, and Terence P. McLaughlin were taken by death.

Following Vatican II, the reorganized Sacred Congregation for Catholic Education convoked a total of three Roman Congresses: one in 1967 to study and reform pontifical universities, faculties, and institutes; one in 1968 to modify and reform ecclesiastical seminaries; and one in 1969 on Catholic universities. J.R. O'Donnell represented English-speaking Canada at the first of these, L.K. Shook at the third. Far-reaching changes of external and internal structure and revisions of academic policies and strategies were as a consequence of these congresses undertaken in many Catholic institutions of higher learning. The institute, in line with this recent development, further revised its statutes and pattern of living with a view to increasing student participation and responsibility in its government, to the involving of a larger number of mature and experienced scholars in its collaborative research, and to pooling its resources more effectively with those of the graduate school of the University of Toronto. With these developments, the institute continued to move toward the fulfilment of its founders' vision of a teaching-researching-publishing body of professional scholars serving learning at its highest level where church and state inevitably and legitimately meet.

THE LIBRARY OF THE PONTIFICAL INSTITUTE

The preceding account presents the measurable chronology of the Pontifical Institute of Mediaeval Studies. It has consciously avoided the complex matter of the library holdings as this deserves separate treatment. The library has been the favourite child of founders, presidents, and council right from the beginning. It is the institute's laboratory and workshop. It establishes the limits to the work which the institute can do and it reflects at the same time the story of what it has accomplished. The holdings of the institute library form a unique special collection. They do not form the largest mediaeval library in the world nor the best supplied with manuscripts. They are, however, in terms of availability and arrangement, and within their own objectives, without equal anywhere.

The basis of the library, historically speaking, was the collection of about 2000 volumes gathered together during the twenties when the department of philosophy of St Michael's College was being developed. This collection contained such series as the *Acta Sanctorum*, both the *Series Latina* and the *Series Graeca* of Migne's *Cursus Patrologiae*, and a selection of incunabula. When the institute was opened in 1929, its best full-time scholar, Gerald B. Phelan, was appointed librarian, and its most handsome gift, that of Frank O'Connor, was assigned to the library. Phelan bought assiduously during the first three years when so many rare and important items were accessible in the bookshops of London, Paris, Rome, and elsewhere. What he acquired in those years is irreplaceable.

In 1932, when he became associate director of studies, Phelan was replaced in the library by his assistant, Robert J. Scollard. Scollard carried on the perceptive purchasing policies of Phelan. He had also, in the six or seven Basilians preparing abroad for the institute faculty and in Gilson himself and in others, purchasing agents of a particularly knowledgeable stamp. In 1939, Scollard introduced the Library of Congress classification and utilized its printed catalogue card service, a refinement not picked up by many Canadian librarians until much later. Scollard also became interested in writing and speaking about the library and has in one way or another preserved much of its history.[15] In 1951 Scollard decided to give more time to the developing of libraries in some of the Basilian houses and resigned from the institute in favour of his assistant, John F. Stapleton. Stapleton, like Scollard, was a qualified librarian and skilful in handling a special collection. The collection rose from 18,000 to 28,000 volumes during the years of his librarianship, 1951 and 1962. In 1962 he was succeeded by Harold B. Gardner. Gardner too was a successful librarian. He had to cope with greatly increased circulation, especially after the opening of the university's Centre for Medieval Studies and in view of the institute's policy of sharing with the university all its facilities. Gardner rearranged the collection, enlarged the reading room and cataloguing areas, and modernized the library in many ways including the introducing of

15 Consult R.J. Scollard, 'A List of Photographic Reproductions of Mediaeval Manuscripts,' *Mediaeval Studies*, 4 (1943), 126–38 and v (1944), 51–74; also 'The Walls are Lined with Books for Study and Research,' *The Catholic Library World*, 16 (1945), 140ff; and 'A Veritable Laboratory,' *Canadian Library Association Bulletin*, May 1951.

ultramodern xeroxing equipment. Gardner also built up a Gilson collection and produced what must soon become the best collection of a living author in America. He was also interested in the entire area of mediaeval bibliography and made the official report of the proceedings of the Conference of Medieval Bibliography held in Providence in 1964.[16] During 1967, Gardner took on special duties for the Basilian Fathers and turned over the institute librarianship to Donald F. Finlay. Finlay was able, in view of special grants over several years from the Canada Council, to step up purchases, especially of reprinted series and monographs. He also supervised the transfer of the collection to its new location in the library of the University of St Michael's College where it is housed and administered as a special collection of national significance.

The library of the Pontifical Institute has not been without recognition, not only for its specialized book collection of now about 40,000 volumes and 120 mediaeval periodical items, but also for its over 390,000 folios of microfilm and for its newly-launched slide collection. The important, if devastating, Williams Report on the resources of Canadian libraries for research paid the Pontifical Institute a conscious and deserved compliment when it singled out mediaeval studies as the only area in the humanities and social sciences in Canada, other than Canadian history, which can be said to provide for research in an outstanding way.[17]

The library has in recent years received a number of memorable gifts: a facsimile of the Vatican's premier manuscript of Holy Scripture, the *Codex Vaticanus* (Codex B) as a gift from Pope Paul VI, a facsimile of the Book of Durrow from the government of Ireland; the 76-volume Realencyclopädie of Pauly-Wissowa from the government of West Germany.

In addition to areas already mentioned, like microfilms, mediaeval periodicals and Gilsoniana, the library has particular depth in early philosophy, history, liturgy, editions of St Thomas, Maurist publications, cartularies, special series and collections (the Rolls, Monumenta Germaniae Historica, the Vienna Corpus, the Corpus Christianorum), old Norse, and old Provençal. In some of these cases the holdings are complete or practically so. Where gaps occur, as in old and middle English, Byzantine studies, and so on, it is because little work has been done at the institute in these areas and purchases have accordingly been

16 Harold B. Gardner, 'Current Trends in Mediaeval Bibliography,' *Mediaeval Studies*, 27 (1965), 309–21

17 E.E. Williams, *Report on Resources of Canadian University Libraries for Research*, Ottawa: NCCU, 1962, 48. See also 25, 26, 27, 28, 49.

light. Projects continue: buying is heavy today in history, in the micro-films of scriptural and philosophical commentaries and in Vatican ar-chival collections which are being systematically filmed on an endow-ment set up by Mrs Harry Hatch. In memory of the first president, the archival collection is now known as the Carr Memorial Collection.

The catalogue of the library has been completely microfilmed and is available in the National Library, Ottawa. Scholars seeking to use the institute's books may do so either by visiting the library itself, as many from all parts of the world do in increasing numbers, or through inter-library loan, on the condition that the book desired is neither irreplace-able nor in actual use. The project started in 1929 is today for practical purposes a national treasure in the public domain as well as a mediae-valist's paradise.

ENVOY

A final series of facts complete the present chronicle. The institute pos-sesses for the use of some future historian a set of records faithfully kept by a succession of secretaries or, as they are normally called in civil universities, registrars: Henry S. Bellisle 1929–32; Edmund J. McCorkell 1932–4; Vincent L. Kennedy 1934–44; George B. Flahiff 1944–52; Joseph C. Wey 1952–61; Robert W. Crooker since 1961. The archives created and preserved by these men will one day provide the fully digested and definitive story of the Pontifical Institute of Mediae-val Studies. The present survey but provides sign posts along a trail that will eventually call for a well-built highway.

St Augustine's College

SCARBOROUGH

(1910) 1964

St Augustine's College is a post-secondary school of arts and philosophy preparing young men for admission to a major seminary. The college was formally established by the archdiocese of Toronto in 1964. Its history extends back into and is part of that of the seminary itself. The college is located on the seminary campus, a property of some 130 acres at 2661 Kingston Road, Scarborough. Combined college and seminary buildings include: the original seminary (opened 1913), the residential annex (opened 1926), and the college proper (opened 1964). Lands and buildings have an estimated value of 12 million dollars. Between 1964 and 1969 the college was affiliated with the University of Ottawa and provided, through Ottawa and (after 1963) St Paul's, accreditation of students in arts and theology. St Augustine's College is now a non-accrediting, non-teaching school of arts and philosophy providing direction, residence, and religious orientation for students intending to enter the major seminary.

St Augustine's Seminary, which pre-dates the college by more than fifty years was undertaken as an 'extension' and regional seminary by archbishop Fergus P. McEvay in 1910.[1] It was designed by the Toronto architect, Arthur Holmes, built under the direction of Martin D. Whelan, rector of St Michael's Cathedral, and made possible by a gift of about half a million dollars by Eugene O'Keefe. The seminary with accommodation for 100 students was opened 28 August 1913. The first rector was John Thomas Kidd, later bishop of London. The original staff, though small, was a good one and had an international air about it. With the rector were several other professors from Canada, John R. Grant, Denis McBride, and Francis J. Morrissey; from the United States were Michael J. Ryan and Cyril Kehoe; from France, John M. Castex; from Ireland, Edward Kissane. Almost all of these held doctorates, two of them the PHD and Kissane, who at the time was only licenced in sacred scripture, was already launched on what was to be a distinguished career in scripture studies.

---

1 See above, 182–4. See also the jubilee booklet: *Fifty Golden Years, 1913–1963: St Augustine's Seminary*, eds. R.J. Dobell and Andrew Stevenson, Toronto: Mission Press, 1963.

St Augustine's was envisaged as a nationally important seminary on the Council of Trent pattern and functioning at the university level. The time was ripe for such an institution in Toronto: the new archbishop, Neil McNeil, was a former professor and president at St Francis Xavier University; and Toronto itself had become somewhat university-conscious as St Michael's College had only recently decided to enter the controversial University of Toronto federation.

Kidd remained rector of St Augustine's until 1925, when he was appointed bishop of Calgary. Succeeding rectors have been Joseph Anthony O'Sullivan, 1925–31 (later bishop of Charlottetown and archbishop of Kingston); Francis Patrick Carroll, 1931–6 (later bishop of Calgary); Edward Michael Brennan, 1936–46; John Henry Ingoldsby, 1946–54; Richard Joseph Dobell, 1954–68. On Dobell's resignation because of ill health, Noel H. Cooper became acting rector until the appointment of John A. O'Mara in 1969.

Events preceding and pointing to the establishing of a St Augustine's College distinct from the seminary are the following: the decision made in December 1938 to register qualified students of philosophy (pre-theology) in the arts department of St Michael's College – a *pro forma* registration as these seminary students took all their instruction in the seminary classrooms; the further decision of 1950 to move these undergraduates to 21 St Mary Street on the St Michael's campus so that they would be in a position to attend lectures in science, a university subject, prescribed at that time for all students of first-year arts.

The move of 1950 brought pre-theologians – those, that is, who had their university entrance – to the university campus. A St Augustine's university residence was set up in the old Basilian scholasticate with Walter Kerr, professor of English at St Augustine's, as its rector. From 1950 to 1964 this house functioned effectively, introducing into the theological programme of the seminary a steady stream of university graduates. It was Cardinal McGuigan's intention to erect a permanent residence for his philosophers near the St Michael's campus and in 1960 he formed a committee consisting of three diocesan priests: Bernard T. Kyte, Denis O'Connor, and Leo G. Smyth, to find and purchase a suitable property. McGuigan's health broke about this time and the committee made little headway. In 1961 McGuigan retired from active duty and a coadjutor archbishop, Philip Francis Pocock was brought to Toronto from Winnipeg.

Shortly after Pocock's arrival it was announced that the archdiocese would establish St Augustine's College on the seminary campus and affiliate it with the University of Ottawa. A variety of factors led to this decision. The St Mary St building had become unusable. Indeed, it was this circumstance that had forced Cardinal McGuigan to take steps to replace it. He had wanted the president of St Michael's, John M. Kelly, to erect a building for diocesan seminarians and to receive them on the same basis as other resident students. When Kelly demurred, the cardinal appointed his residence committee. The diocesan consultors advised Pocock on his coming to Toronto to re-unite the seminary family even if this meant closing the university residence. Pocock and some others felt that an Ottawa affiliation would be more flexible and more adaptable to seminary problems than the existing arrangement with the University of Toronto through St Michael's. He had in mind, among other advantages, that St Augustine's might eventually be able to qualify all or most of its students for federal grants, not just the philosophers enrolled in St Michael's or the theologians who already had a bachelor's degree. Pocock also attached importance to the prestige and sense of well-being the new status would give the seminary as a whole. He had seen this kind of thing happen in London when St Peter's Seminary (indeed, at his suggestion) had successfully applied for affiliation with the University of Western Ontario. Consultation with the head of the seminary, with the president of St Michael's, and with the rector of the university residence brought objections only from Walter Kerr, who thought the existing idea too sound to abandon. Kelly did not attach as much importance to the presence of seminarians on the university campus – for the sake of the campus – as had L.J. Bondy, who made the original arrangement.

Late in 1962 the bishop opened negotiations with Henri Legaré, president of the University of Ottawa, with a view to requesting from the university senate the affiliation of a new St Augustine's College. At the same time he arranged for the financing and construction of the new college building adjacent to the seminary. In June 1964, St Augustine's College was formally affiliated with Ottawa and classes began in September of that year. The agreement of affiliation was made for five years and was renewable; ecclesiastical approbation of that part of the agreement touching pontifical degrees was given at the same time by the Sacred Congregation of Seminaries and Universities, but only for four years.

The new affiliation had some unique clauses. The affiliation was effected between Ottawa and St Augustine's College, not St Augustine's Seminary. The college was recognized as having two divisions: a faculty of arts or philosophy, and a faculty of theology. The rector of the college, Walter Kerr, was responsible only for the philosophy students. The rector of the seminary, Richard Dobell, remained responsible for the theologians. The seminary was linked to Ottawa through the college; and federal grants in favour of the seminary were paid through the college but it was independent of the college in anything pertaining to administration or curriculum. It was subject of course, to supervision by the faculty of theology of the University of Ottawa in academic matters and by the Congregation of Seminaries and Universities in what concerned pontifical degrees. The senate of the University of Ottawa was divided over the wisdom of affiliating St Augustine's and both president Legaré and his successor, Roger Guindon, were uneasy about it.

These arrangements between St Augustine's College and the University of Ottawa preceded by one year Ottawa's own transformation into a provincially-supported university. At this time Ottawa continued its commitment with St Augustine's, as it did in the case of its other affiliates, but it transferred supervision of the administration and curriculum of the seminary division of St Augustine's to St Paul's University. This produced a somewhat awkward legal situation in which St Augustine's College was affiliated with the newly enfranchised (1965) University of Ottawa while its constituent part, St Augustine's Seminary, was the responsibility of St Paul's University, the holder of the old Ottawa charter (1866). This structural change also meant that henceforth the seminary would be dealing with a more sympathetic university administration than would the college.

When the congregation's approbation came up for renewal in 1968, it was extended for one year so as to co-ordinate the renewal dates of the civil agreement and the ecclesiastical approbation. In 1969 St Augustine's College requested that only that part of the civil agreement affecting theology be renewed. The college would continue in existence, it would negotiate with Ottawa and St Paul's in what concerned St Augustine's faculty of theology, but it would not continue to present students for degrees in arts or philosophy. This request was accepted by the University of Ottawa and St Paul's, and that part of the civil agreement affecting undergraduates at St Augustine's was not renewed.

The circumstances leading up to the discontinuance of the undergraduate affiliation were as follows. Registration in St Augustine's College declined from 125 in 1964 to about 40 in 1969. At the same time, there was considerable discontent among undergraduates mainly because they were isolated from both the Ottawa and the various Toronto campuses. At a meeting with the staff, administration, and archbishop during the spring of 1969, the student body asked to be transferred to a university campus. The administration's answer was to arrange the transfer of students to St Michael's College, Scarborough College (a constitutive college of the University of Toronto located near St Augustine's), or Centennial College (a community college of applied arts and technology also near the seminary), according to their choice or qualifications, for their arts programme. At the same time it arranged with Ottawa not to renew the affiliation of the undergraduate department. The present situation of St Augustine's College is that it enrols pre-theologians, provides them with residence, with religious life and exercises, and sends them to the campus of their choice for their university or college work. The new arrangement is one of considerable promise in the context of the current *aggiornamento*, and it may well solve many of the knotty problems besetting Catholic pre-theological education. The college has been described by a hostile critic as 'inoperative.'[2] The truth of the matter is that it has achieved a new kind of operation that may constitute the greatest breakthrough of its history.

Concurrently with this modification of the undergraduate programme, the faculty of theology also entered a new and experimental phase. The major seminary, after months of discussion and uncertainty, became a participating member of the new Toronto School of Theology. This TST is an attempt on the part of all Toronto's major seminaries, Catholic and Protestant, to share their courses and their professors with one another. There is here involved a tremendous overall reduction of course hours and the avoidance of much duplication. It also, in the best ecumenical manner, gives a wider and less confessional character to seminary programmes. St Augustine's, St Basil's, and Regis College are the participating Catholic seminaries. Along with them are several Protestant theologates – Knox, Wycliffe, Emmanuel, and Trinity colleges. The TST operated during 1969–70 with C.D. Jay of Emmanuel as chairman and J.I. Hochban of Regis as secretary. St Augustine's seminarians, like the students of the college, attended lectures on the university campus; St Augustine's professors lectured to a cross-section of theological students in the provincial university. Seminary and college, still distinct in function, but again under one rector, John A. O'Mara, are on the threshold of a new and exciting era alive with hitherto unimagined hopes and unexpected possibilities.[3]

2 John McDonough, 'The Female Principle,' *The Globe Magazine*, Toronto, 20 Sept. 1969, 6

3 The present situation of St Augustine's College closely resembles that of the famous Collegium Americanum in Louvain.

Regis College

1930

Regis College, 3425 Bayview Avenue, Willowdale 433, is a major faculty of theology conducted by the Upper Canadian province of the Society of Jesus. It offers civil degrees in theology (BTH, MTH, STM) through St Mary's University, Halifax, and pontifical degrees (STB, STL) as the Toronto section of the Collegium Immaculatae Conceptionis, Montreal. The English-speaking Jesuits in Canada maintain for their own scholastics two post-secondary institutions: Ignatius College, Guelph, an undergraduate college of arts and sciences; and Regis College, a major theological seminary for college graduates who have completed their philosophical training. Regis offers its theological programmes in collaboration with other major seminaries in the Toronto area, and is an initial member-institution in the ecumenical Toronto School of Theology.

THE PRE-HISTORY OF REGIS COLLEGE

Regis College, a theologate of considerable distinction and scholarship in English-speaking Canada, was established as a scholasticate and house of philosophy only at the relatively late date of 1930. Since the Canadian Jesuits had long maintained a large theologate in Montreal, l'Immaculée Conception, there was until recently no pressing call for a second similar foundation in Ontario. The immediate occasions for establishing an Ontario scholasticate were the success of the English novitiate opened in Guelph in 1913 and the official separation of the Canadian Jesuits into French and English provinces in 1924. There was also, however, a long-standing desire on the part of many Jesuits to have a first-class college in that part of Canada where the early missionaries had once laboured so effectively and where the crippling effects of the suppression of 1773 removed for some time all but their memory.

In a sense Regis College has two pre-histories: that of its academic curriculum which is to be traced through the Montreal Immaculée Conception back into the long tradition of the *ratio studiorum*; the other the long struggle of the Jesuits for an Ontario college.

The first of these pre-histories, the story of the *ratio studiorum*, has limited relevance in the history of post-secondary education in English-speaking Canada, where no Jesuit college has been fully committed to it. Though important in itself as a strategy and as a valid theory of education, there is no call to deal with it in the present study.[1] Suffice it to say that the *ratio studiorum* is really not so inflexibly committed to a limited classical curriculum nor to formalized pedagogy as sometimes charged, and that, regardless of whether it is or not, the programme has not been possible in the context of the much less yielding prescriptions of a different order as set down by the departments of education in Canada's provinces.

The second pre-history is a different matter. During the 1840s and 1850s there were three distinct but abortive moves to establish a Jesuit-administered college in Ontario. The first was that of Pierre Point. Bishop Michael Power succeeded in 1843 in having the provincial of the Paris Jesuits, Pierre Chazelle, send two priests, Pierre Point and Jean-Pierre Choné, to work in Sandwich and its nearby missions. Point soon opened a parish school which he thought might be a step towards founding Upper Canada's first Jesuit college. Circumstances dictated otherwise and Assumption College, when it opened, was not Jesuit.[2]

In 1847 the same Bishop Power brought two German-speaking Jesuits from the Swiss province to Waterloo county to work among the German Catholics who had settled there. These priests were Lucius Cavang and Bernard Fritsch; and they made Wilmot, or St Agatha as it came to be called, their missionary headquarters. They hoped in time to open a college in St Agatha.[3] The mission, however, had in 1852 to be transferred to Guelph where two Jesuit colleagues, John Holzer and Caspar Matoga, took charge. The idea of opening a college persisted, and in 1855 a small College of St Ignatius was actually opened. It had a short career and must have shown some promise in that Bishop John

1 The *ratio atque institutio studiorum Societatis Jesu*, usually called simply the *ratio studiorum* or even the *ratio*, was first draughted about 1585. It was a theory and strategy of education based on the experience of Jesuit professors in Jesuit schools. The *ratio* was issued in its definitive format by the society in 1599. A revised *ratio* was issued in 1832. The *ratio* provided a plan of studies and a detailed system of presentation for use in Jesuit colleges. It featured the wisdom of teaching relatively few but related subjects with a view to liberal training, general culture, and the development of the faculties of the human soul. Although it emphasized teaching disciplines in depth, it was not intended to provide specialized or professional education but only to serve as their background. With the suppression of the order in 1773 the influence of the *ratio* declined; with the restoration in 1814 it revived partially but in a modified and revised form. The *ratio* has influenced most modern educational theory and method and thus indirectly affects the colleges and schools of Canada.
2 See below, 275ff.
3 See below, 305ff.

Farrell, Father Holzer, and others petitioned for and were granted an act of incorporation for it, 9 June 1862.[4] This was not strictly speaking a Jesuit college but it was almost certainly the mind of Bishop Farrell that the Jesuits would run it when they had the men to do so. The college had unfortunately to be given up shortly after its incorporation 'for want of necessary support from the public and the absence of professors.'[5] It provides at least a tenuous and anticipatory link between today's Ignatius College novitiate and the past.

The third move to establish a Jesuit college in the 1840s and early 1850s was more private. In 1849 the Jesuits of Montreal released Remi Tellier from the Collège de Chambéry to join the staff of Regiopolis at Kingston.[6] Tellier remained in Kingston for only one year, then moved on to Toronto where he thought he might open a Jesuit college on property promised for the purpose by Captain John Elmsley. This turned out to be impossible and for the usual reason: the Jesuits had not the men to meet such a commitment.

These early efforts to found a college in Ontario remained in the memory of later Jesuits, particularly those from English-speaking Canada. The first real opportunity to make another try came in 1929 when Michael J. O'Brien, the coadjutor archbishop of Kingston, opened negotiations with William H. Hingston, provincial of the English-speaking province, to have the Jesuits take over Regiopolis College, the archdiocesan high school, and to revive the university dormant since 1869.[7]

Hingston visited Kingston in 1930 to discuss O'Brien's offer. The two men were not entirely at one. O'Brien was concerned to get the university re-opened, to keep it in Kingston, and to have post-secondary instruction given in Kingston. Hingston was more concerned to create a great national Catholic university utilizing all the resources which the Canadian Church could assemble.[8] O'Brien's plans, which were ultimately adopted, did not take into adequate consideration the difficulty of competing with Queen's. Hingston's depended upon the collaboration of existing Catholic colleges and the financial backing of the Ontario hierarchy, neither of which was forthcoming. Articles of agreement between the archbishop and the society were signed 12 June 1931.

4 An Act to Incorporate the College of St Ignatius, Guelph, in Hodgins, *Documentary History*, XVII, 43, 45, 51, 55–7
5 Theobald Spetz, *The Catholic Church in Waterloo County*, Toronto: Catholic Register Press, 1916, 54. See below 305ff. and esp. n.3.
6 See above, 22
7 See above, 25
8 See above, 28ff.

The university act of 1866 was twice revised: in 1931 to place the co-adjutor archbishop on the board of trustees *nominatim*; and in 1934 to revive the old charter's powers in case they had legally lapsed.[9]

A new Jesuit house was thus opened in Kingston in 1931. It was at first only a high school which continued, under Jesuit direction, the school hitherto run by the diocesan clergy. The first rector was Leo J. Nelligan, whose staff consisted of two Jesuit priests (Christopher Keating and Nicholas Quirk), two scholastics, five diocesan priests, and two lay brothers. In 1934 Christopher Keating became rector and in 1938 instruction in arts subjects began. By this time the Jesuit faculty had been enlarged and strengthened; and a few laymen (including in 1935 John Deutsch, former student of Campion and now a graduate student at Queen's) were added.

The arts course proved impossible to maintain, partly because of the proximity of Queen's, partly because of the outbreak of war which curtailed arts registration everywhere, and partly because the high school department was so thriving and demanding that it made the college look like an afterthought. A few students completed the entire arts course and some five or six BAs were granted in 1941 and 1942, after Francis McDonald had succeeded Keating as rector. In 1942 the experiment was discontinued. In the meantime other more promising developments drew the attention of the Jesuits in other directions: the taking over of St Mary's in Halifax[10] and, more significantly, the immediate and encouraging success of the house of philosophy opened in Toronto in 1930.

REGIS COLEGE: THE JESUIT SEMINARY

Regis College, or as it was known then, the Jesuit Seminary, was brought into existence in 1930 in order to make philosophical training at the post-secondary level available to English-speaking scholastics who had made their novitiate at Guelph. The Guelph novitiate, St Stanislaus Novitiate, opened in 1913 on property acquired for the purpose on the Elora Road two miles north of Guelph, was now providing the society with a sufficient number of scholastics to make a house of studies desirable and necessary. The opportunity to open such a house came in 1930 when the Sisters of Loretto moved their motherhouse from 403 Wellington Street in downtown Toronto to Armour Heights.

9 An Act Respecting the University of Regiopolis (21 George v, ch. 137; 2 Apr. 1931); and An Act Respecting the University of Regiopolis (24 George v, ch. 93; 3 Apr. 1934)

10 See above, 70

The Jesuits bought the old Loretto Abbey, opening in it their Collegium Christi Regis.

The abbey was an old building, rich in historical memories, but dilapidated beyond all but minimal repair. The oldest part of the building dated back to 1838 and had been the home of the Jamesons – of Robert Sympson Jameson and (for a few long years) of his wife Anna Murphy – and then of the Frederick Widders, who named it Lyndhurst and who entertained many distinguished guests in it, including in 1860 the Prince of Wales, later Edward VII. The Loretto Sisters acquired it in 1867, renamed it Loretto Abbey, and built eight distinct additions to it between 1871 and 1898.[11] When the Jesuits took it over, 27 June 1930, and moved into it, 5 August 1930, they did so with full knowledge that neither the building nor the location could serve them long.

During the first ten years the seminary had two rectors: Wafer Doyle 1930–4 and Joseph Keating 1934–40. Doyle and Keating saw to it that their students received a good course in philosophy supplemented by training in the physical and natural sciences. The curriculum was internal, that is, met no civil requirements and had no civil accreditation. It satisfied, indeed, more than satisfied the norms of the *ratio studiorum* and all ecclesiastical requirements for admission to theology. The limitation which was to become serious in time was that it was neither understood by nor always recognized by Canadian and American graduate schools.

The first significant adaptation of the seminary's programme came during the rectorship of George Nunan, 1940–7, who in 1943 introduced courses in theology. This expansion of curriculum had two highly beneficial effects: the gathering together of a large and highly competent staff, and the creation of a library of 35,000 volumes which was to become the core of the magnificent theological library owned today by Regis College. On the other hand, the providing of both philosophy and theology on Wellington Street meant some loss of the diversified and international flavour of the earlier training.

Nunan's successors in the rectorship while the seminary remained a downtown college were as follows: Frederick Lynch 1947–51, James Elliott MacGuigan, 1951–6, Gordon George from 1956 until his election as provincial in 1957, and Edward F. Sheridan from 1957 to 1964. It was during Sheridan's rectorship that the move to Willowdale was made.

The sequence of developments under the foregoing rectors was revo-

11 B.W. Connolly, 'After 100 Years – A Jesuit Seminary,' *Loretto Rainbow* 52 (1946), 138–45

lutionary: the seminary was civilly incorporated and its name changed to Regis College in 1954; it received power to issue pontifical degrees in 1956; in 1957 it affiliated with St Mary's University, Halifax; and in 1958 it dropped its school of philosophy and released plans for a new building in Willowdale.

These developments were attributable to two forces: the increasing need for recognized degrees by priests proceeding to graduate studies, and the requirement of the federal government that students had to be enrolled in a provincially recognized degree course in order that the institution enrolling them be eligible for federal grants. The incorporation and change of name in 1954 was a first step towards these objectives. The new name, Regis College, was a happy and ingenious one: it echoed the Latin of the original Collegium Christi Regis; it removed the danger of confusing the Jesuit seminary with Vancouver's Seminary of Christ the King; and it honoured St John Francis Regis, the Jesuit apologist and apostle of the Vivarais.

Then, in 1956, by arrangement with the Sacred Congregation of Seminaries and Universities, Regis College became the Toronto section of the pontifical theological faculty of l'Immaculée Conception, Montreal. This was not an affiliation in the usual sense but the integral possession of a common charter which looked after ecclesiastical accreditation with independence and dignity. Regis has since that time conferred the pontifical bachelor's degree, STB, and the licentiate, STL, in sacred theology.

Civil accreditation came soon after. On 31 January 1957, the Regis faculty of theology was affiliated with St Mary's University. This affiliation took place at the same time as St Stanislaus Novitiate in Guelph changed its name to Ignatius College and assumed the status of an affiliated college of St Mary's with accrediting privileges in arts and science.[12] Through St Mary's, Regis began to offer a civil bachelor's degree in theology, BTH, and two kinds of master's degrees, the MTH for students taking theology as an academic discipline, the STM for those taking it as a pastoral discipline.

It is interesting to observe that when the Canadian Jesuits became convinced of the need for this kind of reorientation of studies, they established a country-wide committee to draught, in the spirit of the *ratio* but for the twentieth century, an *ordinatio* to specify and explain their policy both to themselves and Jesuits elsewhere. This committee,

---

12 Ignatius College has recently been sending all its students to the new University of Guelph, where three Jesuits are on the teaching staff. Ignatius retains but is not using its St Mary's affiliation.

consisting of Gerald Lahey, Lawrence Braceland, Hugh Kierans, Patrick Malone, Eric O'Connor, and Edward Sheridan met from 1959 to 1961. Before the committee's *ordinatio* was ready, but influenced no doubt by its preparation, there came out from the Roman headquarters of the society an *Instructio de junioratu* (dated 8 December 1961) which incorporated many of the committee's considerations and conclusions and which since has become known as 'the *magna charta* of humanistic studies in the society.'[13]

In 1958 the rector of Regis, Edward Sheridan, made two significant announcements. One was that Regis College would discontinue its programme of philosophy, the other that a firm of architects, Peter Dickinson Associates, had completed plans and specifications for a new building in Willowdale.

The dropping of philosophy surprised many but was, nevertheless, deliberate and well-advised policy. In the first place it enabled the Canadian Jesuits to restore their earlier policy of allowing many of their scholastics to spend some of their preparatory years either in the house of studies of another province or on a university campus. Many students and some professors went to the Oregon scholasticate. But some went elsewhere, too, to one or other of the Jesuit houses around the world: Antilles, Austria, north Belgium, Bolivia, France, Germany, Malta, Missouri, Montreal, New York, Spain, and elsewhere. In the second place, Regis was left more free to develop a strong theologate which in its turn brought to Toronto Jesuit students from around the world.

In October 1959 the Wellington St property was sold to the *Evening Telegram*. On 21 March 1961, staff and students moved to Willowdale; and on 15 October of the same year the beautiful new college was formally dedicated. Edward Sheridan remained rector until 1964. Recent rectors have been John Hochban 1964–6, Lionel Stanford 1966–9, and Remi Limoges since 1969. As in the case of other colleges, it was found useful at Regis to separate the offices of rector (religious superior) and president (academic head). The academic administrators during 1969–70 were as follows: president, Frederick E. Crowe; registrar, John Hochban; dean, Colin Maloney.

The Willowdale period, from 1961 on, has been marked by the continued development of a strong staff: Bernard Lonergan, Frederick E. Crowe, David Stanley, and Roderick A. MacKenzie are among the

13 Horatio P. Phelan, 'Fifty Years at Guelph: the Story of Ignatius College, Guelph,' Ignatius College, 1963. This is a typed manuscript of 127 pages, a copy of which is to be found in the archives of Regis College, Willowdale.

better known for their publications and their international postings.[14] But the staff of the sixties has displayed generally a diversity of competence and a depth of scholarship that bespeaks the wisdom, perspicacity, and foresight of the provincial administration for over a generation.

During the late sixties the Jesuits of Regis College had to cope with the problems besetting theologates everywhere – restlessness, activism, withdrawals, and a falling off of vocations – but somewhat less acutely and intensely than most other diocesan and religious seminaries. Their unexpected trial was the common irony of the times, that they located their new facilities at an excessive remove from university resources. They met this situation, however, by entering into full collaboration not only with the other Catholic theologates of Toronto – St Augustine's Seminary, St Basil's College, the University of St Michael's College – but with the ecumenically conceived Toronto School of Theology.[15] They began to transport staff and students daily to the University of Toronto campus so as to provide the combined mobility and involvement which it became fashionable for the modern student, including the theological student, to demand.

14 Bernard J.F. Lonergan is best known for his *Insight: A Study of Human Understanding,* New York and London, 1957. The periodical *Continuum* has devoted an entire issue (vol. ii, no. 3, 1964) to an assessment of his work under the general title 'Spirit as Inquiry,' supplying a full bibliography of his writings to that date, 544–9. He taught at l'Immaculée Conception, Montreal, at Regis, and then in the Pontifical Gregorian University, Rome. He returned to Regis in 1966. During 1969 he was appointed by Pope Paul vi to the new International Theological Commission. The others mentioned are also well known for their scholarly writings: Crowe in systematic theology, Stanley and MacKenzie in sacred scripture. MacKenzie became rector of the Pontifical Biblical Institute, Rome, in 1963.

15 See above 233. The TST went into operation during 1969–70. Its first director was C. Douglas Jay of Emmanuel College, its first registrar John Hochban of Regis College. Hochban was also registrar of Regis.

University of Ottawa

(ST JOSEPH COLLEGE, BYTOWN COLLEGE, OTTAWA COLLEGE)

1848

The University of Ottawa, founded as St Joseph College, Bytown, in 1848, has since 1965 been a provincially supported bilingual, non-sectarian, multi-faculty university. Originally an Oblate foundation, it has Oblates on its board of governors and teaching staff.

The University of Ottawa will be dealt with in detail in two other volumes in this series on higher education in Canada.[1] However, the early history of this university, especially during the period preceding the granting of its royal charter in 1866, is so closely interwoven with the history of Regiopolis, Kingston, and St Michael's, Toronto, that some account seems called for in the present investigation of English church colleges in Canada.

The establishing of a Catholic college at Bytown (now Ottawa) was first broached in the correspondence between Bishop Ignace Bourget of Montreal and bishop-elect Patrick Phelan during 1843.[2] Phelan, founder and first pastor of the parish of Bytown, had just been named co-adjutor to bishop Gaulin of Kingston, who had become incapacitated. Phelan, who had not yet left Bytown, wanted Bourget to invite the Oblate Fathers to take over his parish. He advanced among other reasons that a new French missionary congregation like the Oblates might well extend its work to teaching. Bourget acknowledged Bytown's need for a college and did invite the Oblates to accept the parish. The first Oblate to come to Bytown was Pierre-Adrien Telmon, who assumed his duties as parish priest during 1844. Telmon also wanted a college in Bytown and he had available the counsel of Bishop Phelan, who on removing to Kingston found himself deeply involved in de-

---

1 Robin S. Harris, 'A History of Higher Education in Canada'; Claude Galarneau, 'French Catholic Church Colleges.' These works are still in production.
2 Gaston Carrière, 'Le Collège de Bytown,' *Revue de l'Université d'Ottawa*, 26(1956), 56–78, 224–25, 317–49; also *Histoire documentaire de la Congrégation des Missionnaires Oblats de Marie-Immaculée dans l'Est du Canada 1re Partie, De l'arrivée au Canada à la mort du Fondateur (1841–61)*, II, 9–143. Jean Leflon, *Eugéne de Mazenod*, transl. by F.D. Flanagan, New York: Fordham, III, Part I, 1968, 123–54. J.B. O'Reilly, 'The Pontifical University of Ottawa from its origins to the Civil Charter, 1848–1866,' *Revue de l'Université d'Ottawa*, 19(1949), 119–42. Alexis de Barbezieux, *Histoire de la Province Ecclésiastique d'Ottawa*, Ottawa, 1897, I, 305–9.

veloping the newly-established Regiopolis College. It was Telmon who convinced the founder and superior general of the Oblates, Bishop de Mazenod, that teaching was a normal extension of the missionary apostolate.

During 1845 or 1846 a fine property known as Sandy Hill, located at Theodore (now Laurier) and Wilbrod Streets was offered by M. Louis-Theodore Besserer to the diocese (Kingston) for a college in Bytown.[3] Sandy Hill was in due time deeded over to the diocese of Bytown, but it was not the site selected for the first college building because it was thought to be a little far from the church and because it would require large expenditures for proper development.

No positive move to establish a college was taken until 1847 when Bytown was made a diocese and J.E.B. Guigues, the former superior of the Oblates in Canada, came as its first bishop. Once in Bytown, Guigues acted quickly. His first choice of site was a property close to the cathedral on Nepean Point held by the ordnance department of the army. Failing to get this either as a gift or for a moderate price, he had a wooden building constructed adjacent to the cathedral. The first sod was turned for this building on 10 August 1848. A prospectus issued at the same time announced the opening of a college two months later. Impossible as it may seem today, a small three-storey building costing $250 was opened on 27 September, just two months later. It was called St Joseph College or the College of Bytown. Enrolment as of early October was 55 students including 15 boarders.

This first college building was used from 1848 to 1853. The academic operation was closely watched by Guigues. There was always, of course, a superior or rector: Charles-Edouard Chevalier (1848–9), Napoléon Mignault (1849–51), Augustin Gaudet (1851–3). Here Bytown had a great advantage over Regiopolis. It invariably had during these early years a supply of teachers available: two or three Oblate priests and two or three theologians. The records include the following names: Arthur Mignault, Henri-Joseph Tabaret, Brother Claude-Amable Tisserand, Patrick McGoey (ordained 1849), Thomas O'Boyle, William Corbett (ordained 1854), Joseph John Collins (ordained 1850) – a distribution between French and Irish not unlike the Catholic school constituency of Bytown itself. The first prospectus announced both elementary and advanced education and promised (significantly enough in view of the characteristic tone taken by the institution ever since) an emphasis on the study of both English and French.

3 This property was probably a gift even though a small sum of money sealed the bargain. See Carrière, *Histoire documentaire*, n.3, 9–10.

Guigues lost no time in obtaining civil incorporation. He applied during January 1849 for an act of incorporation and for financial aid. He also had Robert Conroy and others of Bytown submit a separate petition 'praying that the College of Bytown may receive a like support by legislative aid as the other colleges of Upper Canada.'[4] The incorporation came immediately; it vested civil powers in the Roman Catholic bishop of Bytown (Guigues) as president, the superior of the college (Chevalier), the curé of the parish, the director of the college, and other 'necessary' officers. No grants accompanied the act of incorporation; indeed, none came from the government of Upper Canada until 1855 when St Michael's and Bytown both received their first grants of 350 and 200 pounds respectively. Bytown received a grant from the education fund of Lower Canada in 1852 and others from time to time thereafter.

In June 1850 an informative 'statement of the affairs of the college' signed by D. D'Aumaud, curé of Bytown, was submitted to the legislative council by Joseph Bourret. The statement provides the best picture we have of the college during these early years:

First. The Corporation is composed, at the present moment, of five Members (including the Bishop of the Diocese).

Secondly. Five Professors give instruction in the divers Branches mentioned in the Prospectus, published on the 15th of September, 1848: the Reverend Mr Mignault teaches Latin and Mathematics. Mr Carbet [Corbett], the Greek Language and English Literature. Mr Arthur Mignault, Methode. Mr Collins, Mathematics, Drawing, and English. Mr Triol, Elements.

Thirdly. This College has been in operation since the 26th September, 1848. About one hundred scholars, thirty-five of whom are boarders, receive instruction in this Establishment, without reference to origin, or creed: about thirty scholars receive a gratuitous Education. The College occupies, at the present moment a large Wooden House, three stories in height, constructed on the Church Property. A large piece of land, situate in a very fine position between both Towns, has been given by Mr Bissonet [Besserer], for the use of the College. When the resources of the Corporation shall permit, they will lose no time in fulfilling the intentions of the Donor, by building a College thereon, sufficiently large for the wants of the population.

The Corporation hold also, Four Hundred Acres of Land in the Township of Gloucester, at a distance of three leagues from Bytown – Lots Numbers 1 and 2 of the first Concession, on the River Ottawa. This land is not yet

4 An Act to incorporate the Collège de Bytown. (12 Victoria, ch.107; 30 May 1849). See also Hodgins, *Documentary History*, VIII, 10.

cleared. At present very little revenue is derived from it. The only revenue of the College is derived from the payments of the Boarders, and the monthly payments of the other Scholars.

It is only by the sacrifices made by the Bishop, and the devotedness of the Professors that this Institution has been supported up to this day.[5]

Bishop Guigues found the financing of the college very difficult. When his petitions to the legislature of Upper Canada between 1849 and 1851 got no response he wondered whether he ought not try to affiliate Bytown College with the University of Toronto. This was the period when three university bills – a Sherwood Bill and a Boulton Bill, neither of which passed, and the Baldwin Act of 1849 – were introduced, and when the Hincks Bill, passed in 1853 as the University of Toronto Act, was in the draughting stage. Bishop de Charbonnel, who had just opened St. Michael's in Toronto, was equally curious. Guigues had a M. Cazeau look into the matter. Cazeau reported that Bytown College could probably be affiliated if it was given the form and appearance of an institution of higher learning; had at least three or four professors over and above the staff in theology; rendered a complete accounting of receipts and expenditures; had its students receive their degrees from Toronto, and had them take the Toronto examinations. An incorporated college, as Bytown was, should negotiate for affiliation directly through the senate of the University of Toronto, not through the legislature.

The Upper Canadian bishops – Phelan, de Charbonnel, Guigues – were not of one mind about affiliation with the University of Toronto. Guigues took the position that the university was now in a period of transition and would soon become a strictly civil institution. It would shortly, he felt, be giving up its Protestant character and would then be in a position to help places like Bytown develop. De Charbonnel was less sanguine. He wrote to Guigues on 28 December 1852, that the more he examined the provincial university project the less sympathetic he became to it. He had, he said, written the archbishop of Quebec to the effect that the Toronto university project really stood condemned by the decree *de scholis mixtis*[6] because it was in fact affected by both Protestantism and indifferentism. There is no record of Phelan's position but it was probably more hopeful. He and Angus Macdonell were

5 Ibid., IX, 27
6 Carrière, 'Le Collège,' 73. The decree *de scholis mixtis* was passed by the First Provincial Council of Quebec, 1851: *Acta et decreta primi concilii provinciae Quebecensis.* Quebeci: apud Aug. Côté et soc., 1852, p.63: decretum XV. De Charbonnel attended this council.

in the Alexander Macdonell tradition. When the senate of the University of Toronto met on 9 March 1854, Angus Macdonell took his place on the senate and attended subsequent meetings. Although Guigues did not formally request affiliation for Bytown, a place on the senate was nevertheless assigned to Bytown's rector. Tabaret, like Macdonell, accepted his place on the senate.

The College of Bytown's first building had been located on the property of the parish church and was used from 1848 to 1852.[7] During these five years in the hastily constructed school the college had the three superiors named above: Chevalier, Mignault, and Gaudet. All three were Oblates and all seem to have favoured a college structure much like that adopted at St Michael's in Toronto and largely imported from France. The superior in Bytown was really the vice-regent; the bishop retained the name of president of the college.

In 1852 the college moved to a new home, a former dwelling at 365 Sussex Street, near the church. The new college cost £3995, a large amount for the new diocese, and the building was not a good one. It was in fact turned down as a bad risk by an insurance company. The following year, 1853, a new and significant change of superiors took place with the coming of Joseph-Henri Tabaret. Tabaret took office at the young age of 25. He was to remain at the college as superior or director or professor (with the exception of the years 1864–7 when he became Canadian provincial and Father Timothy Ryan served as superior of the College) until his death in 1886. Tabaret was a gifted educator and administrator and probably ranks with the most influential figures in his field in the nineteenth century. His thought reflects the influence of de Mazenod and Newman, his action the perception of issues connatural with genius. The following are to be attributed to his direction: the development of the Sandy Hill property; the assumption by the Oblates of full responsibility for the college; the formulation of a positive seminary policy; the directing of the college away from the provincial university toward autonomy; and the cultivation of the English-speaking constituency with a view to a genuinely bilingual university.

Tabaret became superior in 1853. During his first year in office the University of Toronto Act was passed. He was sometime thereafter, that is, during 1854, named a member of the university senate. It is not known whether he ever attended a meeting, but he never looked to affiliation to solve the problems of Bytown College. The next year,

7 Carrière, 'Le Collège.' O'Reilly gives the date as 1853, probably by confusion with the date of Tabaret's arrival.

1855, the name of the City of Bytown was changed to Ottawa; Tabaret saw to it that the college became at once Ottawa College, although he could not make the change legally effective until the passing of a new act by the parliament of 1861. This same amendment to the act of incorporation contained a provision unusual in its day: it *excluded* the bishop of Bytown and the curé of the parish of Bytown from membership in the corporation of Ottawa College.[8] This need not, of course, be a significant anticipation of today's trend away from *ex officio* ecclesiastical appointments to Catholic colleges; it could just have been a practical means of restricting membership of the corporation to Oblates.

Tabaret's report to the Ontario legislature for 1861 contains a forthright description of the college's threefold programme: preparatory, classical, theological. It supplies pertinent statistics, as, for example, that there were 15 enrolled in theology, 100 in the other two divisions; and that graduates of the college in its 14 years of operation included 36 priests, 15 medical doctors, and 10 lawyers.[9] The same report reveals how precisely bilingualism was made to function in the classical division: 'Translations are simultaneously made in English and French by all the students in the course. This was imperiously demanded of the directors of the institution by the position they occupy in the midst of two countries, where the English and French populations are equally mixed.'

Tabaret's main concern during these exciting years was to get the College away from Sussex Street and over to Sandy Hill. The college had not grown rapidly and was under constant criticism from both its French and Irish constituencies. It was also too closely supervised by Bishop Guigues for its own good. The fault here was not Guigues'. He had actually to convince the Oblate authorities to take on the responsibility for the college. He argued with them that a community dedicated to the external works of the missions would benefit from the atmosphere of study which a college could supply; he also pointed out that the bishop of Toronto, Monseigneur de Charbonnel, had just succeeded in getting the Basilians to leave the cathedral property, and to built and operate at their own risk on donated land at some distance from the cathedral. The Toronto college, he pointed out, was less developed than

8 An Act to Change the Name of the College of Bytown and to Amend the Act Incorporating the Same (24 Victoria, ch.108; 18 May 1861). See also Hodgins, *Documentary History*, XVI, 189.

9 An Act to Amend the Acts Incorporating the College of Ottawa and to Grant Certain Privileges to the Said College (29–30 Victoria, ch.135; 15 Aug. 1866). Hodgins, *Documentary History*, XVII, 174.

that of Bytown and its French-speaking priests did not, like them, have the opportunity of working where half the students were already French-speaking and the other half conscious of the need to learn and speak French. Tabaret needed no convincing; when the provincial and general came round, he was quite ready to accept the financial responsibiltiy for a new building and to move to the new site. The bishop, for his part, gave the Sandy Hill property to the Oblates. This was in 1856. So successful was the move that by 1860–1 a new wing had to be added to the third college building. This addition raises another point.

The matter of theology had from the beginning required particular attention. When the college was opened in 1848, a number of unordained Oblates were sent there to teach and to prepare for ordination. Their needs required attention. There were also possible diocesan candidates for the priesthood to be considered. The college itself was a 'little seminary' but it was not a theologate. Instruction in theology was soon given informally in the bishop's house: four candidates were reading in 1851, three in 1856, six in 1857, and more to come from France. The new wing begun in 1860 was intended to house the Oblates and to serve as a seminary distinct from the college. This was the beginning of the important school of theology maintained by the University of Ottawa and by St Paul University to the present time.

During the late fifties and the sixties there were constant complaints from both Irish and French about language policies. The Irish wanted somewhat less French than they were getting; the French-speaking Canadians, only too aware of their isolation in Ottawa, wanted to exploit an apparent national opportunity: after all, Ottawa was the only really French foundation in Upper Canada. Bishop Guigues was inclined to side with the French, or as he put it with 'l'élément canadien-français, dépourvu de tout enseignement un peu élévé.' He wanted a college which would save 'la langue française en voie de disparaître dans la région de Bytown.'[10] Tabaret struggled to observe a mean. Ottawa has never been without a recurring problem of conflicting constituencies, appearing intermittently over football, or affiliates, or the school of medicine, the pendulum swinging now this way, now that. Tabaret set up the ideal of genuine bilingualism and the constant effort of the university to achieve this ideal has become its most distinguishing characteristic.

Ottawa had an advantage over the colleges in Toronto and Kingston: it was not a ghetto struggling to survive in the shadow of larger and richer institutions. This was a great advantage in the early years because it gave an incentive to go after a charter and to put that charter to

10 Carrière, 'Le College'

work. When confederation became a national certainty, Ottawa sought a civil university charter and was granted it by the Ontario legislature, 15 August 1866.[11] Under this charter, degree-conferring power was granted, ecclesiastical character was acknowledged, and institutional government was place in the hands of a small, strong 'college senate' consisting of the president, four classical college professors (of theology, philosophy, rhetoric, and belle-lettres), the prefect of discipline, and (in a reversal of policy) the bishop of Ottawa. This civil charter was fortified by a pontifical charter granted 5 February 1889 by Pope Leo XIII.

From 1866 to the 1940s, when Ottawa had, exclusive of Tabaret, 18 rectors, the university was rather undistinguished. It was a small bilingual, liberal arts college, racked by nationalist problems and maintaining rather indifferent schools of philosophy, theology, and canon law. Officially bilingual, the overall tendency was to adopt a French rather than an Anglo-Irish flavour. In 1903 all the older buildings were razed in a disastrous fire and were only gradually replaced during the subsequent years. The years 1905–20 were particularly dismal. During the twenties there was some recovery, and considerable during the thirties. Noteworthy, in spite of internal trials, was Ottawa's generous policy towards struggling new foundations both in the neighborhood of Ottawa and in western Canada, affiliating them where possible so that Catholic students, whether of English or French expression, could proceed to a university degree under ecclesiastical auspices.

During the 1930s the university's incorporations were updated: the civil incorporation was revised in 1933 when the bicameral governing structure found in most Canadian universities was introduced; the ecclesiastical incorporation was revised in 1934 to bring the statutes under the papal charter in line with the apostolic constitution *Deus Scientiarum Dominus* of 1931. From the early thirties on, scholarly development became deep and rapid.[12]

The security of Ottawa's relations with its local constituency, particularly the English-speaking part of it, began to be threatened when an Ottawa Association for the Advancement of Learning was established in 1942. The Association opened Carleton College in 1943, obtained a limited charter in 1952, and had the operation transferred into Carleton University in 1957. Not being an ecclesiastical foundation, Carleton qualified for large operating and capital grants from the province of Ontario.

11 For text see Hodgins, *Documentary History*, 19:222–4.
12 Gaston Carrière, 'Bibliographie des professeurs oblats des facultés ecclesiastiques de l'université d'Ottawa (1932–1961),' *Revue de l'Université d'Ottawa*, 32 (1962), 81–104, 215–44

Expansion came to the University of Ottawa during the forties and fifties with the establishing of several new faculties, especially the medical school and the faculty of pure and applied science. At the same time an extensive building programme was launched. But Ottawa was in financial straits trying to expand on private funds and with only limited grants for medicine and science from the government of Ontario.

The twenty-fifth rector of Ottawa, Henri F. Legaré, 1958–64, prepared the university for a change of status. With the recent examples of McMaster and Assumption before him, he engaged Professor James A. Murray of Toronto as planning consultant, and was able in 1963 to place a plan for a new secularized Ottawa University in the hands of his board, senate, and other advisers. The changes recommended by Legaré were carried through under Roger Guindon, who became Ottawa's twenty-sixth Oblate rector in 1964.

The proposed new government bill was common knowledge by February 1965,[13] and was publicly announced by the university 27 May 1965. The bill established a new University of Ottawa and transferred the old Ottawa charter to St Paul University for use by theological and related faculties. St Paul was to be federated with the new state-supported University of Ottawa.

Ottawa ceased to be denominational but was intended, in line with its tradition, 'to promote the advancement of learning ... in accordance with Christian principles,' but without any religious tests. It was to be free from restrictions and control of any outside body, lay or religious. It was also 'to further bilingualism and preserve and develop French culture in Ontario.' The government of the university became similar to that of other state-supported universities in Ontario.

Of special interest in English-speaking Catholic circles was the fate proposed for Ottawa's many affiliates, and especially St Patrick's College, Ottawa, Notre Dame of Canada, Wilcox, Saskatchewan, and St Augustine's Seminary and College, Toronto.[14] In general they were given options: to go with St Paul University, to draw up a new affiliation with the new University of Ottawa, to seek affiliation elsewhere, or to become autonomous. St Patrick's, after some delay, affiliated with

13 *The Globe and Mail*, Toronto, 28 May 1965. For the bill itself see An Act Respecting Université d'Ottawa (13–14 Elizabeth II, ch.137; 22 June 1965).

14 In the spring of 1965, before the new bill passed, the old University of Ottawa had 9 faculties, 4 autonomous schools, 10 affiliates, and a miscellany of related institutes and courses. It held 43 acres of land, and projected a campus of 83 acres along the Rideau canal. It had 4106 full-time students, 610 of them graduate students. Counting part-time, extension, and affiliated students, its grand total of students was 11,991.

Carleton; Notre Dame affiliated with the new Ottawa; St Augustine's Seminary and College affiliated with St Paul's University.

The present university reflects as yet no startling changes from the old one. Oblates are on the faculty. Affiliates have been continued, but reduced in number; the new senate is less disposed to accept affiliates than the old, and is very demanding. The university has, in the loss of the school of social work, which was a project of St Patrick's College and which moved with it to Carleton, suffered a setback which will take some years to remedy. The university's structure resembles the English rather than the French-Canadian pattern, its student body on the other hand is more French than formerly. The president, Roger Guindon, has been continued in office. There is every likelihood that he will be succeeded by a layman, but there will almost certainly be Oblate presidents from time to time. The present chancellor, Madame Georges Vanier, wife of the former governor-general of Canada, has proven an excellent choice for the transitionary period. The prestige of the university is enhanced by the new salary scales made possible by government support: good professors are rarely attracted elsewhere and the scholarly advantages of the capital city are increasingly recognized.

St Patrick's College

OTTAWA

1929

St Patrick's College, Ottawa, is a Catholic college division of the faculty of arts of Carleton University. It is located at 283 Echo Drive in a handsome multipurpose building erected by the English Oblates (St Peter's Province) in 1929, enlarged in 1955, and transferred with other college assets to Carleton University in 1968. St Patrick's continues features distinct from Carleton: a largely Catholic and partly Oblate teaching faculty, a department of religion, and a moderately structured undergraduate arts curriculum. The head of the college and his assistant have the rank of dean and vice-dean in the university.

On 15 March 1926, the Oblates of Mary Immaculate in Canada established their new nation-wide St Peter's Province under its own provincial, W.B. Grant, to serve the order's growing English-speaking constituency.[1] The new province took over missions, parishes, and schools, mainly in western Canada, and St Joseph's parish in Ottawa. During 1929, under the direction of the second provincial, Edward Killian, it opened the high school department of St Patrick's College, Ottawa, in a large new building on Echo Drive. Killian himself served as rector during the first year. He had a staff of four Oblates (Fathers T. Kennedy, L. Bartley, F. Tedrow, P. O'Dwyer) and a school of about 150 boys. In 1930 Thomas Kennedy was rector, and in 1931 D.J. Moriarty. During 1931, arts students were accepted, and during the following year, with Patrick Phelan as rector and first college head, St Patrick's was admitted by the senate of the University of Ottawa as a constituent or integral college in its faculty of arts. The agreement between Ottawa and St Patrick's was confirmed officially by the Sacred Congregation of Seminaries and Universities, 26 October 1932.[2]

St Patrick's arrangement with Ottawa was not quite parallel to that in effect in other Catholic colleges of Canada. It was, unlike Ottawa affiliates (which at this time were numerous) a constituent college; and it offered, unlike St Michael's in Toronto, a full arts programme. It also

1 F.E. Banim, 'The Centenary of the Oblates of Mary Immaculate,' *Report of the Canadian Catholic Historical Association,* 9 (1941–2), 29–33
2 J.J. Kelly to L.K. Shook, 23 Jan. 1962

had a ready-made, if limited, constituency, some of it already enrolled in Ottawa. Indeed, its first task was the rather delicate one of detaching this constituency from the University of Ottawa without creating embarrassment – difficult enough during the economic depression when all Canadian universities and colleges were dependent upon students' fees for their very survival. From a strictly financial point of view, no Catholic college in Canada experienced so trying a beginning as did St Patrick's.

The trouble, however, was not all financial. The appearance of St Patrick's in 1929 came towards the end of a long series of English-French tensions over Catholic education itself which divided the population of much of Ontario but especially of eastern Ontario. It began over primary education but ultimately affected secondary and post-secondary education as well.

During the early years of its history, Ottawa College, and later the University of Ottawa, had two constituencies, an Irish and a French. Tensions existed but were not critical until J.T. Duhamel became bishop of Ottawa in 1874. They increased after he became Archbishop Duhamel in 1886, and reached a serious climax in 1898 when Michael Francis Fallon, pro-Irish vice-rector of the University of Ottawa, was removed from office and made pastor of St Joseph's parish. They became even more serious in 1901 when Fallon was relieved of his pastoral duties in Ottawa and appointed to a post in Buffalo, New York, the result, he said later, 'of a deliberate conspiracy hatched in Montreal and Ottawa.'[3] The issue calmed for a while, then flared again in 1910 because of three provocative events: l'Association Canadienne-Française d'Education d'Ottawa was organized, the exiled Fallon was consecrated bishop of London, and the Orange order launched a bigotted attack on bilingualism in Ontario's school system.[4] The basic rift was between French-speaking and English-speaking Catholics, above all in Ottawa.

From 1910 to 1917 the debate focussed upon the celebrated Regulation 17, and the Instructions 17, which were designed by the department of education of Ontario to assure the primacy of English as the language of instruction in the schools of Ontario, but which divided French and English Catholics over the question of the very nature of separate schools.[5] The debate evoked two interventions by Pope

3 *The Ottawa Citizen*, 20 Mar. 1916
4 Marilyn Barber, 'The Ontario Bilingual School Issue: Source of Conflict,' *Canadian Historical Review*, 47 (1966), 233–4
5 For fuller discussion, see Franklin A. Walker, *Catholic Education and Politics in Ontario*, Toronto: Nelson and Sons, 1964, 123–91 and 227–322; also Margaret Prang, 'Clerics, Politicians, and the Bilingual Schools Issue in Ontario, 1910–1917,' *Canadian Historical Review*, 41 (1960), 281–307.

Benedict xv.[6] After the victory of the conservative party in the elections of June 1923, a solution was reached in line with the principle advocated by D'Arcy Scott as early as 1916 that French and English school supporters should have each their own board – a principle re-stated by the archbishops of Canada in 1919 when they resolved 'that in localities where there exists racial friction between French- and English-speaking Catholics in regard to the management of their Catholic schools, an effort be made to so arrange such schools that the two classes for children be separate under French bilingual and English-speaking teachers.'[7]

Although this solution was not reached politically until 1927 by premier Ferguson, its acceptance was a foregone conclusion. The Oblates as an educational order had already put it into effect at one level when they established St Peter's Province in 1926; and the University of Ottawa and St Patrick's College but applied it at the post-secondary level when they drew up their agreement of 1932.

The college which was established at St Patrick's during 1932 received a shot in the arm with the addition of F.E. Banim and Leo Alphonse Cormican to the teaching staff. These two young men had attended University College, Dublin, and Cambridge University to prepare themselves for high school teaching in Colombo, Ceylon. When this missionary appointment turned out to be unsatisfactory, they were transferred to St Patrick's College, Ottawa. Their training not only strengthened the college staff but also established a bond between St Patrick's and Cambridge which was the prelude of a succession of men who prepared themselves at Cambridge – Hugh McDougall, James Trainor, and James Noonan. The contribution of these men and of John J. Kelly and T. Swift, who prepared themselves at Toronto, and of others who went elsewhere in the United States and Europe has given St Patrick's a strong staff with which to build a scholarly reputation.

Considerable attention was given, during the early years, to the building up of English along the Toronto lines, and philosophy in the traditional Catholic manner. Thus honour courses in English were offered even during the thirties, and by 1941 graduate courses; and two courses in philosophy were prescribed for all students in each year. Unlike other federated Catholic colleges in Canada, St Patrick's could and did from the beginning teach the natural sciences. Chemistry and biology were given special attention, and by 1952 honour courses were

6 See *The Catholic Register*, 8 Feb. 1917; *The Canadian Freeman*, 31 Oct. 1918.
7 Minutes of the Meeting of the Archbishops of Canada at Quebec, Apr. 1919, Kingston Archdiocesan Archives

being given in chemistry. Courses leading to degrees in commerce and
the social sciences were inaugurated in 1936. The rectors during these
years were Patrick Phelan 1932–5, Leo A. Cormican 1935–44, and
Lawrence K. Poupore 1944–53.

A new agreement with Ottawa in 1948 provided for the establishment at St Patrick's of a graduate school of social welfare. Since 1945
the University of Ottawa had been expanding, opening the faculties of
medicine, engineering, and nursing, and planning others. As part of
this expansion, Ottawa gave St Patrick's the right to open one of these
faculties – the school of social welfare. This development was an important one for St Patrick's as it extended its activities outside the
faculty of arts. It was a gratifying one too since Canada's Catholic
social agencies, active in several cities, felt a need for the creation of
such a school. The new school, under the direction of Swithun Bowers,
was subsidized from the beginning by the Ontario government.

The distinctive character of St Patrick's school of social welfare, in
addition to its being English and Catholic, was its commitment to the
block plan whereby the three regular terms of the professional programme were interrupted by two intervening field-work terms which
the student spent in agencies in Ottawa or in one of several cities in
Canada and United States.

Bowers, the first and thus far only director, drew up the programme,
canvassed for students, and signed up the more than 35 field-work
instructors and agencies spread over two provinces and six states.
Under his direction the school developed rapidly and surely. An addition in 1955 to the original college building provided the school of social
welfare with modern facilities separate from those of the high school
and college. This development came during the rectorship of Gerald E.
Cousineau, 1953–6.

When in 1965 the University of Ottawa obtained a new charter and
became a provincially supported university, the administration of St
Patrick's was presented with a serious challenge and several alternatives:[8] it could remain a constituent but separate college; it could integrate fully into the faculty of arts of the new university; or it could
sever relations with the parent university. Ottawa provided time to
assess the situation by granting St Patrick's a status quo position based
on the 1932 and 1948 agreements.[9] In May 1967, the high school department of St Patrick's was moved to a new site, and in July of the
same year the rector, John Kelly, announced that the college division

8 See above, 250
9 University Affairs, 9, n.l. (Oct. 1967), 9

would join Carleton University. Reasons given for this decision were as follows: it was the best means of continuing to serve the same English-speaking Catholic constituency; the denominational college was, as such, experiencing difficulties in meeting administrative financial obligations; Carleton offered professors and students improved opportunities and security. Also important, though not specifically mentioned, was the example of Assumption, and of Ottawa itself, both of which institutions had dared to risk revolutionary change; and the desire to escape the combined English-French and inter-provincial Oblate tensions in which the college had passed its lively if harassed career.

Under the latest agreement both the faculty of arts and the school of social work became integral parts of Carleton University. The St Patrick's faculty of arts became one of three divisions in the faculty of arts of Carleton; the St Patrick's school of social work became the university's school of social work. The continuing St Patrick's division of the faculty of arts maintains a curriculum much like the old one, except that religion and philosophy have, in the contemporary fashion, ceased to be compulsory. The bachelor of commerce degree is no longer offered. All professors of St Patrick's hold Carleton appointments and all its students take Carleton degrees. The assets of St Patrick's, including its building, were transferred to Carleton in 1968. Kelly, as head of the St Patrick's division of the faculty of arts, is in rank and function, dean of a faculty providing undergraduate instruction, and Hugh A. MacDougall is its vice-dean; Swithun Bowers became director of the school of social work of Carleton University, and Carmen L. Couillard assistant director. These two administrators are no longer connected with St Patrick's, and their school has veered away from the block system to the more common structure of Canadian schools.

Although St Patrick's retains no formal religious affiliation, it can still be fairly described as a 'Catholic' undergraduate arts college in that it has a measure of control over appointments and maintains a liaison with the St Peter's Province of the Oblates. It is not limited to describing itself as 'Christian' as Ottawa is; nor is it 'non-teaching' as Assumption is; nor has it disappeared as St Dunstan's legally has. Its permanence will be tested with the passing of the present administrators, for although Carleton is disposed to preserve the Oblate image and tradition, it is not by any agreement obliged to do so.

Loyola College

MONTREAL

1896 (1848)

Loyola College, directed by the Fathers of the Society of Jesus (Upper Canada) and affiliated with the University of Montreal, is located on a fifty-acre property on Sherbrooke Street, Montreal West. Technically a classical college with privileged status, its academic programme is in the tradition of the Anglo-Canadian university colleges modified by the *ratio studiorum*. The college has four faculties: arts, commerce, science and engineering, theology; it grants through the University of Montreal the BA, BSC, and BCOMM degrees. Its buildings, many of them connected, consist of the junior building (1916), the refectory (1916), administration (1916 and 1917), the studium (1933), the chapel and auditorium (1933), the central building (1945, 1947), the Drummond science building (1962), the Brian building for the communication arts and social sciences (1968), and the Jesuit residence (1969). Land and buildings are evaluated at approximately $10,000,000.

BEFORE 1896

The early history of Loyola College is embedded in that of Montreal's Collège Ste-Marie, which had an English-speaking constituency even from its beginning in 1848 when it was founded by the New York–Canada mission of the Paris province (*Provincia Franciae*) of the Society of Jesus. Ste-Marie was the Jesuits' first college in Canada after their restoration; but they had, as is well known, opened a college in Quebec City back in 1635.

On 2 July 1841, the year after he became Montreal's second bishop, Monseigneur Ignace Bourget invited the General of the Society, Jean Roothaan, to re-establish a mission in Canada. During 1842, six priests and three brothers were sent to Montreal from Paris: Fathers Pierre Chazelle, Félix Martin, Paul Luiset, Dominique du Ranquet, Joseph Hanipaut, and Remi Tellier; and Brothers Emmanuel Brenans, Joseph Jenesseaux, and Pierre Tupin. Of these, Chazelle spoke English well, having been superior of a mission and college in Kentucky since 1830; he was already well-known in Montreal when he arrived with his colleagues because he had during 1839 conducted a retreat for the priests of the diocese.

When Bourget brought the Jesuits to Montreal, he intended to install them in the little seminary or college of Chambly established in Montreal by the Sulpicians in 1767. This turned out to be impractical. Instead, the new mission went as a group to the parish of Laprairie on the south bank of the St Lawrence where they replaced the pastor, Michael Power, who had just been named first bishop of Toronto, and from where they attended to retreats and other missions in many parts of Lower and Upper Canada. Chazelle established close rapport with Irish Catholics located in Bytown, Toronto, and the military camp at Sorel. He would also have liked to open a college right in Laprairie, but he was opposed in such a project by the Sulpicians, who saw no need for another little seminary, and by Monseigneur Bourget, who seems already to have envisaged a combined classical and commercial college for laymen in Montreal. In 1848, after the Jesuit mission in Canada had been subdivided, and after Chazelle had moved to other labours in Upper Canada, Félix Martin and four Jesuit companions opened Collège Ste-Marie at 17 St Alexander Street in Montreal.

The newly-founded college received its first students (seven French-speaking; six English-speaking) on 20 September 1848. Most of the students entering were young; that is, between eleven and fourteen years of age, but the programme planned was the full *ratio studiorum* which was to be gradually implemented. The college was at first known as *le petit collège* because of being located in small temporary quarters. The priests lived nearby in a residence attached to St Patrick's parish and supplied them by the Sulpicians. Boarders were accepted from the beginning, although Jesuit tradition favoured day schools. The legal incorporation of this new classical and commercial college was obtained from the legislature in 1852.

Martin's first announcement stated that 'the English and French languages will receive equal attention' and the school was officially known as both Le Collège Ste-Marie and St Mary's College. There is justification for regarding the English-speaking students and staff of the college as providing the early history of Loyola. There was even talk in the beginning of Ste-Marie being developed as an English college. The historian of Loyola writes as follows:

The proportion of English-speaking to French-speaking students at St Mary's College was fairly high. During the fifties, the average maintained in the senior class of philosophy in the classical course was 3 English to 8 French, and in the commercial course, where there were some studies in civil and mechanical engineering, it was preponderantly English. Among the boarders there were many American students, and Father Vignon noted in 1870 that almost two-thirds of the boarders spoke only English.

In those years, serious proposals were made by Father Jean Baptiste Hus and renewed by Fathers Remi Tellier and Jacques Perron that St Mary's should be developed as an English-speaking College. These suggestions were still under discussion in the early seventies when the census of 1871 showed that of Montreal's total population of 115,000, there were 56,856 French speaking and 58,144 English speaking. Practically one-half the English speaking population of Montreal, were then Irish who numbered 28,440.[1]

A parallel dichotomy also existed among the Jesuit faculty. The early mission from *Provincia Franciae* included both Canada and New York and there was considerable exchange of personnel between Ste-Marie and Fordham. Three Fordham presidents had, before their appointment, taught at Ste-Marie: Joseph Shea, William Gockelm, and Patrick Francis Dealy, the tenth, eleventh, and twelfth presidents respectively. The diverse constituencies within the college became strikingly apparent after 1888 when separate classical courses were provided for French and English boys; and it was a matter of some significance when in 1890 Lewis Drummond of Montreal became the first English-speaking rector of Collège Ste-Marie. At this period 'there were, in fact, two colleges in one'[2] and their physical separation in 1896 came as a surprise to no one.

Of importance to Loyola in subsequent years was the academic stature conferred on Collège Ste-Marie by the papal constitution usually referred to as Jamdudum. When the University of Montreal was established as a succursal or dependent branch of Laval, the Holy See extended limited academic privileges to it by a Propaganda decree dated 1 February 1876. Montreal's autonomy was further extended by the decree Jamdudum of 2 February 1889, which was especially concerned with empowering the bishops of the ecclesiastical province of Montreal to nominate the vice-chancellor. Because the Jesuit college of Montreal was old and revered and because, moreover, the University of Montreal was in a way to benefit from the legal disposal of the Jesuit Estates, the same Jamdudum conferred on Collège Ste-Marie special control over its courses and examinations. The pertinent passage of the decree is the following:

Now as there exists in Montreal a College by the name of St Mary's which is administered by the religious of the Society of Jesus, and which is outstanding

1 T.P. Slattery, *Loyola and Montreal*, Montreal: Palm, 1962, 61
2 Ibid., 70

both for the excellence of its teaching and the number of its students, we, lest there be any derogation at all made to the special privileges which have been granted long since to that Society by the Apostolic See, willingly allow its members to organize the examinations of their students, and to give to those they find proficient, a written certificate, stating they are worthy of the degrees which Laval University confers on the young men of equal merit in its affiliated colleges. On presenting this certificate, the University Council will issue to them the diploma granted to the University students who obtain the same degrees.[3]

The autonomy thus provided by Jamdudum placed Collège Ste-Marie in a more favourable academic position in relation to the University than the affiliated classical colleges.

LOYOLA SINCE 1896

In August 1896 a four-page leaflet labelled 'Prospectus' announced that Loyola College, a separate institution for English-speaking boys, would be established at 2084 St Catherine Street at Bleury across from Collège Ste-Marie. The college opened its doors on 2 September with 150 boys enrolled in the three junior years of the classical course. The growth of Loyola was rapid. By its second year of operation, it had to lease an adjacent building to the rear to look after its students. In February 1898 fire damaged these St Catherine Street quarters and the college moved back into Ste-Marie for a month before taking over the Tucker School at 68 Drummond St.

Loyola was planned as a national college and aspired from the beginning to become a university. Its first rector, Father Gregory O'Bryan, a well-known preacher of parish missions, but invalided by a heart attack, was clear on both these points. He was able through his wide contacts to fill the school with students from every part of English-speaking Canada and the eastern United States. His act of incorporation, which the Quebec legislature had ready for royal signature on 10 March 1899,[4] had in its original draught a degree-conferring clause which was only removed in committee and replaced by an affiliation clause after the second reading at the request of Monseigneur J.C.K. Laflamme, rector of Laval. While holding up Loyola's university status Laflamme confirmed its possession of the Jamdudum privileges and affiliated the college with Laval.

3 Ibid., 76
4 Statutes of Quebec, 62 Victoria, ch.78

O'Bryan's next contribution to Loyola came in his second term of office. He was replaced by the more scholarly William Doherty in 1899, but became rector again three months later on Doherty's sudden death. O'Bryan and the treasurer, John Charles Coffee, made the daring and colourful move of buying the 50-acre Decary farm in Notre Dame de Grace near Montreal West. The borrowing of $25,000 to buy the farm was at the time a controversial move, and the farm was often referred to as the Loyola 'melon patch.' Indeed, the property was not at the time of purchase suitable for the even then badly-needed new site, but it was to serve the next generation handsomely.

Loyola's third rector was the distinguished archaeologist Arthur E. Jones. He was appointed rector in 1901 when he was already at work tracing the paths followed by the Jesuit missionaries through Old Huronia. The college still had relatively few senior students or philosophers; actually only 18 during 1900–1, but the appointment of Jones enhanced the prestige of scholarship in the school. He presided over Loyola's seventh commencement, 22 June 1903, when Laval degrees were conferred for the first time on seven Loyola candidates.

In 1904 Adrian C. Turgeon succeeded Jones as rector. He held office for only one year when he was replaced by Gregory O'Bryan, who assumed the office for the third time. As on the earlier occasions O'Bryan had something new to sponsor: this time it was the Loyola Old Boys' Association which he brought into existence in 1906 under the presidency of John T. Hackett, who had just graduated.

From 1907 to 1913 the rector was Alexander A. Gagnieur. The college was during these years functioning well within the classical college tradition, but its core of philosophy students, now running about 40 a year, was assuming more importance in the overall structure. When Thomas J. MacMahon became rector in May 1913, and the administration at last made the decision to build on the Loyola farm, it was the philosophers, by now a reduced wartime class of only 21, who were in 1915 transferred to the unfinished buildings. The rest of the college was moved to Montreal West in the summer of 1916 when the junior building, the refectory building, and part of the administration building were ready.

The new buildings on Sherbrooke Street West, attractively designed and ornamented, were apparently uneconomical and less suitable than they appeared to be from the outside. Their opening was followed by financially difficult, even penurious war years. In 1917 MacMahon was succeeded by his predecessor, Alexander Gagnieur. Four months later

Gagnieur fell ill and the bursar, John Milivay Filion, had to take over as rector. Relief came in 1918 with the end of the war and the appointment of William H. Hingston.

It is not easy to exaggerate the importance of Hingston's rectorship, 1918–25, for Loyola College. In the first place it was no small matter that he should be the son of Sir William Hales Hingston, physician, surgeon, and mayor of Montreal, whose life had become a legend woven into the city's history. Secondly, Father Hingston was a man of almost extravagant courage, precisely the virtue called for in the unpredictable post-war years when a major campaign for funds and status simply had to be undertaken to remove the institution from its penury and frustration. He raised almost $300,000 and he allowed the stadium to be built. Thirdly, and most significant in the long run, he gave a free hand to his dean of studies, Father Edward de la Peza, to reorganize the course of studies in the college, initiating the slow process of transformation from the French classical college to the Anglo-Canadian faculty of arts and science. Loyola students now began to finish their algebra and geometry during the first four years of the course instead of at the end of the sixth year. The first four and the last four years of the programme became distinct units giving Loyola in effect a high school department and an arts programme. The bachelor's degree came to be regarded as the termination of an undergraduate course in a faculty of arts rather than the certificate of university entrance.

Hingston had less success in his attempt to deal with Loyola's constitution. Around 1919–20 it appeared for a time that the college might lose the limited autonomy it had. The University of Montreal was in the process of realizing its own autonomous status and obtained a preparatory rescript from the Holy See, 8 May 1919, which provided canonically for the separating of its ecclesiastical faculties from Laval. It was uncertain how this change would affect Loyola. However, Rome confirmed the privileges of Jamdudum on 5 January 1920, and they were written into the civil charter of the University of Montreal, 14 February 1920. Having made this much ground Hingston judged the time opportune for Loyola to seek its own charter. His bid is described by Slattery as follows:

Then in November 1922, after assurance of support had been privately given and relayed through the offices of the apostolic delegate, Loyola took steps to obtain legal autonomy with the right to grant her own degrees. Premier L.A. Taschereau indicated that he was favourable, and moreover promised a grant of $350,000 to help establish Loyola on its own. Dr B.A. Conroy then sponsored a joint Petition of Loyola College and its Governors to be presented as a bill in the Legislature. But the suffragan bishops of Montreal expressed their opposition, and Loyola was called upon to withdraw her petition.[5]

On this withdrawal a special act confirming the agreement between the University of Montreal and Loyola was passed:

[The University undertakes] to recognize and maintain for the conferring of degrees to the students of Loyola College, the privilege granted by the Pontifical Constitution Jamdudum, just as it has been recognized until now by the Université-Laval of Quebec; and consequently to confer upon the students of the aforesaid College, on presentation of certificates attesting they have undergone successful examinations, the ordinary diplomas which she gives to the students of her affiliated colleges.[6]

Hingston's successor was E.G. Bartlett, who held the office from 1925 to 1930. Bartlett completed the administration building in 1927. He initiated a long period of relative calm and consolidation extending from the late twenties to the sixties under the following rectors: Thomas J. MacMahon (1930–5), Hugh C. McCarthy (1935–40), Edward M. Brown (1940–8), John F. McCaffrey (1948–54), Gerald R. Lahey (1954–9), Patrick G. Malone, since 1959.

This long period of steady development has seen the building of the chapel and auditorium (1933), the central building (1945–7), the Drummond science building (1961–2), and the purchase in 1961 of a new 14-acre site in Côte St Luc for the new high school which will be opened within a few years. The expansion of the physical plant and of the salaried professoriate has in recent years been made possible by gifts from the general public including the Montreal archdiocesan drive of 1948, by regular provincial operational subsidies to classical colleges, by provincial capital and building grants in 1939, 1944, and 1960–1, by the 1959 settlement of the accumulated federal grants, and by a special grant in 1968 to meet capital and operating deficits.

The expansion of the physical plant has been accompanied on the academic level by the emergence of a university structure in specified areas. The present structure began to take form with the opening of the faculty of science in 1943. The rector, Edward Brown, had on 15 December 1942, requested the support of Archbishop Joseph Charbonneau

5 Slattery, Loyola, 187
6 Brief submitted by Loyola College to the Royal Commission of Inquiry on Education, Montreal, Nov. 1961

to support a new move for a charter. Charbonneau felt that he could not acquiesce but encouraged Loyola to establish its own science faculty. The opening of the building was accompanied by the introduction of honours work in chemistry and mathematics and of the first three years of engineering. In 1948 a faculty of commerce was added, and in 1958 honour courses in economics, English, and history. General academic recognition followed these moves. On 22 January 1960, Loyola was admitted to membership in the National Conference of Canadian Universities at a special meeting of the association held in Montreal. It was hoped at the time that the special meeting in Montreal would be useful to Malone, who was preparing another request to the legislature for a provincial charter.

In recent years Loyola has been conducting continuing efforts to achieve complete academic autonomy. Archbishop Charbonneau twice promised to support Loyola's petition to the Quebec legislature: on 7 June 1948, he gave his assurance to Father Brown, and on 29 November 1948, to Father McCaffrey and John T. Hackett. Premier Duplessis stopped this move on 28 January 1949. Attempts were again made in 1954, 1960, and 1961. On this last occasion success seemed assured: Bishop Emmett Carter, Governor-General Georges Vanier, and educators in many parts of Canada were supporting it; a petition signed by 34,000 persons carried the weight of the English-speaking Catholics of Montreal. The issue, however, became incredibly complex when Collège Brébeuf, directed by the Jesuits of the Lower Canadian province, also placed a petition for a charter before the legislature. Premier Lesage decided at the last minute not to deal with these requests in isolation from Quebec's many educational problems at all levels but referred them with the others to a royal commission of inquiry on education set up under the chairmanship of Monsignor Alphonse-Marie Parent, former rector of Laval University.

It was 1964 before the Parent Commission handed down its report. Loyola is dealt with in chapter 7 of the second part of the report. The commission distinguished three kinds of institutions of higher education: unlimited charter universities, limited charter universites, centres for university studies. The first and third categories looked after Quebec's six established universities and their affiliates. The new category of limited charter universities was designed to look after the needs of institutions like Loyola, without actually raising them to full university status. The commission's reasons for suggesting limited charter universities were that such universities would help cope with the problem of numbers and would decentralize higher education. In this last function they would be a sort of antidote to the centralization accepted in so much of the report. Limited charter universities were to provide instruction and to award first degrees (licence or bachelor), serve constituencies of about 2000 students, have on their overall staff about one-third with a doctoral degree in their subject of instruction, and have adequate library and laboratory facilities. This recommendation, no.120 of the report, comes very close to describing Loyola in detail.

Three other recommendations of the report were pertinent:

No.122: We recommend that, for each new limited charter university, the Board of Higher Education appoint an academic advisory committee, made up of university professors and persons familiar with the administration and direction of a university, which will during a limited period of some five years, advise the university on the appointment of principal and of other executive officers, the framing of its charter, the choice of staff, the elaboration of programmes, plans for building and equipment.

No.124: We recommend that every new institution at the university level be constituted as a corporation by a law reserving to the state the appointment of at least the majority of the administrative board, but recognizing the right of teachers' groups, or of persons interested in education for various reasons, to propose to the state the appointment of persons of their choice.

No.126: We recommend that a limited charter university be formed by grouping the facilities of Loyola College, Marianopolis College, Thomas More Institute and St Joseph's Teachers College, in order to constitute a corporation governed by an administrative board appointed by the Lieutenant-Governor-in-Council on the recommendation of the English-speaking Roman Catholic institutions and groups concerned.

The foregoing recommendations leave undetermined the role of the Jesuits in the proposed university. The discussion preliminary to the recommendation assumes that the new university will not be Jesuit: 'We have insisted in earlier paragraphs on the fact that the state should no longer entrust to a private group control over a university when this university is largely financed by the state. The principle applies here also; recognition can of course be given to the services rendered by the Jesuits in the past; this is not an adequate reason to entrust to them in the future entire and exclusive authority over the new institution of higher learning. For the fine work which has been accomplished to date to reach completion it must change, in status and in nature; this is an evolutionary process of fairly frequent occurrence.' From Loyola's point of view much would have to be sacrificed for this very real institutional autonomy: the right to confer degrees after the first one; and the right of the Jesuits to appoint the president and the administration. From the point of view of the other parties to the federation the Jesuits would remain only too strong: they would be one of the groups, and the largest, to nominate officers; they would have large representation in the continuing administration and on the faculty, which would also be assured a voice; and they would, at least at first, own the probable site of the university.[7]

The report appeared in 1964. Malone asked that recommendation 126 be implemented immediately; it was thought that this might happen during the spring or summer of 1965. On 24 July 1965 the revenue minister Eric Kierans announced that the legislature would not consider the matter during the present session. The government, he said, would not act precipitately but would implement the report from the bottom up by expanding primary and secondary institutions first, and dealing with higher education later. He may also have been influenced by the mixed feeling of St Thomas More Institute, St Joseph's Teachers' College, and Marianopolis. The institute and the teachers' college had always been unsure whether their work properly belonged within or without a university. Marianopolis hesitated over two issues: fear that a co-educational Catholic university would offer them little scope for an apostolate other than providing residence; the conviction that the move to Loyola would end forever the possibility of a tie with McGill.

During the months following the publication of the *Parent Report*, the Catholic institutions suggested as participating members of the limited charter university held a series of discussions on possible collaboration and action. In January 1968 it was suggested by Edmund J. Roche, director of the Canadian hierarchy's National Education Office, that there be established 'an English Catholic University in Montreal.'[8] This university would stress the Catholic dimension pretty much in the Catholic University of America tradition. The idea was a good one if the government would help support it. Again Marianopolis was cool to the plan.[9] When the government made a subsidy to Loyola at the end of 1968, the ministry suggested a merger with Sir George Williams, evidence, perhaps, of a lack of enthusiasm for the Catholic dimension.

Important developments at Loyola during recent years include the

7 *Report of the Royal Commission of Inquiry on Education in the Province of Quebec*, 1964. See esp. II, *The Pedagogical Structures*, ch.7, 'Higher Education,' 195–259.

8 Report on Montreal University Question to Most Reverend Norman Gallagher, DD, Auxiliary Bishop of Montreal by Rev. Edmund J. Roche, Director, National Education Office, 2 Jan. 1968. Privately distributed.

9 See below, 271–2

building up of strong departments in history and theology, the strengthening of the lay faculty, the admission of women to full-term regular courses,[10] the establishing of a new communication arts department under J.E. O'Brien. The most recent trend in the college, as in McGill and Toronto, is to subject the entire institution to vigorous self-study. By the end of 1968, one committee was examining college government with a view to expanding the role therein of Loyola's faculty and students; another was studying Loyola's future, probing the impact on the college of the new University of Quebec, of projected university centres, of CEGEPs; still another was studying student life.

While such self-assessment has been proceeding, the college has been growing in numbers (it is now over 3000), and has been falling heavily into debt. The government has been encouraging expansion but making no new grants. Relief came in November 1968 when the Quebec government made Loyola a special grant of nearly $6,000,000 towards capital debt and current operating deficit, possibly saving the college from bankruptcy. Whether the ministry's new policy augurs well for the future remains to be seen, but there could one day be either an independent Loyola, or a Loyola participating in a recognized and supported university complex.

The disturbing uncertainty of Loyola's position in the structure of higher education in Quebec was a major factor in the creation of a sense of insecurity among the staff, students, and constituency. This manifested itself in many ways, but especially in the matter of staff appointments, and largely accounts for the exaggerated importance attached even nationally to the celebrated Santhanam case.

Dr Srinvas Santhanam was hired by Loyola's physics department in 1963 on a two-year contract. The administration was not satisfied with the young physicist but reluctantly renewed his contract, for one compassionate reason or another, a year at a time until 1968. The 1968–9 contract was made so that Santhanam could complete his research in progress before leaving Loyola, which he agreed to do at the end of the academic year.

When the contract was not renewed for 1969–70, Santhanam charged the administration with unfair treatment and asked the Canadian Association of University Teachers to take up his case. CAUT agreed to do so because some of the staff and student body of Loyola saw some substance in the charge of unfairness.

The case gained notoriety in university circles during 1970 when

10 The graduating class of 1965, totalling 199 graduates, included 5 women. *The Montreal Star*, 20 May 1965.

rumours were circulating that the committee established by CAUT to examine the case was going to ask for a censure on Loyola. Santhanam's case was far too weak to justify a censure, but the CAUT committee asked that Loyola and Santhanam agree to submit the issue to binding arbitration. Although binding arbitration was recognized procedure for dealing with dismissal of faculty members holding tenure, it seemed uncalled for in the given situation, which was not a case of dismissal and did not involve tenure. Malone appealed to the AUCC and was upheld: 'We are of the opinion that the recommendation of the CAUT committee for binding arbitration should not be accepted even though we deplore the fact that those who have encouraged Dr Santhanam to seek a redress to which he is not entitled have left him in doubly difficult circumstances.'[11]

The Santhanam case could only have become a heightened issue in the context of Loyola's combined external and internal uncertainties. The task of the next few years for both the college administration and the provincial government is to have Loyola recognized as the public institution it truly is and its problems solved in the public forum.

11 *University Affairs*, 11, no.3, March 1970, 3

Marianopolis College

MONTREAL

1908 (1944)

Marianopolis College is an undergraduate university college affiliated with the University of Montreal, offering programmes leading to the BA and BSC. It provides two common years of general course work and professional prerequisites, and these are followed by two diversified years in the various majors and in honour chemistry. The college, under the direction of the Sisters of the Congregation of Notre Dame, is located at 3647 Peel Street in downtown Montreal adjacent to McGill University. Its campus is a compact arrangement of six buildings on a valuable property on the beautiful slope of Mount Royal. Besides an administration building, and the Drummond-McGregor Residence Hall, there are four academic buildings: Georgian Hall housing the library, student affairs, and guidance offices; Margarita Hall, containing faculty offices and seminar rooms; Good Counsel Hall for departmental offices; and the science building. The college also maintains a lodge at St Hippolyte in the Laurentians for study week-ends and relaxation.

The Congregation of Notre Dame, founded in the seventeenth century by Marguerite Bourgeoys, has a long history in education in the province of Quebec and elsewhere. The present university college was founded in 1908 as Notre Dame Ladies' College and was intended to provide the equivalent of a Quebec classical college education for English-speaking girls. It was opened in the motherhouse of the congregation at Sherbrooke and Atwater Streets in conjunction with but distinct from a second college conducted in the same building for French-speaking girls. These were Quebec's first institutions for the higher education of Catholic women. Notre Dame Ladies' College was affiliated from the beginning with Laval University, but the affiliation was transferred in 1922 to the newly-chartered University of Montreal.

In 1927 the two colleges were moved from the motherhouse to Westmount Avenue where, along with l'Institute Pédagogique also directed by the congregation, they were welded into a single institution called Marguerite Bourgeoys College after the saintly foundress of the congregation. The new arrangement turned out to be unattractive to English-speaking girls in part because of the classroom language problem but even more because the curriculum followed the Quebec pattern for women's colleges and was intended to be terminal, while many of the English-speaking girls were looking for something that would admit them to the graduate and professional programmes of McGill, Toronto, and the American universities. A committee was formed to look into the question. With the consent of Archbishop Charbonneau, the committee recommended the opening of a totally independent college for English-speaking girls. This recommendation led to the removal of these girls from Westmount Avenue and the opening of Marianopolis College in the remodelled Mount St Mary School on Dorchester Street. Lectures began in Marianopolis in September 1944. Four months later, January 1945, the remodelled building was totally destroyed by fire. Very shortly afterwards Marianopolis reopened on its present site on Peel Street. It was incorporated under the Quebec Companies Act in 1946 and again in 1961, remaining an affiliate of Montreal.

At the beginning, the College was administered by its dean. Sister St George (McGuigan) was the first dean, taking office in 1943 a year before the setting up of Marianopolis as distinct from Marguerite Bourgeoys College. She remained dean until 1949. She was succeeded by Sister Alfred of Rome (Baeszler) who was dean from 1949 to 1952. Sister Madeleine of Charity (Noonan) was dean from 1952 to 1966. The present dean, Sister Calista Begnal took over in 1966. In 1960 the office of president was established. Sister Mary MacCormack has been the only president. She has been a strong administrator and has seen the academic and educational project grow encouragingly. By 1969 the college enrolled over 400 women, 100 of them in residence, graduating nearly 100 women a year. Marianopolis offered these women challenging programmes in the arts and sciences, including advanced chemistry, philosophy, and theology which the college features, and even a contemporary discipline like structural, descriptive, and historical linguistics both theoretical and applied. For its relatively small enrolment, it provided a teaching faculty of 59 persons, some of them quite distinguished professors and one-third of them holding a doctorate. The college provided a selective but adequate undergraduate library of 28,632 volumes, plus 446 accumulating serials and collections of records and microfilms – rather good, considering the availability of Montreal's other downtown libraries and galleries.

Sister Mary MacCormack has been confronted with a series of complex institutional problems, mainly structural. The first of these was amalgamation: should Marianopolis amalgamate with Loyola, or with a proposed Montreal Catholic university, or with Sir George Williams, or with McGill? The second problem involved co-education: should

Marianopolis remain a women's college, or should it admit men? The two problems, of course, amalgamation and co-education, are related.

Pressure was early brought to bear on Marianopolis to throw in its lot with Loyola. At one stage, a few years back, it looked as though this might happen. The girls of Marianopolis went regularly to Loyola for science instruction and laboratory work. The administration of Marianopolis seriously considered acquiring a property adjacent to the Loyola campus. To have moved would not likely at that time have been a mistake in that the *Parent Report* on education in Quebec encouraged consolidation of resources. It might even, though this is pure conjecture, have won Loyola its charter.

But the move was not made, and for strong reasons: it would have been a rejection of the college tradition which located Marianopolis downtown and restricted it to women; it would have threatened the college with loss of identity, especially given the extraordinary vigour of Loyola's administration; more seriously, the move would have created in Montreal West a strong non-French, committed Irish academic enclave which could not serve the overall interests of Montreal and would therefore have been politically disastrous.

Loyola's counter move, admitting women to its courses over the objections of Marianopolis, was right; Loyola needed this particular constituency for its own academic integrity. Marianopolis would have been perfectly in order had it even then begun to accept men into its student body. Bold moves of this kind create healthy rivalry; any inconvenience entailed is quickly removed by time, especially in a large growing urban area. In any event, the affiliation of Marianopolis with Loyola either then or now without at the same time creating a common campus was and is unthinkable. A divided campus could only repeat the remote and anomalous University of Montreal connection, indefensible except as a stopgap pending the granting of the various charters called for.

Throughout 1967 and 1968 a new alternative was presented to Marianopolis – that it become part of an English-speaking Catholic university centre. Such a centre would hope to include, in addition to Marianopolis, Loyola, the Thomas More Institute, and St Joseph's Teachers' College. The plan was put forward in January 1968 by Edmund J. Roche, director of the National Education Office of the Canadian Catholic Conference of bishops, after consultation with all the administrations concerned.[1] Although the document was addressed to

1 Report on Montreal University Question to Most Reverend Norman Gallagher, DD, Auxiliary Bishop of Montreal by Rev. Edmund J. Roche, Director, National Education Office, 2 Jan. 1968. Privately distributed. See above, 266.

a different problem, that of the wisdom of establishing an English-speaking Catholic university in Montreal, and although it was inspired by high ideals, it was defective on a basic point, the kind of ownership religious orders or dioceses have over properties provided by the faithful (which includes the orders and diocesan officials themselves) for educational purposes. The proposal called for the setting up of a new university board which would buy the holdings of the Jesuit Fathers in Loyola, and presumably the holdings of the Sisters of Notre Dame if they came into the plan – or alternatively allowing the sisters to sell their property and keep the income – and which would provide tenure, full salaries, and pensions for participating religious. The plan presumes a kind of ownership over Catholic colleges which orders and dioceses do not possess. Religious are entitled in a case of reorganization like this to recover their debt but no more. The surplus belongs to the continuing Catholic operation.[2] Marianopolis dropped out of these discussions at an early date and was not one of the participating parties named in Roches's proposal.

The oldest amalgamation with which Marianopolis has been concerned is one with McGill University. When the college opened on its present site, there was hope that one day it might become part of McGill. In the time of Sister St George, however, the very suggestion was anathema to chancery and to the University of Montreal. Only the Montreal affiliation was acceptable. There has been a steady relaxation of this attitude especially since 1967 when Cardinal Léger approved of a non-denominational board for the University of Montreal, a lay president, and the termination of pontifical status. In the ordinary course of events, this kind of openness ought to have facilitated negotiations with McGill. Thus far it has not, partly because of the Catholic University proposal, partly because of the new attitude present among the French-Canadians of Montreal that a large English-speaking complex in the city's centre is a kind of affront to the true character of Montreal as a whole. At the moment, an amalgamation of Marianopolis and McGill can only accentuate McGill's English image. Negotiations would be much easier if the *Parent Report* had encouraged co-operation, even amalgamation, as a solution to the problems of the English-language universities of Montreal.

Marianopolis has never shown any inclination to amalgamate with Sir George Williams, but when in November 1968 the government assisted Loyola with a special grant, the suggestion was officially put forward that Loyola and Sir George Williams look into the possibility

2 See below, 420

of a merger. Subsequently, there was talk of including Marianopolis in such a proposed merger. The question remains open.

Perhaps pertinent here is the reflection, not uncommon today, that the very language of amalgamations, mergers, and affiliations in the traditional sense is an outmoded form of discourse. It might be more expedient to seek expression for Marianopolis's true function in public education. Since the college is not likely to become a university in its own right, and since its ties with Montreal (as they would be also with Loyola or Sir George Williams) are but a legal fiction, it should either become a constituent and integral part of McGill (on whose campus it is for all practical purposes located) or it should be given its own limited charter.

The commissioners who prepared the *Parent Report* thought in terms of function, as have the legislators who implemented it, particularly in devising their colleges of general and vocational education (CEGEPs). It is doubtful that Marianopolis should be only a CEGEP, although the CEGEP function should be part of its service to its constituency. It should probably be part of the whole experimental policy of the department of education, a project, for example, where educational ideas for the future could be tested.

Sister Mary MacCormack's other problem has been the question of deciding whether Marianopolis should go co-educational. The heads and boards of women's colleges everywhere have been asking themselves the same question. Many feel that the trend away from women's colleges is only part of the temper of the times and that these colleges will like other fashions be re-accepted. But the issue probably runs deeper. Higher education in the twentieth century requires a broader milieu than any college, and *a fortiori* any college of men or women only, can provide. A college is a sort of project, in the sense that a school of medicine, a research centre, or any faculty is a project. It must inhere in a complementing conglomerate and is quite lost without catholicity of environment. The university itself only with difficulty provides such a milieu. But it does provide it in a stumbling sort of way and an isolated project does not.

If this is the case with colleges as such it is doubly so of women's colleges, not merely because women want to be where the men are, but because modern women, like modern men, need the university as it needs them. Especially is this latter true. Universities need women for the richer development of their own scholarship. Women have too much to offer universities to be isolated even in the finest of segregated colleges. Awareness of all this brought Marianopolis to the stage where it could no longer tolerate its own restrictions. In the fall of 1969 the college admitted men for the first time – the token number of 10. The move was judged successful enough that in 1970 one-fifth of the 300 freshmen admitted were men.

At the same time that it opened its doors to men, Marianopolis also immersed itself more deeply in the higher educational systems of the province by offering its own CEGEP equivalent, or, as it is known within the college, CEGEP 'M'.[3] When the CEGEP programme was initiated in Quebec, it was officially estimated that the programme would be taken up only by French institutions. At one stage, it appeared that there would be by 1971 some 70 institutions participating in the programme, only one of them – Dawson College – being English-speaking.[4] But McGill, Bishops, and Marianopolis have bolstered the project by initiating their own equivalents – a significant acceptance of provincial educational structure. Marianopolis enters the seventies in a refreshing burst of enthusiasm and expansion.

3 Re the college of general and vocational education (CEGEP) see 'Quebec Completes Structure for Universal Post-Secondary Education,' *University Affairs*, 10, no.5 (Apr. 1969), 1–2.
4 'McGill Announces Policy for 1969 Admissions,' *University Affairs*, 10, no.4 (Feb. 1969), 19

Assumption University

WINDSOR

1857 (1963)

Assumption University, as operating since 1963, is a federated university in the University of Windsor. It is located along Huron Line on the west side of the Windsor campus. It consists of one large unit which houses the residence of the Basilian faculty, the administrative offices, the chapel, and chaplain facilities. The university is not exercising its degree-conferring powers, and is not enrolling or registering students, but is experimenting with new patterns intended to serve the Church and Church-related disciplines by collaborating with a large, flourishing, multifaculty secular university which is at the same time its own creation.

BEGINNINGS TO 1870

Assumption College opened on 10 February 1857, a combined common school and college with 26 boarders and 60 day scholars. The school and college building was undertaken by Angus MacDonell and was well under way when the Jesuit Father, Pierre Point, came to Assumption parish. Point finished the first college building and opened it in 1857. In charge of the common school when it went into the college building in February 1857 was Theodore Girardot, a school teacher from France. Point himself was probably head of the college *pro tempore*.[1]

Assumption took its name from the Sandwich parish which in its turn had taken it from the Settlement of L'Assomption, the Jesuit mission to the Wyandots or Hurons on either side of the Detroit River. The Jesuits had left the area after the suppression but had been restored to the parish of the Assumption by Bishop Michael Power in 1843. Point, in charge of the parish after the restoration, built the parish church and then, between 1855 and the beginning of 1857, a college building into which the common school also moved.[2]

While the college building was still under construction, Sandwich

---

1 L.K. Shook, 'The Coming of the Basilians to Assumption College: Early Expansion of St Michael's College, *Report of the Canadian Catholic Historical Association*, 18(1951), 59–73

2 E.J. Lajeunesse, *The Windsor Border Region*, Toronto: The Champlain Society, 1960; also his 'Sermon Preached in Assumption Church,' Windsor, 4 Feb. 1957, in Scollard, *Historical Notes*, XXIX, 27–8

became part of the new diocese of London and came under the jurisdiction of Bishop Pierre-Adolphe Pinsonneault. It was Pinsonneault's intention to make Sandwich rather than London his see, which meant making the parish church his cathedral and the college a diocesan institution. With this in mind he approached Joseph Malbos, the Basilian treasurer of St Michael's College in Toronto, inviting him to come to Sandwich as superior of the college. Malbos consulted his Basilian superiors and accepted the invitation. He did not, however, consult Bishop de Charbonnel, to whom he was, as treasurer of the college, also responsible. De Charbonnel was in Europe at the time. In late October or early November 1857, Malbos went to Sandwich under the following contract: that he was to be superior of Assumption College, that the college was to be operated *aux périls et risques* of the bishop of London, and that the arrangements were to be regarded as tentative and exploratory binding for one year only.[3]

Although French was the language of the people of Assumption parish and of the common school, it was Pinsonneault's intention that the college, at least after Point was out of the picture, should be predominantly English. The bishop thought of the college as serving the diocese of London as a whole and as supporting itself by drawing students also from dioceses in Michigan and Ohio.[4] The first advertisement placed in the Toronto papers stated that English and French were to be on equal footing.[5] But Malbos was sought out as superior because he had quickly acquired facility in English after coming out from France. Pinsonneault also expressly stated in a letter of 1859 that 'in order not to complicate courses, English was to be the principal language as in Toronto, French the accessory.'[6]

Malbos conducted the college until the end of the academic year. Available records indicate that he was the only priest on the staff. Mr Girardot was teaching in the common school, and at least seven ecclesiastical students were doing some teaching in the college.[7] It is possible too that assistance was given by Jesuits on the parish staff. The year

3 Tourvieille to Soulerin, Nov. 1857, *Registre 1855–1860*, 171. See Shook, 'The Coming of the Basilians,' 63.

4 Pinsonneault to Soulerin, 28 Sept. 1858, Basilian Archives, Toronto; see Scollard, *Historical Notes*, VI, 99–102.

5 *The Toronto Mirror*, 31 July 1857

6 Pinsonneault to Malbos, 21 Sept. 1859; see Scollard, *Historical Notes*, VI, 107–8.

7 *Dunigan's American Catholic Almanac and List of Clergy*, New York: Edward Dunigan and his brother, 1858, p.185. The eight ecclesiastical students were John Shea, J. Murphy (ordained July 1858), W. Oram, P. Fauteux (ordained 1859), A. Saivaudet, J.T. Wagner (ordained 1860), and Joseph Girard (ordained 1860).

seems to have been a good one academically, and both Malbos and Pinsonneault faced 1858–9 with hope and confidence.[8]

Very important for the future of Assumption was the incorporation of the college. Pinsonneault and Malbos applied for incorporation at the beginning of the session of parliament, 26 February 1858; the public act incorporating the college was given royal assent on 16 August of the same year.[9] Malbos was the first superior under the terms of the act. With this act Assumption became eligible for government grants in favour of higher education. Its name was included among the colleges qualifying for assistance when a payment was authorized for 1860. The first grant received was in the amount of $400.[10]

Malbos was still in Sandwich at the opening of 1858–9. He left suddenly for France in late October or early November 1858, terminating his superiorship. His departure was occasioned by several factors: his failure to obtain either recruits or a commitment from the Basilians, personality clashes with the staff, continued opposition from de Charbonnel, and tensions between Pinsonneault and the Jesuits over the proposal to move the episcopal see from London to Sandwich.[11]

The departure of Malbos did not mean the closing of the college. The bishop expected to have him back before long and in the meantime brought Father C. Fracton from Sarnia to serve as superior. The bishop also secured on 2 February 1859 a pontifical brief authorizing the transference of his see to Sandwich. By the following October the Jesuits had left the parish and the bishop had moved in.

From this time until 1870 the records are scanty. Nothing is known of Fracton's superiorship. In 1862 the college was placed under the direction of the Benedictines, an arrangement which lasted for only one academic year. It was a discouraging time for an American order to take over Assumption because the effects of the civil war on the college's enrolment were already beginning to be felt, and the financial pressures in Canada were severe.[12] When the Benedictines left in May 1863, the status of Assumption as a college became most uncertain. It is not, for

8 *The Canadian Freeman*, 23 July 1858, gives a brief account of the closing exercises for the past year. The following issue of *The Canadian Freeman*, 30 July 1858, carries both an announcement for 1858–9 and an article on the prospects of the college.

9 An Act to Incorporate Assumption College, Sandwich, in the Diocese of London (21 Victoria, ch.136; 16 Aug. 1858)

10 Hodgins, *Documentary History*, xv, 34

11 Pinsonneault to Malbos, 21 Sept. 1859; see Scollard, *Historical Notes*, vi, 103–12.

12 O'Connor to Soulerin, 1 Dec. 1868, calls them 'bad managers' and he seems to have in mind their financial difficulties. See Scollard, *Historical Notes*, vi, 155.

example, listed in the Catholic Church directories between 1864 and 1870. The common school was there, certainly, and Girardot was in charge of it. Headship of the college seems to have been largely nominal. Father L. Musart was brought from London and is called 'Bishop's Chaplain' in 1866, the year of Pinsonneault's resignation. Musart is also called on one occasion, superior of Assumption.[13] The responsibility, however, was Girardot's, and college registration must have reached the vanishing point. Another name attached to the headship in the late sixties was P.D. Laurent, pastor of Amherstburg and dean of the district, but also, apparently, pastor of Assumption. So far as the college was concerned, he was probably a figurehead. At any rate, following the government's apportioning of grants for 1867, according to O'Connor, 'the premier found out that the college consisted only of an ordinary school' and refused to turn over the subsidy of $1500.[14] The new bishop, John Walsh, when it became clear that he was successfully negotiating for the return of the Basilian Fathers to Assumption, succeeded in getting the subsidy, which he immediately applied to the mortgage. The concordat made with the Basilians speaks of their obligation to 'rouvrir le college de Sandwich.'[15]

When J.M. Bruyère, Walsh's vicar general, was negotiating with the Basilians just prior to their returning to Sandwich, he spoke of the present (April 1870) status of the college as follows: 'Assumption College, although its personnel is extremely limited, has at the moment 52 boarders under the supervision of Rev. Father Laurent who is both pastor of the parish and superior of the college. This gentleman is assisted by Mr Girardot, a teacher, and by three ecclesiastical students.'[16] Bruyère is not understating the case. Father Laurent was pastor of Amherstburg and dean of the western end of the diocese. It is possible that he was on leave in 1870 to look after the college.[17] Bruyère at any rate speaks of the college as existing and as being the responsibility of Dean Laurent rather than of Girardot. There was little enough for Denis

13 From 'L'Assumption College and Church, Sandwich,' in *The Evening Record*, 18 July 1890; in Scollard *Historical Notes*, xxvi, 76.

14 O'Connor to Soulerin, 1 Dec. 1868, in Scollard, *Historical Notes*, vi, 155; and Bruyère, 25 Apr. 1870, in Scollard, *Historical Notes*, viii, 10, 12, 15

15 Concordat of 27 Sept. 1869; Scollard, *Historical Notes*, vi, 208

16 Bruyère to Soulerin, 28 Apr. 1870; Scollard, *Historical Notes*, viii, 10; see also O'Connor to Soulerin, 25 Jan. 1869, vi, 186.

17 In a history of the parish of St. John the Baptist, Amherstburg, Vincent Donnelly speaks of the absence of Father Laurent from Amherstburg 'from January 1870 till November 1870.' *Border Cities Star*, 7 July 1928; see Scollard, *Historical Notes*, xxvi, 88. It is unlikely that this absence had anything to do with Assumption College.

O'Connor and his colleagues to take over when they arrived in Sandwich during the summer of 1870.

THE INDEPENDENT COLLEGE: 1870–1919

In June 1868, Bishop Walsh formally invited the Basilian Fathers to take over the direction of Assumption College.[18] Preliminary negotiations dealt mainly with the state of the property, the amount of land to go with the college, the direction of Assumption parish, the separation of the college from the common school, and the threatened cessation of government grants following Canadian confederation. The negotiations concluded with the concordat of 27 September 1869, by which Bishop Walsh agreed to turn over to the Basilians the building and land of college and parish for 499 years, also to release to them, so that they could meet mortgage payments, some of the parish revenues which ought ordinarily to have gone to him, and by which the Basilians committed themselves to establish a college with classical and commercial courses of the kind being given at St Michael's in Toronto.[19]

Assumption reopened in September 1870 with Denis O'Connor as superior and econome, Jean J. Aboulin and Charles J. Faure in the parish, and a group of unordained theological students – Robert McBrady, James Scanlon, John Quinlan, and James Mannix – to teach the various courses and look after the study hall and the dormitory. The staff had to work hard and to put up with poor lodging; but they were happy and confident about their prospects for success.

O'Connor's major problem was money, which he borrowed from Annonay, from a Windsor businessman, and from St Michael's. Charles Vincent, the superior in Toronto, was not generous to the new Assumption with men: he held back two prospective teachers, Mr Kennedy and Mr Foy, who had been designated for Assumption by the superior general.[20] But he came through with a no-interest loan. Inadequate enrolment was a worry too. During the first three years, there were only about 40 boarders – all perhaps that the rundown buildings could properly accommodate – but almost no day scholars. Sandwich residents would attend the common school, which was free, but they would not go to college. Very few boarders came from the whole diocese of London. Most students were Americans, and they tended to be interested in the commercial, not the classical course. Yet Assumption

18 Eleven letters dealing with these negotiations are in the general archives of the Basilian Fathers. See Scollard, *Historical Notes*, VI.
19 For text see Scollard, *Historical Notes*, VI, 206–10.
20 O'Connor to Soulerin, 1 Nov. 1870; Scollard, *Historical Notes*, VIII, 33–43

managed to remain a college of the St Michael's type, with a few students taking philosophy, and a few theology, which O'Connor himself seems to have taught. The following excerpt from a letter to J.M. Soulerin, the superior general, written about two months after opening, gives a frank and informative picture:

I am glad, too, to be able to report favourably of the masters. I have only four classes, two Latin and two English. I did not want to establish too many at first. I can establish them as they will be required. All the masters have had no experience in teaching, except one who taught for a few months in Toronto. Yet they are all very devoted to their work, and their boys are making a reasonable progress. The masters also study well themselves and I am generally content with the manner in which they observe the rules.

I see by your letter that you think I have Kennedy and Foy here. Such is not the case. You ought to know Father Vincent well enough to know that he first looks out for himself. I was not at all satisfied with the way he served me here. In your first letter, accepting Sandwich, you told him to send Father Frachon or Father Chalandard along with me; he was not willing to do so. You intended Mr Foy for Sandwich and Father Vincent would not let him come, though I asked for him especially, as he is able to teach drawing. Consequently I have no drawing master, though some pupils have asked to learn it. When it was a question of sending Father Aboulin here, he never let me know anything about it until he wrote to tell me he was coming. All this did not please me much in the beginning, but now that I see things are going pretty well I am more reconciled. The only thing I complain of now is that I have too much to do. I have to teach theology, moral and dogmatic, philosophy, catechism on Sundays, to preach every Sunday in English at early Mass, besides performing my duties as superior and econome.[21]

O'Connor's regime was, in spite of years of national depression, marked by material progress. In 1873 he bought a farm of 108 acres, paying $1000 for it. The occasion of making the purchase was an increase in the cost of wood – it had gone up to $50 a cord – and his method of coping with the annoying expense was to buy a wooded farm with money he could borrow from Annonay. The same year his boarders rose to 71, and the following year he actually had to refuse 24. This last statistic caused him in 1875 to put up a new wing, again borrowing, not only from Annonay but from Toronto and Owen Sound as well. He made a second addition to the college building during 1883–4. The confidence O'Connor was able to inspire in his projects is one of the stirring features of his launching of Assumption.

21 Scollard, *Historical Notes*, VIII, 38–40

O'Connor was a stern disciplinarian and a shrewd judge of character. He was a bulwark of defence for all Basilians during the trying years when Bishop Lynch of Toronto became unfriendly and tried to replace the Basilians there with Vincentians.[22] He also held good men on his staff when they came his way: notably Robert McBrady, Michael Ferguson (whom Lynch drove out of Toronto), and Daniel Cushing, men who must always remain on any list of Canada's distinguished educators.

O'Connor remained in charge of Assumption until 1890 when, on 19 October, he was consecrated bishop of London, successor to his admired friend of many years, John Walsh, who had just been transferred to the archbishopric of Toronto. O'Connor's contribution to Assumption was material, organizational, and moral. Although he left behind in 1890 a debt of $90,000, he also left a well-run college, with a presentable building and with remarkable prestige. He was not a man of ideas. He saw his task as transferring to Sandwich what he had known in Toronto, and he fulfilled it. He could never have carried out the daring Teefy-Carr changes effected in Toronto. Carr refers to O'Connor as among those who were dubious that adopting the departments curriculum would work.[23]

The regime begun by O'Connor was continued with varying success by three successors: Daniel Cushing 1890–1901, Robert McBrady 1901–7, and Francis Forster 1907–19. Cushing and McBrady introduced no substantial changes of policy but continued the material development of the college. Cushing was O'Connor-trained, having joined O'Connor's staff in 1871 as a teaching scholastic. He was superior of St Michael's in Toronto for short terms immediately preceding and shortly following his eleven-year stint as superior of Assumption. He was a kindly, soft-spoken, but firm man who was much-loved as superior, and who built up a large student body, paying off in the meantime some of O'Connor's debt. McBrady was also an O'Connor-trained man, having been on his original staff. He became subsequently a brilliant classicist and a distinguished speaker. He was more daring than Cushing in that he initiated the practice of assigning professors to a subject rather than to a class, but was less beloved and a poor administrator. His chief contribution to Assumption was the building of the lovely chapel wing, initiated but not fully paid for by the alumni.

Francis Forster, who became superior in 1907, was stronger, more venturesome, and more successful than his two predecessors. Like

22 See above, 239–41
23 Carr to Scollard, 21 Mar. 1963; Scollard, *Historical Notes*, xix, 105–6

O'Connor, he was a builder. He erected two new buildings in 1914: St Michael's Hall, a much-needed residence, named in memory of Michael Ferguson, and St Denis Hall, a gymnasium in honour of Denis O'Connor. Forster also guided Assumption through two crises: the great war of 1914 to 1918, which seriously affected the college division, and a controversy with the town of Sandwich which tried to impose unfair rates and taxes on the college during his superiorship. Forster's 'Statement to the Catholic Men of Sandwich' in which he rebuked the citizens of Sandwich for their injustice and inhospitality towards Assumption and the Basilians is in its own way a sort of classic.[24]

THE AFFILIATED COLLEGE: 1919–53

Forster tried to do for Assumption what Henry Carr had done some years before for St Michael's – bring it into the twentieth century. Shortly after taking office Forster adapted the high school curriculum to the regulations of the department of education. Then in 1914 he wrote to Nicholas Roche, provincial of the Basilians in America, raising the matter of federation with Western University (now University of Western Ontario). Roche was immediately encouraging, but Bishop Michael F. Fallon of London was quite annoyed when he first heard about it. Fallon was convinced that independent Catholic universities were preferable to federated colleges, and he criticized the *Catholic Register*, of Toronto, for creating, in an editorial entitled 'An Educational Centre,' published in the issue of 29 June 1916, the impression that the Catholic University in Washington did not offer Canada a viable pattern for Catholic university education.[25]

Forster's hope of bringing Assumption into Western gained momentum when two London laymen, Major Albert Murphy and Philip Pocock, sided with him and won the bishop over. Three other factors influenced the bishop: the Ursuline College of Chatham also wanted to affiliate with Western, affiliation might very well provide reason for moving both colleges to London, and Western University needed and wanted affiliates. Forster did not see affiliation through, but when he left Sandwich in 1919 (to devote himself full-time to his duties as provincial of the Basilians, a post he had occupied since 1916) it was taken for granted that federation would take place. Joseph T. Muckle's appointment as superior of Assumption in 1919 seems to have been pri-

24 Preserved in the general archives of the Basilian Fathers; see Scollard, *Historical Notes*, XIV, 169–214.
25 M.F. Fallon, bishop of London, to the *Catholic Register*, 15 July 1916. Fallon is complaining about the misuse of an article written by Bishop T.J. Shahan, rector of Catholic University of America and published in *The Catholic World*, June 1916. See above, 29.

marily to have a Toronto man in Windsor to carry through affiliation.

Fallon officially applied for the affiliation of both Assumption and the Ursuline College in a letter to C.R. Somerville, chairman of the board of governors, 18 September 1919. A committee consisting of W. Sherwood Fox, Dr K.P.R. Neville, Philip Pocock, C.R. Somerville, and A.T. Little studied the request for the board. Three weeks later, 8 October 1919, the affiliation agreement between Western and Assumption was signed by J.T. Muckle for Assumption and by W. Sherwood Fox and W.H. Chapman, vice-chairman of the board, for Western.[26]

The terms of the agreement were modelled on the Toronto federation, but the basis of the agreement was affiliation, not federation. Assumption was not a university, and was not on the London campus, factors which modified its relation to the university. Besides, Huron college, the theological college out of which Western came into existence, was itself only an affiliated college.[27] Assumption did not move to London as Fallon hoped it would. Indeed, Fallon wrote in a letter published in Asumption's *Golden Jubilee Volume* (1920, p. 69) that the moving of the arts department to London was 'a necessary part of the understanding.' Muckle may possibly have raised Fallon's hope on this score; but Forster, by this time superior general of the Basilians, seems never to have seriously considered such a transfer.

Muckle remained at Assumption until the fall of 1922 when he peremptorily resigned and moved to Houston. The reasons for this resignation were complex. He was in the first place, though an excellent scholar, an over-sensitive person. And the summer of 1922 was a period of great tension at Assumption. The Basilian chapter, held in Toronto in July, radically changed the constitutions and the rule of the community, including the method of observing poverty. Some priests on the staff disapproved of these changes and were almost certainly going to take up the option, given all Basilians at this time, of seeking incardination in some diocese. In the midst of this, a decision of Muckle's on a matter raised by one of his professors, Charles E. Coughlin (permission to have a piano in his room), was unwittingly overruled by the superior general. Apprehensive of further and more serious troubles, Muckle resigned.

The troubles expected by Muckle came during the first year of the superiorship of his successor, Daniel L. Dillon. Four Assumption priests, Fathers Rogers, Coughlin, Sheridan, and Plomer left the Basilians; two of them, Plomer and Coughlin, using the occasion for an

26 Agreement of Affiliation of Assumption College, Sandwich, with Western University; Scollard, *Historical Notes*, xiv, 154–61.

27 J.J. and R.D. Talman, *'Western' – 1878–1953*, London, Ontario, 1953, 129–30

acrimonious attack on the community, which was countered by an equally acrimonious rejoinder from Alphonse McIntyre, a lay member of the teaching staff. Dillon's patience and strength at this time endeared him to his confreres to his dying day. The affair meant, unfortunately, that Dillon had to go through the six years of his superiorship seriously short-handed and with personnel troubles always threatening. It also meant that from 1923 on, when Bishop Fallon pulled his prospective theologians out of Assumption and placed them in his new St Peters School of Theology,[28] and withdrew his support from Assumption, that Dillon had to cope with a highly unpleasant situation, at one stage involving even the attempted cancellation of the faculties of his priests. The real dispute was less between Dillon and the bishop than between Forster and the bishop. And this difference was accentuated by still another dispute between Forster's brother, a pastor in the diocese of London, and Bishop Fallon, which ultimately forced the brother to transfer from London to the diocese of Detroit. Tension remained until the death of Forster in 1929 and of Fallon in 1931.

Dillon made a major material contribution to Assumption when in 1928 he opened a modern high school building, relieving serious overcrowding. This building, later known as Dillon Hall, became a sort of *cause célèbre* when mechanical defects in its planning and construction came to light. However, it was a solid structure and withstood remodelling. It still houses several departments of the faculty of arts and sciences in the University of Windsor.

In 1928 Vincent L. Kennedy succeeded Dillon as superior. The college was both large and active throughout Kennedy's presidency. Personnel troubles continued, accentuated by the very difficult economic situation produced by the great depression of 1929 and following. Kennedy was a good university man, indeed, a better university man than Dillon. He left office after a three-year term, going to Strasbourg and Rome to study liturgy and archaeology in preparation for a post offered him at the Pontifical Institute of Mediaeval Studies. On Kennedy's leaving, Dillon returned as superior, but only for a short time; his health gave out under the fierce economic strain and he suffered a major heart attack. His term was filled out by his assistant, Thomas A. MacDonald, who was superior of Assumption from 1932 until 1940.

MacDonald was a maritimer who knew very well the meaning of hard work and poverty. He found himself, when Dillon's health broke, in an impossible and preposterous situation. The credit of the college had been extended to the breaking point, revenues had dropped alarm-

28 See below, 294–5

ingly, and the normal services (heat, light, water, telephone) were on the point of being cut off. Dillon and MacDonald tided the institution over the immediate crisis by telephoning Bellisle and apprising him of the situation. Bellisle sent in the next mail an interest-free loan of $15,000 to meet the service bills.[29] The next step was taken by Mac-Donald alone. He called in the principal creditors to obtain their consent for major and drastic refinancing. The banks came to MacDonald's aid, and Assumption avoided bankruptcy. Superior and faculty dug in their heels for a long hard tug against heavy odds. The work of rehabilitation went slowly but surely and Assumption fought its way out of a depression much deeper than that besetting Canada as a whole. Had Assumption not been a Church institution, and had it not had Mac-Donald, it would almost certainly have collapsed.

It is not surprising that between 1932 and 1940 Assumption undertook few major projects. But there was life in the institution and important things happened. There was, for example, an almost complete recovery of morale as the entire faculty assumed the burden of rebuilding. One of Assumption's grandest undertakings got under way during 1933–4 when Stanley Murphy launched, with Fulton Sheen as his first speaker, the extraordinary Christian Culture Series, which in 1969 entered its thirty-sixth successful year. The project involved the college significantly with its local constituency. In 1934 Holy Names College was affiliated with Assumption to look after women students. Holy Names was established out of St Mary's Academy (founded 1864). The new women's college division was for the time being housed in the Academy in South Windsor. In 1950 it was moved to two buildings adjacent to the campus. The lean years invited other projects too – summer courses, night courses, athletic projects – which kept men busy and created an important *esprit de corps*. Concurrently, MacDonald worked hard on public relations, especially with the priests of Windsor and with the London diocese generally. Tensions created by the problems of the twenties largely disappeared during the thirties.

MacDonald's refinancing was built around the development of a large paying high school, filled residences, and maximum Sunday work by all Basilians. It was not university-centred. In spite of this, Mac-Donald maintained strong ties with Western, so much so that he was able to repay Bellisle's generosity handsomely when he got the authorities of Western to enrol the American freshmen of St Michael's, when the traditional attendance of Americans at St Michael's was threatened by the University of Toronto's decision to conform with the provincial

29 See above, 170

department's plan to make grade XIII the normal university admission requirement. When MacDonald left Assumption, it was to continue as an experienced financier both as bursar of St Michael's and as general bursar of the Basilian Fathers.

In 1940 Vincent J. Guinan, long a member of the faculty of Assumption, became superior. Although he had to cope with the special problems of the war years when arts departments worked under discouraging difficulties, his superiorship marks the extrication of the college from the grip of depression. In Guinan's Assumption the college passed the high school in institutional importance; from his time on, moreover, Assumption was to cease being a kind of reflection or shadow of St Michael's. Guinan was succeeded in 1946 by John H. O'Loane, who headed the college until 1952. The Guinan-O'Loane development from 1940 to 1952 has its special consistency and continuity – it is the period of the flourishing of the affiliated Assumption and of its preparation for an independent existence as an autonomous Catholic university.

The 1940–50 period is marked by a series of events that changed the whole character of Assumption. One of the first such events was the establishing of a Pius XI School of Social Studies in which Edwin C. Garvey and Désiré Barath, a layman, sought to bring the influence of Assumption to bear on the significant labour force of the Windsor area. Although the movement was short-lived and always controversial, it was the first real indication that Assumption had arrived as a shaping force among the people of Canada. The school was followed by an intensified interest in extension courses, in summer and night courses, and in continuing education generally – later, to be sure, but comparable with the movements that took place some 20 years before in Edmonton and Antigonish. A new confidence came to Assumption so that Guinan could announce during 1944–5 that the institution was going to conduct a drive for $750,000 in order to erect a new arts and sciences building. In the same year, early, that is, in 1945, the seventy-fifth anniversary of O'Connor's coming to Sandwich, the University of Western Ontario agreed to hold a convocation in Windsor, conferring an honorary degree on Father W.G. Rogers, president of Assumption's alumni association. These were important events, possibly the real beginnings of 'the university movement.' Guinan's drive actually served, especially as supported by LeBel to whom O'Loane entrusted most of the specifically college business, to alert the people of Windsor to the college's potential; and the work among them of fellow citizens like George Weller, Roy Coyle, Eli Goldin, James Barth, and William

Furlong, who brought Protestants and Jews into the college constituency, effectively making of Assumption a regional centre for post-secondary education.

An important contributing factor to this changing relation with Windsor was the increased flow of local high school and collegiate graduates from every ethnic and religious background into the Assumption orbit, with an accompanying modification of the sectarian character of staff and student body and with new demands for increased facilities. Guinan had air force huts moved to the campus for temporary relief. With the aid of competent colleagues, particularly Francis Ruth, he planned and started construction on the first of Assumption's great modern units, its $375,000 Memorial Science building, which was opened by O'Loane in 1948. Memorable and heroic on the part of staff and students was the enthusiastic use of the makeshift huts and of spaces in the gymnasium for the holding of classes and the providing of services and facilities.

ASSUMPTION UNIVERSITY: 1953 TO THE PRESENT

There was also a deeper aspect to the movement now stirring the members of the college community. It was an interest in and concern for structure. Should Assumption be an affiliate? Should it be a specifically Catholic institution? Was its real future tied to the Essex county constituency which it served? Different men thought differently, and, without allowing feelings to run too high, everyone knew that change was in the wind, but no one knew exactly where that change would take them. This was not an administrators' movement: it was taking place within the faculty at large and especially in the thinking of Cornelius Crowley, Edwin Garvey, Alex Grant, Carlisle LeBel, Daniel Mulvihill, John Murphy, Peter Swan, and Leonard McCann.

LeBel was not sure at first whether his colleagues were for or against him on this matter of maintaining the Western affiliation. In the spring of 1953, at a meeting of all local Basilians, he got his answer. One of the priests, Adrian Record, noting that the discussion was getting particularly hot, and thinking LeBel might misinterpret the expression of such varied opinions, called for a vote of confidence. To everyone's amazement, the vote was unanimous. Disagreement over detail was no sign that his subjects distrusted him or that they did not feel that the time for action had come. Most agreed too on the essential point that the college should abandon affiliation and should seek its own university charter.

This was also what people in Windsor knowledgeable in university affairs wanted; and their attitude was probably the strongest of all forces behind the movement. Along with this force came a change of attitude towards affiliation by the administration in London, and particularly by President George Edward Hall. All affiliated colleges were conscious of this change and were worried about it. Assumption located so far away, and giving all its own instruction in any case, was in a better position than the others to do something about it. When Carlisle LeBel was named superior in 1952, it became evident that change was likely to be deep and radical; and by his time change was the more possible in that O'Loane had considerably enlarged the teaching staff, even in 1952 succeeding in getting the Basilian Fathers to increase their Assumption appointments from 32 to 40.

LeBel took office on 1 July 1952. On 2 April 1953 Assumption's original act of incorporation was amended by the province of Ontario so as to give the college independent status and full university powers.[30] The only qualification was a temporary one; the title 'university' was not to be used until a minimum of one more college was added. The Assumption University of 1953 remained a Catholic university. It had a board of governors which was exclusively Basilian; a board of regents, which was a non-denominational citizens' board of advisers on finances and general policy; it had also a senate enlarged to include representatives from all local educational institutions and religious groups. But everyone knew that the change was not yet complete. For one thing the Basilian Fathers had neither the will nor the manpower to accept responsibility for a large university. For another, the province had no intention of departing from a policy, rigidly adhered to since 1867, of refusing to grant public funds to a denominational university.

For the time being, Assumption turned to a procedure followed in Hamilton, Ontario, whereby McMaster University, which was Baptist, maintained a non-sectarian affiliate, Hamilton College, to which instruction in science was entrusted and which the Ontario government was willing to subsidize because it had a non-denominational board. On this pattern, Assumption encouraged the founding of Essex College with a non-denominational board and entrusted to it instruction in the sciences, mathematics, business, nursing, and engineering. Essex College came into being in 1956; at the same time Assumption University amended its title to Assumption University of Windsor.[31] Essex College had its own separate board of governors. It was also one of three colleges affiliated with Assumption at that time. The other two were Holy

30 An Act Respecting Assumption College (2 Elizabeth II, ch.III; 2 Apr. 1953)
31 An Act Respecting Assumption College (2 Elizabeth II, ch.94, 28 Mar. 1956)

Names College, a women's division in operation since 1934, and Holy Redeemer College, the house of studies of the Redemptorist Fathers.

Assumption University (1953), or Assumption University of Windsor (1956), had a relatively lively if short career. Its first significant move was to effect the long-contemplated separation of the university and high school: in 1955 the first unit of the high school was moved to a site on Huron Line, south of the university; the following year the second unit was moved; in 1957 the high school was given its own independent administration with George J. Thompson as superior, W. Oscar Regan as first councillor, Ronald J. Cullen as principal, and John J. Gaughan as treasurer.

Other significant steps taken by Assumption were the following: on 3 June 1954, the new university's first convocation took place and an honorary degree was conferred on the Hon. Leslie M. Frost, prime minister of Ontario; in 1956, when the word Windsor was added to the legal name, three colleges were affiliated: Essex College, Holy Names College, which had carried on arts work since 1934, and Holy Redeemer College, the new house of studies of the Redemptorist Fathers; 1957 was declared a centennial year, one hundred years after Malbos came to the college at the request of Pinsonneault; during 1957 and 1958 a new university library was built and formally opened on 11 September 1958, by Sir Philip Robert Morris, vice-chancellor of Bristol; in 1959 the Canadian-American Seminar was initiated by John Francis Boland; in 1961 two large buildings were opened, the new Essex Engineering building and the University Centre, the latter by General Georges Vanier, the governor-general of Canada; in June 1962, the Sisters of the Holy Names relinquished direction of their college and Assumption took it over as a university women's residence, renaming it Electa Hall in memory of the foundress of the arts division of Holy Names.

Unique and altogether extraordinary among the moves made by Assumption University of Windsor was the affiliation of Canterbury College on 4 November 1957. This affiliation was in the first instance requested by representatives of the synod of the diocese of Huron of the Anglican Church of Canada. Canterbury was given the right to teach its own courses in theology, philosophy, and mediaeval history. The event was received with enthusiasm everywhere.[32]

LeBel ceased to be superior of Assumption in 1958 but he remained president of the university. The superiorship was taken over by Francis

32 See 'Signing of Affiliation Agreement between Assumption University of Windsor and Canterbury College,' *Alumni Times: Quarterly Publication of Assumption University of Windsor*, II, no.5 (1957), 3–11.

L. Burns from 1958 to 1961; by E.J. McCorkell 1961–4, D.J. Mulvihill 1964–7, and E.R. Malley since 1967. Fathers Mulvihill and Malley have also, as will appear, been presidents of the present Assumption University.

During the fall of 1962 plans were made to reorganize Assumption University of Windsor, making it a civil university eligible for government support. A University of Windsor bill was put through the Ontario legislature in December 1962 to become effective 1 July 1963.[33] By this act the University of Windsor came into existence as a new non-denominational university; Assumption University remained in existence but as a non-teaching, Catholic university in federation with the University of Windsor. The changeover was effected gently: the chancellor of Assumption, Bishop J.C. Cody, was named first chancellor of the new University of Windsor, and E.C. LeBel, president of Assumption became first president of Windsor: both of these were continuing appointments by an understanding with the board; the statutes provided means of choosing their successors. Bishop Cody died before July 1963, and never actually served as chancellor of the University of Windsor although Bishop Emmett Carter acted for him at the fall convocation of 1963; the second chancellor of the new university was the Hon. Keiller MacKay, former lieutenant-governor of Ontario. LeBel became Windsor's first president and remained in office until a year later when he reached retirement age. The second president, J. Francis Leddy, took office in 1964.

The petitioners for the new University of Windsor were the boards of governors and regents of the former Assumption University of Windsor and the board of directors of Essex College. The first board of governors of the new University of Windsor were named by the new act, and 13 of them came from the then existing board of directors of Essex College and the board of regents of Assumption University. This new board had 30 members, six of whom (and their successors) were to be named by the board of governors of the continuing Assumption University. While Assumption became a federated university in the University of Windsor (November 1963), dropping the name Windsor from its own title, [34] Canterbury College and Holy Redeemer College, became affiliated colleges (10 October and 18 December 1963); and Iona College, sponsored by the United Church of Canada, was affiliated to the University of Windsor, 1 May 1964. The latest Univer-

33 An Act to Incorporate the University of Windsor (11–12 Elizabeth II, ch.194; 19 Dec. 1962)

34 An Act Respecting Assumption University (12–13 Elizabeth II, ch.125; 25 Mar. 1964)

sity of Windsor Act was passed in the spring of 1969. Its main purpose was to increase the size of the board of governors to 32, allocating 4 places to members of the university's teaching staff.[35]

It is impossible to exaggerate the role of Carlisle LeBel in the development of the modern universities of Assumption and Windsor. Although he did not himself start the development, nor carry it through alone, he supplied from about 1946 on much of the vision and drive. Above all, he, more than anyone else, suffered, faced, and overcame the countless blocks thrown in the way of his development by colleagues, by Basilians, by the department of education, and by the universities of Ontario. With each step and with each victory, his personal prestige increased and sympathy for Assumption and Windsor grew. Two occasions stand out as especially significant in demonstrating his personal role: the charter dinner held in Windsor, 21 April 1953, when Sidney Smith, president of the University of Toronto, was principal speaker; and the testimonial dinner in Windsor, 23 May 1964, on the occasion of LeBel's retirement.

LeBel, of course, had invaluable support from his own men. Norbert Ruth, for example, draughted most of the plans and presented them to committees of government and universities. Ruth has also published the best and clearest analyses of the university's structural changes and its long-range objectives.[36] Also collaborating closely with LeBel were Daniel Mulvihill, Cornelius Crowley, and Frank De Marco.

The subsequent history of the University of Windsor does not belong in the present study. Worthy of mention, however, is that this university, because of Assumption's role in forming it, and because of the special interests of Assumption between 1953 and 1962, provides for the teaching of theology, even of denominational theology, on its campus.

Assumption University is carrying on from the old buildings on Huron Line. It is perhaps best described as an administration with a role. Whether that role will turn out to be practical and important remains to be seen, but there are indications that it well may. Assumption today is a Catholic university with a charter, a faculty, and almost

35 An Act Respecting the University of Windsor (18 Elizabeth II, ch.169; 1 Apr. 1969)

36 Norbert J. Ruth, 'Assumption University and the University of Windsor,' *The Basilian Teacher*, 8(1964), 155–68; also 'The University of Windsor,' *Journal of Higher Education*, 38(1967), 90–5; 'The University of Windsor,' in *Were the Dean's Windows Rusty?*, ed. Gerard Mulligan, Montreal, 1917, 93–104. The Hon. John P. Robarts, prime minister of Ontario, paying tribute to the men responsible for the University of Windsor, speaks of N.J. Ruth, 'whose great skill is attested by the wording of the Act itself.' Statement made in the house on Ontario University Affairs, Thursday, 21 Mar. 1963.

no students. Its charter is held against the day, which it hopes will never arrive, when a charter may be needed. Assumption's faculty is engaged in teaching, not in Assumption itself, but in the provincially-supported University of Windsor, where it finds a broader constituency than any denominational institution could ever provide. It has also a Catholic faculty with a felt responsibility for the whole people of God in the Windsor area. It has certain material resources: some land and a building; some capital which has come from the sale of superfluous buildings and which remains even after a huge indebtedness has been removed; and the salaries of Basilians teaching in the University of Windsor. These resources Assumption is directing to educational works: publication, research, scholarships, fellowships, and other activities pertinent to the making of Catholic scholars, works which most Catholic universities have to neglect in the sheer struggle for survival. Above all, Assumption has been able to assume a special concern for all theology. In forging the institutional teaching of theology, it has in fact restored it to the genuine university milieu where it properly belongs. There are emerging patterns in all this, patterns capable of rescuing the Church from the excessive and perhaps impossible burden of supporting mass education at the post-secondary level.

King's College

(ST PETER'S SEMINARY:
COLLEGE OF CHRIST THE KING)

1912

King's College is a Catholic liberal arts college affiliated with the University of Western Ontario, London. It is located in a beautiful stone building at Waterloo Street North and Epworth Avenue, a few blocks from the university campus and a little west of St Peter's Seminary. Although King's is now the affiliate, and the pre-theology department of St Peter's Seminary is now the subsidiary, the college really took its origin from the seminary and its history properly begins with the opening of the seminary in the cathedral rectory in 1912.

St Peter's Seminary came into existence as follows. Archbishop F.P. McEvay of Toronto, attending the Council of Quebec in 1909, heard Francis Clement Kelley, the Prince Edward Islander who founded the Catholic Church Extension Society of the United States, expound convincingly on the case for establishing in Canada and the United States 'Extension Seminaries,' that is, reasonably large seminaries to provide priests not only for local dioceses but for the home missions generally. McEvay resolved to found such a seminary in Toronto and enlisted the support of neighbouring bishops, including Michael F. Fallon, bishop of London.

Fallon went along with the idea with some enthusiasm. He urged McEvay to train his own faculty rather than to rely heavily on Europeans. He also encouraged him to send Francis J. Morrissey to Rome to study, while he himself also sent off two of his young priests, J.G. Labelle and F.J. Brennan. The three were designated for teaching posts in the proposed extension seminary. When the cornerstone of St Augustine's Seminary was laid, 23 October 1910, Fallon preached the sermon. McEvay died in May 1911. Fallon decided not to collaborate quite so fully with McEvay's successor Archbishop Neil McNeil, because he felt that McNeil would not likely allow him much voice in the conduct of the seminary. Accordingly, he brought Labelle and Brennan back from Rome for parish work where they were sorely needed. Fallon still intended to send his theologians to Toronto as soon as the new seminary was opened. In the meantime, he had eighteen students taking theology in the grand seminary in Montreal and two in Ottawa.

During the following year, 1911–12, it was reported to Fallon that one of the professors of Montreal's grand seminary had, during spiritual lecture, spoken of him as anti-French. It was a sore point. Fallon had, in 1898, before he was a bishop, been forced out of the vice-rectorship of the University of Ottawa on just such a charge. Now in 1910 and 1911 the charge was being revived because he was thought by some to be too sympathetic towards the Ontario government's Regulation 17, which was to assure that English would be the language of instruction in Ontario's schools. Fallon was disturbed that his own seminarians in Montreal were exposed to such criticism of their bishop. He discussed the grand seminary with his cathedral staff, regretting especially that there was no way of his getting to know his future priests, nor of their knowing him. Monsignor J.T. Aylward, rector of the cathedral, suggested that he pull his students out of Montreal and Ottawa and provide them with theology in his own rectory. The rectory, Aylward said, was large enough and teaching staff could be put together. The decision to bring his theologians to London was made on the spot, and in September 1912, St Peter's Seminary opened in the cathedral rectory with Labelle teaching scripture and canon law, Brennan moral theology, Denis O'Connor dogma, and E.L. Tierney, the bishop's secretary, teaching sacred liturgy. The bishop himself presided at table, at weekly oral examinations, and at predication classes. In charge of the seminary and its first rector was J.V. Tobin, a brilliant but unsettled priest who was rector for only one year. There have been subsequently but three rectors of St Peter's: Denis O'Connor (later Bishop O'Connor of Peterborough) from 1913 to 1930; A.P. Mahoney from 1930 to 1966; and James J. Carrigan since 1966.

The seminary remained strictly a theologate until 1926. In 1923, however, St Peter's School of Philosophy was separately established under the following circumstances. Most candidates for London diocese were sent for their philosophy to Assumption College in Windsor. In 1919, Fallon applied to the University of Western Ontario for the affiliation of Assumption College for men and Ursuline College for women. It was his idea that Assumption and Ursuline should move their university divisions from Sandwich and Chatham respectively to London. Ursuline College moved to Brescia Hall in 1920; Assumption did not move. The superior of Assumption, J.T. Muckle, seems to have given the bishop some reason to hope that Assumption might move. The superior general of the Basilians, however, Francis Forster, was adamantly opposed to it. Muckle resigned from Assumption in the fall of 1922, and during the summer of 1923, Fallon notified his prospective theologians enrolled in philosophy at Assumption that they should report in September, not at Assumption, but at St Peter's School of Philosophy which was opening in the former monstery of the Precious Blood in London at 572 Queen's Avenue near William Street. The School of Philosophy opened in September with 20 students at various stages of their philosophy, most of them, including Philip F. Pocock and Lester A. Wemple, being withdrawals from Assumption. President of the School of Philosophy was Monsignor Denis O'Connor, who taught ontology; resident principal was F.J. Brennan, who taught ethics. Other professors were J.B. Ffoulkes, cosmology, J.H. Pocock, logic, L.M. Forristal, psychology and history of philosophy, and W.T. Flannery, criteriology. Of these professors only Brennan and Ffoulkes lived in the school, and two men, Ffoulkes and Flannery, had just returned from studies in Rome.

The students took only their philosophy and religious knowledge in St Peter's. For their other arts subjects – Latin, French, English, History, library science (or alternative) – they went to regular lectures in the University of Western Ontario. Their registration in the university was arranged through Brescia Hall. Although the seminary was not yet affiliated with the university, it had worked out an *ad hoc* arrangement approximating affiliation.

In 1926 the new St Peter's Seminary opened in Sunshine Park, donated by Sir Philip Pocock, off Waterloo Street. It was built to house and provide college facilities for both philosophers and theologians. For philosophers the procedure was as before: philosophy at the seminary, the other arts subjects at the university, and registration through Brescia. The idea was by now taking hold that a full college staff should be trained. With this in view, Thomas J. McCarthy (later Bishop McCarthy) began special studies in English and theology, William F. Simpson in French, and Anthony J. Durand in English. Another development at this time was the decision of the Resurrectionist Fathers to send their scholastics to London for their university course. They built St Thomas Scholasticate on the seminary grounds in 1930. Their scholastics were registered like the diocesan seminarians, through Brescia, and took their courses in the same way. Bishop Fallon died in 1931 before any essential change was made in the academic status of the seminary. He was succeeded by John Thomas Kidd, bishop of Calgary.

During the thirties there was from time to time talk of the Resurrectionists asking the university to affiliate their Kitchener college, St Jerome's. The university was getting a little sensitive about the increase of Catholic institutions around the campus. There was a consensus that no religious denomination should have more than one affiliated college. The Catholic constituency already had two, albeit one for men and one for women, and two other institutions in London and Holy Names in Windsor (and even St Michael's in Toronto), using Western's charter in one way or another. The Resurrectionists made overtures to the university after the middle thirties but were given no encouragement. It was at this somewhat unlikely moment that Philip F. Pocock of the seminary staff urged Bishop Kidd to apply to the board of governors of the university for direct affiliation of the arts department of St Peter's Seminary. To the surprise of the seminary faculty, the request was granted in late 1937; the affiliation of the seminary became effective with the opening of the 1939-40 academic year.

This was the beginning of a new and exhilarating period in London. It was also the period in which awareness spread that only women and candidates for the priesthood were properly provided in London with Catholic college facilities. The forties passed and half the fifties before anything was effectively done. The great barrier now, of course, was the multiplicity of Catholic affiliates. There was amelioration of this situation in 1953 when Assumption withdrew from affiliation and acquired independent university status. It was only two years later, 1955, that St Peter's Seminary opened for laymen its subsidiary, the College of Christ the King. It was located on seminary property but closer to the university campus than the seminary building. The college was provided with its own separate administration. T.J. McCarthy was named first dean of Christ the King College, and directed its establishment. He was named bishop of Nelson during August 1955, just before the college actually opened in its new buildings. L.A. Wemple, also of the seminary staff, succeeded McCarthy as dean and guided the new college through its early years. The nucleus of a separate staff was found for the first year, and a system of collaboration with St Peter's and Brescia was worked out.

There were those, and among them Wemple, who would have preferred to open the laymen's college on the ample Brescia campus. Bishop Cody opposed this plan. Where the college ought to be located remains a problem. Its present land allotment is too small. However, there is room for expansion on the seminary property and some day this may be opened up. The university's own expansion has brought the college closer to the centre of things than it was when opened.

During the first year of operation, 1955-6, the college had as was to be expected to cope with inexperience, lack of money to acquire and maintain adequate staff, and too little space for a college operation. The pressure was relieved during the second year when P.E. Crunican, S.E. McGuire, and E.P. Laroque (priests of the diocese) returned from graduate studies; it was further relieved in subsequent years as lay professors – D.A. Lenardon, F.M. Wieden, C.J. Treacy, and others – joined the teaching staff.

The immediate effect of the appearance of the College of Christ the King was a fuller integration of the Catholic constituency into the university, particularly into the honour course system. The college functioned with reasonable success in the academic order, but with recurring misgivings on the part of students and faculty about ecclesiastical government. While Wemple was careful not to allow college policy to be directed from the seminary, the situation of a laymen's college functioning as a subsidiary of a seminary invited criticism. The diocesan authorities on their part were in some consternation when they learned how much more costly a modern college is to run than a Tridentine seminary. The seminary, however, was above criticism as an academic body. It maintained a strong pre-theological arts course and was in 1964 admitted to full membership in the National Conference of Canadian Universities and Colleges, known since 1965 as the Association of Universities and Colleges of Canada.

During 1964 and 1965 it became evident that the seminary and college would have to work out a new arrangement. Some advisers wanted an offer from Western to buy the college buildings for the university expansion to be accepted. The college, they said, could move to Brescia to form one co-educational college with it. Bishop Carter was not sure that the Brescia property really offered a better long-term location than the present college property. Instead of amalgamation, two other important steps were taken during 1965 and 1966. First, the old affiliation of St Peter's with Western was transferred to Christ the King, now called simply King's College, and St Peter's took the subsidiary position. E.P. Laroque, who succeeded Wemple as dean just prior to this change, became dean of King's College; and what was formerly St Peter's Seminary College became the pre-theology division of King's. This change enhanced the campus prestige of the laymen's college.

Secondly, a university parish was established on the University of Western Ontario campus with a view to attending to the pastoral needs of all the Catholics of the university. A property was bought by the bishop from Brescia, directly opposite the main building, as the site of a projected chapel and student centre. The university parish was expected to expand and extend the scope of Western's Newman Club, which had always functioned apart from Christ the King's College and the seminary. R.T.A. Murphy was named pastor of the university parish, and was given two or three diocesan associates to be jointly responsible with him for meeting the pastoral needs of university students. It was felt that the appointment of scholarly men with academic positions to a university parish might very well be an advance over the traditional Newman Club movement. The parish holds Sunday masses in Middlesex College. At present, the priests assigned to the parish are living at Holy Spirit Centre adjacent to the campus. The strategy of the parish is to distinguish campus pastoral activity from the academic, yet to place it in the hands of men at home and active in academic circles.

Two significant announcements came during 1968. First, King's College got its first lay head when Owen Carrigan was named principal and dean. Secondly, it was announced that King's would accept henceforth women students. Both moves are in the spirit of the times. The first encourages the staff, especially the lay staff, and may facilitate certain types of co-operation with the university. The second was not welcomed by Brescia, but it has not interefered with academic collaboration. It is still an open question whether the future of Catholic education on the London campus will not call for an amalgamation of the two colleges and perhaps a closer integration into the academic life of the university.

Brescia College

(URSULINE COLLEGE, BRESCIA HALL)

1919

Brescia College, a Catholic women's college of arts in affiliation with the University of Western Ontario, London, was founded in 1919 by Mother Clare, general of the Ursulines, and Bishop Fallon. The college is located on Western Road on an elevated property of about 120 acres immediately adjacent to the university campus. Brescia is a four-building complex: the new Brescia Hall erected in stone in 1925 including the new wing of 1950; the cottage once used for domestics is now a small residence; Mary Manor, a residence unit purchased from George Gunn in 1961; the St James Memorial academic and administrative unit put up in 1963. Student body and staff approximate four hundred persons.

The Ursulines who direct Brescia College are religious sisters whose main work is the education of young women. The order, founded by St Angela Merici in Brescia, Italy, in 1535, has had a complex and interesting history. At first its members lived with their parents; they were later reorganized into a cloistered community; still later they became missionary and their schools and colleges spread throughout the world. The Ursulines who came to Ontario were brought to America in 1853 from La Faouet in Brittany by Mother Mary Xavier Yvonne Le Bihan to serve especially the needs of Indians.[1] They opened a primary and secondary school for girls in Chatham in 1861 and had it incorporated in the province of Ontario, 15 August 1866.[2] Ursuline College at Chatham was a 'young ladies' college' providing, besides academic work, instruction in fine arts, music, painting, and needlework. A large building was erected on Grand Avenue, Chatham, in 1870, since known, from the lovely grove on its east side, as 'The Pines.'

When in 1919 Bishop Michael Fallon modified his earlier unsympathetic views on the affiliating and federating of Catholic colleges with provincial institutions,[3] he applied to Western University, London, for

1 Mother M. St Paul, *From Desenzano to 'The Pines,'* Toronto: Macmillan, 1941; also Mother Mercedes, 'The History of the Ursulines in Ontario,' unpublished MA thesis, University of Western Ontario, 1937
2 An Act to Incorporate the Ursuline Academy of Chatham (29-30 Victoria, ch.142; 15 Aug. 1866), J.G. Hodgins, *Documentary History,* XIX, 228
3 See above, 29 and 282

the affiliation of Ursuline College and Assumption College so that women and men in his diocese might proceed to university degrees in Catholic institutions. It was his idea that Ursuline and Assumption should move their university divisions to London, locating them on or near the campus. Fallon's request for the two affiliations was granted almost immediately by the Western board. Articles of agreement were subsequently signed by all concerned, and, on behalf of Ursuline College, by Mother M. Clare Gaukler, general of the Ursulines.

The nature of these articles of agreement was in part determined by the Western University Act of 1908 (Statutes of Ontario) chapter 125, and in part by the university's desire to enlarge its constituency and its fear that Fallon might, as he suggested he might, seek affiliation with Toronto. Ursuline College thus became a college of arts in the faculty of arts of Western. It was given representation on the board of governors and the senate; it was expected to maintain admission requirements identical with those of the university; its students were released from payment of tuition (though not of incidental fees) for courses taken in the university. Ursuline was also permitted to provide substitute curricula and examinations in philosophy, history, and religious knowledge. The college agreed to pay a small tuition fee, $5.50 for a major course, $3.00 for a minor, for college students enrolling in university subjects, and to collect a similar fee from the university for university students enrolling in college courses. The college normally sent its instructors, prior to examinations in subjects whose curricula and examinations were identical with those of the university, to a pre-conference of instructors and examiners.[4]

During 1919–20 the university division of Ursuline College remained in Chatham at 'The Pines' with Mother St Anne Lachance as the first dean, and with a small staff of sisters supplemented by a part-time lecturer in philosophy and religious knowledge who commuted from St Peter's Seminary in London. After one year the university division was moved to the original Brescia Hall in London: the Whiskard residence on the corner of Wolfe and Wellington streets, opposite Victoria Park. In 1922 honours work in French, English, and history was initiated. As early as 1925, with the help of a gift from Mother Clare's mother, Mrs Josephine Gaukler of Grosse Point, Michigan, the new stone building on Western Road was erected near the campus.[5] A wing containing library stacks, lecture rooms, and home economics laboratories was added to Brescia Hall in 1950.

4 These are the terms of agreement between Assumption and Western. See Scollard, *Historical Notes*, XIV, 154–61.
5 J.J. and R.D. Talman, *'Western' – 1878–1953*, London, 1953, 132

In 1923, when Bishop Fallon recalled his philosophy students from Assumption and provided for their further education by opening at the seminary in London a St Peter's School of Philosophy,[6] he arranged to register them in Brescia Hall so that they would receive academic credit for their work. In this way the teaching staff of St Peter's was introduced to the life of Western; henceforth some St Peter's professors represented Brescia on a number of university committees and boards. This took place while Mother St Anne was still dean. She was replaced in 1926 by Mother Immaculate Dwyer, who followed similar policies. Thus when the Resurrectionists built St Thomas Scholasticate on the university campus in 1930, they registered their clerics in Western University through Brescia. When Mother Immaculate's deanship was terminated in 1933, Mother St Anne returned to office, continuing as dean until 1938 when she fell ill. Mother Francis Clare Connor filled out the last year of her term; that is, 1938–9. During Mother St Anne's second term, Brescia organized a course in home economics which was offered to students of Brescia and the university. This course was first given during 1936–7. As set up, home economics took two forms: it was a constituent subject in a programme for the bachelor of arts degree; and it was a diploma programme for girls not proceeding to a university degree. The diploma course was dropped after a few years because it was not functioning at the university level; in the bachelor's programme, however, home economics developed as both a pass subject and a subject of concentration. Brescia provided and continues to provide the department of home economics for the entire university.

The last development, important for Brescia and unique in Canadian universities was largely the work of Mother St James Hickey, dean of the college 1939–45 and 1947–56. Under her policies, relations with the university were clear and strong, and the consolidation of the position of home economics has furnished the college community with a project around which to establish an *esprit de corps*. Mother St James was a strong community woman who saw to it that the Ursulines benefited intellectually from the operation of Brescia. She encouraged sisters to get into graduate studies and to strengthen their competence by acquiring higher degrees. The scholarly courses of Sister St Michael Guinan, in philosophy and psychology; of Sister Dolores Kuntz in clinical psychology; and of Sister Corona Sharpe in literature are in large part of her making.[7] Mother St James also arranged to have Ursulines, located

6 See above, 283 and 294–5
7 Sister St Michael Guinan, head until 1 July 1968 of Brescia's combined department of philosophy and psychology; she has published in learned journals and popular magazines and has submitted communications and papers to international and national congresses. During 1968–9 she served as an executive officer

in Windsor and other centres, take extension work through Brescia, and then to have those who showed promise given an opportunity to carry on graduate studies. She worked hard at recruiting and brought what was in the thirties a relatively small enrolment to 250 in the fifties.

Mother Marie Rosier twice succeeded Mother St James as dean, holding the office from 1945 to 1947, and from 1956 to 1963. She was herself succeeded in 1963 by Sister Dominica Dietrich. These two deans brought the college through a period of adjustment and reassessment. Mother Marie ran into serious difficulties which led to a revision of the articles of affiliation in 1962. The difficulties were first given public expression in the *Conran Report*, 1959, which devoted considerable and unsympathetic attention to the current status of psychology, sociology, and the social sciences generally as college offerings. The matter came up when Christ the King offered a course in psychology without previous consultation with the university department, which chose to make an issue of it. Could such sciences be given for credit in an affiliated college? Philosophy, of course, could be given under the original articles of agreement. But did philosophy include psychology as the department of the affiliated college seemed to think? Further clarification and specification seemed necessary, especially in that recently-appointed heads of university departments – often Americans – were less clear about and less sympathetic towards the Canadian type of affiliation based as it was on denominational distinctions.

The revision of 1962–3 introduced a number of changes into affiliation arrangements. Students could henceforth take a maximum of only two (not four as formerly) courses in religious knowledge for credit towards their BA. Colleges were no longer to give courses providing professional training – pre-science, pre-medicine – but could continue to offer pre-business, pre-nursing, and secretarial courses. Colleges now accepted the quota principle: an overall enrolment quota of 500 per college, and specified quotas in subjects where facilities were a controlling factor. Payment for courses taken in the university by college students or in the college by university students was raised to eighty dollars a course. Colleges were authorized to keep all their federal grant.

(research) in the Office on Aging in Ontario's department of social and family services. When Sister St Michael resigned her headship in 1968 to be free for research at Queen's Park, Toronto, Sister Dolores Kuntz succeeded her in psychology, Dr P.E. Cavanagh of London diocese succeeded her in philosophy. Sister Corona Sharpe, author of *The Confidante of Henry James: Evolution and Moral Value of a Fictive Character*, Notre Dame, 1963, and of numerous articles in learned journals (see F.E.L. Priestly, *The Humanities in Canada*, Toronto, 1964, and R.M. Wiles, *The Humanities in Canada: Supplement*, Toronto, 1966), is in Brescia's department of English.

Most touchy in the revised arrangements was the reorganizing of the so-called x courses. Since 1934 college courses in philosophy and religious knowledge had an x attached to the course number. Brescia's courses in home economics and sociology 39 (sociology of the family) were known as x courses from the beginning. An x was attached to psychology 20 for the year 1935–6 but not subsequently. The course, however, continued to be given by the college for credit. The x was reintroduced into psychology in 1960–1, that is, following the submission of the *Conran Report*. After the affiliation agreement of 1962, x courses could still be taken for credit towards the BA by students of the affiliated college itself but not (without special permission) by other university students, which was a curtailment.

Brescia was not seriously affected by the general reorganization, partly because few women were enrolled in pre-professional courses, partly because the college was the official custodian for the university of the department of home economics. Christ the King and Huron suffered somewhat from the curtailment.

Sister Dominica opened in 1963, fulfilling a dream of her predecessor who planned it carefully, the new St James Memorial building with increased library, administrative, faculty, student, and academic facilities. This addition brought buildings more or less into line with numbers, then approaching and soon to pass the four hundred mark. Sister Dominica remained dean until the summer of 1969 when she was elected general of the Ursulines. She was succeeded as dean by Sister Arlene Walker, professor of sociology and former registrar and librarian.

Brescia's campus problems in the late sixties were more basic: should Brescia remain an exclusively women's college, and how should it react to a new decision make by King's in 1967 to go co-educational? Like Marianopolis and Mount St Vincent, Brescia opted to remain a women's college partly because of the religious order's tradition, partly because of a conviction that there is a place for women's colleges and that they will come back. Brescia had not been petty in the matter. In the early days it had enrolled the men of St Peter's Seminary and of St Thomas Scholasticate as a service to the Church. Brescia had not resisted the expansion of St Peter's when Christ the King College was added as a lay division because the sisters realized that London's Catholic constituency needed a laymen's college and no competition for students was involved. But when the situation at Christ the King deteriorated financially, administratively, and academically to the point where reorganization became imperative, conflicting issues did arise. The solution, the creation in 1968 of a co-educational King's College, placed on the campus a college capable of rendering Brescia redundant. For Brescia to reply by itself going co-educational could be doubly redundant.

After considerable soul-searching Brescia decided to accept the whole development of King's College as historically valid and to rely on goodwill and collaboration to redress possible injury. Accordingly Brescia and King's agreed not to duplicate each other's courses in the upper years, and to duplicate only populous courses in the early years. Both Catholic colleges began to make greater use of university facilities, especially in science, to the advantage as it turned out, of all three parties concerned. Buses then began to move students to and from Brescia, King's, and the university before and after every lecture.

When federal grants were dropped in 1967, Brescia and the Ontario government found themselves with a unique problem. Brescia conducted the university's department of home economics. Should the Ontario government make operational grants as it would to other provincially-supported universities? Or should it deal with Brescia as a denominational college and so discriminate against home economics at Western? The decision was to double grants to Brescia for students in home economics. The solution was just; but the principle which the government saved appeared, in the context of honest collaboration, somewhat ridiculous.

By 1970 Brescia College was moving towards stricter screening of students, a more aggressive Canadianism, and a larger lay faculty. It was maintaining, however, its emphasis on the traditional vocation of the Ursulines, the education of Catholic women.

University of St Jerome's College

WATERLOO

1865

St Jerome's College is a federated arts college in the University of Waterloo, Waterloo, Ontario, and is located along the west side of Laurel Creek on the large new university campus. The college is under the direction of the Resurrectionist Fathers, and is co-educational. It is a complex of three buildings: a classroom and administration building, a men's residence, and Notre Dame Hall, a women's residence. St Jerome's is governed by its own board of governors and by the senate of the university. It offers in its own lecture rooms courses in classics, economics, English, French, history, mathematics, philosophy, political science, psychology, sociology, and theology; other subjects are available through the university. St Jerome's has had a university charter since 1959 but holds its degree-conferring powers, except in theology, in abeyance. Associated with St Jerome's are Resurrection College and St Eugene's College for students preparing for the priesthood or the religious life. The School Sisters of Notre Dame conduct the women's residence.

The first St Jerome's College was established in 1865 in St Agatha (or Wilmot), four miles west of Waterloo in Wilmot township. St Agatha was the chief parish centre of the German Catholic settlers in the Berlin-Waterloo area.[1] There had been Catholics in this part of western Ontario from about 1826 and German priests from about 1833.[2] First talk of a college began after 1847 when Bishop Michael Power succeeded in getting a few German-speaking Jesuit missionaries to come from the continent. It was thought that a small college might possibly be built at St Agatha or New Germany. This became impossible when the Jesuits shifted the centre of their missionary activity to the Guelph area.[3] The Jesuits were replaced in the Berlin area by the Resurrection-

1 Theobald Spetz, *The Catholic Church in Waterloo County*, Toronto: Catholic Register Press, 1916
2 John Louis Wiriath was the first priest in charge; after him came Peter Schneider, and then Simon Sanderl. Spetz, *The Catholic Church in Waterloo County*, 4–22.
3 A college was started in Guelph about 1855. See An Act to Incorporate the College of St Ignatius, Guelph, which received royal assent, 9 June 1962. Hodgins, *Documentary History*, XVII, 43, 45, 51, 55–7. The act, submitted by bishop John

ists whom Bishop de Charbonnel brought from Rome. The first Resurrectionist to come to Canada was Eugene Funcken, who was despatched to St Agatha immediately after his ordination to the priesthood, 6 July 1857. With him came one ecclesiastical student, Edward Glowacki. Funcken and Glowacki, like the Jesuits, felt that the district needed a college in order to provide its own priests.

The first step towards establishing a college can be seen in the action of Bishop John Farrell when in 1859 he sent David Fennessey to St Agatha to learn German from Father Funcken. Farrell had been a student at St Michael's in Toronto and he planned on becoming a priest. He not only learned German from Funcken but taught him English in return. He also taught Latin and some other high school subjects to local boys in the dining room of the St Agatha rectory .

In 1864 Louis Funcken, a brother of Eugene's and also a Resurrectionist, came to St Agatha to start the college. Louis had been educated in Holland and ordained there. He had afterwards taken his doctorate in theology at the Sapienza – then the pontifical University of Rome. He was an indomitable kind of man who, although deaf from a childhood illness, forced himself to get an education in spite of his handicap. He acquired as first home for the college a log house belonging to Joseph Wey and located on the Waterloo road a mile and a quarter east of the village. In January 1865 he opened St Jerome's College.

The first staff consisted of two Resurrectionists: Louis Funcken in charge, David Fennessey (not yet ordained) his assistant. They were joined in October by a third confrere, Ludwig Elena from Trent, Austria, who had just been ordained. The beginning was not an easy one: Funcken had constantly to take on mission assignments; there were almost no funds; and there were students of varied preparation. Many of the boys whom Fennessey had taught in the rectory were now enrolled in the new college.

Bishop Farrell succeeded in having St Jerome's College incorporated by the Ontario legislature 15 August 1866.[4] A few months later, just before the end of the year, the college was transferred from the Wey residence near St Agatha to a house beside the church in Berlin, to which a 40 by 50 foot addition was made. Enrolment at the time of the

Farrell of Hamilton and five others, gives the name of only one Jesuit, John Holzer. The act also states that a college 'hath been established' since 1855. Spetz, p.54, says that the college was given up 'for want of necessary support from the public and the absence of professors.'

4 An Act to Incorporate the College of Saint Jerome, in the town of Berlin (29th and 30th Victoria, ch.134). Hodgins, *Documentary History*, XVII, 221–2.

move to Berlin was 46: 40 boarders from Ontario and six day scholars.[5]

Louis Funcken's rectorship of St Jerome's College, or Berlin College as it was usually called in his time, extended over a period of 25 years, 1865–90. The curriculum was essentially that of the classical colleges elsewhere in Canada, perhaps a little less complete but solid enough in some areas, particularly in Latin. The programme was designed for boys who intended to be priests, and especially Resurrectionists. This meant that it ought to equip them to complete their studies in Rome where they could live in the Resurrectionist residence and attend a pontifical university, especially the Sapienza.

A typical case would seem to be that of Theobald Spetz. He was a student of St Jerome's from 1866 to 1870. He then spent a year at St Agatha, and another teaching at St Mary's College, Kentucky, for which the Resurrectionists were also responsible. In 1872 he went to Rome. He required five years for his doctorate, which he completed in 1879.[6] He may have begun philosophy before leaving Canada, but he seems to have had to complete it in Rome before being admitted to theology.

The seventies were Funcken's most trying years. He received a few priests from the headquarters of the order in Rome, but they were quickly absorbed into parish work locally or sent to St Mary's College in Kentucky. He had, like the other college heads in Canada, to employ advanced students to teach the younger, and he had also to call on grammar school teachers – as in the case of C.V. Levermann teaching in Berlin – to come to the college to teach after hours. He had a good deal of bad luck with unordained clerics sent to him from Rome, losing many of them by sickness, death, or withdrawal from the order. In addition to all this, he had to serve as local parish priest, and even to tour the United States in search of funds to keep his college open. It is hardly surprising that by 1878 the college was reduced to some 20 or 25 students.[7] Had it not a religious order like the Resurrectionists behind it, it would surely have failed.

Better times came to St Jerome's in 1879 when Theobald Spetz returned from Rome to take up his teaching post. Spetz was the first locally-trained boy to return from studies in Rome to teach in Berlin College. He was followed in the next few years by William Kloepfer, Joseph Schweitzer, Anthony Weiler, and John Steffan. With this more

5 E.F. Donohoe, 'St Jerome's College: Historical Sketch,' in *Waterloo Historical Society, 28th Annual Report, 1940*, Kitchener, 1941, 101–10

6 Spetz, *The Catholic Church in Waterloo County*, 259–60

7 Donohoe, 'St Jerome's College,' 106

permanent kind of reinforcement by men who knew and understood the pioneer background of the central Ontario student, the college at last began to prosper.

In 1881 a small addition was made to the original building. By 1883, the college enrolled about 70 boarders and a small number of day scholars. In 1887 a new four-storey building was erected beside the original Berlin College, and its opening, which coincided with the twenty-fifth anniversary of Louis Funcken's ordination, was made a gala affair. Only two years later, that is, in 1889, an addition had to be made even to this new building doubling its size. The same year Funcken's health failed and he died at Roermond, Holland, where he had gone to recuperate. At the time of his death, St Jerome's enrolled 90 boarders.

Funcken's own education provides a rather good idea of what the Resurrectionists had in mind in training a boy during the later nineteenth century. Funcken studied first at Secular College, Roermond, Holland, then at the Roermond Seminary where he was ordained in 1862. He proceeded to the Resurrectionist residence in Rome from which he did his doctoral studies in theology at the Sapienza. This was the pattern for Spetz's education too, and for that of many a boy well into the twentieth century. The pattern has disappeared from the present St Jerome's but traces of it may be seen in the programme of Resurrection College.

Funcken was succeeded as president by Theobald Spetz, 1890–1901, by John Fehrenbach, 1901–5, and by Albert L. Zinger, 1905–19. This long period was a satisfying one in the old tradition. Early in Fehrenbach's presidency, a new act was obtained from the Ontario legislature.[8] This act made no essential changes other than to remove the bishop from the corporation. The original corporation had been set up in 1866. The property of the college was never transferred to it, possibly because the bishop, who was at its head, might conceivably take it out of the hands of the Resurrectionists. Hence the awkward device had been followed of placing property in the name of individual Resurrectionists and held by them in trust for the college. Moreover, officers of the corporation had never been re-elected since the passing of the original bill. It was thus more than possible that the original corporation had actually lapsed. When Fehrenbach became president in 1901, he settled this somewhat involved problem by having the legislature pass a new act.

8 An Act Respecting the Corporation of the College of St Jerome, Berlin (3 Edward VII, ch.133; 12 June 1903)

With the presidency of Zinger in 1905, St Jerome's entered what is, with the exception of the present, the greatest period in its history. Zinger was aware of curriculum modifications in Toronto and elsewhere. He appears to have considered introducing similar changes at St Jerome's, and at a meeting of the college board held on 31 January 1906 he proposed that steps be taken to have the provincial minister of education give official approval to the college course. When he had to report at the meeting of 29 March 1906 that there was 'no encouragement' from the department, he made a further motion that the necessary changes be made to have students take the matriculation examination 'at the end of a three-years course.'[9] After these early attempts to modify the traditional programme, Zinger seems to have resolved to make the best of the traditional college programme.

In 1908 Zinger erected the large administration building on Duke Street. Immediately afterward he undertook the gymnasium on College Street. Enrolment at this time reached 150 boarders and 30 day scholars. He strengthened and enlarged the curriculum but adapted it very little. The college still directed much of its attention to younger boys and to candidates for the priesthood. It was still a classical college in the older sense but with German and Italian rather than the French or British ties of other Catholic colleges of Canada.

Zinger was also a good president for local public relations. He succeeded in strengthening the image of the college in its own constituency, a task not easily achieved in an essentially rural community with little orientation towards higher education. One of his very successful efforts, in view at least of subsequent events, was his engaging in 1909 or so the brilliant young local lawyer, W.L.M. King, to give lectures at St Jerome's in economics.

Towards the end of his presidency, Zinger arranged with St Mary's College, Kentucky, to have their bachelor's degree conferred on St Jerome's students who had completed the full college programme. Although it was awkward negotiating across the border in this way, the step was useful. St Mary's degrees were recognized by the University of St Louis and therefore by most other American colleges. The arrangement with St Mary's College lasted until 1936.

Zinger's three successors in the presidency, William Beninger 1919–26, Leo Siess 1926–9, and Robert Dehler 1929–36, conducted a holding operation, academically speaking, and a declining one, in terms of post-secondary enrolment. The college was very badly hurt by the depres-

9 Meeting of the college board: College Board Minute Book 1897–1919, Archives of St Jerome's College

sion of the late twenties and thirties and tended more and more to become a high school operation.

In 1930 the Canadian Resurrectionists built their new St Thomas Scholasticate on the grounds of St Peter's Seminary, London.[10] This was a significant event in shaping the St Jerome's of the future.

In the early years, candidates had received much of their formation, and especially their theological training, in Rome. The war of 1914–18 had forced a change, and clerics were thereafter usually sent to St Louis to receive their formation with scholastics from Chicago and St Louis, among whom German and Polish traditions were still strong. Canadian Resurrectionists, realizing that their work and interests were different from their confreres' in the western states, sought and obtained during the twenties the appointment of Albert Zinger as a delegate-general. This was the first step towards establishing a separate province. The next and decisive step was setting up their own scholasticate in London. Henceforth young Resurrectionists took their theology in St Peter's and passed part of their academic life on the campus of the University of Western Ontario. A new generation of Resurrectionists appeared who were less committed to an almost exclusive concern with ecclesiastical education.

Meanwhile, St Jerome's continued to be more and more high school conscious. In 1936, William Borho succeeded Dehler as president. Almost immediately he discontinued post-secondary education at St Jerome's and completely adapted the high school department to the Ontario system, qualifying teachers at the College of Education in Toronto and conforming to the directives of the inspectors of the Ontario department of education.

Borho remained president until 1941. He was succeeded by F.M. Weiler who held the office from 1941 to 1948. Weiler revived post-secondary education in 1947, restoring it, however, not as the old classical course, but as an arts faculty affiliated with the University of Ottawa, which he arranged with the help and encouragement of Bishop Joseph F. Ryan of Hamilton. This restoration of post-secondary teaching was accompanied by the passing of a new St Jerome's College Act by the legislature which gave the college the legal powers required by the revived and changed academic status.[11]

Once under way in a contemporary mode, the revolution at St Jerome's moved rapidly. In 1948 the most aggressive of all St Jerome's presidents, C.L. Siegfried, came to office. By 1953 he reconciled his

10 See above, 294 and 300
11 An Act Respecting St Jerome's College (2 George VI, ch.137; 3 Apr. 1947)

confreres to the long overdue separation of the high school and college departments. The buildings in downtown Kitchener were turned over to the high school and the college moved to a new campus at Kingsdale, the eastern extremity of Kitchener. The new campus was built with the help of Bishop Ryan, who raised funds throughout the diocese for the project. In his mind and in the minds of many, the campus was to be a compromise between the new and the old St Jerome's. It was to accommodate the new faculty of arts recently affiliated with Ottawa, and it was also to accommodate a new version of the ecclesiastical minor seminary, one not tied to the restrictive demands of either a university or a department of education, but which was attractive to veterans returning from World War II and other late vocations which were around in abundance.

The new college at Kingsdale was an immediate success. Particularly successful was the intensive programme in Latin and other disciplines for late or inadequately prepared candidates for the priesthood. Kingsdale's enrolment soon reached 240 students, larger than the faculty of arts. Candidates for the intensive Latin and pre-theology course came from all over Canada and the United States, many of them supported by the GI bill of rights and other veterans' allowance plans.

When the college campus was moved to Kingsdale in 1953, Siegfried gave up the presidency and was replaced by Jerome Arnold, who held the office until 1955. In that year Siegfried began his second term as president which lasted until 1965. These years, 1955 to 1965, proved to be the most revolutionary in St Jerome's long history.

During the fall of 1955, Joseph Gerald Hagey, first lay president of the United Lutheran Church's Waterloo College, took steps to set up a non-denomination affiliate so as to be eligible for government aid to science and engineering under what by now had become known as the McMaster Plan. McMaster, a Baptist university, had established Hamilton College as a non-denominational affiliate and through it received provincial subsidies for science and engineering. Hagey solicited the help of industrialists and businessmen and was able to establish on 4 April 1956 the Waterloo College Associate Faculties. By June he had affiliated the Associate Faculties with Waterloo College.

At a meeting of the board of the Associate Faculties, 25 April 1956, it was decided that the board would entertain a petition from St Jerome's for an association that would make 'the facilities of this board available to St Jerome's on a favorable basis.'[12] It was felt that consoli-

12 For a full account see James Scott, *Of Mud and Dreams*, Toronto: Ryerson, 1927, 29ff.

dation and collaboration of all constituencies concerned might even bring a university to Waterloo county. Siegfried showed immediate interest in this local university development.

Once aware of the possibilities of the proposed university development, Siegfried never looked back. He threw his full support behind the new undertaking. By July 1957 negotiations were so far advanced that Hagey began enrolling engineers in the Associated Faculties, using the Waterloo College affiliation with Western to assure his students of academic credit. Siegfried closely followed the successful application of St Michael's during 1958 for a university charter which would give it degree-conferring powers without disturbing its federated status in the University of Toronto.[13] He now saw clearly the legal pattern for the projected university in Waterloo. Thus, on 5 March 1959, three private bills, all sponsored by John J. Wintermeyer, formally established The University of St Jerome's College, The University of Waterloo, and The Waterloo Lutheran University.[14] It was Wintermeyer's, and the minister of education's, first intention that both St Jerome's and Waterloo Lutheran be federated colleges in the University of Waterloo. At the last moment, Waterloo Lutheran withdrew from the three-party arrangement, deciding not to hold its degree-conferring powers in abeyance but to strike off on its own. St Jerome's stayed with the federation idea, and formally federated its faculty of arts as a college in the University of Waterloo on 18 June 1960.

St Jerome's experienced no serious problems during the course of its negotiations with Waterloo College and the Associate Faculties. At one stage Waterloo College asked to be the new university's only federated college, with St Jerome's being but an affiliate. The request, however, was quickly dropped when Siegfried objected. Later, after the breakdown of relations between Waterloo College and the new university, St Jerome's had to turn down the university's request that it operate the entire arts programme until such time as the university was ready to take it over. Both of these were but trifling incidents. St Jerome's greatest problem was probably a psychological one – the irony of having to move the faculty of arts away from Kingsdale so few years after taking it to the beautiful and convenient campus, and having to leave behind its successful programme of intensive Latin for prospective theologians.

13 Ibid., 36; and see above, 195
14 An Act Respecting St Jerome's College (7–8 Elizabeth II, ch.139; 5 Mar. 1959). An Act Respecting the University of Waterloo (7–8 Elizabeth II, ch.140; 5 Mar. 1959). An Act Respecting Waterloo Lutheran University (7–8 Elizabeth II, ch.142: 5 Mar. 1959).

Following federation in 1960, St Jerome's remained at Kingsdale for two more years, moving in 1962 to its three-building complex erected on a campus site along the west bank of Laurel Creek, which Siegfried had himself selected shortly after the property was acquired for the university.

Siegfried's academic arrangements with the University of Waterloo were also highly satisfactory. Curriculum programming was made the responsibility of the university's faculty of arts, the college reserving the right to teach as many subjects as it wished or could afford. As a federated college, St Jerome's provided about two-thirds of the instruction of its own students in its own classrooms. At the same time it admitted to its classes a substantial number of university students. Financial arrangements have thus far been satisfactory. Overall enrolment, which was 85 in 1960 at Kingsdale, reached nearly 400 during 1969–70 on the university campus. In 1965, Siegfried gave up the presidency and was succeeded by John R. Finn.

When the arts faculty left Kingsdale in 1962, the institution which was left behind was renamed Resurrection College. Its constituency was the group of pre-theologians preparing for seminaries throughout America. This group of students had been quite numerous at one stage, and was in a real way the operation providing much of St Jerome's continuity with the past. It was given its own rector in 1962, Bernard J. Murphy, subsequently named bishop of Bermuda. The rector since 1967 has been Gordon R. Lang. After 1962 registration in Resurrection College declined rapidly. The reason was twofold: the end of veteran enrolment, and the seminary crisis subsequent to Vatican II. Plans were made for the ultimate disposal of the property and the removal of the small operation to St Eugene's College where those students requiring university courses (and there have always been some such students at Resurrection College) were once more near the St Jerome's campus.

St Eugene's College is a small house of philosophy for scholastics of the Congregation of the Resurrection. It was built in 1964 near St Jerome's but just off the university campus, and has been under the direction of C.L. Siegfried ever since. Scholastics attend lectures at St Jerome's and the University of Waterloo. Resurrection College, St Eugene's College, and the campus residence for women conducted by the School Sisters of Notre Dame, are the constituent parts of the greater University of St Jerome's College.

IV
WESTERN CANADA

St Paul's College

WINNIPEG

1926

St Paul's College, in affiliation with the University of Manitoba and under the direction of the Jesuit Fathers of Upper Canada, is located on the large Fort Garry campus of the provincial university. Its five adjoining buildings, beautifully designed by the Canadian architect, Peter Thornton, include an administration wing, lecture rooms and library, chapel, students' centre, and faculty residence. St Paul's offers BA and BSC degrees, general and honour, through the university's faculty of arts and science.

ST PAUL'S UNDER THE OBLATES

The college is, in its origins, very much the personal creation of Alfred Arthur Sinnott, first archbishop of Winnipeg, appointed to that see from the secretariat of the apostolic delegation in Ottawa. Sinnott, a man of considerable education, was familiar with college work from two years spent on the staff of St Dunstan's, Charlottetown, before being called to Ottawa. He seems to have envisaged the founding of a college from the moment he took over the archdiocese of Winnipeg in December 1916, but it was not actually until 1926 that he at last succeeded in purchasing the fifteen-year-old YMCA building on Selkirk Avenue, Winnipeg, and then in getting, on 18 August, the commitment of Father Paul Hilland, acting-provincial of the new Oblate province of St Mary, to take on the task of founding a college. St Paul's opened on 15 September 1926, with a staff of six, composed of four Oblate priests – Alphonse Simon, Alfred J. Schimonowski, James Schnerch, S. Puchniak – one Oblate brother, J. Simon; and one diocesan cleric, Joseph E. Campbell, who was preparing for orders.

Alphonse Simon was the first rector, holding that office until 1931 when the Oblates gave up the college.[1] Simon's St Paul's was a classical college, somewhat adapted to the demands of Manitoba's school system; that is, it covered four years of high school and two of philosophy or arts. St Paul's had no degree-conferring charter, but the first administration arranged to have those who completed philosophy with

---

1 During the 1960s Alphonse Simon was director of King's Retreat House, Buffalo, Minnesota.

an agreed-upon selection of courses to be admitted to advanced standing in the University of Manitoba where they could complete their course and qualify for their degree. The St Paul's of Simon's time was not deeply immersed in college work: there were no philosophy students among the 100 registered in 1926, and no more than a dozen in 1930 when 224 students in all were registered. However, the full programme from first-year high school to second-year arts was in operation that year, and 27 candidates had been sent on to study for the priesthood; only a few, unfortunately, for the archdiocese, which was in sore need of priests.

Relations between Sinnott and the Oblates were never easy, but there was considerable co-operation between the diocesan and religious priests on the staff. The number of the former became surprisingly large, considering the shortage of priests in Winnipeg. Diocesan priests serving at one time or another under Simon included Joseph E. Campbell, Gaston St Jacques, James K. MacIsaac, J.A. Mullaly, James H. Fitzgerald, and J.E. Cahill.

During 1931 Archbishop Sinnott became even more deeply involved in college affairs. Characteristically, he acquired the old Manitoba College building from the United Church without even his own chancellor knowing that the deal was in process. It was an excellent purchase, however. The building had been erected by the Presbyterians in 1882 at Vaughan and Ellice in downtown Winnipeg to serve as a school. It was not longer needed since Manitoba College, which dropped its arts course in 1914, merged with Wesley College following the church union of 1925. Dr John MacKay, who had been principal of Manitoba College, was favourable to the sale of the buildings to Archbishop Sinnott. It was at this time that both Sinnott and the Oblates agreed that a change of administration in the college was necessary. When the college reopened for the fall term 1931, it became a diocesan college. Sinnott seemed to have in mind a kind of western Canadian St Francis Xavier. He had written to H.P. MacPherson, president of St Francis Xavier University, for help in finding a new rector. He is said to have had his eye on Father Jimmie Tompkins. MacPherson, however, recommended Cornelius B. Collins of Providence, Rhode Island, whom he knew well and on whom he conferred an LLD before sending him to Winnipeg to become St Paul's second rector.

THE DIOCESAN COLLEGE

Collins's rectorship, 1931 to 1933, got off to a promising start. Not only did it begin in a new location, but with formal affiliation with the University of Manitoba by arrangements begun and completed during October 1931.[2] This affiliation was in line with the principles operative in Manitoba since the University of Manitoba Amendment Act of 1917 which reversed earlier policy and tended to relegate the denominational colleges to the periphery of the university while allowing them generous autonomy over their own courses and academic structure. There were objections to the admission of St Paul's to affiliation voiced in the University Council by W.A. McIntyre. His objections were on principle: affiliation may restore the denominational colleges to domination; and the providing of special courses is divisive and unnecessary.[3] But strong support came from Dr MacKay, formerly head of Manitoba but then of United College, from the Anglican Archbishop Matheson, still in 1931 chancellor of the provincial university, and from Monsignor A.A. Cherrier, vicar general of the archdiocese and long-time representative of the St Boniface constituency on the board of governors. St Paul's was acknowledged to have the staff and equipment necessary to meet the standards of the university and its course in scholastic philosophy was, like that of St Boniface, specifically accepted by the University Council.

Collins's regime began auspiciously enough. His staff of 15 included eight priests, one of them Michael Pontarelli from Chicago, and seven laymen. There was still very little distinctinction made between high school and college, and the new building, renovated under the direction of Father A.D. Rheaume of chancery, was at once filled to capacity with a large school of residents and day scholars. The arts faculty still only embraced two years of philosophy with four men in second year (Vivian Carey, Alphonse Minvielle, Frank Strosewski, Leonard Delaney) and eight in first year. Of the eight beginning university work, three were from Winnipeg (Edgar O'Brien, Russell Manning, William Jordan) and three were from Saskatchewan (Sebastian Leibel, Jerome Volk, Joseph Lambertus). The two remaining residents were native Manitobans. The year was no sooner begun than there was talk of an addition to the building; the first sod of this addition was turned by Monsignor Cherrier on 25 May 1932.

Collins's two-year regime was marked by the domination of a sports conscious high school, by the departure of Fathers MacIsaac and Fitzgerald from the staff, and by the acquiring of a debt of $90,000 for building and faculty salaries. It was quite clear that local resources

2 Minutes of the University Council, 13 Oct. 1931, 47–8; Minutes of the Board of Governors, 14 Oct. 1931
3 W.L. Morton, *One University: A History of the University of Manitoba*, Toronto: McClelland and Stewart, 1957, 145

could not furnish qualified men in adequate numbers for a university college nor provide for the financing demanded in a non-religious economy. Sinnott approached both the Jesuits of Upper Canada and the Basilians of Toronto with invitations to take over the college. The general council of the Basilians was divided on the issue and for a long time no answer came from Father Henry Carr. When at length Carr indicated through a verbal message sent to the archbishop through Father MacIsaac, who spent 1932–3 studying philosophy in Toronto, that the Basilians would take on the college, the Jesuit provincial had already accepted Archbishop Sinnott's offer. With the end of the academic year 1932–3 Collins returned to Providence, and in September John Samuel Holland took over as St Paul's third rector.

ST PAUL'S UNDER THE JESUITS

The bringing of the Jesuits to St Paul's required more than a formal invitation. The Upper Canadian province of the order had no surplus priests, there was no strong feeling in favour of a college in the west, and the prospect of assuming responsibility for paying off a debt of $90,000 on an insolvent operation during the depth of national economic depression was appalling. Archbishop Sinnott dealt directly with the Roman generalate, bringing as much pressure to bear on the provincial council as he could, which proved to be adequate. The Jesuits of Upper Canada took over both the direction of the college and its debt during the summer of 1933, and appointed Holland as rector. Holland was accompanied to Winnipeg by a staff of three Jesuits: E.G. Bartlett, F. Joseph McDonald, and Christoper Keating. A number of teachers, diocesan priests, and laymen who were on the staff during Collins's regime continued to serve under the Jesuit administration. By a happy coincidence, Sidney Earle Smith became president of the University of Manitoba during 1934. Father Holland and Smith, both new arrivals on the educational scene in Manitoba, became close friends – an important factor in the subsequent development of St Paul's.

Father Holland's St Paul's was a downtown high school to which a college with neither money nor prestige was attached. Holland and his successors have pursued a courageous and constant expansionary policy. They have opened a new college on the Fort Garry campus, a new and independent high school in Bellaire, and have profitably disposed of the original property.

There has been a consistency about their policies and problems which invites analysis of the years 1933 to the present as a unit. The Jesuit rectors have been as follows: James Samuel Holland, 1933–41; Raymond Sutton, 1941–5; Joseph P. Monaghan, 1945–51; Cecil C. Ryan, 1951–8; Hugh P. Kierans, 1958–64; Desmond Burke-Gaffney 1964–9. The present rector, John E. Page, was appointed during the summer of 1969. The first three of these men were downtown rectors conducting both a high school and a college, but with constantly increasing emphasis on the college division. During 1957–8, the last year of Ryan's rectorship, the college department was transferred to Fort Garry. Recent rectors, Kierans, Burke-Gaffney, and Page, have been occupied exclusively with college administration.

The development of St Paul's under the Jesuits can be examined under four headings: the move to Fort Garry; the trend towards co-education; the university pastorate; the growing pains of affiliation.

The move to Fort Garry

Certainly, the move to Fort Garry has been the most spectacular development of the Jesuit regime and constitutes a successful modern instance in a long series of not always equally felicitous operations. The question of the site of the University of Manitoba was from the beginning a sensitive one. The University of Manitoba was established in 1877 as an examining rather than a teaching body. It possessed at first no property, no building, and a ridiculously low annual grant of $200. The university, as a legal entity, conducted such business as it had in a room rented from the Historical and Scientific Society of Manitoba, and later, during the nineties, in the McIntyre Block. Only in 1901 was a building opened for the teaching of the natural sciences on the Old Driving Park property of 6.6 acres on Broadway. By 1904 the university had acquired some inadequate buildings of its own and a few university professors. It was located on the Broadway site, but most of its members looked to the day when it would go elsewhere. Some would move it to Tuxedo where the Agricultural College was located. When in 1913 the Agricultural College was moved to St Vital (Fort Garry) on the Red River, seven miles south from downtown Winnipeg, the university seemed on the point of moving too. It had an option on the Tuxedo site which the Agricultural College was leaving and held a signed lease on 37 acres on the St Vital as well. Nothing came of much discussing and manoeuvring. Not until 1929 was the decision made to locate on the 663-acre site in Fort Garry occupied by the Agricultural College since 1913. University buildings began slowly to appear on the campus: an arts building for senior students in 1930, a science building in 1931. Only in 1950–1 were the first two years of arts and science offered at Fort Garry. This year, however, was a time of soul-searching for the affiliated colleges, especially those in downtown Winnipeg. Should they, as predominantly city colleges, remain close to their city constituency, or should they follow the university to Fort Garry?

United College, the strongest of the affiliates, a composite of the former Presbyterian Manitoba College and the Methodist Wesley College, elected to remain permanently on its downtown site. For St Paul's the choice was not so clear-cut. The opportunity to separate the college from the high school was attractive, and the building at Vaughan and Ellice Streets was entirely inadequate. But a decision that invited city students to change their registration to United rather than commute seven miles each day might well turn out not to be a service to Catholic education. Moreover, the removal of a Jesuit college to the campus of a state university was tantamount to endorsing university affiliation, regarded by many inside and outside the order as an educational structure foreign to traditional Jesuit principles. The final decision to move to Fort Garry was Archbishop Pocock's. He had first-hand experience of affiliation and federation at London and Saskatoon. He was also eager to co-operate with the Manitoba government wherever he reasonably could, in the hope of one day solving the vexed Manitoba school question. Father Ryan, the college rector, and the provincial council of the order decided in 1956 to accede to Pocock's request and to move St Paul's to Fort Garry, a meaningful decision for Catholic education in western Canada. W.L. Morton, university historian and later first provost of University College, wrote as follows about the move in 1957 before it had actually been carried out:

To the historian of the university, however, perhaps the most significant example of this new harmony and purpose was the decision of St John's and St Paul's colleges to build on the campus. By 1956 it was certain that these two colleges at least would be housed at Fort Garry in appropriate and beautiful buildings, with quadrangle, cloister, and chapel, in a matter of a year or two. This consummation of the original idea of the University, if only partial while United College remained on its downtown site, was still a heartening fulfilment of destiny. It bade fair to realize the physical neighbourhood indispensible to intellectual exchange and it would restore to the university something of that companionship of religion and learning to which it was originally committed.[4]

A further argument for the removal of St Paul's to the university campus was a strong desire to give more integrity to the undergraduate programme of the college. St Paul's had become affiliated to the uni-

4 Ibid., 191

versity in 1931, that is, at precisely the time the university decided to remove its senior students in arts and science to Fort Garry. During the following years there was a tendency for those who entered St Paul's to discontinue after two years, either to enter a professional faculty or, in a few cases, to complete their course at the university. The pattern was not a healthy one, either for the college or for the men whose education was involved. Many felt, as indeed turned out to be the case, that the locating of the college on the university campus would put an end to the practice.

Co-education

A corollary of the move of St Paul's to Fort Garry was a commitment of the college to the principle of co-education. In Winnipeg, as in so many of the Catholic colleges elsewhere in Canada, the college education of men and women was provided for in separate colleges. St Mary's College for women, conducted by the Sisters of the Holy Names of Jesus and Mary, was in operation before St Paul's. St Mary's applied for affiliation with the university of Manitoba in 1925,[5] but the application was refused on the ground that the University of Manitoba did not affiliate women's colleges. In 1926, however, St Mary's made arrangements to provide their college students with university registration through the Collège Saint-Boniface. After St Paul's became an affiliated college in 1931, requests began to come from time to time for the use of facilities by St Mary's girls. When Father Holland was rector he was quite firm in refusing to enrol any women in St Paul's. He felt that there was some affront to the sisters involved in any arrangements in favour of St Mary's girls. In 1936, Collège Saint-Joseph requested to be allowed to qualify women students for university credit through St Paul's. St Joseph's was a French school and might have been expected to make arrangements through Saint-Boniface, but another of Manitoba's regulations would not permit an affiliated college to sponsor more than one women's college. Sidney Smith suggested a switch whereby St Mary's would enrol its students through St Paul's and leave Saint-Boniface free to sponsor St Joseph's. In August 1936, St Mary's became the women's division of St Paul's, and relations between the two were for the most part rather good. There was some exchange of instruction, and women were sometimes admitted to lectures in individual courses at St Paul's. There was occasional pressure on St Paul's to allow individual women to bypass St Mary's and enrol directly in the men's college. When St Paul's moved to the Fort Garry campus in 1958, it became co-educational and soon had almost as many women as

5 Minutes of the University Council, 22 Jan. 1925

St Mary's, without, however, reducing St Mary's enrolment. The distance between the two colleges now rendered impossible the earlier practice of sharing staff and facilities. In 1962 the Sisters were already thinking of withdrawing from university work. 'In conjunction with our Archbishop,' wrote the dean 28 January 1962, 'and the authorities at St Paul's we are trying to decide what is best for the future of Catholic education in this province, and the decision, when it comes, may mean the end of our college as it now exists.'[6] St Mary's withdrew from college education during 1963. The St Paul's of 1963–4 was completely co-educational, although it listed only three women on its teaching staff, one of them being Sister Mary Judith Anne of the Sisters of the Holy Name. Sister Judith Anne remained a member of the St Paul's department of English until 1970.

The university pastorate

The university pastorate for Catholic students only began when the first two years of arts and science were moved to Fort Garry in 1950. A Newman Club was set up from the beginning and a chaplain supplied by the Jesuits of St Paul's, who were still in the city. When St Paul's moved to Fort Garry in 1958, the club was but an indifferent one, nor did it immediately prosper when the Catholic college appeared on the campus. In fact it became more difficult to contact Catholics enrolled in university departments and to elicit their interest in Newmanism after the opening of the college than it was before. University students felt that the club was now dominated by the Catholic college students and began avoiding it. Newmanism at Fort Garry did not achieve the effectiveness it had in Saskatoon, which was a disappointment to Archbishop Pocock, who had come from Saskatoon to Winnipeg, and who hoped to create in the archdiocese an equally lively operation. The two situations were very different: in Saskatoon it was the club which appeared first and the college which grew out of it; moreover, Saskatoon had no Catholic campus residence and the club was able to take over functions not looked after by anyone else; Saskatoon also had a group of excellent lay teachers within and without the university who wanted an active club. Winnipeg lacked most of these advantages.

Winnipeg also had a more complex ethnic problem. Ukrainian students in university courses were numerous and they preferred to patronize Gamma Rho, the Fort Garry chapter of Obnova.[7] The resultant

6 Judith Anne to Shook, 30 Jan. 1962.
7 Obnova ('renewal') is an international Ukrainian students organization affiliated with Pax Romana.

fragmentation of effort along ethnic lines though understandable curtails Catholic action. The situation was further complicated when the
orthodox Ukrainians had their St Andrew's College made an associate
college of the university in 1962. Two years later when the lovely St
Andrew's residence and theologate was opened on the campus, it was
feared that Newman might lose even its uniate Ukrainians.

The situation, however, actually began to improve in 1964. The university provided for the appointment of a 'resident university Catholic
chaplain.' This gave the Newman Club chaplain, still a Jesuit, university recognition and dissociated his assignment from St Paul's. Since
that time St Paul's has appointed Alexander Baran, chaplain of Gamma
Rho, to its religious studies and history departments, and has designated him a member of the college administration. The unique pastoral
problem of the Fort Garry campus is moving to its necessarily unique
solution.

Affiliation's growing pains

The affiliation of St Paul's with the University of Manitoba was
negotiated by the archdiocese back in 1931. The terms of agreement
were broad and flexible, with no arbitrary limiting of college teaching
to a narrow list of subjects or courses. St Paul's, St John's, Wesley, and
Manitoba (United, after 1938; University of Winnipeg since 1967)
taught in practice any subject in arts and science for which they could
provide instruction. The university senate had, of course, to approve
the college selection. In the case of St Paul's, some courses were provided in science even during the thirties and forties. Indeed, it was
characteristic of Manitoba affiliations from the beginning (and notably
in the cases of St Boniface and United) that students took all or nearly
all their instruction in their own college. So much was this so that the
question was sometimes asked whether affiliation was of any financial
advantage to the colleges.

The removal of the university to Fort Garry affected colleges in two
ways: those electing to remain where they were – Brandon, St Boniface,
United – became even more independent; those accompanying the
university to its new campus – St John's and St Paul's – became less so.
For the latter, some re-negotiation of the terms and details of affiliation
was only to be expected, and it was bound to be in the direction of integrated instruction. St Paul's drew up such an agreement with the university 1 May 1957 which was subsequently approved by the legislature 4 October 1957.

Resistance to college independence in the area of instruction seems to have come in the first instance from the university departments. Chairmen began to feel that colleges ought not be permitted to provide senior work (courses of the last two years) or honours work in any subject, or science courses or graduate work. Here the departments and the colleges did not see eye to eye. Although the controversy concerned all the colleges, Kierans figured prominently in the debates, and St Paul's viewed the issue as serious. The early sixties were marked by worry and tension.

The colleges maintained throughout the campus controversy that university regulations covering the matter of instruction should be generous towards them rather than miserable. And so, indeed, the matter turned out in the long run. By 1964–5, the colleges found themselves providing more subjects and courses than they could finance. In that year the St Paul's calendar listed 15 departments, yet the entire staff totalled only 31. For two of the departments announced, sociology and zoology, no instructors were named; and some staff members were working in more than one department: Adam Giesinger in chemistry and mathematics, Robert L. Bennett in classics and French, Charles Kane in classics and English, Vincent J. Jensen in history and political science, Philip Leah in mathematics and philosophy, Paul Forstner in German and political science. This doubling of fields made good sense in the given cases but, being out of line with the rigid and perhaps absurd departmentalism rampant in the sixties, it caused increased tension. During these years, 1964 to 1967, a quiet revolution took place on the Fort Garry campus, completely revising the situation of the denominational colleges. There were a few 'incidents.' Philip Leah, for example, a highly competent Jesuit mathematician who was given no scope to function in his specialty, withdrew from the university in disgust and took a post in the department of mathematics in the University of Toronto. There was also, however, a positive step on the part of the provincial government: the naming of a committee on college structure, to report to the province's Council of Higher Learning. This committee was chaired by Professor B. Lionel Funt, and its recommendations proved to be the basis of deep and apparently lasting change.[8]

Significant among the proposals of the *Funt Report* were the following: that there be a community of constituent colleges each with an appropriate area of emphasis; that there be provision made in the university for the identity, growth, flexibility of status, and government financing of its colleges; that faculty and student membership be

8 *Report of the Committee on College Structure: The Council of Higher Learning (The Funt Report 1967)*

primarily in the university, secondarily and voluntarily in the college; and that there be contractual arrangements between colleges and the university designed to leave colleges some real autonomy but promoting at the same time the use of university-wide services.

Two colleges accepted the principles of the *Funt Report*, St John's in a letter to the minister of education, 7 June 1967, and St Paul's in a letter of 10 July 1967. The rector and the dean of St Paul's, Desmond Burke-Gaffney and Lawrence Braceland, threw themselves wholeheartedly into its full implementation. By 28 March 1968 they prepared a 'Letter of Intent and Arrangement' with the University of Manitoba; and on 1 April, just four days later, put the new arrangements into operation.

The Letter of Intent was concerned largely with the academic and financial administrative detail necessary to put the recommendations of the *Funt Report* to work. The letter was signed on behalf of St Paul's by Burke-Gaffney as rector and C.M. Keenan as comptroller, Signatories for the university's board of governors were Peter D. Curry and W.J. Condo. Life at St Paul's began to change immediately. Students planning to attend during 1968–9 applied for membership. They became eligible for membership if they took a stipulated minimum number of courses in departments represented in the college; three such courses in the first year, three (or two under certain conditions) in the second, one in the third. The solution tended to reduce the size of student membership in the college but it preserved, perhaps even strengthened, the college community. The community became slightly less representative of the Catholic constituency than formerly; and the college's power in the university as a whole was possibly reduced. However, the burden of financing education was more evenly spread, because the college staffs became full members of their university department where their salaries originated.

The Letter of Intent was an important document. It was the memorandum or arrangement under which the college operated experimentally within the university until the spring of 1970 when the experiment was formalized by the agreement of 11 June with the university, and legal establishment by the government of a 'Board of Management' of St Paul's. By this time St Paul's was eligible for both operating and capital grants from the provincial government.

During the course of the foregoing negotiations St Paul's had also to work out an agreement about the amount of credit to be given to students for courses in religion. This too reached crisis proportions and was then resolved. Under new arrangements there were two types of courses: religious studies which was credit-bearing, theology which was not. Courses were provided in both religious studies and theology in all years. The former were structured to serve the academic curiosity of Christians generally; the latter were designed for Catholic students who wanted to know their religion in some depth. Catholics were strongly urged to take a course in theology each year, especially if they were not taking a credit course in religious studies. It is probably in this area that St Paul's programme is most removed from traditional practice in Jesuit colleges elsewhere.

The religious programme flourished on the Fort Garry campus and the university introduced the scholarly study of religion as a humanistic discipline with both minor and major programmes at the undergraduate level. In 1970 the university department of religion was offering a total of 16 courses by a staff of nine professors. Among this staff were two of Catholic training: the Jesuit, John C. Hanley, professor of modern Catholic theology, and Dr Klaus K. Klostermaier, professor of the history of religions.

St Paul's is today one of Canada's leading Catholic colleges offering students and professors an attractive role in both Catholic and Canadian education.

Campion College

UNIVERSITY OF SASKATCHEWAN: REGINA CAMPUS

1917

Campion College, Regina, Saskatchewan, is a federated Catholic college of the University of Saskatchewan on the Regina campus. It is an undergraduate liberal arts college offering courses leading to the BA in arts and science. The college has a staff of its own, and many facilities, including chapel, common rooms, cafeteria, and library, but neither classrooms nor students' residence. The college moved to the Regina campus early in 1968 into a modern concrete building valued at $2,000,000 and matching in design and material the other buildings of the university campus.

Campion owes its existence to the zeal and determination of Olivier-Elzéar Mathieu, first bishop, and later archbishop, of Regina. Before his appointment to Regina in 1911, Mathieu had been, since 1878, professor of philosophy, and from 1899 to 1908 rector magnificus of Laval University. Named bishop of Regina in 1911, he resolved to bring Catholic colleges to the prairies. He was encouraged in his resolution by George Daly, rector of Holy Rosary cathedral, Regina.[1] During 1917 Mathieu and Daly laid the foundations for two colleges, one at Gravelbourg for the French, the other at Regina for the English.

Daly contacted the Jesuit rector of St Boniface College, Gregory Fere, suggesting that the Jesuits consider establishing a college and high school in Regina. Fere visited Regina during 1917 to examine Daly's plans and then recommended the project to J.M. Filion, provincial of the Canadian Jesuits.[2] Filion was instrumental in having Thomas Mac-Mahon appointed first rector of the proposed college. In the meantime, Mathieu obtained from the provincial legislature an act of incorporation of a 'Catholic College of Regina.'[3] He also put at the disposal of the Jesuits eleven acres of property in the city of Regina which had

1 See above, 29–30
2 The Jesuits had but one province in Canada until 1924 when the English-language Province of Upper Canada was established. Father Fere, a gold medalist in medicine from the University of Toronto, was one of the most distinguished Jesuits to work in education in the Canadian west. After playing a role in the founding of Campion, he was a member of its faculty for many years and is responsible for its assembling a library beyond what is usual in small colleges.
3 Statutes of Saskatchewan, 15 Dec. 1917

some time before been signed over to the archbishop of St Boniface by two Catholic laymen for the development of the Church in Regina.[4]

MacMahon arrived in Regina in June 1918. He rented two houses on 13th Avenue, opposite the cathedral, and opened classes in September. Six boys registered during the fall of 1918; by the end of the year 24 were registered. The staff consisted of three Jesuits: Father MacMahon, Mr Gwyn, Brother La Flamme. In 1919–20, with 30 students in attendance, the school was moved to two larger houses on Argyle and 8th Avenue. The large donated site at Albert and 23rd became available in 1921, and a small new building was ready for occupancy during late 1922. In 1922 Joseph Leahy was appointed Campion's second rector. His first move was to add a new wing to the building with $14,000 obtained in a drive and $10,000 given by Archbishop Mathieu.

During 1923 Campion was recognized as a junior college of the University of Saskatchewan. Students could, if they wished, transfer to Saskatchewan with advanced standing, that is, enter the second year of a three-year arts course. A further arrangement was then negotiated with the University of Manitoba for recognition of the instruction given in the final two years and for the conferring of the bachelor's degree.

Campion's third rector, George F. Bradly, was appointed during the summer of 1924. He presided in 1926 at Campion's first graduation exercises in which Leonard Krisch and Orville Kristweiser received their BA. Courses carrying credit towards the BA continued to be offered at Campion up to the beginning of World War II, that is, during the rectorships of John S. Holland (1930–4) and Leo J. Burns (1934–9).

R.A. MacGillivray succeeded Burns as rector in 1939. He had only a high school to conduct during these war years but it was an active and expanding one. Campion, however, maintained its junior college affiliation with Saskatchewan. Its arrangement for higher work was no longer with Manitoba but with Montreal. MacGillivray was succeeded in 1945 by V. Murphy, who added a fine new wing to the building in 1948. College classes were resumed in the fall of 1948 when F.J. Boyle took over as Campion's eighth rector, but only at the junior college level. The situation remained unchanged throughout the rectorships of R.C. Johnston, 1954–7, and J.J.Farrell, 1957–60. The high school continued to expand and to be prosperous; the college was a holding operation.

Under Farrell, who is well remembered for his important addition of

4 *The Northwest Review*, 45th anniversary edition, 1930, 36. See also: 50th anniversary edition, 1935, 49.

a gymnasium-auditorium to Campion's physical plant, a new dawn began to break for the college department as word circulated that the University of Saskatchewan was about to establish a second campus around Regina College. Farrell wrote to President Spinks, 25 July 1960, formally requesting the federation of Campion with the Regina branch of the university on a basis identical with that of St Thomas More College with the parent university at Saskatoon.

Some months after the receipt of this letter, a joint committee of representatives from the board, the senate, and the arts council began to meet to study the request. By this time, Campion had a new rector, Angus J. MacDougall, who took over in September 1960. MacDougall set forth in detail in a letter of 1 March 1961 what kind of federation he would like to have. He asked, in effect, for full federated status, distinct from a junior college arrangement, with right to the fees of college students, with the privilege of having college lectures in university lecture rooms, with college buildings located eventually on the campus, and with the understanding that federal grants would go to the university until such time as a college building was constructed.

The request from Farrell and MacDougall was dealt with slowly, not so much because Campion and St Thomas More were not in parallel situations, but because Regina and Saskatoon were not. Regina was not yet sufficiently established, the committee felt, to cope with a federated college from a secure position. However, the Campion request was never rejected. On 12 September 1963, the committee recommended the Campion federation, asking that it not become effective before 1 July 1966, thus providing for the Regina branch certain temporal priorities which would serve its interests. This recommendation was formally adopted by the university during 1964, and the Campion federation went into effect during 1966 while the college was still at its high school campus.

After the request for federation, and when there was reason to hope it might be given a favourable reply, the Jesuits strengthened the college staff with the appointment of Peter W. Nash, a distinguished young philosopher who, it was hoped, might obtain an appointment on the university staff even before federation went into effect. This was indeed what happened. Nash was named to the new university's department of philosophy, and he was also, in 1963, appointed rector of Campion succeeding MacDougall, who was elected provincial of the Upper Canadian province.

While Campion was negotiating for federation, the university had two other requests to deal with, and these made the case of Campion a little delicate: the Ukrainian diocese of Saskatchewan requested the affiliation as a junior college of its St Joseph's College at Yorkton, which was staffed by the Christian Brothers; and the German Oblates, wishing to move their candidates out of Lebret, requesting affiliation for a college at Sutherland near Saskatoon. The university ultimately accepted the Yorkton junior college as an affiliate in Saskatoon but not the proposed Sutherland scholasticate. But the very number of these applications was somewhat embarrassing to Dean Leddy and President Spinks and made them all the more cautious about accepting Campion.

Campion had one other delicate matter come up in 1965, after its acceptance into the university was final. Collège Mathieu decided to phase out its college operation in Gravelburg and make arrangements for its French constituents to become part of the Regina campus, possibly in a French Catholic college incorporated right into the university. A fairly ambitious bilingual project was proposed by the French oblates for consideration by the university. Had this project been implemented it could have been both competitive and embarrassing for Campion. The project proposed by Collège Mathieu was not taken up. The idea of a bilingual consortium has, however, been taken over in a different form, one unrelated to church colleges, by the university itself; and some professors have been brought to Regina from France to implement it. It was helpful to Campion not to have the two Catholic projects put into operation at the same time on the same campus.

Since 1966, Campion has completed its campus building and separated from its high school. The college moved to the Regina campus during the fall of 1967 and was formally opened in January 1968. It is functioning today as a fully federated co-educational college in the University of Saskatchewan.

Notre Dame of Canada

WILCOX

1933

Notre Dame of Canada, formerly of Saskatchewan, traces the history of its uniquely rugged *universitas studiorum* back to 1927. It is located in the sparsely inhabited village of Wilcox, about twenty-eight miles south of Regina in the heart of Canada's best wheat belt. Notre Dame provides a high school course (to grade XII, Saskatchewan) and a three-year general arts programme within the pattern of the curriculum of the University of Ottawa, with which it has been affiliated since 1933. The campus contains a total of about twenty buildings of which the newer and more permanent are the following: Lane Hall, the library and arts building acquired in 1938; Varsity Hall, the assembly and dining room, 1956; Edith Hall, the women's residence, 1964; Fred Hill Hall and Max Bell Hall, men's residences, 1968; Chapel of St Augustine, 1960; the Tower of God, 1962; Carr Hall and McCraken Hall, 1960 and 1964, for the high school; and the arena, 1969. The buildings, with their water, gas, and sewerage, and the 100 acres of village land have cost about $4,000,000.

The origins of Notre Dame of Canada can only be dealt with in relation to the biography of its founder and only president to date, Athol Murray, priest of the archdiocese of Toronto on loan to Regina.[1] Murray, born 1892, motherless at four, was raised and motivated by his convert father, a Toronto carpet manufacturer and founder of the Argonaut Rowing Club. Murray was sent to various Toronto schools, then to St Hyacinthe and Laval for his college education. At Laval he became an admirer of Olivier E. Mathieu, professor of philosophy there since 1878 and rector magnificus 1899–1908. Athol Murray knew Mathieu best at the very moment of his appointment as first bishop of Regina, 31 July 1911, one of a series of ecclesiastical appointments designed to ease the tension between French- and English-speaking Catholics following the Eucharistic Congress in Montreal in 1910. Through Mathieu, Murray's attention was focused upon philosophy and upon the Canadian west.

In 1913 Murray attended Osgoode Hall and was articled to Thomas

---

1 Much of the material in this sketch has been obtained *viva voce* from Athol Murray himself. For further biographical material see Hanlon, 'The Salty Priest of the Prairies' Notre Dame,' *The Canadian*, 2 (12 Feb. 1966), 6ff.

Cowper Robinette. In 1915 he changed his mind about law and entered the new St Augustine's Seminary. Ordained in 1918, he worked in Orillia and Penetanguishene where he became part of public movements to erect a Champlain statue in the Orillia park and to hold a tercentenary of Canada's French missionaries celebrated in Midland in 1921. Appointed to St John's parish in Toronto, he met Mathieu again in 1922 when he and his father entertained the visiting archbishop at the National Club. Murray was not surprised to receive and was eager to accept the invitation, when it came in 1923, to go to Regina as chancellor.

Between 1923 and 1927 Murray served as Mathieu's chancellor. He became thoroughly familiar with the archbishop's conviction that the development of Catholicism in the west would be dependent upon the founding of Catholic colleges. Mathieu personally founded three classical colleges for boys: Collège Mathieu at Gravelbourg for French-speaking boys, entrusted to the Oblates; Campion College at Regina for English-speaking boys, entrusted to the Jesuits of Upper Canada; St Joseph's College at Yorkton, a junior college for Ukrainians and entrusted to the Christian Brothers. Murray was familiar with these new foundations and also saw, as chancellor, the affiliation in 1925 of Regina's Sacred Heart Academy for girls as a junior college of the University of Saskatchewan with the prospect of ultimately offering undergraduate training. Murray shared Mathieu's love of philosophy and confidence in the classical college. When the archbishop's health failed in 1927 and discordant discussions about who his successors should be and whether Regina ought not to go to an English-speaking bishop, were rampant, Murray was urged to leave chancery and return to Toronto. He left chancery but asked to be allowed to establish a new parish at Wilcox, south of Regina. He opened St Augustine's Church in 1927 and brought in four Sisters of St Louis to staff a parish school for the children of the village.

How Notre Dame came to be attached to this school is a separate story. While Murray was serving as chancellor in Regina, he began working with a group of boys, largely Protestant, all of whom had in some minor way skirmished with the local police. For them, and for other boys who found life in the city rather boring, he founded a boy's club which he called (with his father in mind) the Regina Argos, and he worked out a rather elaborate athletic programme for them. He had to leave them behind when he went to Wilcox. The years of depression and drought which began towards the end of the twenties and continued in the thirties made the presence of Murray more essential to his Argos then than before his appointment to Wilcox. The solution which he proposed was not to return to the Argos but to bring the Argos to Wilcox. With this in mind, he had a new high school programme attached to the sisters' school, provided makeshift accommodation for 17 boys in his five-room rectory, and assumed personal responsibility for the additional instruction required. The new arrangement became a 'college'; and, since its athletic programme chronologically preceded its academic, he borrowed a name already celebrated in athletic circles, and called his school 'Notre Dame' of Saskatchewan.

In the early thirties the original boys of Notre Dame began to finish their high school courses, but poverty and depression fell heavier upon them than before. The obvious and most charitable procedure was to continue their programme into arts. With Mathieu's experience behind him, Murray sought and obtained in 1933 an affiliation for Notre Dame with the University of Ottawa. It was at this moment that the college of today came fully into existence.

Life at Notre Dame was, and is, unique in the annals of education. It was a life built around principles realistically, even brutally, applied. The 'primacy of the spiritual' was not only stated as an objective, but its contrary made unthinkable in an atmosphere where the material amenities were so completely lacking. Subsidiary mottos like 'for God and Canada' and 'for freest action under divine law' were given full existence: Christian philosophy and Canadian patriotism were extravagantly and dramatically heralded, and the reins of discipline and ethic were so completely placed in the hands of older students that the daily regime acquired a fantastically unconventional though not disorderly character.

At first the 17 boys were accommodated in the small rectory and cooked and ate in its basement. Then Prairie field granaries were brought in, and shacks erected and maintained by the boys themselves. In 1933 those who could do so were paying $18.00 a month for their board, room, and tuition. There were absolutely no buildings which could be described as permanent, and none designed with a school in mind.

Classes were held in the Sisters' school when this was possible, or wherever 'Père,' as Father Murray was always called, set himself up. A staff gradually formed around Murray. Its size and quality varied sharply from year to year, but some distinguished men became associated with the college: Denis Solleroz was from Louvain; Leo Sullivan, William Slavik, and Jack Murphy had master's degrees and were devoted to poverty and the 'cause'; many others came and went, most of

them making an intellectual contribution and accepting the unusual
material conditions as unavoidable if not actually desirable. Three
priests in addition to Murray, Peter D'Aoust, Jack Molloy, and James
Weisperber have given their most valuable years to the project. So
have at least three laymen: 'Cy' MacDonald, now of the Saskatchewan
legislature, and Hugh Carr and Frank Germann still on the teaching
staff.

The boys and men of Notre Dame tended to preserve something of
the club spirit of the Argos. They were the 'hounds' of Notre Dame.
Yet the school was always co-educational. The children enrolled in the
sisters' school always included girls. There were usually some girls in
high school. The arts division has never had many women, but usually
there have been a few. Of 46 arts students enrolled during 1964–5,
three were women. The first formal building, Memorare Hall, was a
frame house put up for the girls. The story of its construction is a kind
of tragi-comedy. When the frame house was completed in a suitable
and convenient location, the town council discovered to its annoyance
that Memorare stood right in the middle of what their plans described
as a right-of-way. The unusual name, Memorare, may have come from
the well-known prayer to Our Lady, but it is usually said to carry a
number of special overtones serving to remind students that they are
on their own, and rectors and councilmen that they should watch where
they build.

An account of the buildings standing on the present campus tells the
real story of the college. The boys have lived until just recently in
makeshift quarters described as Claggett Hall, Dwyer Hall, and Tiger,
each recording some gift or paying tribute to some former student. The
oldest building surviving is Lane Hall. It was built originally by a
Canadian bank and acquired by the college for $500 after the bank
failed. It is named Lane Hall in honour of a San Diego sportsman and
hunter, once owner of the San Diego Padres, who helped the college
in its early years and whose crucial telegram is preserved inside the
front door: 'You may draw on me First National Bank San Diego for
whatever you are short on that building. Answer collect. H.V. Lane.
April 30, 1938.'

Lane Hall became the first permanent building at Notre Dame and
has served as its arts building and library. It contains a number of staff
offices, a common room, and seminar rooms. Above all, it houses a
book collection unique by any standard, if fairly rated higher for its
research than for its undergraduate facilities. Wolf describes it accu-
rately as follows:

'The library has grown from Father Murray's own, selected with the digestive care of a true bookworm, into something extraordinary through purchase and donation. It is surprising to find on the prairie priceless manuscripts, more than 500 incunabula – books printed before 1500 – as well as standard works. Among the pigskin, sheepskin and calfskin vellum manuscripts is a fifty-three-page treatise by Thomas Aquinas. It is bound in wooden covers, with a chain for locking it to desk or belt, and a collector would have a difficult time putting a price on it.

'Among the books are John Peter Schoeffer's 1462 *Chronicles of the Kings of France*; the *Convivia* of Franciscus Philelphus of 1477, a rare copy, well authenticated, and highly valued; a 1482 Golden Legend of the Saints, or Flowers of the Saints, which, marginal notes indicate, might have been the very copy read by St Ignatius Loyola while convalescing from a leg wound at Pampeluna in 1521, and the famed three-volume Frankfurt edition of Martin Luther's Bible in German.'[2]

The oldest building actually erected for college use is Varsity Hall, and it marks a critical turning point in the history of Notre Dame. During 1955 one of the huts was destroyed by fire. A meeting of the staff discussed two alternatives: should Notre Dame remain primitive, or had the time come for brick and mortar? Varsity Hall went up in brick and mortar on funds supplied by the Canada Council and the will of Rex Beach. Beach's connection with Notre Dame is highly interesting but not surprising. He began visiting Wilcox in 1936, wrote about it a number of times, and fully subscribed to the educational and social views it represented. On his death he left Notre Dame the revenue from one-tenth of his million-dollar estate. It was this revenue that financed the loan required to complete Varsity Hall. The building itself is a low spacious brick structure resembling a gymnasium or an armoury. It houses a number of offices including 'Père' Murray's, the kitchen, dining hall, domestic and academic services, and the Rex Beach Museum – an extraordinary collection of pieces of great interest drawn from all quarters of the globe. The building itself was opened in 1956; the Rex Beach Depository, in 1960. The building houses a series of portraits of outstanding men, chiefly Canadians, painted by the distinguished Canadian artist, Nicholas de Grandmaison.

The new church or chapel of St Augustine, built 1960, though still a parish church for the dwindling village population of Wilcox, is designed and used as a collegiate building. The windows of this chapel

2 Bill Wolf, 'Toughest College in the Land,' *Saturday Evening Post*, 10 Apr. 1964, 37

executed in splendid stained glass by Marjorie Nazer of Toronto and Georgetown, Gollifer of Ottawa, and André Rault of Rennes, record Christian humanism from Leo, Benedict, Augustine, Gregory, through Aquinas, Francis, and More, to Brébeuf, Newman, and Henry Carr. Rare editions of St Augustine lie open in pulpit and lectern, and fragments of the world's great architectural achievements are woven into brickwork and plaster. Outside and separate from the chapel, stands the Tower of God, a modern belfry, with its lower structure built around an altar to the Unknown God, enclosed by a Moslem Wall, a Wall of Israel, a Wall of Great Affirmation, and a Wall of Christ, recording by text and relic the impact of world religions on the mind of man.[3]

A large classroom building, Carr Hall, opened in October 1960 by the Rt. Hon. Lester Pearson, houses grades I–IX, the lower school. It is living evidence of the integration of education at all its levels encountered on the Wilcox campus. It also speaks Murray's admiration for the contribution of Henry Carr to the academic life of Canada. Closely associated with Carr Hall is McCusker Hall, which was opened for grades XI and XII in 1964. It is a modern high school building, an important part of the total campus complex and a tribute to a staunch supporter of Notre Dame, Brigadier Emmett A. McCusker, MD. It is no accident that Murray associates Carr and McCusker. Both men are Canadians; both reached the top of professional life – McCusker in the army and medicine, Carr in the Church and education; and both are honoured in athletic circles, the one for creating the Regina Roughriders, the other for pioneering St Michael's hockey and rugby champions.

Another, and the loveliest building on the campus, is Edith Hall. Its name pays tribute to Sister Edith, the only English-speaking sister of the four who came to Wilcox in 1927 and the only one of them staying on into the sixties. The building replaces Memorare Hall, the so-called 'snakepit,' for women students, and stands on the same disputed right-of-way. It provides excellent private accommodation for a total of 100 artswomen and high school girls, as well as a convent for the sisters. It was opened in March 1964, the same year as McCusker Hall, and contributes to the more conventional appearance which the campus is beginning to take.

3 These materials come from a series of splendid brochures by Athol Murray and published without date: *Mathieu: For God and Country*, Wilcox n.d., pp.12; *The Witness of Michaelangelo's Sybils*, Wilcox, n.d., pp.12; *Design of God*, Wilcox, n.d., pp.8; *The Ephesus Grotto of Notre Dame*, Wilcox, n.d., pp.12. See also items in *The Laocoon*, 2 (1945), and 2 (1946).

Notre Dame's civil incorporation dates only from 1949.[4] Under this act, Notre Dame has a non-denominational board of governors which controls the affairs of the college. The archbishop is not its chancellor *ex officio* as in most of the older Catholic institutions. Indeed, the board usually names two chancellors, a Canadian and an American. The decisive voice in all matters academic and financial has always been its founder's. The civil act does not establish Notre Dame within the provincial structure of education, but leaves intact its highly cherished affiliation with Ottawa. Neither does the act set up a council or a senate as these also are felt to be supplied by Ottawa. When Ottawa became a non-denominational state-supported university in 1965, Notre Dame elected to go with the new university and remains on Ottawa's much reduced list of affiliates.

During 1964–5 Notre Dame enrolled 148 high school students and 46 arts students paying a combined board and tuition fee of only $600. Its staff numbered twelve: three priests, two sisters, two unmarried and five married teachers or professors. The corresponding statistics for 1969 are: 240 high school students, 62 arts students; a staff of 15: three priests, two sisters, nine laymen. The arts programme has been perforce limited. For the most part, no options are provided for students, though the programme actually is a carefully considered selection of the options listed in Ottawa's calendar. Arts students take the following programme: first year: English, French, history (modern), calculus, history of education, philosophy (one half course), and religion(one half course); second year: English, Greek classics in translation, economics, philosophy (two and one-half courses), religion (one half course); third year: English, general and social ethics, history of philosophy, religion (one half course), political science *or* Latin classics in translation. Classroom work is done largely in seminars, but English and religion are given in cycles as lectures to the entire student body. The more obvious serious gaps for the generality of college students are in science and foreign languages. Most graduates who continue further enter law, journalism, education, and social welfare. A few have entered seminaries.

The spirit of Notre Dame of Canada is a curious imaginative healthy blend of the ecclesiastical and non-ecclesiastical. The people of God are certainly afforded a priority befitting 'the free initiative of the sons of God.'[5] God's people rate the skilful attention of the artist in stained

4 Statutes of the Province of Saskatchewan, 1949, ch.95
5 See the Laocoon objective as stated in the Augustine number of *The Laocoon: An Athenaeum Quarterly*, 2 (no. 3, 1945–6), 2.

glass if under whatever title they can be called 'western': Leo, Gregory, Benedict, Thomas More, Newman, Gilson, Dawson, Carr, Rose Fraser of Lovat, and Our Lady of the Wheat.[6] Ecclesiastical too is Notre Dame's recognition of Augustine as wisdom's spokesman, of Thomas Aquinas as the philosopher, of Maritain as the living commentator.

But the college rejects where it can do so with dignity rigid and formal church attachments: it is not diocesan, not a religious-order foundation; there is little of the clerical in the dress or atmosphere of its campus; its chancellor is not either *ex offico* or in fact the archbishop of Regina; religious symbol, though plentiful on the campus, is largely non-denominational: Tower of God, grotto of Panaya Kapulu at Ephesus, Laocoon, the Sibyls.[7] The commission appointed in 1969 by the Catholic colleges and universities of Canada to make a self-study was not received at Wilcox, which claimed not to fall under its terms of reference.

Two unsolved questions must be raised about this young eccentric institution. What will happen when Murray retires? Is its ultra-provincial affiliation to remain viable? Both questions must have an answer soon. When Murray steps down, the board of governors will have to replace him. They will probably carry out his recommendation, if he lets his will be known. Some think Murray wants to be succeeded by David Bauer, former St Michael's hockey star and member of the Canadian National Hockey executive. Certainly there is no reason why a college president should have to be an academic. If Murray has Bauer in mind, the choice is hardly atypical, and it gives special significance to the recent building of an excellent arena at Wilcox. Bauer could be as unconventional and as visionary a president as Murray himself – and as well-loved by the same Canadian public. Bauer's appointment is at this stage sheer conjecture. As for the civil and academic status of the college, the province of Saskatchewan should give some kind of recognition to Notre Dame's contribution to society: it should either grant Notre Dame a charter or provide it with some suitably autonomous *modus vivendi* in the provincial university.

There are those who feel that Notre Dame's existence depends upon a depressed economy, and that its survival into the seventies is an anachronism. It is to be hoped that this is not the case. Notre Dame of Canada is a refreshing exception and an exciting challenge in an age of increasing institutional conformity.

6 *The Stained Glass at Notre Dame*, Wilcox, Saskatchewan, n.d., a brochure on the windows of the college chapel

7 See Athol Murray's brochures: *Designs of God, The Ephesus Grotto of Notre Dame*, various issues of *The Laocoon*, and *The Witness of Michaelangelo's Sibyls*.

St Thomas More College

St Thomas More College, in federation with the University of Saskatchewan, provides instruction and credit in specified college subjects and
presents, through the university's college of arts and sciences and
faculty of graduate studies, candidates for the bachelor's and master's
degrees. The college was founded in 1936. It was civilly incorporated in
1943 and its status as a federated college clearly set forth in the statutes
of the senate of the university during May 1953. It is located at 1437
College Drive, Saskatoon, on a small site consisting of four building
lots adjacent to the campus and convenient to the main arts buildings of
the university. The property is administered by the Basilian Fathers;
part of it is owned by the corporation of St Thomas More College, and
part is leased by the corporation from the university. The college has
its own student body and also provides credit courses for some non-
college students of the university. It maintains a large public chapel and
a Newman Club but no classrooms or residences. It has, as a supplement
and complement to the university facilities at its service, its own faculty
and library. The college is housed in one large handsome stone building
opened in three stages in 1957, 1964, and 1969 at a cost of approximately $3,000,000.

SCHOLASTIC PHILOSOPHY FOUNDATION AND NEWMAN SOCIETY

In a lenten pastoral letter of 1919, Bishop Albert Pascal, of Prince Albert, expressed the opinion that his diocese ought to have a Catholic
college on the campus of the University of Saskatchewan and in affiliation with it.[1] This is the first recorded mention of a Catholic university
college in Saskatoon. On 4 April 1926, a delegation of 14 laymen waited
on Bishop Joseph-Henri Prudhomme to seek his authorization for their
negotiating with the president of the university for the establishment
of a Catholic college. They had already privately consulted President
Walter C. Murray and knew that he was sympathetic towards a move
that implied real expansion of the university.

Bishop Prudhomme received the delegation gladly and urged them to
negotiate with the president. Prudhomme spoke to the Oblates about

1 Chancery Files of the Diocese of Saskatoon

the possibility of their conducting such a college. The bishop's approach to the Oblates was not successful. The laymen worked somewhat more effectively. They approached many bishops in eastern Canada and some scholars abroad in search of a possible professor to come to Saskatoon and accept a post in the department of philosophy of the university, which the president assured them he would procure as a first practical step towards a college. Archbishop Neil McNeil of Toronto promised the laymen that he would lend Saskatoon one of his young priests, Basil Markle, who had just returned to Toronto from graduate studies in Rome.

During September 1926 the president drew up a contract for the university with Dr Markle and the archbishop. Markle began during 1926–7 a series of courses in scholastic philosophy for the philosophy department of the university. This was the first official appearance of the Church on the campus. By December 1926 the Newman Society was formed following discussions between Markle and the 'committee of 14.' The Society was a senior off-campus group and its purpose was to promote Catholic education on the campus. It described itself as the Scholastic Philosophy Foundation and the Newman Society.[2] Student members formed the Junior Newman Club.

In May 1927 steps were taken to find a base of operations. Four building lots were acquired adjacent to the campus close to the arts building. The lots cost $2400; the wooden clubhouse erected shortly afterwards cost $14,000. The full cost of land and buildings was provided by the diocese and the title of property and building was vested in the episcopal corporation. It was expected that the money would one day be repaid.

These arrangements, well-intentioned as they were, turned out unhappily because there was no committed revenue for the campus venture. Dr Markle paid rental to live in the clubhouse and also paid the light, power, and fuel bills. What he could turn over of his personal salary of only $1350 a year was all the Newman Society had beyond, of course, small membership fees. The precarious arrangement suffered a setback during 1933 when the president of the university, in an economy move, reduced Markle's salary by one-third. At one point the building was to be put up for sale to pay arrears in taxes and was only saved by a personal gift from Archbishop McNeil of Toronto. The project, consisting of a Newman Club, a professor on the university staff,

2 This and much of the early background material comes from an unsigned memorandum in the Chancery Files, Saskatoon. The memorandum, though unsigned, was probably prepared by J.J. Leddy, father of J.F. Leddy, dean of arts at the University of Saskatchewan and later president of the University of Windsor.

and an active Catholic centre for the Saskatoon constituency, was an admirable one. But two basic flaws placed it in jeopardy: the effectively involved group was local rather than province-wide; and there was no major academic facility, especially no book collection, to attract and hold the scholarly.

On 9 June 1933, the diocese of Saskatoon was cut off from Prince Albert and made an independent diocese under Bishop Gerald C. Murray. A year later the apostolic delegate visited Saskatoon and asked that a full statement of complaints and suggestions from the Scholastic Philosophy Foundation be prepared. The foundation hoped ultimately to see a Catholic college established, but was in favour for the present of negotiating with the university to have Dr Markle's courses placed in a department of scholastic philosophy distinct from the regular university department. Behind this suggestion lay a difference of opinion between Markle and the department of philosophy, and between the 'committee of 14,' that is, the group of laymen behind the Newman Foundation, and the university itself.

From the time Markle came to the campus he devoted himself completely to his courses in philosophy and to the service of the members of the Newman Club. He was immensely popular with students generally and with the Catholics of Saskatoon but less so with his university colleagues, particularly the members of his department. Enrolment in Markle's courses was always high and they became more and more popular with non-Catholic and professional students. About 50 per cent of the Catholic students of the university enrolled in his courses and they represented about 60 per cent of the number actually taking them. There were objections from the department that he marked too easily and from the theological colleges that he was proselytizing. Markle maintained that he simply taught his courses as well as he could, worked with his students personally, and succeeded in eliciting their maximum effort. One cannot be sure what the real situation was. However, on Markle's part, and among many junior members of Newman, and especially among the committee who controlled the Newman Society, there was a great deal of antipathy and distrust shown towards the university. It was felt that the university regarded a course in scholastic philosophy as an indefensible privilege in a public university and that it was constantly seeking an excuse to dislodge it. When the university actually approached the diocese to buy the Newman building in order to house its new department of music, the worst motives were suspected by the members of the club. The entire situation became too unhealthy for genuine educational activity.

At the end of the academic year 1934–5, Bishop Murray approached President Murray to obtain higher academic rank for Dr Markle. The bishop felt that a show of confidence on the part of the university in Markle's work was both called for in itself and likely to relieve much of the tension. The president suggested what had long been talked about, the establishment of an affiliated college in the university.

Over 1935–6 the bishop, the president, and Henry Carr, superior general of the Basilian Fathers, discussed the founding of a college. A meeting was arranged for 21 February 1936 but postponed because Carr fell ill. The decisive meeting was held on 6 March from which date St Thomas Aquinas (later St Thomas More) College became a certainty. The initiative was taken by the president of the university, and Carr always maintained that Walter Murray was the real founder and planner of the Catholic college. In fact, so much of the actual planning for the college was left to the president that Carr and the bishop quite overlooked the need for looking to the details of its financing.

ST THOMAS MORE COLLEGE

The university senate in a meeting of 7 May 1936 set up a committee consisting of its local Saskatoon members to negotiate with the authorities of St Thomas the academic terms of its affiliation with the university. This committee agreed on 13 July to present the following terms to the senate: the university to lease a site of three to five acres to the college at a nominal rental; the college principal to be a member of senate; college students to be admitted to university classes; college instruction in classics, French, German, English, economics, history, philosophy, and other subjects agreed upon, to be recognized; the university to confer its BA on college students who have satisfied its requirements; the university to provide for the giving of MA credit courses by college professors. These terms were formally accepted by the entire senate on 13 May 1937. In the meantime, that is, on 23 June 1936, the board of governors agreed to forego the fees of college students in arts, pre-law, and pre-medicine; to hand over to the college financial responsibility for instruction provided by the college including Markle's courses; to collect, however, fees for any professional students exercising the privilege of substituting college for corresponding university courses; and to provide classrooms for college lectures until accommodation became available in the college. These arrangements were, in principle, modelled on those already in operation in Toronto.[3] But there were advantages for

3 This is specifically stated a number of times in the minutes and memoranda of the 1936 meetings of the senate and the board of governors. See also Bernard Daly, 'Memories of a House,' *Chelsea Annual, 1956,* Saskatoon, 1956, 101–11.

the college over the Toronto plan: the list of college subjects was not so rigid, giving the college a chance to adapt with the times; the college staff were not cut off from pre-medical students and the club itself served to keep the college administration closer to students in the professional faculties; and what was at first a makeshift – the giving of college lectures in university classrooms – a variation built into St Thomas More federation structure later by Basil Sullivan and Joseph O'Donnell, turned out to be both unique in Canada and highly successful as a campus arrangement.

In 1936 the new college came into existence. It was placed under the patronage of St Thomas More, just canonized, and was located in the existing Newman Club building. E. Leonard Rush was the first principal. In many ways he was an extraordinary and inimitable founder. A man of personal brilliance, linguistic competence, musical talent, and urbane sophistication, he was a good choice to establish the kind of college his university colleagues could respect. For the first two years he was short-handed. He had only one Basilian with him, G.F. Anglin, whose quiet, unassuming, persevering manner complemented and completed Rush's effusiveness. With them, of course, was Basil Markle, who was still professor of scholastic philosophy but who was not attached to the college although it was responsible for his meagre salary of $900. Eugene Cullinane was added to the staff in 1938 and Eugene Carlyle LeBel in 1940.

Rush had little revenue with which to run the college or to pay Markle. Nor had he any details from Carr as to how the college was set up or where he was to live. The general council, on the recommendation of the general chapter of 1936 accepted the Saskatoon college in August 1936 'without recompense,' that is, expected no tax or revenue from its operation, at least during the early years. The bishop took this to mean that the Basilians would also provide for the expenses of any priests sent to Saskatoon and cover any deficit. 'No recompense' was one thing; to provide livelihood and a subsidy was quite another. In any event, Rush and Anglin found themselves trying to start a college with the fees from 39 students, such casual revenue as they could pick up from Sunday work and mass intentions, or any gifts they could solicit. To complicate matters further, the bishop thought the two Basilians were going to live with him and be supported in this way. When Rush and Anglin reached Saskatoon they stayed only for a very short time with the bishop, then, at the urging of President Murray, who felt that the Basilians should have a presence on the campus, moved into the tiny club-become-college. Since this move took place in Markle's absence, it turned out to be embarrassing on his return. It also meant that college expenses would be a little higher. No college has opened with less preparation or less exchange of information.

Somehow or other the operation went along reasonably smoothly, although the bishop was puzzled at being called on from time to time for 'loans.' In 1938 he enquired about these 'loans,' referred to the debt on Newman Hall of $19,000, asked why in two years Rush had paid no rental, taxes, interest, and why he was borrowing from him. He asked for the repayment of loans by 1 December 1938. On top of this, Markle wanted his salary. This was in the summer of 1938. Rush went to Toronto to see the general council only to find that Carr had not told them any more about the arrangements than he had told either him or the bishop. There just seemed to have been no arrangements.

Carr wrote two letters to the bishop after a meeting of the general council on Labour Day. The first, written 8 September 1938, runs as follows: 'I am more sorry than I can say at the way things have turned out financially. I suppose things went too easily, and were bound to run into worries. I really do not know what to suggest to Your Excellency. As I said in the telegram, the general chapter approved of taking over St Thomas More College on the understanding that we would not be involved financially in any way. The chapter looked on the project as a missionary work of charity, and was willing, and formally decided, to provide Basilians for the staff according as they were needed and could be spared, and without remuneration.'[4] The second letter, five days later, suggested that the Basilians withdraw from St Thomas More and that Markle be made head of the college; or that if the Basilians remain in Saskatoon, they work under Markle.[5] Carr's alternatives were not tried. Now that the troubles were in the open they could be coped with. Rush stayed on as principal until 1941.

Apart from these financial matters, the college moved along rather well. Rush found Markle difficult, as Markle found Rush, but the college made a good impression on the university. There was still a publicity problem as there was in the days of the Foundation. Many Catholic students coming to Saskatoon had no idea that the college existed; others ignored the college under the impression that it was something other than the university. The numbers registered during Rush's time were as follows: 39 during 1936–7; 41 during 1937–8; 50 during 1938–9; 52 during 1939–40; 43 during 1940–1. These were low numbers, and growth was not encouraging. The college, however, assumed what were to be its lasting patterns during these years: it was both an

4 Carr to Murray, 6 Sept. 1938. Chancery Files, Saskatoon
5 Carr to Murray, 11 Sept. 1938, Chancery Files, Saskatoon

arts college and a Newman club; it was co-educational; it was not a residence for students; it had no lecture halls; it acquired prestige on the university campus far beyond what is usual for newly-created affiliated colleges; it also generated a warm community pattern of living.

Rush's term as principal, and also as religious superior of the Basilians at St Thomas More, terminated in 1941. He was replaced by Edmund J. McCorkell, twice superior and president of St Michael's in Toronto.[6] McCorkell brought vast experience to the post. He remained principal for only one year as he was elected superior general, replacing Carr, in the general chapter of 1942. Carr, probably by choice, took McCorkell's place in Saskatoon in the fall of 1942.

During McCorkell's year as principal and for the first few years of Carr's term, the staff of St Thomas More was enriched by the presence of Joseph E. McGahey, the originator of many of the social and religious traditions of the college and Newman club. McGahey had been invalided from his Canadian army chaplaincy by a serious coronary; he had also spent six months as a chaplain in the experimental Newman Hall at the University of Illinois, Urbana. He brought a wealth of experience in literature, labour relations, dramatics, athletics, spiritual guidance, and philosophy. He created at St Thomas More the challengingly intellectual but warm and friendly common-room spirit which tradition and legend associate with the English college, and which has been genuinely characteristic of St Thomas More since the McGahey years, 1941 to 1945.[7]

Carr was principal from 1942 to 1949.[8] His regime began with an unusual kind of act – the buying of the college. Bishop Murray wrote McCorkell in June of 1942 telling him that it was the desire of the bishops of Saskatchewan that the Basilians take over the college as a permanent foundation. The buildings and the property belonged to the diocese, and the diocese was carrying a debt of $16,500 on them at four per cent interest, about $650 annually. The Basilians were asked either to assume half the annual interest or to take over the debt and buy the buildings at $7500. The general council, no doubt anxious to please Carr, agreed at its meeting of 8 October 1942, after Carr had become principal, to assume the debt and purchase the property at $7500. With Carr's principalship, then, the Basilians began to operate St Thomas

6 See above, 165–74
7 See J.F. Leddy, 'Two Great Priests: A Tribute,' *Chelsea Annual, 1956,* Saskatoon, 1956, 112–20. This tribute honours Basil Markle, died 22 July 1956 and Joseph E. McGahey, died 2 Dec. 1945.
8 See E.J. McCorkell, *Henry Carr: Revolutionary,* Toronto, Griffin House, 1969, ch.II, 107–29.

More at their own risks. It was a period of fantastic economies – Carr himself stoked the furnace – and of tremendous enthusiasm kindled by McGahey.

Carr immediately had the college incorporated. The bill, which received assent 1 April 1943, named Carr, Mallon, McGahey, and Cullinane – all Basilians – as members of the corporation, described the college as 'in affiliation' and authorized it to have a Roman Catholic chapel and to be tax-exempt 'save and except special assessment taxes under part XII of *The City Act*.'[9]

The same year, 1943, Carr also opened an extension to the wooden building constructed earlier for the Newman Foundation.

The seven years of Carr's principalship were marked by his personal relations not only with the students of the college and university but with the men of Saskatoon. Markle had maintained excellent rapport with the Saskatoon constituency. Carr too was able to do the same. But whereas Markle was inclined to encourage them to fight for their rights against the university establishment, Carr drew them into the university family. That the group came to be called in Carr's time the Forum indicates the level of discussion maintained. Carr also grew close to his university colleagues and became the centre of regular Saturday luncheons at the Bessborough which both senior and younger professors attended.

In 1944 Philip F. Pocock became the second bishop of Saskatoon. Pocock had been a student of Assumption, indeed, was one of those pulled out of Assumption by Bishop Fallon when he opened St Peter's School of Philosophy in London in 1923.[10] Pocock knew the Basilians well and had something of Murray's confidence in them. He also knew the problems of affiliation inside out, having himself been the member of the staff of St Peter's Seminary who suggested to Fallon in 1919 that the time had come for an application for direct affiliation of the seminary with the University of Western Ontario. Now, in Saskatoon, Pocock and Carr became fast, understanding friends. With J.F. Leddy, Pocock played a significant role in the consolidation of St Thomas More. This consolidation was further promoted in 1947 when Michael C. O'Neill, a graduate of St Michael's during the 'Carr years,' became, on leaving his chaplaincy in the Canadian army, archbishop of Regina and metropolitan of the dioceses of Saskatchewan.[11]

9 Bill no. 04 of 1943, An Act to Incorporate St Thomas More College, the Legislature of Saskatchewan

10 See above, 295

11 Henry Carr, 'Address Given at the Silver Jubilee of St Thomas More College, Saskatoon, 9 February 1961,' R.J.Scollard, *Historical Notes*, XIX, 179–91

During Carr's principalship, St Thomas More College gradually ceased to be a pioneer project in higher education. It came of age, and Carr began to feel that he had done all he could for it. Then in 1945 a new and unquestionably pioneer project began to attract Carr's interest: Norman MacKenzie, president of the University of British Columbia, visited Carr and President Walter P. Thompson in Saskatoon to examine at first hand the affiliation structure they had fashioned. Mackenzie had in mind providing something similar in Vancouver.[12] At the same time Archbishop Duke began to regard Carr as his personal adviser on the same project. Carr became more and more restless in Saskatoon and could hardly wait for his seven-year appointment to come to an end. When it did, in 1949, the general council, considerate of his wishes, moved him to Toronto where he was 'in waiting' for developments in British Columbia. Basil F. Sullivan, for many years registrar of St Michael's in Toronto, was appointed Carr's successor as superior and principal of St Thomas More.

During Sullivan's principalship three significant events took place: St Thomas More was given the status of a federated college; a general campaign for building funds was launched; and the new permanent stone building was designed and its construction begun.

When Sullivan was at St Michael's he came to realize that federation had certain advantages over simple affiliation: a high degree of partnership and integration into the academic project, relative equality of status and increased self-respect, and legal responsibility and commitment. It is not surprising that he sought federation for St Thomas More; and it is a sign of confidence in the college that the university was willing to grant it, recognizing that the college was already central to its own structure and existence.

In April 1953, S.R. Laycock, dean of education and chairman of the senate's committee on affiliation, informed Sullivan that his committee was recommending the establishment of federation as a new status in the university, and that this status be given to St Thomas More, even if this called for an amendment to the university act.[13] In May 1953, the senate announced the establishment of the new category and declared its requirements to be as follows: that a federated college must be authorized to give credit courses in at least four departments of the college of arts and sciences; that members of the college teaching staff

12 See below, 375–6
13 S.R. Laycock to B.F. Sullivan, 6 Apr. 1953; also the solicitor's opinion on the matter in P.H. Maguire to S.R. Laycock, 30 Mar. 1953. The solicitor thought an amendment to the act was necessary; the senate handled the matter finally as a special statute of its own.

be members of the faculty of arts and sciences; that the college be situated on or adjacent to the university campus. These regulations, and the admission of St Thomas More to a new status were introduced into the statutes of the senate in November 1953.[14]

In 1953 the college launched a major building campaign, seeking $500,000 for a permanent college building. The campaign was chaired by the Hon. Mr Justice E.M. Culliton, with Emmett M. Hall QC as vice-chairman. The appeal went throughout the province and even into neighbouring provinces. The response, however, was but fair ($350,000 was raised), evidence that the college still had only partly succeeded in acquiring the broad constituency so sadly wanting at the time of its inception. St Thomas More College had been founded in part to cope with the disproportion between the two to five per cent Catholic men in public and professional life and the fifteen per cent which Catholics formed of the general population of the province. The statistics for Saskatoon in 1935 revealed a situation like the following: dentists, one Catholic out of 26; doctors, two out of 50; lawyers, three out of 50; teachers in the collegiates, one out of 90. By 1953 there were 151 students in St Thomas More College and 530 members in its Newman Club. Graduates of the college and club over 17 years included 81 engineers, 41 teachers, 32 lawyers, 13 doctors. These, of course, were spread over the province, but they were evidence (along with graduates in farming, business, pharmacy, nursing etc.) that the college had made a measurable impact on its constituency. The campaign should probably have done better. Where pledges fell short, however, the great generosity of the contractors supplied.

The new building was the corollary and the end of the campaign. It was designed by E.J. Gilbert and Peter Thornton and built by the Shannon brothers. It was in stone, matching nearby university buildings, and featuring a chapel, an auditorium, club facilities, a small library, and staff accommodations. It provided no student residence and no classrooms. Carr was as pleased with these two omissions as he was with the handsome building itself; for him it meant that Sullivan and O'Donnell had faith in the special kind of college he and the other founders had called into existence.

Sullivan's term as principal came to an end in 1955 before the building was completed. His successor was Joseph L. O'Donnell, who had collaborated with him at every step of the planning of the new college. O'Donnell, like McGahey, made a unique cultural contribution. His

14 See Statutes of the Senate of the University of Saskatchewan, 1962, ch.XVIII, 16–17, and ch.XXIV, 19–20.

academic field was English literature, his specialty Shakespeare and the drama. His student productions of plays old and new had for years been famous for their professional character. Since coming west he had added a new dimension to the life of the college, the university, and the city through a series of important dramatic productions. As superior and principal he kept in touch with both literature and dramatics as well as looking after the new building. The building itself was put into use during the winter of 1956–7 and was formally opened 7 March 1957.

With the appearance of the new college building St Thomas More entered a new and perhaps more sophisticated pattern of living. Most surprising, perhaps, was the use made of the small but attractive library. The book collection at this time amounted to only 2500 volumes, but they were properly classified by the librarian, Bernard Black, and the nucleus of special collections of Moreana, Shakespeareana, and other pertinent materials instituted; a new scholarship developed which was stimulated from two other sources.

Stimulation came in the first instance from the addition during the fifties of new staff. The Basilian Fathers continued to be generous in sending men of academic stature: Robert Miller, Alphonse Malone, Leonard Kennedy, Francis Burns, Robert Finn, Robert Montague among others; laymen were hired as funds became available: Frederick Flahiff, R.F. and Mrs (Judith) Kennedy, Dominic Baker-Smith, James Penna, and others. In both groups the turnover was large, partly because of the sense of isolation from other scholars and from great libraries, partly because of the long and severe winters. But the exceptions are notable – Paul Mallon, Joseph O'Donnell – and some of the faculty have distinguished themselves both in scholarship and endurance.

The second stimulation to scholarship came from professor, later dean, J.F. Leddy, who wanted to see some specialized development at St Thomas More comparable in spirit and depth with the Toronto project at the Pontifical Institute of Mediaeval Studies. So we find him writing as follows to O'Donnell: 'In view of the increase in enrolment in St Thomas More College and the additions to the staff of the college in recent years, I wonder whether it is not time to consider some expansion in the offerings in the field of philosophy.'[15] In pressing this matter Leddy had also in mind removing an academic concession to St Thomas More whereby philosophy majors offered a psychology course as one of their four courses in philosophy. Following this communication, renewed efforts were made to further strengthen philosophy. Robert M. Montague and Basil F. Sullivan joined the staff the next year.

15 Leddy to O'Donnell, 10 Dec. 1957, Archives of St Thomas More College

One change introduced by O'Donnell affected finances and was occasioned by the erection of the permanent college building. When federal grants were initiated in 1951, Basil Sullivan decided to turn over to the university the entire grant made in favour of St Thomas More. He felt, and Carr agreed, that the university had been generous to the college in many ways. The college had been collecting tuition, yet doing but a part of the teaching of its students and holding classes in university buildings. Besides, there was no financial problem at the moment. With construction of the new building, conditions were altered. In a letter of 3 December 1956, O'Donnell asked the president if the college might retain 40 per cent of the federal grant so as to be able to cope with new financial obligations. The proposal was acceptable both to the president and the board of governors.[16]

In 1961, Peter Swan succeeded O'Donnell as principal. Swan was, like Sullivan, an extremely knowledgeable university administrator. He was registrar of Assumption College when it got its charter in 1953 and during the short but exciting career of Assumption University of Windsor. He was in disagreement with the policy that led to the founding of the new University of Windsor and welcomed a new appointment. He brought with him to Saskatoon in 1961 an unusual knowledge of the Canadian university scene.

Swan's principalship was a period of increased enrolment. In O'Donnell's last year the full-time enrolment was 391; it rose to 529 in 1961 and 802 in 1966 nearly 1000 in 1969. This means that Swan had to become involved in staff development and organized use of the university's facilities. He had also, following his Assumption experience, to give time to assessing the relationship of the college to the university with a view to preserving its Christian character and some Basilian control. In 1962 he outlined in a letter to Edwin Garvey the nature of the college as he found it on coming to Saskatoon: legally guaranteed by simple statutes of the senate; smooth operating procedures resulting from practice and a sort of 'gentleman's agreement'; classrooms provided by the university, offices by the college; departments varying from complete integration of staffs in English to almost complete dissociation in philosophy; availability of college courses to students in the professional faculties of the university. These, he concluded, pointed to 'an advance over that of St Michael's College.'[17]

Swan planned in his first year at Saskatoon on an addition to the

---

16 O'Donnell to Thompson, 3 Dec. 1956, Thomson to O'Donnell, 14 Jan. 1957; Archives of St Thomas More College
17 Swan to Garvey, 4 July 1962; Archives of St Thomas More College

north end of the new building: what he most wanted was a library of some size and excellence, and staff offices more or less separated from the Newman Club facilities. He engaged the assistant architect of the original building, Peter Thornton of Vancouver, and the same contractor, The Shannons of Saskatoon. The enlarged building was opened 6 February 1964. Its striking feature both for design and contents was its library, which was enriched at the time of its opening by 'The Leddy Collection,' some 2000 titles collected by J.J. Leddy and given to the college by his son Francis, dean of the college of arts and science. Five years later, on 5 October 1969, Swan opened still another new wing, the east wing, providing seminar rooms, lounges and offices, and completing a finely balanced and self-contained college complex.

In 1966 Swan introduced an important change in the civil corporation, opening it to all faculty with tenure (Basilian and non-Basilian) and to representatives of the alumni. In 1968 he added new government machinery – a forum and a collegium. These were experimental bodies designed to harmonize college and university governments, the forum being a faculty-administrative body to generate discussion and to facilitate communication within the college, the collegium being a senior academic and administrative body to formulate policies within the college and between the college and the university's senate and councils.

The college of Swan's regime was a well-run, sophisticated institution with prestige within and without the university. It provided instruction for certain outside groups, especially the nurses of local Catholic hospitals, and some correspondence work for teachers improving their academic qualifications. It also served as a *pied à terre* for the students of the bishop's St Pius x Seminary, established in 1958 to prepare students for admission to major seminaries and moved to quarters adjacent to the university in 1966. The college now shared, since the opening of the Regina branch of the University of Saskatchewan, its educational objectives in Saskatchewan with Campion College. One significant academic change to take place was that St Thomas More professors offered an increased number of advanced courses: where six such courses were offered in 1963, twenty-five were being offered in 1970. Since advanced courses were not normally duplicated on the campus, the attendance of university students in St Thomas More courses increased considerably.

St Joseph's College

YORKTON

1920 (1964)

St Joseph's Junior College, Yorkton, Saskatchewan, is a high school and junior college directed by the Brothers of the Christian Schools(De la Salle) for the Ukrainian diocese of Saskatchewan. It offers, in addition to the full high school programme, courses in arts and science and in education, for credit through the University of Saskatchewan, with which it has been affiliated since 1964.

St Joseph's College was founded by the Christian Brothers of Toronto at the request of Nicetas Budka, Ruthenian Greek Catholic bishop of Canada. The bishop was concerned about the lack of educational facilities for all people in his district but especially for his Ukrainians, who had special needs which required special attention, especially while the children were young and being brought into communication with their fellow Canadians.

Thus it was that Brother Ansbert and several colleagues opened a complete school, grades 1 to 12 in Yorkton in 1920. During the forties the elementary school division was dropped and St Joseph's became a high school only, mainly residential. During 1964, on the request of Brothers Justin and Isadore, the University of Saskatchewan admitted St Joseph's, Yorkton, to its family as an affiliated college, that is, permitted it to teach for credit courses in arts and science, and in education. Students can be admitted from this programme to the second year of a three-year course in arts and science.

The junior college first operated during the academic year, 1964–5, when evening classes were offered. The numbers taking these courses proved to be large and day courses for full-time students were planned for 1965–6. The day courses were less well attended than the evening ones. After three years of operation, day courses were dropped and full-time students were integrated into the evening courses, being permitted to take a full year's work by following five courses simultaneously. This arrangement has proven satisfactory. Enrolment in evening courses during 1969–70 was 319, which was gratifying to those conducting them.

The principals of St Joseph's between 1920 and 1964, before it was a junior college, were Brothers Ansbert, Stanislaus (two separate terms), Anthony, Aloysius, Justin, Methodius, and Justin. Following Justin's second term the affiliation went into effect with Brother Isadore first rector of the junior college. He was succeeded in 1969 by Brother Justin. With the last appointment, the office of religious superior and principal were separated, Brother Raymond becoming superior of the religious house. Teaching in the college department during 1969–70 were Brothers Justin, Michael, and Methodius.

St Peter's College

MUENSTER

1925

St Peter's College, Muenster, Saskatchewan, is a junior college in the University of Saskatchewan conducted by the Benedictines of St Peter's Abbey. The college offers a full high school programme and one year of general arts for day and evening students. The college serves an ecclesiastical district, comprising 50 townships in the Muenster-Humboldt area, headed by the abbot of St Peter's, who is designated as *abbas nullius diocesis*.

St Peter's Abbey was established in 1921 by a group of Benedictines from St John's Abbey, Collegeville, Minnesota. St Peter's was officially erected by Pope Benedict xv, 6 May 1921, under Abbot Michael Ott. The monastic school, intended to serve the abbey's clerics and the boys of the district, was opened during 1921–2 with 10 priest teachers and about 50 students. Abbot Michael was, *ex officio*, the first president of the college and Matthew Michel was the first rector. The curriculum followed during the first year was tailored to the ability and needs of the varied group of pioneer students; it was revised during the second year so as to serve effectively students proceeding towards high school graduation.

During 1923–4, Lewis Gwynn of the Jesuits joined the staff as an oblate and was immediately appointed rector succeeding Matthew. Gwynn emphasized as the school's wisest policy the meeting of departmental regulations to the end of grade xII. He also opened negotiations with president Walter Murray of the University of Saskatchewan for the accreditation of St Peter's as a junior college. Gwyn was rector for only one year and did not complete his negotiations. His successor, Wilfrid Hergott, renewed the petition in a letter written to Murray in February 1925. Murray felt that the request was reasonable. The students of the abbey school who completed grade xII were already eligible for admission to second-year arts; if they took an additional year's work at the college level, they could be admitted to the two final years of the general course programme.

Murray visited Muenster personally on 14 May 1925 and wrote in August that there was 'no difficulty with regard to the recognition of work in Latin, French, German, English,' and that if St Peter's was 'willing to teach philosophy' the junior college arrangement was 'acceptable.'[1] An agreement went into effect during the fall of 1925 when Latin, German, French, English, history, and mathematics were taught for university credit. Philosophy was added to the list of subjects in the fall of 1926.

Thus by the end of 1926 St Peter's was offering both senior high school and junior college programmes. The junior college programme, however, served a limited purpose in that it was mainly followed by Benedictine clerics and by candidates for the order who on completing it normally transferred not to Saskatchewan but to St John's Abbey, Collegeville, where they took their bachelor's degree.

Principals of St Peter's have been as follows: Wilfrid Hergott 1924–7, 1928–31; Matthew Michel 1927–8, 1931–5; Xavier Benning 1935–60; Albert Ruetz 1960–6; Vincent Morrison since 1966. Successors to Abbot Michael Ott and presidents of the college have been abbots Severin Gertkin 1927–60, and Jerome Weber, since 1960.

The college programme was curtailed during the fifties when the University of Saskatchewan raised its admission requirement to grade XII, which meant that junior college students at St Peter's really only took one year of university work before transferring to the second year of a three-year university programme.

A further university modification, carried out during 1968–9, established both three- and four-year programmes. The junior colleges are hopeful that this will ultimately result in their being allowed to reintroduce two university years into their junior college programme.

The university has always taken a generous attitude towards St Peter's. At present it permits the junior college professors to set and mark their own examinations, subject to revision by the university departments concerned. It also permits St Peter's to provide evening courses. These tokens of confidence have resulted, since Morrison became principal[2] in 1966, in rapid development and enthusiasm. During 1968–9 the student body included, over and above the high school registration, 46 full-time and 100 evening-class university students.

1 See the following letters in the archives of St Peter's: Hergott to Thompson 16 Feb. 1925, Thompson to Hergott 17 Feb. 1925, Thompson to Hergott 24 Aug. 1925.
2 The title of rector was changed to principal when Morrison took over.

St Joseph's College

EDMONTON

1926

St Joseph's College, affiliated with the University of Alberta and operated by a board of governors consisting of representatives lay and
clerical from the archdiocese of Edmonton, the diocese of Calgary, the
Basilian Fathers, and the University of Alberta, is located on a property
of slightly over three acres on the south side of 89th Street facing the
medical building and main campus of the university. The assessment
value of the land and buildings is about $550,000 and the replacement
value, about 1½ million. The college provides credit courses of its own
in philosophy and theology, one of its priest members holds a university appointment in economics, and the college operates a residence and
a Catholic Centre with a library and chapel facilities for Catholic students of the entire university.

When Archbishop Henry Joseph O'Leary was appointed to Edmonton
in 1920, he planned to have a Catholic college in the University of
Alberta. He is known to have expressed this intention to Archbishop
Neil McNeil of Toronto, to the Basilian Fathers, to the Brothers of the
Christian Schools, and to the Carnegie Corporation of New York. The
Carnegie Corporation was anxious to explore the possibilities of uni-
versity federation and offered the archbishop a grant of $100,000 to-
wards his college provided he could match it. The Basilians sent Father
V.J. Murphy to discuss the matter with O'Leary, and the Christian
Brothers sent Brother Bernard. Little is known about Murphy's visit:
he had been a bursar at St Michael's, Toronto, and no doubt, shared
the good bursar's fear of institutional debt. No action followed his visit.
Brother Bernard, Visitor of the District of Toronto, held much more
fruitful discussions with O'Leary, and he spoke in favour of the archbishop's project with his Toronto colleagues, who had no post-secondary foundations in Canada and were keenly interested in an Edmonton
college.

Brother Alfred went to Edmonton in September 1925 to plan a university college and to organize a campaign to raise the archbishop's
matching grant. Alfred was an excellent choice for this particular chore,
having a host of friends across Canada, being familiar, as were few

Catholic churchmen of his generation, with local history in Canada, and endowed with a lively blending of imagination and courage. The public campaign was launched on 22 October 1925, under a large committee of which Henry J. Roche was chairman and Alfred executive secretary. The objective was raised by January 1926; the Carnegie Corporation paid its commitment; and the University of Alberta, with the consent of the provincial government, agreed to transfer to the new college – which was to be called St Joseph's – a site near the campus.

On 8 April 1926, St Joseph's College was civilly incorporated by the legislature. The act provided for a board of governors which was to own the college and was to be responsible for its operation. This board was a small one of eight persons: Archbishop H.J. O'Leary, Bishop J.T. Kidd of Calgary, Brother Rogation, Brother Alfred, The Honourable Justice N.D. Beck, Patrick Burns, and the dean of arts of the University, who at that time was W.A.R. Kerr. This was an interesting board. The including of the bishops of Edmonton and Calgary indicated precisely the ecclesiastical responsibility; and the including of two university functionaries, Chancellor Beck and Dean Kerr, acknowledged the public nature of the board. It was known by April 1926 that Brother Rogation was to be the first rector of St Joseph's and he joined the board *ex officio*. Brother Alfred and Patrick Burns were financial advisors. The board of governors was clearly intended to be an active, responsible board. It was really not such even from the beginning. The board tended to abdicate its responsibilities; this was to be one of the many problems facing the brothers, but one for which they and the archbishop were responsible. By contrast today's board at St Joseph's is as effective a one as is to be found in Canada.

On 28 April 1926, an agreement was drawn up between the boards of the university and the college by which 5.6 acres of land located on the south side of 89th Street, opposite the medical school, was turned over to the college under the usual conditions that it be used for educational purposes and that it be properly maintained. This deed was a reasonable one, and the site of a respectable size. Time has seen a later, more niggardly, university board nibble away under one pretext or another at this original land grant and an irresponsible college board negotiate away the college's birthright.

There were other clauses in the agreement. Instruction given in the college was to lead towards the degrees of BA and BSC in the faculty of arts. The college was to be an affiliate of the university and the rector was to sit on the university senate. Academically significant was the clause that 'the college shall have the right, should it so decide, to teach

Roman Catholic students the subjects of history and philosophy (including ethics).' There were precautions taken regarding standards, and it was specifically stated that the teaching of additional subjects in the college might be agreed upon from time to time. Unique at this early date was the provision for two kinds of college teaching: one in the university by college personnel who might be given a university appointment and salary, one in the college by college personnel with some remitting of fees by the university for such work done. These terms indicate a considerable degree of good will on the part of the university and gave those responsible for the new college every reason to expect that their venture would be a successful one.

The college board's inaugural meeting was held shortly after the foregoing agreement was arranged. The board approved the agreement and took the wise precaution to have the agreement specifically state that the term 'college students' be taken to include both men and women. St Joseph's College, on the insistence of its board, was co-educational from the beginning. At this inaugural meeting, Edward Underwood was selected as architect for the new college building, but he must actually have been selected some time before, since, on the following day, 13 May, a resolution of the university senate approved the affiliation of St Joseph's, and, on 14 May, the first sod was turned by Archbishop O'Leary in the presence of the lieutenant-governor of the province, of President H.M. Tory, and of a host of university, municipal, and provincial dignitaries. The building was to include some classrooms, Newman Club facilities, a gymnasium, and (later) a permanent chapel. The building was to cost in the neighbourhood of $200,000 and to house 100 boarders and provide cafeteria service for 250 students.

Brother Rogation was rector of St Joseph's from 1927 to 1933. His term began with the opening of the building in September 1927, but he seems already to have been in Edmonton during 1926–7. The first staff began to arrive in September: Brothers Philip and Xavier on the 4th, Brother Aloysius a day or two before. Philip and Aloysius were to be the academic backbone of the new staff, and their appointment to Edmonton was promising. The first staff had six brothers on it: Rogation, Philip, Aloysius, Xavier, Pius, Joseph. Rogation was a distinguished member of the order who had opened several classical colleges in Cuba, was fluent in Spanish, and a student of literature. He had been with the Toronto Separate School Board for ten years before his appointment to Edmonton. He was obviously selected as a rector for his experience in administration. Philip, on the other hand, was already an able student of psychology. He was appointed to the staff of the university and began teaching, according to the college journal, on 6 October 1927. He has subsequently been professor of psychology in Queen's University, in Western, in Fordham, and in Assumption University of Windsor, where he was head of the department until his retirement. His appointment to St Joseph's was an admirable one, and he was obviously a university man. Aloysius was an advanced student of Spanish when he came to St Joseph's. He had his MA in modern languages from the University of Toronto and was a doctoral candidate at the Catholic University of America. Xavier and Pius were not ready for university teaching. Joseph came to Edmonton primarily to look after the chancel choir in the cathedral and to assist with music around the college.

By 5 October 1927, all rooms in St Joseph's College had been taken and there was a waiting list of 12. It was on this day that lectures began for freshmen and also for what the college's 'Daily Journal' refers to as the 'High School Department.' The brothers had decided to teach matriculation courses at the college for university students deficient in one or more high school subjects. These courses were open to any students of the university who wished to take them. The brothers were experienced high school teachers, and one can see how they might take on this work, particularly as they knew that the financing of St Joseph's would not be easy. Tactically and psychologically it was unwise. The high school attachments of Catholic colleges have been their bane. The administration of St Joseph's was rash to get involved in high school work during the opening year.

On 6 November 1927, the new St Joseph's College building was formally opened by Andrea Cassulo, apostolic delegate to Canada. Brother Rogation's address on the occasion, printed in the *Western Catholic*, outlined the kind of programme which the college administration had in mind. Most of its teaching would ultimately be done in the university. Some brothers were joining the university staff. There were to be no 'divinity courses.' Matriculation subjects were to be taught for a time. There were to be college courses in history and philosophy.

The registration as of 20 April 1928, that is, towards the end of the first year of operation, was reported to the third annual meeting of the board as follows: 'total registration of resident students, including students attending the short course, is 104. Of this total, 80 are in residence at this date. University registration by faculty shows 16 in medicine, 16 in agriculture, 14 in arts, 8 in commerce, 7 in applied science, 5 in dentistry, 4 in pharmacy, 2 in graduate studies, 6 in combined courses. The high school students number 10 in residence and 26 attending classes.'

There was in the first year an attempt to create a lively interest in athletics. The well-known Edmonton athlete, Miles Palmer, was engaged as athletic instructor of St Joseph's College. By October, Palmer was also coaching the football team of the University of Alberta. It is recorded in the 'Daily Journal' for Monday, 12 November that 'Mr Miles Palmer held his first gym class at 8:45 p.m. consisting of twenty-one girls.'

The second year of operation, 1928-9, proved a trying one for the brothers. It started off with a tragedy: Brother Aloysius, who had gone to California to take a summer course and to prepare his doctoral thesis for publication, died suddenly. This was both a personal and a severe academic loss because it meant forfeiting a salary towards the operating of the college.

The original plan was to construct the college chapel during 1928-9. The loss of Brother Aloysius made this more difficult, but the administration decided to go ahead with this all-important facility. The board met twice to deal with the matter. At a special meeting on 26 December 1928, the board voted to float a bond issue in the amount of $60,000 so that the chapel might go up. A second meeting on 26 March 1929, revealed that the bond issue had become unnecessary as the university was willing to make a direct loan in the same amount at 5½ per cent interest payable over twenty years. The board decided to borrow from the university. The chapel was erected and the college went into the difficult thirties with what proved to be a rising debt.

The other issue of the early part of 1929 was the ordeal of an extraordinary visitation. For some reason not quite clear, but probably because some important individual or some significant institution had lodged a complaint to the effect that St Joseph's was not adhering sufficiently closely to canon law or to customs approved by the Sacred Congregation of Seminaries and Universities or the Congregation of Religious, an official visitor (the Jesuit father, Francis M. Connell) was sent to investigate the college and to report on conditions found in it. A supplement to the college's 'Daily Journal' bitterly notes that the visitor looked in vain for the non-existent swimming pool where mixed bathing was said to take place.

Connell's major concern seems to have been to investigate the relatively large number of non-Catholics admitted into residence. This, no doubt, was the nub of the original complaint. The brothers were, of course, primarily interested in serving Catholic students, but they rightly opened their facilities to others as called for by fraternal charity, by their location in the provincial university and by financial necessity. The brothers were at a disadvantage when the official visitor arrived because Archbishop O'Leary was in Rome and because they were annoyed and shocked both that such ridiculous charges should be made and that they should receive such formidable attention.

Following the visitation Rome asked that non-Catholic students taken into residence be restricted to five. This directive resulted in the college having now to take 20 high school students rather than 10 into residence, and the total number of residents reached only 82, about 20 short of capacity. The visitation itself was an indignity, and the subsequent directive forced the college to expand the one service which as a university college it ought never to have started. In 1931 the college reconsidered its policy and dropped the high school department.

The thirties were years of growing debt in all institutions and St Joseph's was no exception. During 1931 the board owed $67,000, and this figure rose to $87,000 by 1939. The brothers ran the college economically, keeping the operation within the revenue, but could not avoid some capital outlay. The year 1929–30 was typical of the following decade: revenue from room, board, cafeteria, dining room, salaries was $31,000; expenditures were $28,300, leaving a small credit balance of $2800 for capital investment.

Brother Rogation's term as rector ended in 1933. He remained on the staff, teaching Spanish, and was replaced as rector by Brother Memorian. Memorian was more of an academic man than Rogation, though less scholarly than some of his staff, notably than Philip. He was interested in Church history and spoke frequently on historical subjects throughout the province. His report to the board in 1934 provides an excellent picture of the life and work in the college. The report describes the five kinds of work carried on by the college: (1) it provides pastoral services and instructions through a chaplain. (2) It gives academic courses in scholastic philosophy (1927 on), and provides occasional lectures in legal and medical ethics. (3) It conducts two societies: the Historical Evidence Guild, the Catholic Truth Society. (4) It has a library of 3000 volumes on ethics, apologetics, philosophy, church history, religious knowledge. (5) It provides personal counselling to all who seek it. The only work not as yet taken up was that of a formal Newman Club. Such a club was organized in 1938. The college which Memorian describes is a good operation but a holding one. Circumstances then seemed not to favour concentration on the developing of a distinctive scholarly tradition. Perhaps the university failed the college in not encouraging it to develop in areas likely to fall under its special competence. The college, for example, offered its first credit course in religion during 1929–30. Students who took the course were entitled to exemption from one of the courses prescribed in divisions A or B of the university calendar. Religion was a 'credit,' and was strictly limited (as it still is) to one course in a student's entire programme. It was not treated like other disciplines, say anthropology. It is true that the brothers were free to develop some other area like philosophy or history or a discipline of their own choosing. Their efforts to develop philosophy were equally stalemated by the faculty of education (Board Minutes, 12 June 1946). The brothers failed to develop a characteristic area. But they sent good men to Edmonton during these and later years. Philip and Aloysius have already been mentioned. Also distinguished for their scholarship have been brothers Anselm (philosophy), Ansbert, Aloysius, Mark, and Bonaventure; and for their administrative skill, Prudent, Luke, and others.

In 1939 Brother Ansbert became the third rector of St Joseph's. He was a good financier and seems to have been the force behind a move made by the board in 1940 to transfer the full responsibility for the college property to the Brothers of the Christian Schools of Ontario. Brother Austin, who was provincial at the time, attended the board meeting and favoured the move. At the next meeting, however, twenty months later, the new provincial, Brother Prudent, was in attendance, and he reported that his executive was not willing to assume further obligations and would not take over the college property. Ansbert's financial reports continued to be good ones. When his six-year term as rector ended in 1945, he had cut back the debt by $43,000. His successor, Brother Prudent, removed the debt to the university in 1949. Most of the outstanding debt in 1949 seems to have been owed by the board to the Christian Brothers, though whether this was for an actual loan, for contributed services, or for salary turned in to the college is not clear from the minutes. Clear, however, from other sources (Prudent to Shook, 22 October 1965), is that the brothers received very little recompense for their very hard work in Edmonton. The tax paid by the college to the Toronto province of the order even as late as 1959 for four active men was only $3000; and by 1963 when the financial situation was much better only amounted to $8000.

During Brother Prudent's rectorship the college encountered difficulty with the university over its site. During the spring of 1946 the college was asked to surrender about half the land it held. This was a frustrating demand, and should neither have been made nor concurred with. It imposed totally new limitations on the future development of the college. Brother Prudent and the board countered the demand for surrender of property with a demand for reimbursement, which was equally preposterous. If the college board could make a case for selling back the property, then there was an even better case for its giving it back – and this it had ultimately to do, though some barter of services was arranged. In first making the demand, President Newton said he needed two acres of the college property to be able to carry out the new plans for the expanding university. His attitude in the matter was harsh, and his bitter reply to the Board's counter demand crushed them entirely.

The history of St Joseph's in the 1950s is not marked by the vitality which characterized most of the other Catholic institutions during the same period. There was no structural evolution, no building expansion, and academic deepening and broadening was not evident. Brother Luke succeeded Brother Prudent as rector in 1951, and was succeeded by Brother Aloysius in 1957. Brother Prudent returned as rector in 1959 and held office until 1963.

A gratifying bolstering of the faculty came in 1957 when Aloysius took over as rector and Brother Bonaventure joined the staff in history. The academic strengthening had been sought by Ansbert and Prudent, and Bonaventure's coming gave satisfaction to all concerned. Bonaventure Miner is one of Canada's distinguished Catholic historians. He holds a doctorate in mediaeval history from the University of London. He has become a producing scholar with creative contributions in *Mediaeval Studies* (Toronto), *British Journal of Educational Studies* (London), *Report of the Canadian Catholic Historical Association* (Ottawa), and the *Innes Review* (Glasgow). When he was appointed to St Joseph's, he had to turn down an offer from Assumption University of Windsor. When the brothers left St Joseph's in 1963 he stayed on into the Basilian regime. Late in 1963 he accepted a post at LaSalle College, Philadelphia; and in 1967 he joined the department of history of the University of Windsor.

In spite of the coming of Bonaventure in 1957 and the return of Prudent as rector in 1959, it became increasingly evident that the direction of the college was destined to pass into other hands. The minutes of the meetings of the board begin as far back as 1953 to show ominous signs of a coming change. The minutes of 29 June 1953 contain the cryptic remark: 'During the past year as there was not a brother to act as bursar, there was a deficiency on the Board.' At the annual meeting of 1954 there was no bishop present. Bishop Carroll had been ill and missing meetings frequently. Calgary, in any event, was becoming less interested in St Joseph's. Perhaps the time had come for Calgary to have its own college, as it was to have its own branch of the university. Archbishop MacDonald of Edmonton was also ill, though still far from his retirement. The thirtieth annual meeting of the board was held 18 September 1955; the thirty-first, three years later on 6 August 1958, when a 'capital expenditures' programme was belatedly and ineffectively discussed. In June 1961 the board noted that it had not yet applied for the capital funds held for it by the Canada Council; and in 1962 a suggestion coming from a new member of the board, Dr. William Shandro, that the gymnasium be turned into a library, was unfavourably received by Brother Prudent. In simple fact, the board had, under Archbishop Jordan and Dr Shandro, suddenly come to life and was determined to take drastic steps to revitalize the college. The brothers had now only one established scholar, Brother Bonaventure, on the staff, and seemed not to have the depth in scholarly men to continue university work. There seemed also to be a desire on the part of the board to have priests on the staff of St Joseph's.

The last significant interest of the brothers was the proposed department of religion. Over the years there had been some change for the better so far as religion was concerned, and St Joseph's College had been responsible in some degree for it. More recently a number of denominations had established active religious clubs at the university and appointed official chaplains. The university's attitude toward religion became one of increasing interest. So we find in the minutes of the meeting held in Calgary by the university senate, 17 November 1961, the following: 'The motion to establish a Religious Center was then PUT AND CARRIED, and the Motion to establish a Department of Religion as an integral part of the academic life of the University was PUT AND CARRIED.'

The original committee appointed to investigate this matter was headed by Dr Cragg, vice-president of the university, and Dr J.J. Thompson, principal of St Stephen's College (United Church of Canada). The Catholic view was expressed by Brother Prudent, rector of St Joseph's College, who consulted Archbishop Jordan on the stand to be taken. Brother Prudent was one of some six university officials called together by Dr Thompson to a preliminary meeting in Edmonton to prepare for the session of the senate in Calgary.

Subsequent to the Calgary meeting Professor F.C. Burkill was brought to the university campus attached for 1964–5 to the department of philosophy. This development belongs to the next regime. The brothers gave up direction of the college at the end of 1962–3, and the Basilian fathers of Toronto replaced them.

J. Wilfrid Dore became the first Basilian rector of St Joseph's College. He arrived in Edmonton 12 August 1963 and took office on the 16th. He was accompanied by Russell A.J. Pendergast, and followed in 1964 by James E. Daley. Dore came with long experience in university work behind him. He had taught rational psychology and philosophy in Toronto for many years and had acquired an enviable reputation as student counsellor and disciplinarian. He came to St Joseph's in the proven role of a senior professor and from the first maintained that role on the new campus. He was a man of exquisite taste who supervised the almost total alteration of the old facilties, giving privileged status where he could do so to academics and scholarship. He agreed with Dr Shandro that something had to be done about the library, and he converted much of the old east wing of the building into a reading room and the gymnasium into commodious stacks.

St Joseph's College, from the point of view of the Basilians, is a promising institution. Dore was in administration and teaching; Daley's appointment was full-time in the college; Pendergast full-time in the university's department of economics. When the house was opened some Basilian scholastics were sent there for their university work: a good move, well received by the university and one which healthily diversified the training of such candidates for the order. Some priests have also been appointed to Edmonton to pursue graduate studies.

Ill health forced Dore's resignation from the rectorship, though not from teaching, in July 1965. The new Basilian rector was Robert M. Montague, also a man of varied experience: a lieutenant-commander in the Royal Canadian Navy who captained HMCS *Port Hope* in World War II, and professor of philosophy and sociology at St Thomas More College in Saskatoon from 1957 to 1965. Montague's was a promising appointment. After two years of active leadership he became a victim of cancer and died during October 1968. His policy was to focus aggressively on creating a college life as close to the university programme as possible without building up sharply distinct college departments. St Joseph's gained considerably in prestige and influence under his direction. Following his death, the rectorship was taken over for a few months by a non-resident encumbent, Robert Finn, the representative of the western Canadian region on the general council of the order and the principal of St Mark's College in Vancouver. The present rector, Joseph B. Courtney, took over in June 1969.

The great issue affecting the college in recent years has been the move in the university towards a department of religious studies. Following the coming of Professor Burkill to the campus in 1964, a kind of pro-department was conducted for two or three years. Burkill was replaced in 1967 by Charles Davis, the English theologian who had publicly left the Catholic Church shortly after Vatican II. The appointment was embarrassing to the St Joseph's people but resulted in no difficult situations with Davis himself or his policies. In 1968 Davis was named head of the new department of religious studies, essentially a department of comparative religions. The only other professor in the department was Dr V. Prittipaul, a young Hindu theologian of great promise. The sad part of the new department was that circumstances tended to keep the St Joseph's people aloof from its activities to their loss and that of the department. The Basilians strengthened the department of religion at St Joseph's in 1969 by appointing to the faculty J.J. Francis Firth, holder of a doctoral degree from the Pontifical Institute of Mediaeval Studies, and an established and publishing scholar. The college, however, was still handicapped by the manpower crisis that had struck the Basilians, and which will have to be solved before a college like St Joseph's can achieve its potential.

Newman Theological College: St Joseph's Seminary

EDMONTON

1917 (1927, 1969)

Newman Theological College is a private university college established within St Joseph's Major Seminary to look after academic programmes and accreditation. Newman serves not only diocesan seminarians enrolled in St Joseph's but also other students, lay and clerical, enrolled directly in the college. The college offers two degree programmes: one leading to the MTH, intended primarily but not exclusively for candidates for the priesthood; and one leading to the MRSC (master of religious science) for prospective teachers, specialists, and research students in theology. The college also comprises a Pastoral Renewal Center which looks after continuing education and special curricula of a formal and full-time nature; and a school of theology to provide informal programmes and to serve the needs of serious but less qualified students. The college and seminary are located in a handsome complex of modern buildings on highway 2 north (the Saint Albert Trail) midway between Edmonton and St Albert. The seminary dates from 1927, the college from 1969.

St Joseph's Seminary of the archdiocese of Edmonton took its origin from within the Scolasticat des Oblats de Marie Immaculée. The scholasticate was established in 1917 to look after the needs of the order's own candidates, French and English, in western Canada. It was located at the corner of 110th Street and 100th Avenue in Edmonton.[1]

The scholasticate of the Oblates was not Edmonton's first seminary. A strictly French-speaking seminary, Le Séminaire de la Sainte Famille, was established in 1900 to prepare and train priests for the diocese of St Albert, of which Edmonton was at that time one of four districts or divisions. The early seminary decreased in importance as the proportion between the English and French population of the area shifted, and was ultimately absorbed into the Oblate juniorate in the city.

1 R.A. MacLean, 'The History of the Roman Catholic Church in Edmonton' (unpublished master's thesis in history, University of Alberta, Edmonton, 1958). See esp. 120–3.

Edmonton became a separate ecclesiastical diocese in 1912. The Oblates decided to open a scholasticate of philosophy and theology in Edmonton in 1917 primarily to educate the order's own candidates from the west. This scholasticate was located at the corner of 110th Street and 100th Avenue near the cathedral.

The first superior of the scholasticate was Michel Mérer. Mérer was a pioneer of the church in Alberta, who had worked closely and effectively with two of St Albert's bishops, Vital-Justin Grandin (d.1902) and Emile Legal (d.1920). Legal became archbishop of Edmonton in 1912. Mérer's work had always centred around Edmonton, and he was a fine selection for the superiorship of the new scholasticate when it was opened in 1917. The new seminary was intended to be bilingual; thus its first faculty of five priests and two brothers included not only Michel Mérer, François-Xavier Blanchin, P.F. Boileau, and Jean-Baptist Salles, but also Thomas Schnerch, Thomas Kennedy, and William B. Grant. When the scholasticate opened it had 18 students in residence. Most of these were Oblate scholastics; but at least one – Emile Tessier – was a diocesan seminarian.

By 1919 the student body consisted of 23 scholastics and three seminarians. These diocesan seminarians can be said to have constituted in germ the future seminary. When François-Xavier Blanchin succeeded Mérer as superior in 1921, there were seven priests and two brothers on the staff, 46 scholastics and 21 seminarians enrolled as students.

From 1921 to 1927, the scholasticate continued as an Oblate house of studies and theologate. The superiors were as follows: François-Xavier Blanchin 1921–3, Bernard McKenna 1923–4, William Patton 1924–6, and Thomas Kennedy 1926–7. Kennedy filled out Patton's term after the latter's accidental death. By Kennedy's time the numbers enrolled were 35 scholastics, 40 seminarians; that is, the house was more diocesan than Oblate.[2]

In 1927 the archbishop of Edmonton, Henry Joseph O'Leary, took over the scholasticate from the Oblates and opened St Joseph's Seminary in September of the same year. There were at this time 66 diocesan seminarians enrolled. O'Leary named as first rector of St Joseph's Seminary his vicar general, James Charles McGuigan, whom he had brought from Charlottetown to Edmonton a short time after his own nomination as archbishop.[3]

2 Data is taken from the entries in Kenedy's *American Catholic Directory* for the years 1917–27.
3 Henry Joseph O'Leary, born in Richibouctou, NB, 1879, ordained 21 Sept. 1901, named bishop of Charlottetown 20 Jan. 1913, named archbishop of Edmonton 7 Sept. 1920, d.1938.

Along with McGuigan on the staff of the new seminary were eight other professors including Henri Lacoste, an Oblate who had been on the staff of the scholasticate during the preceding year. Lacoste was, during 1927–8, vice-rector of St Joseph's and professor of dogmatic theology. He along with the older students preserved the link between the old and new dispensations. Meanwhile, the Oblates moved their scholasticate to Lebret, Saskatchewan.

In 1930 McGuigan was named second archbishop of Regina. He was succeeded as rector of St Joseph's Seminary by Michael C. O'Neill, professor of sacred scripture, a young man for the post but one with a great deal of practical experience behind him.[4] O'Neill guided the seminary from 1930 to 1939 when he enlisted in the chaplain service of the Canadian army. He was succeeded as rector by Howard Griffin, who held the office from 1939 until his death, 4 January 1965.

The period 1927 to 1965 under McGuigan, O'Neill, and Griffin was one of personal and curricular consolidation. Numbers declined slightly during the thirties and considerably during the war years of the forties when enrolment dropped to 35. During the fifties numbers again increased, passing a total of 100 students. The programme offered in St Joseph's varied little over the period: two years of philosophy for those who required it, and four years of theology. The seminary remained in its old building on 110th Street near the cathedral until the summer of 1957 when the present lovely buildings, comprising five wings extending from a central lobby, were opened on the St Albert Trail a few miles north of Edmonton.

Aloysius Schoen became rector of St Joseph's on 6 February 1965 and held office until the summer of 1969. Schoen had to cope with the serious decline of enrolment of the late sixties. In 1968 he discontinued the school of philosophy, making St Joseph's a major seminary only. In 1968 there began a rather radical re-orientation of the seminary programme in line with the progressive policies of Archbishop Anthony Jordan.[5] A corporation of priests and laymen was formed and a bill presented to the Alberta legislature to incorporate the theology depart-

4 Michael Cornelius O'Neill, born in Kemptville, Ont., 1898; moved to Ottawa; entered active service during World War I; attended St Michael's College, University of Toronto, taking the BA in 1924; studied theology at St Augustine's Seminary; ordained for Edmonton in 1927; rector of major seminary 1930. Subsequent to his rectorship, entered the chaplain service in the Canadian army, becoming senior RC chaplain; named archbishop of Regina 4 Dec. 1947.

5 Anthony Jordan, born in Broxburn, Scot.; ordained as an Oblate 23 June 1929; became vicar apostolic of Prince Rupert 23 June 1945, and coadjutor archbishop of Edmonton 17 Apr. 1955 under John Hugh MacDonald. He succeeded to the see 11 Aug. 1964. His policies relating to higher education have been courageous and aggressive.

ment of the seminary as Newman Theological College.[6] The bill, passed in April 1969, placed the new college in the hands of a strong board which appointed major officers including the chancellor. The bill also gave Newman College a limited charter empowering it to grant degrees in theology and to establish a senate and council. Programmes were set up leading to the MTH for the theologians of St Joseph's Seminary, and for other students too, and to the MRSC for students clerical and lay hoping to teach religion in universities, colleges, and schools or to move into research. The college did not replace the seminary but took over most of its academic and all of its accrediting functions.

Schoen himself gave up the rectorship, or as it was by then being called, the principalship, in the summer of 1969. He was succeeded by Principal Oswald Fuchs, a Franciscan well-known in Edmonton. Fuchs had been guardian of St Francis Friary and prefect of studies in the College of St Anthony, the Franciscans' western Canadian house of studies. His appointment as principal of Newman Theological College was personal. It did not mean that the institution was being transferred from the diocese to the Franciscans. Fuchs was engaged to guide the restructured college and seminary during a crucial period when attention had to focus on contemporary disciplines, and far-reaching changes in courses and in seminary life. During 1969–70, the staff comprised nine full-time and two part-time professors. The student body comprised 24 diocesan seminarians, 18 other full-time students, and 54 part-time students.

The first staff of Newman Theological College consisted of eleven professors, nine of them full-time, six of them religious, two of these religious sisters. It was a reasonably good staff, measured in terms of the academic degrees held by the faculty and the publications of the senior men.[7] The experiment of 1969 added a significant dimension to the revised major seminary picture in Canadian Catholic education.

6 An Act to Incorporate Newman Theological College; the Legislative Assembly of Alberta; second session, 16th legislature, 18 Elizabeth II, Bill Pr. 4, 29 Apr. 1969

7 The staff of Newman Theological College 1969–70: Camille Dozois, STD, author of articles on theology and the church in the *Revue de l'Université d'Ottawa, The Humanities Association Bulletin,* and the *New Catholic Encyclopedia;* Laurence Frizzell, STL, LSS; Oswald Fuchs, MA, PHD, author of *The Psychology of Habit According to William of Ockham,* Louvain, Nauwelaerts, 1952; Sister Lina Gaudette, MED, PHD; James Gibson, STL, DIPL LIT; Donald MacDonald, STL, PHD; Sister Frances MacDonald, MA; Michael O'Callaghan, STL; Francis Patsula, JCL; Henry Peet, MA; Fernand Thibault, STL.

St Mark's College

VANCOUVER

1956

St Mark's College in the University of British Columbia is an affiliated theological college existing under the provisions of the University of British Columbia Act of 1908. Prolonged negotiations preceded civil incorporation and affiliation with the university in 1956. The college is held by a Board of Management and operated for the board by the Basilian Fathers, several of whom are or have been members of the staff of the university, though not by reason of their college appointment. St Mark's is located at 5960 Chancellor Boulevard on a five-acre site leased at nominal rental from the university for 999 years. Three college buildings have been erected: an administration building, containing chapel, dining rooms, and other facilities, 1957; Duke Hall (formerly Durieu), a combined residence and Newman Club, also in 1957; Carr Hall (formerly Demers), a combined residence and library, 1960. Duke Hall and Carr Hall were sold to UBC in 1970. The college may offer, in addition to professional and academic programmes in theology, university courses in religious studies at the undergraduate level; it also conducts the Newman Club of the university and provides specialized library and study facilities for Catholic students of all university faculties. Basilian Fathers holding academic appointments in the university live at the college. The overall investment in buildings and facilities exclusive of land and training of personnel, is estimated at about one million dollars.

BEFORE INCORPORATION: 1938–55

It was always known that there would one day be a Catholic college or university in Vancouver. When the Christian Brothers of Ireland opened Vancouver College high school, in 1925, they were assured by Archbishop Timothy Casey that no other Catholic college would be permitted to open in the city while the brothers' school was still struggling to establish itself. The brothers on their part agreed not to move into university education without first informing the archbishop that they were about to do so. A typical 'Archbishop Casey contract,' it is not recorded in the chancery files, but older clerics know that it was made.[1] The point of it is that everyone knew in 1925 (and long before) that there would one day be a Catholic college or university in Vancouver. During these early years, the Jesuits acquired a 15-acre property in West Point Grey. They were not sure that they wanted to establish a college, but they knew that someone ought to be taking steps against the day when it would have to be done.[2] Archbishop W.M. Duke took over the see of Vancouver in 1931, and shared the same views about the ultimate certainty of a college in Vancouver; but with one additional conviction – that it would come about in his time.

The first tentative enquiry about the possibility of placing an affiliated college in the University of British Columbia was made by Archbishop Duke sometime during 1937.[3] On 21 January 1938, the university senate returned a negative answer: 'A privilege could not be extended to one church college that could not be given to another.' That the privilege could not be given was felt to be written into the original University of British Columbia act which states: 'The University shall be strictly non-sectarian in principle, and no religious creed or dogma shall be taught.' (Section 79) This prescription was to remain on the books until 1964 when the word 'taught' was replaced by 'inculcated.'

On 4 December 1940, Duke wrote to the Honourable George M. Weir, minister of education, asking whether the department could help him with his request to the senate. What Duke wanted was a Roman Catholic arts college offering certain subjects only. He was at this time in constant touch with Henry Carr, the superior general of the Basilian Fathers. The meeting asked for was held in the minister's office in the Vancouver Court House, under the chairmanship of Dr Willis, superintendent of education. Carr attended this meeting.[4] It became clear on this occasion that the university senate had previously interpreted the request of the archbishop to be for a theological college. Only now did they realize that what the archbishop had in mind was an arts college. However, after a series of meetings in 1941 the answer was still negative.

---

1 Forget to McCorkell, 26 Feb. 1943, archives of the Basilian Fathers, Toronto
2 Ibid. Father Forget writes: 'I well remember when the Jesuits came and made an attempt to start a college in Vancouver, and even secured the land for it; but what was the reason for their change of mind, I cannot say.'
3 Some documents referring to this and other matters treated in the following pages are to be found in the files in the chancery office of the archdiocese of Vancouver. A summary of documents relating to negotiations at various times is to be found in the archives of the Basilian Fathers, Toronto, and also in the archives of St Michael's College, Toronto.
4 To the Basilian Fathers' copy of the summary referred to in note 1, Carr appends a note where he says: 'I remember vividly being present at the meeting in the Minister's room in the Court House on March 14, 1941.'

On Weir's urging, the senate appointed in the fall of 1941 a committee to consider a request of Archbishop Duke for an affiliated Catholic college. The committee met on 10 December 1941, with the following present: Judge Harvey (chairman), President Klinck, Archbishop Duke, Dean Buchanan, Professor Finlayson, Professor Sedgewick, Mrs Farris, Mr Fisher. Dr Klinck said after the meeting that he did not think it had much affected the mind of the committee. All knew that the committee would report negatively. The senate at its meeting of 18 February 1942 again rejected the request for an affiliated Catholic college. After the summer of 1942, when Carr's term as superior general was over and he was appointed to Saskatoon, Duke began to consider him as his personal adviser.[5]

The committee's unreceptivity forced Duke to give consideration to the most logical alternative, a university of his own. In a letter to Premier John Hart, dated 16 December 1942, that is, before the senate's meeting, he asked for an interview to discuss the possibility of 'a charter for a Catholic university.' He mentioned this also to the new minister of education, the honourable H.G. Perry. Duke was serious about a university charter, and in some of his moods thought a charter preferable to affiliation. On the same day as his letter to Hart, 16 December, he wrote also to Bishop John C. Cody of Victoria: 'Confidentially, I intend to go ahead on my own regarding the university, but will keep you advised.' He also approached the Basilian Fathers and the Congregation of the Holy Cross about the wisdom and viability of such a project. The hurdles were actually insuperable: the government was committed to a 'one-university' policy, the Catholic constituency was not powerful, the orders were short of competent university men. However, a meeting of Duke, Cody, and Perry to discuss the possibility of a charter was held on 23 March 1942; and, although Perry said he thought the request a legitimate one which he would present to his colleagues and would personally support, nothing came of it.

Meanwhile, the notion of an affiliated college was also kept alive, and the archbishop repeatedly urged Premier Hart and Mr Perry to bring pressure to bear on the university president and the senate. There was a feeling that the university's attitude towards affiliation might soften after Norman MacKenzie replaced Dr Klinck as president during 1943. MacKenzie knew Carr personally and had some practical experience of religious federation in Toronto. He also expressed complete willingness to discuss with President Walter P. Thompson and ex-president Murray the working out of college federation in Saskatoon.

5 See above, 349

In March 1945, MacKenzie visited Saskatoon to examine at first hand the kind of federation existing there. 'President Thompson,' Carr wrote to Duke, 13 March 1945, 'told president MacKenzie that the arrangement works with entire satisfaction and is the only solution of a very difficult problem.' MacKenzie went into every angle of the affiliated college proposal during 1945. He became convinced that the request for a Saskatoon arrangement stood no chance with the UBC senate and board and that all provision for teaching secular subjects in a college with a view to university credit would have to be dropped. The college he envisaged would have to be built personally around Basilians teaching as competent and qualified scholars in the university departments under regular university contracts. It would not be a teaching college and would have to construct its particular ethos in some other way, possibly utilizing the theological college status as enjoyed by Protestant colleges on the campus. This was, of course, not what the archbishop had in mind. He already had a major seminary, the Seminary of Christ the King, to look after the professional training of priests, and Catholic laymen had no great need for the kind of college that could only take them to a BD or to a diploma in religion. Carr, however, came over to MacKenzie's position; that is, that the senate should only be asked for something it could legitimately be expected to concede under the university act. The archbishop finally accepted this as the most prudent policy. After these discussions in 1945, there were no further requests for a teaching college of either the Saskatoon or Toronto type. There was, however, a continuing view that the government should be asked to grant a separate charter for a Catholic university. A private bill was ready for presentation to the legislature in November 1945, but its reading was postponed in view of another approach to the senate planned for the spring of 1946.

The negotiations of 1946, although they broke down, are nevertheless of special importance in this pre-history of St Mark's. The senate appointed a new committee on the affiliation of a Roman Catholic college which included the following members: Mr Hamber (the chancellor), Dean Finlayson (arts), Dean Buchanan (science), Dean Curtis (law), Professor Sedgewick, Mr Lord, Mrs Haskett, Brigadier Lett. The president invited to a preliminary informal meeting in his office on 7 May 1946, Archbishop Duke, Mr Woods (the registrar), Dean Curtis, and Carr. Here it was decided that the first move should be to get university posts for Basilians in three subjects, philosophy, history, and economics; one Basilian would come in the first year; two in the second; three in the third. The university would pay for the actual teaching done. The large senate committee met on 9 May and decided to recommend to the senate at its August meeting that it approve the foregoing procedure. By August, however, new problems had arisen; the new alumni members of senate were particularly unsympathetic; and two ministers, Joseph E. Brown and H.R. Trumpour, gave notice that they would ask the same concessions for their respective denominations. By early 1947, the new negotiations had completely broken down.

A fresh start was made nearly two years later, in October 1948. The archbishop was again ready to seek an independent charter; failing in this he would seek affiliation with an eastern university. A gathering of lay Catholics in Rosary Hall, 20 October 1947, established a committee of the British Columbia Catholic Educational Association consisting of five members: three UBC alumni (Joseph E. Brown, A. E. Branca, and David A. Steele) and two other members (P.D. Murphy and Miss E. Hughes). The BCCEA was anxious to ward off the establishing of an independent university and made formal representation to the senate for the addition of new courses in philosophy, history, and economics available to all students but taught by qualified Basilians in UBC classrooms for UBC credit. They promised to find funds for the erection of a Catholic residence for out-of-town students. Again a senate committee was set up, this time under Professor Angus. The discussion in committee and in the senate centred upon the appointing of a priest to the department of philosophy. On 9 May 1950, the following resolution came from the senate: 'That the president be requested to advise the board of governors that the senate does not view with favour the proposal to appoint a lecturer of a particular faith for the express purpose of teaching a course in scholastic philosophy.' A letter from MacKenzie, written 18 May 1950, to Mr E. Davie Fulton in Ottawa expressed regret at the senate resolution. The BCCEA continued to urge the MacKenzie modifications in one form or another during the next two years. When in March 1952 (to look ahead) the senate was beginning to look more kindly on the affiliation of a Catholic college, its procedure was to reconstitute the earlier Angus Committee which in its turn approved in principle on 4 March 1952, the 1948 recommendations of the Catholic Educational Association.

During the summer and fall of 1950 a new kind of approach was made. MacKenzie and Carr had often noticed during the trying committee meetings on the proposed college, that on the occasions when the name of the Pontifical Institute of Mediaeval Studies came up, it never failed to create an awareness that there was a very real kind of scholarly contribution which a small college could make to the intellectual life of a large university campus. At the June meeting of the Royal Society of Canada, Joseph T. Muckle of the Pontifical Institute suggested to MacKenzie that Etienne Gilson, a co-founder of the institute along with Carr, McCorkell, and Gerald B. Phelan, should be invited to give guest lectures on the UBC campus. Shortly after, both McCorkell and MacKenzie wrote to Gilson, who was summering at Vermenton, outside Paris. Gilson agreed to visit UBC and lecture on 'The Place of Mediaeval Studies in the History of Western Civilization.' Arrangements for the visit were made by Professor Geoffrey Andrew. The lecture was given 16 November 1950 on the campus at noon hour before a huge audience, with discussion meetings following in the afternoon and evening. One of the subjects discussed was academic liberty; and the unresolved question was which course really assured such liberty.

Gilson's lecture at the UBC was certainly an important event in itself. Whether it had anything to do with subsequent developments or not is impossible to tell. Within the next two months MacKenzie took a new tack: he decided on his own responsibility to encourage one of the departments to take Father Carr on as a special lecturer, trusting that the senate and board of governors would, since all would be regular procedure, confirm the appointment in the normal way.

On 17 January 1951, Duke wrote to McCorkell as follows: 'The president of the University has signified his willingness to take a priest on the staff, but he could not provide a salary ... I would be glad to give the salary of an assistant ($25 a month) and accommodation at the cathedral, if one of the fathers could possibly undertake this work to help soften the way for an affiliated college. If Father Carr could possibly come himself as a beginning, it would mean a lot to the meeting of the new senate in April of this year.' The phrase 'could not provide a salary' simply means that MacKenzie was in no position to guarantee that a salary would be paid and that the issue was not to be debated or conditioned on the salary factor. It is not likely that MacKenzie ever had in mind to take on qualified priest-professors without paying them for services rendered, though fear of something like this seems to have lurked in Father Carr's mind and in the minds of some of the Basilian councillors.

The year 1951 turned out to be the decisive one in this area of university appointments. In the letter cited above Duke referred to MacKenzie's offer as a 'beam of light,' and the general council of the Basilian Fathers considered it significant enough for action. They gave Carr an official 'obedience' to go to Vancouver in the fall 'to accept an appointment from the University of British Columbia to its staff in philosophy.' MacKenzie was in Europe a great part of the summer of 1951 and there was considerable confusion about the procedure of arranging the appointment. It came ultimately, not in philosophy from Dean Chant but in classics from Professor Logan. Carr was engaged as a special lecturer to teach Latin 202 (Cicero) during the first term, Latin 304 (Juvenal) during the second term, and four hours of Greek throughout the year. The important thing, MacKenzie insisted, was to get on the staff; the subject of instruction was secondary. There was no question here of competence or incompetence: Carr was a graduate in classics at the University of Toronto and had taught Latin and Greek in St Michael's for many years. Carr began teaching before the contract was officially drawn up and without any decision about salary.

The opening of the fall term in late September was the occasion of a rather celebrated incident in the annals of higher education in Canada. Carr met his first class on 25 September, with 20 students in attendance, 8 men and 12 women. After class he stopped in to speak to Professor Logan, who told him the president wanted to see him. With embarrassment MacKenzie explained to Carr that his appointment had only been provisionally approved at the previous night's meeting of the board. There was objection to his wearing clerical attire in university lecture rooms. For the present the board wanted Carr to lecture in lay attire; if he could not do so, then his appointment was to be deferred a month for further consideration.

This particular turn of affairs was unexpected, and Carr asked for a few hours to think the matter over. The archbishop was away, so Carr had to make his own decision. By evening he had decided that he ought to lecture in lay attire. After all, he argued with himself, sisters had doffed their habits in Saskatchewan schools during the days of the Anderson government; priests in Mexico were not wearing clerical clothes; and a priest who played golf usually did so in suitable sports togs. It would be a pity to allow a trifling thing like dress to spoil all that had been achieved after years of effort. So he got in touch with his friends David and Dorothy Steele and they helped him borrow appropriate apparel from a mutual bachelor friend, Bill Kerr. They took the clothing out to Carr's office at the university and left it there where he could change before going to class. The following day, to his own and MacKenzie's satisfaction, he met his second class, complying with the board's request that he teach in lay attire.

The matter did not end here. University students realized that they had an excellent *casus belli* with the administration. Carr spent one day calming the members of Newman Club; but he was helpless against the staff of the campus paper, *Ubyssey*. In due course, both campus and city papers publicized the episode of his dress, to his own embarrassment, to be sure, but much more to that of his new colleagues. The issue died down gradually, and the matter was dropped before the opening of the second term. Carr continued to wear his lay dress for a short time in order to leave the impression that the action taken by the board had not been all that objectionable.

During November 1951 the board of governors allotted Carr a salary of $2000 for his services as a special lecturer in classics, and the official contract with the university was dated 2 January 1952, six days before Carr's 72nd birthday. Carr himself regarded the terms as eminently satisfactory; he was particularly pleased that MacKenzie did not reduce the salary when the half course on Juvenal had to be dropped.

The years immediately following 1952 saw no essential change in Catholic higher education in Vancouver. From time to time there was talk of the archbishop's opening a Catholic university, but nothing ever came of it. Meanwhile the Basilian Fathers and the University of British Columbia worked out their *modus operandi*. During 1951–2 Father Michael Oliver had joined Father Carr in Vancouver,[6] and a staff residence was acquired at 4620 West Second Avenue in the Point Grey area. The following year, 1952–3, Oliver took over the direction of the Newman Club from Patrick Hennessey, the Redemptorist. In the spring of 1954 arrangements were made for the appointment of Father James Hanrahan, who joined the history department in September of that year. In 1955 Father Elliott Allen joined the department of philosophy. Both Hanrahan and Allen had been doctoral students in Toronto and were working at the Pontifical Institute of Mediaeval Studies. They were welcome additions to the university staff, and they were part of an experiment, which the Basilians were glad to carry out, for placing religious priests on the staffs of secular universities in English-speaking Canada. Since 1955 there have been further Basilian appointments to the university: Gerald F. McGuigan joined the department of economics in 1958; Gareth Poupore, the department of history in 1960. In 1962 Francis Firth began lecturing in religious studies. Father Garr resigned his special lectureship in 1958; Allen and Poupore moved on to Toronto and Rochester respectively, and Hanrahan took two years leave of

6 See M.J. Oliver, 'The Vancouver Story,' *The Basilian Teacher*, 8(1964), 315–22.

absence to carry on research in Europe. A practical and satisfactory method of co-ordinating community and university appointments had been worked out.

THE INCORPORATION OF ST MARK'S COLLEGE

During the late fall of 1954 and the spring and summer of 1955, plans were formulated by which a Catholic theological college would be legally incorporated by the legislature and then affiliated with the university.[7]

In November 1954 Archbishop Johnson told Carr that he was planning a public bill. He set forth what he had in mind in an important letter of 4 April 1955: 'My own idea is a "theological" college teaching religion as a required course, directing the students to the courses now taught by priests and which will be taught by priests in the university. The remainder of courses will have to be given in the regular departments of the University of British Columbia. All this will lead to a university BA plus a religion or theology degree.' Carr hoped that such a college could be established, but it was, he felt, something more than the UBC notion of a theological college. The university took a theological college to be one which gave instruction in theology. The university allowed its own students credit for one course taken in a theological college and credit for three courses in the case of students who expressed the intention of proceeding to a theological degree after graduating from the university.

On 11 May 1955, the proposed incorporation of a Catholic college and the bishop's notion of what it would be like got before the senate but was not favourably received. In an important letter of 24 June 1955, Carr asked the archbishop to lower his sights and ask for exactly what the other theological colleges had. Johnson agreed. A joint committee of members appointed by the senate and the archbishop met on 7 July and went on record as favouring the incorporating of such a college.

Although it was a fact that a theological college could do very little for those Catholic students who were not going on in theology, that is, for the majority of Catholic students, still the case was not really so hopeless as it seemed on the surface to be. There was already a movement under way to establish within the university itself a department of religious studies on the 'Iowa Plan.' It was clear to Carr that if such a movement made real headway the new Catholic college would share the

---

7 Important are the following: Johnson to Carr 4 Apr. 1955: Carr to Flahiff 14 Apr. 1955; Carr to Johnson 24 June 1955: all in the archives of the Basilian Fathers, Toronto.

concessions made to the existing theological colleges. This is all set forth clearly in the letter of 24 June, mentioned above:

We ask for the status of a theological college for St Mark's College, precisely as the calendar defines such a college, on exactly the same terms as the other theological colleges enjoy. ... As for the other things we consider desirable, we place all our confidence in the project of courses in religion upon which the Committee of the President on Spiritual Values is at present working. ... The college so constituted would give us everything we need. It would be different from St Michael's and different from St Thomas More College. In some respects it would be better than either. For example, in St Thomas More there are no courses for credit in religion; at Toronto courses in religion are only open to students in arts. Here, if the proposed plan goes through, these courses will be open to the students of all faculties.

On 18 August 1955, Johnson formally invited the Basilian Fathers to establish a residential college on the UBC campus, and on 3 September 1955, the invitation was accepted by George B. Flahiff, the superior general. A bill was prepared for the legislature. Before its actual passing in March 1956, three other issues had to be dealt with: the effect of the establishing of a Catholic theological college on the already existing Seminary of Christ the King, the securing of a reasonable number of Basilian appointments in the university; and financial arrangements between the archdiocese and the Basilian Fathers of Vancouver.

When Duke and Carr had undertaken to establish a Catholic college in the university, they had not in mind a theological college in the sense so familiar to Protestant denominations. They wanted a college for Catholic laymen, and they had no intention of interfering in any way with either the operation or development of professional seminaries. Yet, as their thinking had gradually been modified to conform with the non-Catholic concept of theological college, there was a sense in which their college presented a kind of threat to the existing diocesan seminary, and there was an understandable restlessness at Mission City, where the Benedictines were operating the Seminary of Christ the King.

This seminary, the first theologate established in the archdiocese of Vancouver, was opened by the Benedictines at Burnaby in 1940. At the opening ceremony, Dr Klinck, president of UBC, attended and spoke. Among other things, he expressed regret that so significant an educational institution was not being placed on the campus of the university. The notion that the seminary ought at least to be affiliated with a university often presented itself to the seminary administration; especially after 1952 when provision was made for the payment of federated grants to properly affiliated and federated seminaries and theological colleges. Between 1951 and 1953 Christ the King sought affiliation with Laval, Montreal, Ottawa, and Assumption without success. Affiliation was not actually sought with UBC, possibly in view of what was felt in Catholic circles as the intransigence of that university, but also because of the negotiations already going on over St Mark's College. Now that it was becoming apparent that St Mark's was to be established, not as a liberal arts college like St Michael's or St Thomas More but as a theological college, there was need for the precise definition of the relationship between the two institutions both for their own sakes and for the information of the public.

Abbot Eugene Medved of Westminster Abbey, Mission City, BC, on 5 November 1955 issued a formal statement at a public meeting recommending 'that in any act drawn up to affiliate St Mark's Theological College explicit mention be made of the Seminary of Christ the King at Mission City.' Abbot Medved would even 'be willing to go as far as to make the seminary subsidiary to St Mark's' although the 'more forthright' approach would be to incorporate the seminary itself and provide a role for St Mark's at the undergraduate level.

This turn of affairs led Carr to enquire of MacKenzie whether St Mark's could actually be established only as an undergraduate body not taking on the responsibility of giving professional theological courses. MacKenzie saw no reason why St Mark's had actually to provide more than that part of theological and religious studies pertaining to the undergraduate faculties of the university. If it only provided such work for university undergraduates, it would not *de facto* invade the area which Christ the King regarded as its own nor would it be unjustified in thinking of itself rather as an 'arts' college, albeit of a unique kind. If St Mark's held its theological privileges in abeyance and exercised only its 'arts' privileges, it would be in effect a kind of arts college. The idea appealed to Carr and he was quite willing to see the college assume in its beginnings a somewhat restricted existence of this kind. In his heart Carr thought of St Mark's as an undergraduate arts college: undergraduate because it would offer no advanced theological degrees, its students would be undergraduates, and the priests on its faculty would be teaching in undergraduate departments of the university. The St Mark's he envisaged offered no threat to the role of Christ the King in the archdiocese of Vancouver. The fears expressed by Medved gradually subsided.

The matter of continuing and additional university appointments was settled shortly after this seminary episode. Father Hanrahan who had been lecturing in history for two years had his time-table increased in what was to Carr a gratifying way. The head of the history department asked Hanrahan, as reported by Carr to the superior general on 19 January 1956, not only to continue in this department but to take over during the following year, when Professor Albert Cook would be on sabbatical, the course on the Renaissance and Reformation. This Carr rightly took as evidence of complete confidence in the competence and scholarly integrity of Father Hanrahan. On 9 February Carr wrote again with the news that Father Elliott Allen would be giving in the department of philosophy a course in the history of mediaeval philosophy. Regular appointments like these in history and philosophy, and Carr's own special appointment, assured St Mark's of an active if indirect role in the academic life of the university.

In February 1956 the financial arrangements first came up. Archbishop Johnson wrote Father Flahiff on 9 February that he planned a major diocesan drive with funds in the amount of $200,000 earmarked for St Mark's. He told Flahiff that he would expect the Basilians to be liable for a similar amount now or in the future. Flahiff replied that the General Council of the Basilians accepted no liability for its individual houses as the Congregation was not centrally financed. Each house was responsible for its own financing. Following this exchange, arrangements were made for a bank loan guaranteed by the archbishop for the erection of the first college building.

The act of incorporation of St Mark's was given its third reading in the legislature on 2 March 1956, and was formally signed by the lieutenant-governor on 2 August. The pertinent clauses were the following:

2 The college may affiliate with the University of British Columbia pursuant to the provisions of the 'British Columbia University Act.'

7 The affairs of the College shall be managed by a Board of Management consisting of not less than five and not more than thirty members, and the following shall constitute the first Board of Management: The Most Reverend William Mark Duke, DD, LLD; the Most Reverend Martin Michael Johnson, DD; the Right Reverend Thomas Melville Nichol, DP; the Very Reverend John Edward Brown; the Very Reverend Henry Carr, CSB, BA, LLD; the Reverend Michael Joseph Oliver, CSB, BA, PHN ... The Board of Management appoints principals, professors etc. The Board of Management can delegate its authority to an Order ... The principal or other head shall be a priest of the Roman Catholic Church or a member of some Roman Catholic teaching order.

15 The Senate of the College shall have power to provide for the granting of and to grant degrees in theology only, including honorary degrees and certificates of proficiency in theology as the Senate may determine.[8]

On 22 March 1956, Archbishop Duke, on the nomination of the superior general of the Basilian Fathers, appointed Carr first principal of St Mark's. On 3 May Carr wrote to MacKenzie asking him to present to the board of governors a request for a site for St Mark's. On 8 July a contract was signed with the Doyle Construction Company for college buildings costing $409,802. On 23 July a formal application for the affiliation of this college was forwarded to the university and was approved by the board on 27 August. The first two units were opened in the fall of 1957: the combined administration and priests' residence wing; and the residence for 50 men and a Newman Centre, now known as Duke Hall. These were located on Chancellor Boulevard and West-brook near Union College. Designed by the local architect, Peter Thornton, they were a handsome addition to the university campus. A third unit, Carr Hall, a combined residence for 53 men and a college library, was added in 1960.

THE AFFILIATED THEOLOGICAL COLLEGE

In contrast with the long period of negotiations, the history of St Mark's as an affiliated college has been peaceful and prosperous, with very little adjustment necessary between administrations. Carr's principal-ship, which began in 1956, continued to the summer of 1961. He opened the second residence unit in 1960. The second unit, only slightly larger than the first, 53 students as against 50, went up in circumstances highly gratifying to Carr and the board in that the university worked out a formula which provided in effect a capital grant towards its construction. The university was anxious to see residences go up, and also wished to be sure that they would be used indefinitely for university students. It 'leased' all rooms in both the original and the new building at the rate of $25.00 a year per student for forty years and paid the lease in advance. It was the payment of this lease in the amount of $103,000 that made the erection of the new building possible. Carr named the residences Durieu and Demers after the first British Colum-bia bishops. Following Carr's death in 1963, the residences were re-named Duke Hall and Carr Hall. Included in the second residence was a college library which was stocked not only with the needs of under-

8 An Act to Incorporate St Mark's College, 2 Mar. 1956, No.47, Legislature of the Province of British Columbia

graduate students in mind but with the development of an appropriate college specialty in the history of the Church and Christian thought.

In 1961 Father Edwin Garvey succeeded Carr as principal of St Mark's. The appointment proved an interesting one for clarifying the relations between the college and the university. Garvey was a distinguished professor of philosophy, having his doctorate from the University of Toronto and having been head of the department of philosophy at Assumption University. There was a presumption that he would be given Allen's university post since Allen was leaving St Mark's for Windsor. The presumption, however, was unfounded; Barnett Savery, head of the department of philosophy, would not recommend the appointment to the president. It was a rather salutary test case, both from the point of view of the liberty of a department head and from that of the general council of the Basilians, who realized that any appointment to St Mark's would require advance extra-canonical negotiations. Garvey remained principal of St Mark's until 1964. He devoted the time he would otherwise have spent in university lecturing to pursuing some of his earlier interests, particularly the notion of education in a pluralist society and the social doctrines of the Church. He lectured in these subjects in Vancouver, Victoria, Nelson, and Kamloops, helping to create a laity willing and ready to assume responsibility for school boards when Archbishop Johnson called on them to save his grade school system. It became apparent that there were unexpected advantages in not having the principal on the university staff. When Father E. Carlisle LeBel succeeded Garvey in 1964, a university appointment for the principal was not even considered.

The buildings at St Mark's do not include a women's residence, a serious gap in the institution since women are otherwise active and prominent in college and Newman Club activities. Carr was always dubious about the wisdom and propriety of a women's residence on the college campus. Apart from his personal misgivings, however, neither the means nor the occasion have yet appeared to erect one. During the pre-incorporation negotiations Carr spoke with more than one mother-general and mother-provincial on the subject, but only on the basis of their coming to the university on the invitation of St Mark's and as a strictly private venture. In 1964, Garvey's last year as principal, 'Yorkeen,' the private home of Stanley S. McKeen at 6251 NW Marine Drive, went on the market and was immediately purchased by St Mark's for a women's residence. It was a large and lovely home about a quarter of a mile from St Mark's. The task of remodelling Yorkeen was more extensive and costly than anticipated. The university was also interested in the mansion and ultimately acquired it at cost. Following this episode, the college regarded itself as more or less committed to a women's residence and planned on locating it, when funds became available, at the north end of its present site. Today priorities are changing, and a women's residence seems unlikely.

St Mark's has through its short history been trying to establish itself effectively into UBC's admittedly complex system of religious education which is constructed around two distinct sequences. The older sequence, provided by denominational colleges, embraces the religious knowledge courses. Traditionally an undergraduate student has been allowed to take one course in religious knowledge, given by a theological college, for credit towards his bachelor's degree. The only exception to this was the undergraduate who indicated that he intended to enter theology upon graduation. Such a pre-theological student could take four religious knowledge courses for credit. In practice, the four-course programme enabled a pre-theological student to cover most of his first-year theology before entering a theological college because many of the religious knowledge options made available to undergraduates were actually professional courses programmed for professional theological students. This did not make for ideal religious knowledge courses for the undergraduates not proceeding to theology – unimportant, perhaps, since they could in any event take only one such course.

As early as 1952 there was a movement afoot in the university to introduce a second sequence in a university department of religion set up along the lines of the 'Iowa Plan.' This was an elaborate plan worked out at the University of Iowa to provide a series of optional, non-denominational courses in religion intended to bring to an end the anomalous situation existing in state universities whereby students were handicapped by the 'exclusion of large bodies of vital importance for their complete understanding of human behaviour and institutions.'[9] The movement to establish a university department of religion at UBC was initiated by the Board of Management of the Alumni Association, which in 1952 appointed a committee to study the matter. On the committee were Mary MacDougall, M.J. Oliver, R.C.S. Ripley, L.W. Shemilt, John Grant, Joseph Brown, Leon Tessler, M.W. Steinberg, and W.G. Black. The committee's recommendations were sent to the president and in 1954 a Senate Committee on Religious Studies was appointed. It was, in fact, the encouraging reception given on all sides to this committee that reconciled Carr to accepting the status of theologi-

9 W.G. Black, 'New Courses in Religious Studies,' UBC *Alumni Chronicle*, 10(spring, 1956), 20–1

cal college for St Mark's. This committee gave as its opinion that the university could, under the UBC act, set up a department of religious studies charged to teach a 'generalized approach to religion' free from any indoctrination. The senate passed a bill to set up such a department, 19 October 1955, and Professor William Nicholls became its head. Through 1955–6 proposed courses were sent before a committee of the new department. Carr submitted for consideration a course in early Christian thought and was thrilled when it was accepted by the committee during August 1957, and later by the curriculum committee of the senate. Carr offered this course, religious studies 305, as a special lecturer during 1957–8 and continued to give it until it was taken over by Francis Firth in 1962.

Thus during the early sixties two kinds of courses were in operation: courses in religious knowledge and courses in religious studies. The former were provided by the theological colleges and were sometimes identical with courses taken by theological students in first-year theology. The latter, courses in religious studies, were provided by the university's department of religious studies and were non-denominational in character.

During LeBel's principalship, 1964–8, an effort was made to develop St Mark's potential both by providing courses within the college leading to the MA in theology, and by obtaining posts for one or more men in the university's department of religion. Accordingly, college courses were given by Francis Firth, Andrew Maloney, Neil Kelly, and others, and a small number of students proceeded to their MA through St Mark's. The maximum of such students registered at the same time has been six; two only were registered during 1968–9, both of whom completed their degree requirements. At the same time, Firth held a part-time appointment in the university's department of religion from 1962–7, turning it over, by arrangement with Nicholls, the department head, to Andrew Maloney for 1967–8 when Firth went to Toronto to complete his doctoral thesis. Maloney and Nicholls fell out several times over curriculum and salary. The following year, 1968–9, after Maloney had gone and Firth returned, the univeristy appointment in religious studies was no longer open. In 1969 Firth transferred from St Mark's to St Joseph's in Edmonton. Prospects for the immediate development of either college courses in theology or university courses in religion are no longer bright.

In some ways, the year 1962–3 was St Mark's best year in university affiliation. Four members of St Mark's staff held university appointments: James Hanrahan and Gareth Poupore in history, Gerald

McGuigan in economics, and Francis Firth in religious studies. The number of appointments steadily declined after 1963: Poupore left for Rochester in the summer of 1963; courses in religious studies were terminated in 1968; Hanrahan was elected assistant superior general of the Basilians at the chapter of 1967 and had to ask in 1968 for indefinite leave of absence; in 1969 McGuigan resigned from the department of economics to take a post in Erindale College of the University of Toronto. During 1969–70 no professor from St Mark's held a university post. The situation was not necessarily permanent. The Hanrahan and McGuigan withdrawals were regretted by all concerned: Hanrahan felt called to fill an immediate need of the Basilian Fathers; McGuigan had carried on so successful a series of experimental programmes and curriculum studies at UBC that his new competence really called for sharing his experience with other Canadian universities. It is likely that when the Basilians have professors of similar competence available, posts will again be found for them in the University of British Columbia, provided of course that St Mark's can survive the present critical years.

It should be stated here with some emphasis that St Mark's has other functions than to provide courses in the University of British Columbia, even though this function constitutes an important privilege and is essential to the particular type of affiliation worked out by Carr and his associates with that university. First among these 'other functions' has been, until 1970, the conducting of residences for 103 Catholic students in the university, residences which have now been sold to the university. St Mark's also operates a large and reasonably successful Newman Centre for the Catholic students on the campus; it provides a limited amount of theological instruction within the college as well as in certain non-university institutions in Vancouver. Highly important is the fact that St Mark's is a *domus formata*, a Basilian religious house, in which Basilians not on the university staff also live and from which they carry on their special apostolates: Michael J. Oliver, for example, has used St Mark's as his base in chaplaining convents, establishing a parish and Newman house in Calgary, editing the British Columbia *Catholic Directory*; and David Bauer has carried on from this same base his unique and important work as coach of the Olympic hockey team in 1964, and active member ever since of the Canadian National Hockey Executive and the National Advisory Council on Fitness and Amateur Sports. These and other members of St Mark's, like Neil Kelly and Carlisle LeBel, have in addition to administering a busy operation, taken on programmes of pastoral, ecumenical, and adult education in the Vancouver area. It remains to be seen, however, whether the Basilians of St Mark's will be able to return to posts in the University of British Columbia or maintain their present operation as a viable apostolate. It would seem that they must do so if the college is to continue its most distinctive and experimental academic character – a theological college which uses other than formal programmes in theology to keep Christian wisdom relevant on the campus of a provincial university.

By 1968 it became clear to LeBel that the principalship of St Mark's at its present stage of development ought to be filled by a trained theologian, which he was not. He resigned as principal, though not as superior of the religious house, and was succeeded by Robert Finn, former professor of philosophy and theology at St Thomas More, Saskatoon, who was regional representative for western Canada on the general council of the Basilian Fathers. Since such significant Basilian appointments as regional representative and college principal were not usually made concurrently, Finn's going to St Mark's appeared to mean that an emergency situation had arisen and that the Basilians were planning to phase out the operation.

There was ground to suspect an emergency, for although St Mark's had been a challenging experiment in many areas of college administration it had been particularly so in the economic. In no Canadian city of the importance of Vancouver had Catholics achieved comparable results for so many students at so little expense. There were 593 Catholic students in the University of British Columbia in 1954 (268 in arts and science, 79 in engineering, 42 in commerce, 42 in graduate studies); there were 700 in 1956, 900 in 1957, when the Hungarian Sopron University set up its school of forestry; there were 1300 in 1958, 1425 in 1963, and about 2000 in 1969. In good years, better than 50 per cent of these Catholics were reached through the university courses, the Newman Centre, and the specialized library. During 1969, when the classroom was removed as a factor, perhaps 25 per cent were reached. The total outlay of capital by the archdiocese for university education had been approximately $250,000 (raised in 1956 in a general campaign for Catholic education which grossed $1,250,000). The debt of over $250,000 still remaining on the buildings in 1969 was the responsibility of the board of management; the interest on this debt ($23,000 a year) was paid by the Basilians of St Mark's out of their normal income, that is, out of university salaries, room and board of residents, club dues, and casual income. The Catholic constituency in Vancouver had not had to over-extend itself to carry on its university experiment.

On the other hand, if UBC had been 'tough' on St Mark's in the area of administrative negotiation, it had been generous in sharing its public funds through the land lease, rental subsidy for residences, and payment of salaries to priests for university courses.

Finn's principalship opened with a major renewal of policy: the board decided to give up its residences and to focus attention upon the college's other presences on the campus. Thus during 1970 the two Catholic residence halls were sold to the university to house its departments of urban affairs and extension. The college realized from the sale approximately $548,000, enough to liquidate its debts to the bank and to the university, which had subsidized the residences at the time of their erection, to cover the cost of re-modelling the main administration building which it retained, and to allocate the somewhat meagre sum of $60,000 to establish an endowment fund.[10]

In spite of this retrenchment, the college operation, consisting of a Catholic student centre, a theological programme aimed at the total university community, and a catechetical programme for the Vancouver archdiocese remains valid. If plans go through, it will collaborate with the other church colleges at UBC to establish a Vancouver School of Theology. All of which means that it would be a mistake on the part of university and ecclesiastical administrators to set aside lightly the basic structure created in 1956. It may well be the enduring pattern in university affiliations.

10 *The Basilian Intercom*, 1, no. 2(1970), 1

Seminary of Christ the King

MISSION CITY

1931 (1951, 1966)

The Seminary of Christ the King, under the direction of the Benedictines of Westminster Abbey, Mission City, BC, is both a major and a minor seminary devoted exclusively to candidates for the priesthood, especially from the archdiocese of Vancouver and from the Benedictines. In the minor seminary, a programme in arts and philosophy is provided, in the major seminary a full programme in theology. The seminary grants bachelor's degrees in arts and theology.

The Seminary of Christ the King was opened as a minor seminary by William Mark Duke, the archbishop of Vancouver, in Ladner, BC, 31 October 1931. The seminary was at first only a high school, but plans called for a seminary of philosophy, and even in due time a major theological seminary. Duke named as first rector of Christ the King, Francis Chaloner, an English priest who had come out to Canada to work in Vancouver. Also appointed were J.P. Kane as bursar and a staff of two or three other priests. In the first year of operation, 1931–2, 18 students of high school age were enrolled.

Throughout the next eight years, during which the seminary remained under diocesan direction, Chaloner was the only rector; there were, however, frequent changes among the other members of the staff. The student body reached 31 in 1934 but dropped to 26 in 1935, and remained at about that number until the coming of the Benedictines.

In 1939 Chaloner was transferred to the chaplaincy of St Paul's Hospital in Vancouver. At the same time Archbishop Duke invited the Benedictines of the Swiss-American congregation, who were at St Benedict's Abbey, Mount Angel, Oregon, to send a small group of men to start a foundation in his archdiocese and to take over the operation of his seminary. This group came to Ladner and conducted the seminary there for one year. Cyril Lebold was superior of the house, and Eugene Medved, one of his able associates, became the new rector of the seminary.

The following year the Benedictines set up their priory in New Westminster as a dependent of Mount Angel. At the same time they acquired in their own name a property at 3912 Deer Lake Avenue, adjacent to the priory, and moved the seminary from Ladner to New Westminster. Medved remained rector for a time, but became more and more immersed in monastic affairs. In 1944 he was succeeded as seminary rector by Luke Eberle. At this time the student body of the seminary was 46 and there were seven professors.

On 1 June 1948, the priory, in view of a papal rescript, became an independent conventual priory with Eugene Medved as first conventual prior. In 1950 Wilfred Sowerby replaced Eberle as rector of the seminary and was to hold that office until 1969. Medved and Sowerby have shaped the course of monastery and seminary. These two men opened a major seminary division of Christ the King in 1951, providing for a full programme of theology. The double seminary had now a staff of ten and a student body of 65. These numbers were to continue mounting until in the early sixties, the staff increased to 14, the student body to 93.

On 12 February 1953, the priory became Westminster Abbey, with Eugene Medved as first abbot. In 1954, the year after Westminster became an abbey, the Benedictines again moved both monastery and seminary, this time to its present location at Mission City, 45 miles inland from Vancouver, along the Fraser River. Sowerby became prior at this time, but remained rector of the seminary. He was given some relief in 1957 when Placidus Sander was given the directorship of the minor seminary and Augustine Kalberer became subprior of the abbey and vice-rector of the major seminary.

The seminary had good years under Sowerby but was constantly – as was St Mark's at the same time and for the same reason – frustrated by the unreceptive attitude of the government's department of education towards post-secondary colleges outside the university. In 1966, however, the breakthrough came, and on 1 April an act giving Christ the King a limited charter, that is, one empowering it to grant the bachelor of arts degree and degrees in theology, received royal assent. Unfortunately this development coincided with the decline of enrolment which was afflicting Christ the King as all other seminaries, but it has opened possibilities for hopeful long-range planning.

In August 1969, Sowerby was replaced as rector of Christ the King by the vice-rector, Augustine Kalberer. It is the intention of Augustine, and of the new coadjutor archbishop of Vancouver, James Carney, to take every step necessary to adjust the seminary to the changing times and to renew it as a shaping force in the Church of Vancouver.

Christ the King, as a seminary, has its distinctive characteristics among the institutions of English-speaking Canada. These flow in some special way from its association with the Benedictines. It is deeply dedicated to liturgy, to Christian creative art, and to church music – the areas of special competence of Eugene Medved, Dunstan Massey, and Basil Foote respectively. It faces the uncertain future armed with fine traditions in these important areas. It is Augustine's resolve, and Carney's too, to place emphasis in the days ahead on professional planning and scholarship.

Notre Dame University of Nelson

NELSON

1950

Notre Dame University of Nelson is located in the eastern interior of British Columbia where it serves primarily, though neither exclusively nor mostly, students from the Kootenays and from the Okanagan Valley. It occupies about 60 acres on 10th Street between Davies Street and Gordon Road at the edge of Nelson. The university offers three degree programmes: one to the BA and BSC through a general course with major subjects in a fully established faculty of Arts and Sciences; one to the BED in elementary or in secondary education; one to the BSC in Medical Record Library Science. Present buildings on the campus include Patinaude (formerly Bonaventure) Hall, an administration and classroom building which was put up in two stages, the first during 1953–4, the second during 1959–60; La Salette Hall, originally a men's but now a women's residence built in 1955–6; two men's residences, St Martin's Hall, 1961, and McCarthy Hall, 1964; and a large dining lounge, auditorium, and facilities building, Maryhall, opened in 1964. A library and science building opened during 1965–6. The present buildings and property are valued at about $3,500,000. They are located near the base of lovely Mount St Francis and overlook the west arm of Lake Kootenay.

JOHNSON, CARTIER, AND ROYCE

The initial step in the founding of Notre Dame, Nelson, was taken in the spring of 1950 by Bishop Martin M. Johnson. Johnson came to Nelson as its first bishop in 1936. During the forties he followed with interest the struggle of Archbishop Duke of Vancouver to establish either a college in the University of British Columbia or an independent Catholic university. Although he had become aware of the hurdles to be taken in founding a college in British Columbia, he was also aware, as the president of the University of British Columbia and the minister of education were not, that Canada had to have such foundations. In his own diocese it was possible and inexpensive for students to attend college in Spokane, and as many were going to the United States as were going to Vancouver. The best of those who went across the border did not come back. Some of Gonzaga University's most distinguished graduates were Kootenay boys, and most of them are now American citizens. Johnson wanted at the very least to keep his Canadian vocations in the country, so he set his mind on having a local Catholic college regardless of whether Vancouver approved or Victoria granted it a charter. In the spring of 1950 Johnson was looking for a staff. He got no encouragement from the over-committed religious orders and decided to recruit laymen. He interviewed one young Canadian couple, John and Mary Wilson, who that year were at Cambridge University. Their willingness to come to Nelson when John completed his doctorate inspired the bishop to get his college opened; he wanted to have something started when they were ready to join him. With this in mind he lined up Albert L. Cartier and Father Peter D'Aoust, who had been teaching at Wilcox, Saskatchewan.

Cartier had been a Christian Brother. He was a graduate of the University of Toronto and had his master's degree in philosophy. He had taught successfully as a brother in the University of Alberta, and as a layman at Notre Dame of Saskatchewan. He had by this time acquired some very definite ideas about what was needed in Catholic higher education. It should be rooted in the humanities; it should focus upon the person of man; it should eschew sectarianism, seeking to be known as Christian rather than as Catholic; and it should cultivate, not merely tolerate, adult education. Cartier was aggressive in his methods, a leader rather than a disciple. He had not got along well with Athol Murray in Wilcox but hoped to do better with Johnson, who seemed willing to give him a free hand.

During the summer of 1950 the opening of Notre Dame was announced and the appointment of Cartier as its dean. Cartier spent the summer at Lourdes Camp near Nelson helping with the leadership courses provided by the diocese for its boys and girls. It took some courage on his part to assume the active headship of an impoverished college with little prospect of attracting good students and with no legal academic existence, whether by incorporation, charter, or affiliation. What appealed to Cartier, as to the Wilsons, was the missionary character of the undertaking.

Cartier's plan was to begin with first-year arts only, and to have his students write British Columbia's grade XIII examinations. This would look after one year's accreditation. He would add second-year arts as soon as some kind of affiliation could be obtained. His thinking did not go beyond a two-year programme following which students would complete their course elsewhere. By this time, they would be thinking men and committed Christians.[1]

Notre Dame opened on 6 September 1950, with eleven students in attendance, in Choquette's unoccupied bakery building. Johnson was its real, if unofficial, head. He asked the rector of the cathedral, Father W. Harrison, to be general superintendent and advisor of the college (*The Prospector*, 8 September 1950), and he named Cartier its dean. Cartier and Father D'Aoust did all the teaching. The first year of operation was a disaster. The students were provided with one kind of programme, in line with Cartier's convictions about Catholic education, and they were examined by the department of education on the basis of another. The experience considerably shook the bishop's confidence in his dean.

Cartier worked with Johnson for the next three years. During 1951–2 two more teachers, Martin L. Brown and John Thomas, joined the staff, but the Wilsons decided not to come. The academic situation of the 24 students now in attendance was rescued when Gonzaga University in Spokane granted Notre Dame affiliation, recognizing its first two years and permitting its students to transfer to the Spokane campus for their third and fourth years. Johnson and Cartier would have preferred affiliation with the University of British Columbia or Ottawa. The University of British Columbia, which they approached first, would not consider it, and Ottawa could only refuse under the circumstances. In the meantime, the college was moved to the more spacious diocesan hall on Mill Street. In this second year of operation, 92 per cent of the grade XIII papers written by Notre Dame students were passed.

Something of the nature of Cartier's ideas can be seen from an episode related by Henry Carr in a letter to E.J. McCorkell, 16 January 1952.[2] Carr had not yet founded St Mark's, but he was already on the staff of the University of British Columbia. Cartier had sent Carr a 150-word telegram stating that his college enrolment in Nelson was only 21 and that he wished to improve the situation of the college by offering during the coming summer a leadership course for teachers. Takers were available, probably more than 100 of them, if academic credit were forthcoming. Teachers of the area were most anxious to improve their standing with the department of education. Would Father Carr

1 The missionary side of Cartier is clear from accounts of the founding of Notre Dame in *The Prospector*, Nelson's Catholic weekly. See *The Prospector*, 15 June 1950, and subsequent issues. *The Prospector* is the best bibliographical reference for the history of Notre Dame.

2 Carr to McCorkell, 16 Jan. 1952, Archives of the Basilian Fathers, Toronto

speak to President MacKenzie and to the registrar, Mr Wood, about having Gonzaga credits recognized also by the University of British Columbia? Carr told McCorkell that he saw no chance of Cartier's request being sent on to the university senate with a recommendation. But MacKenzie and Wood were worried by it. The establishment of Notre Dame and Duke's threat to open a Holy Rosary College in Vancouver were 'annoyances to the university' which, Carr went on, 'strengthened my position here, and favour something like a Catholic college at the University.' Notre Dame's struggle for existence and recognition was part of a general move for some kind of Catholic education at the higher level in the province.

During Cartier's third year in Nelson, 1952–3, Notre Dame won its first concession from the provincial authorities when Premier Bennett placed its name on the list of British Columbia institutions eligible to receive federal grants. Robert Edward Sommers, later minister of lands and forests, took up the cause which Johnson and Cartier were pressing hard, and succeeded, over the objections of MacKenzie, in getting the premier's approval.

During 1953–4, Bishop Johnson opened a campaign for $400,000. This was a large amount to seek by public appeal in Nelson; and the bishop would likely not have risked it except that he had learned privately that the estate of Mr Rintoul would likely come to the diocese for educational purposes. The diocese acquired the present forest property at the outskirts of Nelson; and Cartier, the staff, and the students themselves erected temporary living quarters and the first wing of the present administration and classroom building. Throughout this busy year classes continued to be held in the cathedral hall in the centre of Nelson, with staff and students constantly commuting between campus and classrooms.

It was the success of the diocesan campaign which was the cause of Cartier's leaving the college. He had worked hard at a low salary and felt that he was entitled to direct how the new money should be spent. He had also recently been part of a co-operative housing project in Nelson and had come to fancy himself as perhaps a better financier than the bishop was willing to concede. At any rate, Cartier and some other members of the staff submitted their resignations over the matter of the disposition of the campaign funds, an action which threatened the very existence of the college and which was a serious embarrassment to the bishop. The college was kept alive by the kindness of the Jesuits of Gonzaga, who released Father James Royce to run Notre Dame during 1954–5.

Royce had academic status and experience. He was quite happy to
come to Notre Dame for a year because he hoped he might find leisure
to complete a textbook in psychology on which he had been working
for several years. Though Notre Dame was in a sense only his secondary
interest, it owed its survival to him. He was able to cope with the faculty
crisis because he was able to find substitute teachers. Moreover, he
brought to the institution awareness of the meaning of university standards. In Royce's short term as rector – he preferred this traditional
Jesuit designation of his office – less attention was given to construction by student labour and to the missionary aspects of college education and more to the integrity of a college curriculum. Two buildings
were begun during 1954–5: a men's residence and a chapel. The end of
the year brought a complete change of administration: in May 1955
Bishop Johnson was named auxiliary archbishop of Vancouver, and
Royce returned to his American province.

MCCARTHY, GALLAGHER, AND SMITH

Bishop Thomas Joseph McCarthy came to Nelson in the fall of 1955.
He had been a successful teacher at St Peter's Seminary, London, and
had spent his last few months arranging for the opening of Christ the
King College in the University of Western Ontario, having already
been designated its first dean. He was, from the point of view of the
struggling young college, an ideal appointment to Nelson. He took the
college, financially and academically, completely into his own hands.
He kept an office in the college, was to be found in it every day, and
was in fact principal and president as well as chancellor. He brought
Father John (Jack) Gallagher from Montreal as dean. Gallagher lasted
one year. A year later McCarthy got Father Lawrence Smith to take
over. This arrangement worked rather well. McCarthy wanted to run
the college, and Smith, a victim of painful ulcers, had in any case to live
as a partial invalid. The new regime differed from the preceding (and
from today's) in that McCarthy had both understanding of and sympathy for the principle of affiliation, and he feared that an autonomous
college in Nelson was not really viable. He made it his objective to com-
bine economy and standards in a small institution. Coming to the
diocese in the wake of a successful campaign, he was committed to new
buildings, yet was in no position to seek new funds for a few years. He
worked hard himself and was reconciled to a two-year programme and
to the Gonzaga affiliation. This was practical economy but made the
assembling of a strong faculty almost impossible; and the prestige of
the college, like its enrolment, remained too low. Only in McCarthy's

last year as bishop of Nelson did college affairs begin to show the kind of improvement that has been gaining momentum ever since. The new wing, Bonaventure Hall, which was to provide overall classroom and residence accommodation for 240 students, was begun in 1958; and a board of advisors was established to broaden policies and increase public support. By the beginning of 1958–9, McCarthy's last autumn in Nelson, there were stirrings of the new vitality of the sixties.

DOYLE AND AQUINAS THOMAS

On 9 November 1958, McCarthy was appointed first bishop of St Catharines, and he left Nelson before the end of the month. On 10 December, Wilfred Emmett Doyle was installed as bishop of Nelson. By the following autumn, 1959, Father Aquinas Thomas came to Notre Dame with the appointment of rector. Doyle was prepared to raise large sums of money for the college, and the new rector to introduce revolutionary policies.

Aquinas Thomas was a member of the Franciscan Fathers of the Atonement. He had made his seminary course in New York State and taken his licence in theology, his master's degree, and his doctorate in psychology at the Catholic University of America. His first interest in coming to Canada in 1957 was the introducing of modern methods into the missions serving the Indians of the Columbia River valley. In 1959 he accepted for one year only 'the invitation of Bishop Doyle to head Notre Dame College.' The story after 1959 became one of the rapid expansion of a two-year junior college into a Catholic university of the kind better known in the United States than Canada.

The expansionary policies became evident in 1961 when a large new men's residence, St Martin's Hall, named for Martin Johnson, was opened; the former men's residence, built back in 1955–6, was now converted to a women's residence and re-named La Salette Hall. Until this time women students had lived in private homes in Nelson. In the same year, 1961, the academic programme was extended to cover third- and fourth-year arts, and the affiliation was transferred from Gonzaga to St Francis Xavier University. From the national point of view this was a significant change. Authorities at Gonzaga expressed regret at the transfer but had resisted any earlier move in Nelson to add the higher college years. The St Francis Xavier affiliation was short-lived as the British Columbia legislature, in a complete reversal of long-standing policies, began to grant new university charters. Simon Fraser, then still to be built in Burnaby, Victoria College on Vancouver Island, and Notre Dame in Nelson, were each given autonomous university status. Notre Dame became at the same time Notre Dame of Nelson. Under the charter of 1963, Aquinas Thomas became the first president of Notre Dame University of Nelson.

The university charter of 1963 increased the tempo of expansionary policy. In 1964 a second men's residence, McCarthy Hall, and a large facilities and dining building, Maryhall, were opened. Plans for still other buildings were already on the draughting board in readiness for the flow of students from the United States and other parts of Canada. By 1966, Notre Dame had 455 students enrolled, 90 per cent of them residential and 47 per cent non-Catholic. By 1968 this number was 541. Enquiries about admission to the university became very numerous; in 1966 they were in excess of 1100. This phenomenal increase was accounted for by the employment of an active development officer, by uninvolved and perhaps inadequately scrutinized admission requirements at the junior matriculation level, by increased academic offerings. Another real factor was the unusual kind of publicity which accompanied the announcement in 1964 that the Canadian Amateur Ski Association had selected Notre Dame University as the home of the Canadian National Ski Team. Later, Notre Dame became the assembly point of the summer ski camps. Both NDU and the ski team achieved distinction in 1967 when Nancy Greene won the first world cup in skiing. The team remained at Nelson until 1969 when the headquarters were transferred to Montreal and the academic arrangements for skiers were phased out. Notre Dame also initiated in 1964 the policy (the first Canadian university to do so openly) of giving full-time athletic scholarships. The first student to graduate on such a policy was Murray Owen, who got his BA in October 1967.

The university at first operated under a provincial act passed in 1963. This act provided for a chancellor and vice-chancellor, the bishop and vicar general of the diocese respectively. Notre Dame thus became one of the few universities in Canada to retain the office of vice-chancellor as distinct from that of president. Appointing a diocesan official to the vice-chancellorship strengthened the role of the diocese in the operation of the university. Probably it over-strengthened it. At least an amendment to the act was passed in 1965 which reduced the power of the bishop over the board of governors. The governors were originally named by the chancellor, but the board now became a self-continuing body with power to name the president, all officers of the university, and most of the advisory board. By a still later amendment, passed in 1968, the bishop, though *ex officio* on the board, was no longer *ex officio* chancellor. This office was opened to any member of the board, and was to be held for three years. Unusual in the act was the failure to provide for a senate or its equivalent. Academic matters were divided between a university council and the board of governors itself. The board conferred academic degrees, including honorary degrees. During 1967, when students were pressuring for representation, two were placed on the board of advisors, and one or two on most major university committees. No student was placed on the board of governors.

The academic divisions were as follows. First, a faculty of arts and science offering major and general programmes to the BA and B SC, but no honours courses. Second, a school of education which since 1964 has provided fully-accredited teacher-training programmes for both elementary and secondary school teachers. These programmes were four and five years in duration, respectively, from junior matriculation and lead to the B ED degree. The school of education was not a distinct and separate faculty and many of its courses were provided by the faculty of arts and science. Third, there was established a paramedical programme in medical records library science, leading to a four-year B SC degree, with the third year spent in hospital internship. This course was experimental, being the only library science degree course of its kind offered in Canada. Fourth, there were several two-year pre-professional and diploma courses designed for students planning to go to other universities for professional training.

During 1964–5 Aquinas Thomas, with the support of Dean D.F. Larder, instituted in the higher years an imaginatively worked out seminar-tutorial system of study. Designed to stimulate depth in individual investigation, interdepartmental study, and a taste for intellectual experiment and discovery, it vitalized academic life. Notre Dame, with small upper classes, was at the ideal stage for such development. Moreover, seminar-tutorials compensated for the shortage of fully-trained and experienced teaching personnel, an acute situation then as now. Of a total faculty of 42 in 1965, some eighteen were pre-masters, a mere half dozen post-doctoral. On the other hand, the faculty displayed a remarkable diversity of background; in a total of eight priests, three orders and several dioceses were represented; four religious sisters came from three different orders; and the staff, young and green by some standards, represented most Canadian universities and other centres like Harvard, Exeter, Louvain, Cardiff, Rome, and Paris.

More than most Catholic institutions in Canada, Notre Dame of Nelson gives evidence of careful knowledgeable planning. Every aspect of its operation and evaluation has been schematized by the president for examination and comment by staff and students. Such a document goes far towards removing vast areas of procedural and technical ignorance which tend to handicap university teachers in the presence of their colleagues on the administration.

Notre Dame of Nelson is still only on the point of entering its stabilizing period and can only be examined and judged as a new institution. Until 1964 it gave no degrees; its commencements before that date were strictly ceremonial. The first real convocation was held in 1964 when seven candidates were given degrees – six BAS and one BSC. The convocation of 1965 was a significant and gala affair. Eight candidates (six for the BA, two for the BSC) received earned degrees, and two honorary degrees were conferred, one on Premier W.A.C. Bennett, whose government chartered the university, the other on Archbishop Martin Johnson, who founded it. By 1968, 45 candidates received their bachelor's degrees.

The new university has problems in three areas; its local constituency, its faculty, its finances. The first problem is difficult only in that it is almost intangible. Local students make up only ten per cent of the enrolment; the city of Nelson is indifferent and many Nelson students try to go away to college; and a strong Trail-Nelson rivalry constantly threatens to produce another college in the area. A junior college for the Okanagan valley opened in 1968. Geographical jealousy and local indifference are accentuated by the religious commitment of Notre Dame, and especially by its name. The university ought to be called the University of Kootenay, or of Eastern British Columbia, or of the Rockies. The 'Notre Dame' image comes to Canada laden with overtones of athletic prowess and Catholic triumphalism, both of which militate against unqualified acceptance by the general public. Granting these problems, Notre Dame has contributed in depth to local development in eastern BC.

The second problem is qualifying and retaining the faculty. This problem is being squarely faced. Salaries are being brought into line, though they are not yet good. A compulsory sabbatical programme was introduced by Aquinas Thomas to assure that the teacher with only a BA would go on sabbatical leave with half salary after three years service; that one with only an MA would return to studies after five years; and that the professor with his PHD would be allowed to take a sabbatical after five and would have to do so after eight years. During 1964–5 five faculty members were on sabbatical leave, and a total of eleven had by that time taken advantage of the arrangement. Staff security is further strengthened by group insurance and a compulsory pension plan. Improving library facilities are now also making it possible for a faculty man to increase his competence during the academic year. It will, however, remain difficult to hold highly qualified men until graduate programmes are under way.

The final problem, financing, is a grave one in Nelson. The university enjoys the regular government grants but is without adequate operating grants. These must come or the university will have eventually to cut back. Bishop and president are taking extraordinary steps to find *ad hoc* funds. During 1964–5, for example, they raised enough money to permit the library to spend $100,000 on the purchase of books alone, exclusive of salaries and overhead. Such extraordinary efforts, however, must become the rule, and for this the overall pace must be accelerated. Projected in the autumn of 1965 was the first phase (for 1200 students) of a large seven-storey library building, to be completed in three stages. The first phase was to start within a year but had to be delayed because of the cost. Instead a series of temporary buildings were erected in 1967 and they house the 50,000 volume collection. Completed in the meantime is a second women's residence, called Marianne Hall. A residence is revenue-producing, but the library is not. Pertinent statistics record the rising scale of costs. More than in the case of any other Catholic institution in Canada, the signs point inevitably to Notre Dame of Nelson following within a short time the precedent set by Assumption and Ottawa. It is preparing for such an event by pointing out from time to time its non-denominational character. When, for example, in 1968, the announcement came out that the bishop of Nelson was no longer *ex officio* chancellor, the editor of *University Affairs* reported that the university had taken another step 'to shed the image of a private Catholic college.'[3] In the spring of 1969 Hugh L. Keenleyside became chancellor, replacing Bishop Doyle, whose term expired at the end of 1968. Keenleyside had been a member of the board of UBC. On accepting the chancellorship of Notre Dame he expressed the opinion that government money should no longer be spent on expanding a developed university like UBC but on smaller, weaker institutions like Notre Dame. Many think he was forecasting government policy, which they see taking shape in the announcement made in 1969 that Notre Dame is one member of the consortium of six universities taking over the federal government's Queen Elizabeth telescope project at Mount Koban, a transfer calling for the spending of $10,000,000 by the consortium to complete the project. At the end of the 1968–9 academic year, Aquinas Thomas resigned from office and D.F. Larder, the dean of studies, became acting president. Aquinas

3 *University Affairs*, vol.10, no.2 (1968), 23

Thomas joined the department of religion at King's College, London. Larder carried on until 30 June 1970 when the presidency was taken over by Dr R.L. Kaller, head of the department of mathematics on the Regina campus of the University of Saskatchewan. Kaller's acceptance of the Nelson post was contingent upon his not taking over until January 1971. During the last six months of 1970 Notre Dame operated without a president, even an acting one. The executive of the board of governors conducted the business of the university as a day-to-day operation tended by the dean of studies, the business manager, and the treasurer of the university.

𝔓rince 𝔊eorge 𝔆ollege

PRINCE GEORGE

1963

Prince George College is a junior college, located in north-central British Columbia, serving some 50,000 people and authorized by its provincial incorporation to provide tuition in the first two years of arts and science. For their final years students may transfer to the University of British Columbia where they are given credit for their first two years' work after successful completion of their third year. The college plant consists of a combined high school and college building of modern construction, of an auditorium and gymnasium and of several hostel-type student residences. The complex, although small, is new and attractive, and has attached to it a large property of some 3000 acres on College Road (Highway 16) at the west end of Prince George. The buildings and land have a value of about $1,000,000.

The college is part of a large active missionary project of bishop John Fergus O'Grady, vicar apostolic of Prince Rupert, a project which has drawn volunteer workers from among university graduates across Canada.

The college has evolved with local Catholic education. During the late 1950s the incipient college consisted only of a small high school section located in the Sacred Heart parish school. In 1960 the high school was moved to the St Mary's parish school, which was larger. In 1963 it was given its own building on Highway 16 and the small college division was added. During the first full year of operation, 1964–5, Prince George College had 35 students enrolled, some of them Indians: there were six students in first-year arts, five in second. The high school and college had a staff of eight: two Oblates (Edward Green, principal, and L. MacLennan) three sisters of St Ann, and three lay teachers. Vincent Vychinis, PHD Chicago, was the most highly qualified professor. In June 1968, because of low registration, the college activity was suspended. Circumstances will determine whether and when it will reopen.

The arts or college division when established had no affiliation of any kind, and no real commitment to recognize its instruction from any chartered institution. The establishment, however, was not foolhardy; it was simply called for by the special conditions obtaining in the missionary vicariate: the need to serve a pioneer community, the conviction that even university education falls within the broad scope of a missionary programme, the desire to raise the sights of Canada's Indian population. Prince George is not intended to replace the university but to orientate a section of society towards the university. The pattern of northern universities has been accepted in Ontario; the future will no doubt see the same pattern extended to other Canadian northlands.

The college itself is a bishop's college. O'Grady is the president and chairman of the non-denominational board on which the faculty has representation; and all lay members on the board are non-Catholic. The board's power is at present nominal. It has been anticipated, however, especially if and when the incorporation obtained from the province, 26 March 1966, becomes a full degree-conferring charter, that the real power would lie with the board. In the meantime, Bishop O'Grady has no intention of undertaking to finance a university. His suspending the operation may well only mean that he has thus far been thinking a little ahead of his time.

V
DIRECTIONS

CONTEMPORARY DIRECTIONS

The preceding chronicles deal with the establishment and growth of those Canadian institutions which can today be fairly described as either Catholic universities or Catholic university colleges. What is the future of such institutions? Are they to remain church-related? And if so what is to be the character of their church-relationship? Will those that survive become public rather than private institutions? Or indeed are they already public institutions? And should the state take, or be given, more responsibility for them than at present? Is their contribution to the higher education of Canadian Catholics or to the advancement of scholarship worth the sacrifice necessary to maintain them? These and similar questions call for investigation and comment, by way of conclusion to the historical survey.

CHURCH-RELATIONSHIP

Church-relationship in the sense of general church policy towards universities and university colleges has changed considerably during the century and a half which spans their composite life. At the beginning of this period, that is, from 1820 to 1870, the Church felt that all non-Catholic universities were hostile to the Catholic religion: the Protestant universities as themselves denominational and sectarian strongholds, the secular as the propaganda arm of militant liberalism and atheism. The statement of the Canadian bishops, made at the First Council of Quebec in 1851, on the subject of 'mixed schools,' strikes a harsh and controversial tone:

Mixed schools are those into which Catholic and non-Catholic boys are admitted indiscriminately, and in which they are taught either no religion at all or false religion. We (the bishops of British North America) regard such schools as entirely dangerous in that they foster the spread of irreverence or, as it is commonly called, indifference. Hence we earnestly ask pastors of souls to direct the faithful entrusted to their care away from these schools.

Where boys must attend mixed schools because no Catholic schools exist, pastors and parents should see to it that their boys do not slowly absorb the poison of error to the detriment of their faith and innocence.

Let us, the bishops, be alert that Catholics of this ecclesiastical province retain their right to their own schools, colleges and universities.

Let us take special pains to have a teachers' college or normal school to form teachers of sound doctrine and good morals.[1]

Some softening of this attitude appeared in Canada during the seventies. In the Maritimes it took the very moderate form of collaboration in the University of Halifax;[2] in Toronto it became the now historic negotiations between J.R. Teefy and the University of Toronto for a federated theological college.[3] Depending upon the point of view, these instances, and particularly the latter, were either a victory over prejudice or a compromise with evil. Neither the Halifax nor the Toronto experiment, however, was thought of as a concession to the mixed school.

Federation and affiliation of Catholic university colleges became a controversial issue. Many of the bishops were not sure about it at all. Bishop Michael Fallon criticized federation in 1916, but changed his mind about it in 1919.[4] Bishop Morrison of Antigonish 'exiled' Jimmie Tompkins for promoting it too vigorously[5] and succeeded in 1922 in extracting a condemnation of the principle from the maritime hierarchy. When Morrison consulted the Roman Congregation on the matter in 1923, he was given the opinion that affiliation with a Protestant university should be discouraged but not affiliation with a state university. Later in the same decade the Congregation approved of St Mary's seeking affiliation with Dalhousie.[6]

There was little real softening of the Roman attitude towards mixed schools before 1929. Pius XI writes as follows in his encyclical on the *Christian Education of Youth*: 'Let no one say that in a nation where there are different religious beliefs, it is impossible to provide for public instruction otherwise than by neutral or mixed schools.'[7] He had not in mind here either to praise or blame the affiliating of university colleges. He wished rather to insist that history has shown that it is possible for the Church to create great Christian schools in any age and under varying circumstances and that the prospect of the Church's having her own Christian schools today should not be abandoned.

A change even towards mixed schools seems to have come after 1929,

1 *Acta et decreta primi concilii provinciae Quebecensis, 1851*, Quebec: Aug. Côté, 1852, Decretum xv, 'De scholis mixtis,' 63
2 See above, 162, 78–9 3 See above, 141–4
4 See above, 29, 282, 299 5 See above, 87
6 See above, 66–7
7 Pius XI, *Christian Education of Youth*, 31 Dec. 1929, in *Four Great Encyclicals*, The Paulist Press: New York, n.d., 64

that is, after the pact with Mussolini and the publication of *Deus scientiarum Dominus*,[8] possibly because the pact did not disapprove of Italy's state universities and because the apostolic constitution created confidence in the ultimate sufficiency for the Church's need of the rather select group of pontifical universities *in urbe* reformed and re-established by the new sacred constitution.

A spectacular change of outlook has been apparent since Vatican II, 1962–5. The council's Declaration on Christian Education, although faithful to the conviction that Catholic schools and universities should where possible be maintained, seems to take for granted that many schools will in fact be mixed. It speaks of the school as establishing a centre engaging 'the joint participation of families, teachers, various kinds of cultural, civic and religious groups, civil society and the entire human community.' Again, in speaking of the Church's obligations to the moral and religious education of the young: 'To those large numbers of them who are being trained in schools which are not Catholic, she needs to be present with her special affection.' It speaks of the Church's 'cordial esteem for those Catholic schools ... which contain large numbers of non-Catholic students.' Special thought, sympathetic and hopeful, is given to other than Catholic institutions: 'In their care for the religious development of all their sons, bishops should take appropriate counsel together and see to it that at colleges and universities which are not Catholic residences and centres where priests, religious, and laymen who have been judiciously chosen and trained can serve as on-campus sources of spiritual and intellectual assistance to young college people. Whether they attend a college or university which is Catholic or otherwise, young people of special ability who appear suited for teaching and research should be trained with particular care and urged to undertake a teaching career.'[9]

There was held in Rome during April 1969, under the aegis of the re-organized Congregation for Catholic Education (formerly the Congregation of Seminaries and Universities) an international congress of Catholic universities. The congress prepared an important position paper which is a sort of semi-official statement of what the Catholic universities of the world now consider themselves to be in relation to

8 *Deus scientiarum dominus*, an apostolic constitution issued 24 May 1931, and promulgated in the *Acta Apostolicae Sedis* of July of the same year. The purpose of the constitution was to strengthen the pontifical universities by establishing in detail statutes covering standards of admission, instruction and examining of students, competence of professors, and economic and administrative stability.

9 *Gravissimum educationis*, 10: see W.M. Abbott and Joseph Gallagher, *The Documents of Vatican II*, New York: Association Press, 1966, 649.

one another, to secular universities, to governments, and to the institutional church.

Among many positions adopted by the delegates to the congress were the following:

1 That the Catholic university is a true university, that is, an institution located at the centre of society for research and teaching at the highest level.

2 That the specification or special dimension 'Catholic' is not inconsistent with the nature of the university as such (being comparable to such specifications as 'state,' 'national,' 'private,' 'land-grant,' 'free,' 'commonwealth' and so on), and that it serves to specify the nature of the community of individuals served. The important thing is to assure that there will continue to be reflection upon human knowledge in the light of faith and revelation, and also to assure that attention will be given to areas of knowledge sometimes neglected by other universities.

3 That they are 'Catholic' as maintaining the presence of Christ in the university world and as sympathetic to the Church's magisterium properly used and within the terms of their own statutes and the academic procedures and customs of their particular country.

4 That there must be conceded to Catholic universities, by church, state and society, the kind of autonomy properly attaching to any university in view of its teaching and research functions.

5 That Catholic universities are not and cannot be univocal in structure or in objectives even within the same country; that they need not be (and frequently are not) canonically erected; and that they are open to categorization according to the kind and level of instruction provided, the number of faculties established, and their particular relation to ecclesiastical and civil society.[10]

These positions indicate much similarity of objective as between Catholic and other institutions of higher learning, and a vital understanding of the role which national cultures and customs must play in the formation of all of them. This makes clear that the Church has no quarrel with the Canadian situation. Denominational universities and university colleges may describe themselves as Catholic and be so in fact, even though they can attend to but a portion of the Church's needs. Of some interest is whether universities which have formally abandoned Church-relationship in order to be eligible for full public support

10 Congressus internationalis delegatorum universitatum Catholicarum, Rome, 25 April–1 May 1969, Position Paper, 31–2

– as in Ottawa, Windsor, Charlottetown – are, in view of their history and the composition of their boards, still in any real sense Catholic universities. Does being a Catholic university prevent them from being true state universities in the best sense of the word, or, contrariwise, is there any reason why a state or public-supported university, provided that it is true to its own nature, cannot also be a real Catholic university – providing community for its Catholic members and seeing to the welfare of all so-called 'Catholic' studies including even theology? In view of the progress made in a hundred and fifty years in Canada and in the Church and in the state universities, one is inclined to assert strongly that there is not.

Of further interest is whether the Church ought not begin positively to encourage the affiliation of Catholic university colleges on the ground that an affiliated Catholic college is less likely than the autonomous institution to gravitate toward secularism. In other words, is St Thomas, Fredericton, more actively Catholic than St Mary's, Halifax, or St Paul's, Winnipeg, than Notre Dame of Nelson? This is an open question, of course. From one point of view the affiliated college 'protests' its catholicity in a non-religious milieu. From quite another, affiliation and federation may well be obsolete, the survival of a disappearing denominational situation. All in all, it does not seem proper that the Church should take any position for or against an accidental structure like federation. The Church's only concern can be man's learning in the context of his faith and religious experience.

This brings us to the question of Church-relationship in the more limited sense of influence exerted by chancery offices or religious orders on the governance and operation of universities and colleges.

In the early days, the bishop was in complete control and governed the Catholic college in his diocese either *per se* or *per alios*. He called the college into existence and he provided the academic and administrative staffs from among his own clergy or got a religious order to provide them for him. He was chancellor in the case of universities and he was sometimes, though not so much in the case of colleges run by religious orders, the source of funds. All this has changed. No bishop and few orders can now seriously think of staffing colleges or universities. Educating under title of religion a few boys and girls as prospective priests, nuns, and professional leaders is one thing, providing for the education of society at large quite another. Gone, by reason of the numbers involved if for no other reason, is the practical possibility of the bishops retaining any 'right to their own schools, colleges and universities' as called for by the decree *de scholis mixtis* in 1851. Numbers, however, are not the only problem. The Church is now faced with a whole new way of thinking about vocations, about the role of the laity, about apostolates, ecumenism, and theology itself, which is so different from anything encountered before as to constitute revolution.

The case of vocations is typical. The earliest colleges certainly produced them, but the phenomenon turned out to be transitory. The more fully colleges realized their strictly educational function the less effective they became as minor seminaries. Bishops and people alike had looked to them for something not in their nature to produce. A college education seems rather to have two immediate and measurable effects: it alerts students to a host of social activities other than the ministry, and it modifies the taste for a strictly ecclesiastical manner of living. University graduates tend to view the ecclesiastical life as overly formalized and even as rendered static by a well-meaning, rugged, and heroic clergy. So far as vocations are concerned today, Church-related colleges play but a minor role in assuring the Church of adequate numbers of priests, nuns, and brothers. This is a factor very much affecting the structural aspect of Church-relationship.

There are those who think that this will change. The colleges and universities, they say, will one day supply the Church with the vocations she requires. When the need for them becomes apparent, young men will hear again the call of God and give themselves to the Church in sufficient numbers. Others feel, however, that this situation will arise only when radical changes are made in ecclesiastical discipline: when the commitment to the clerical state becomes temporary, when celibacy is no longer made (in the west) a *sine qua non* of the priesthood, and when the ministry is opened to women as well as men. This same group feels that present discipline is based on a 'static' or at the very best a 'developing' theology, and that until there appears a 'liberating' theology, there will be no substantial increase of vocations. The colleges, they say, must cultivate this 'liberating' non-sectarian theology. Close attention to many of the chronicles provided above, of St Augustine's, Holy Heart, Newman Theological, and St Peter's, among the major seminaries, and of St Michael's among the university colleges, will show that this change is on the way in Canada. It will be even more clear when Canada's French-language universities, and especially when St Paul's University, Ottawa, are dealt with by Claude Galarneau.

The college and university situation, as it affects the laity, is rather different. The laity has assumed a new importance in the contemporary Church and in contemporary society. The colleges have done much to create an informed laity adequate to render priest-professors and priest-administrators almost entirely dispensible. The making available of this new and competent personnel compensates in part for the shrinkage of vocations. It is not far-fetched to speak of phasing out the teaching orders or at least the teaching programmes of these orders, as having now become but the wake of a mercy ship whose mission has been successfully accomplished.

The termination of the kind of Church-relationship that brought with it the contributed services of an academic staff presents serious financial problems to the institutions concerned. A whole new method of financing has now to be worked out and this calls for the discovery of some new arrangement with governments and departments of university affairs. If and when the formula is found, it will mean giving a totally different interpretation to the expression 'Church-related.' It is doubtful that Ottawa, Windsor, and Charlottetown have arrived at the best solution so far as either church or state is concerned, although they have found working solutions. Most professors in the surviving Catholic colleges, and particularly the lay professors, dread the surrendering of Catholic autonomy in favour of the departmental mould and state conformity. There is no reason to suppose that the increased importance of laymen will mean the end of Church-related colleges, unless of course, these laymen are starved out of existence by a situation in which the government is unwilling to accept the realities of a pluralist society.

The increased importance of the lay professors in Catholic colleges has, at least in English-speaking Canada, created relatively little hostility among the priest-professors. This is to be attributed in part to a new concept of apostolic work taking hold among priests and religious since Vatican II. Many now feel that a truly valid religious apostolate is to be especially sought in neglected areas of society. Foreign missions still qualify under this condition, so does work in the inner city or among oppressed minorities, even work with the underground church. Schools, education, scholarship, research, in the minds of many, qualify only ambivalently; and this is rendering the various commitments made years ago by teaching orders difficult to honour. The arguments put forth are that the state is not *de facto* neglecting education and that the contributed services of priests and religious have been rendered unnecessary by the available supply of competent Catholic laymen. The position is still under debate. But if there is any clearly definable educational apostolate left, it seems to reside in special assignments, dedication to learning itself, education of the handicapped, and the creation of Christian community in educational institutions of all kinds. It does not seem to consist in providing teaching staffs and administrations.

The mere cutting down of the cost of operating Catholic colleges by taking over the financial burdens which properly belong to the state carries little weight with prospective priests and religious and seems out of place in the affluent society.

It is pertinent to note here three significant contemporary phenomena: the movement of priests and religious out of traditionally Catholic institutions into the secular universities;[11] the movement of some established lay professors out of the secular universities into Catholic post-secondary institutions – seminaries, colleges, universities; the increased proportional enrolment of Catholic students in secular universities. What, from the point of view of the future of Catholic colleges and universities, do these phenomena mean?

The first means that many priests and religious think (and who can say wrongly?) that a valid apostolate in Catholic higher education is to be found in that field, perhaps an even more important apostolate than in the Catholic university or college. The second means that Catholic colleges are becoming academically stronger and that their administrations are willing to use their resources to pay competitive salaries – a conclusion whose corollary is that unless resources are considerably expanded (which seems unlikely) the Catholic college operation, although better than it has been, must become somewhat smaller too. The third phenomenon, the increased proportional enrolment of Catholic students in secular universities, means that there will also be a corresponding proportional reduction in the number of Catholic colleges in the future. These hard facts do not point to the total disappearance of Catholic colleges and universities in Canada but to a real and relative curtailment of their operation and to the need of transferring their basic functions into the large public university.

Of what functions is it here a question? Mainly three: providing an academic community of which Christ is the centre; providing a place and facilities for the study of theology and religion and also for the study of disciplines especially important for these; and providing a forum for the truly great scholar in these fields.

11 Many priests and religious now hold secular posts: many priests formerly on the staffs of Assumption, Ottawa, and St Dunstan's are now in the universities of Windsor, Ottawa, and Prince Edward Island; agreements made by St Mark's, St Joseph's, St Paul's, and others call for the appointment of priests to secular posts; priests on the staff of St Michael's are sometimes cross-appointed to Toronto's graduate school; many individuals (with or without an understanding with chancery or order), have located themselves in secular institutions: Swithun Bowers, Charles Davis, Lawrence Elmer, James Howard, Genesius Jones, Alfred Keogh, Philip Leah, John McDonough, Gerald McGuigan, Hugh MacKinnon, Marion Norman, Michael Quealey, Kenneth Robitaille, Roland Teske, J.A. Theuws, to select only a few names at random.

Catholics need no longer fear that such functions cannot and will not be assumed by the secular universities. Similar services are being provided for other groups, professional, political, and practical. After all, there will be a community of which Christ is the centre if men who love Christ take him there; and Christ can be taken to the public campus as easily as to the Tridentine seminary! As for the study of religion pure and undefiled, can this only exist, as it has tended up to now in Canada to do, in a context of sectarianism?

An answer to this last question is beginning to be articulated. Religion is now emerging on the university campus as an academic discipline. This is no mere transfer of denominational and sectarian studies – or of true religion diluted or distorted by them – to a public campus. It is happening right on the public campus as a convergence of interest in religion, from within a wide range of disciplines, on human religious experience and behaviour. This seems no longer to be that history-of-religion mentality which has been on public campuses for years – the so-called 'zoo-complex' concerned to examine all denominational forms as demonstrating variety of species. Rather it is now a case of discipline after discipline coming to the point where it wishes to proceed on the assumption that there is a very real human discipline and human experience called religion, revealed or not is beside the issue, which should be examined in depth by a university community committed to freedom of inquiry. A whole literature on this development is appearing.[12]

This is the direction the study of religion is taking today, and many Canadian Catholic colleges and universities would like to become part of it. Catholic theology is struggling to leave the sectarian enclave where it has been doubly imprisoned: by the Reformation sects which rejected it, and by the counter-Reformation sect formed to preserve it. That St Michael's, Regis, and St Augustine's are part of the new Toronto School of Theology, that Holy Heart is reaching out to King's and Pine Hill, that seminary staffs want to be on the university campus are but denominational versions of the movement towards the study of religion as human experience taking place on the secular campus. One wonders whether in Canada something cannot be made of all this. Can, at least, federation and affiliation on the denominational principle – the best that could be managed in 1906 – be replaced by an integration which respects the religious principle, that is, provides for the identity at all levels of the university's structure of groups sharing a common religious

12 Claude Welch, 'Reflections on the Academic Study of Religion: Patterns, Problems, and Prospects,' *ACLS Newsletter*, 19 (Oct. 1968), 1–9; and 'Council on the Study of Religion,' *ACLS Newsletter*, 20 (May 1969), 11–14

experience? This could, it seems, be achieved within already emerging university structures by transforming denominational colleges into constituent colleges in which full consultation precedes pertinent appointments.

This would mean, of course, that Church-relationship on the institutional basis – bishop as chancellor, president named by an ecclesiastical body, probably even control of appointments – would disappear, save perhaps in one or two strictly ecclesiastical institutions. At any rate, the devising of something better than exists now must lie within the ingenuity of man.

To speculate, Church-relationship in the near future will likely be as follows: There will remain a few (one or two) English-Canadian Catholic universities in the traditional sense – with ecclesiastical control, maintaining two to four faculties plus an institute or two to look after special disciplines or projects designed to serve the interests or needs of the Church. There will also be a few (three or five) strong major seminaries whose students will come to them, not from minor seminaries nor from their own division of philosophy, but from the universities; and whose curriculum will provide theology and related subjects in a new wider context of non-theological disciplines, but especially sociology and scientific psychology. These seminaries will be located on secular campuses, when possible, and will maintain close relations with secular and Catholic universities. Their governance will be largely ecclesiastical and their staffs will be appointed on the basis of competence, not of religious affiliation. The other colleges and universities will be integrated into the large secular provincial universities but as ecclesial communities (possibly called colleges) concerned to advance learning itself, and to dedicate both the acquisition and the advancement of learning to God. These communities or colleges will strive to demonstrate to the scholarly world that its interdisciplinary dialogue, now carried on largely within its own closed academic circle, will gain, not lose, from a Christian vision of wisdom that accepts the essential unity of all truth and the ultimate harmony of faith and science. There may also exist a few autonomous, post-doctoral institutes of advanced studies in specialized areas to provide professors and professional scholars with fellowships and facilities necessary for their personal development and for the carrying out of research projects in the service of learning, of society, and of the Church.

GOVERNMENTS AND CATHOLIC COLLEGES

No one can read through the chronicles of Canada's Catholic universities and colleges without being aware of the indebtedness of these institutions to governments for their existence and survival. Governments have been if anything too uncritical of what have sometimes been irresponsible requests for a bill of incorporation. They have also on some occasions incorporated colleges, as in the case of St Michael's College and Ottawa College, knowing full well that incorporation was but the prelude to a request for a subsidy.

Governments have not, however, been generous with degree-granting charters. In the case of Ontario, Quebec, and the western provinces, they have until recently been unwilling to grant a Catholic college a charter. The two charters granted in 1866 to Ottawa and Regiopolis were possible only in the special circumstances preceding Confederation. Assumption's charter came only after prolonged and persistent pressure. Loyola has never succeeded in getting one.[13]

The general policy of 'incorporation, yes: a charter, no' has had diversified effects: in the case of St Michael's and some others, it has been the occasion of academic health and national prestige; in other cases, Loyola and Assumption among others, it tended to hold the small institution to an inferior legal status and limit its effectiveness as a means to improve the social and economic lot of its constituency; in some cases, affiliation turned out to be a makeshift arrangement, one that gave the small college the sense of being a nuisance to the establishment. In other words, the right to exist does entail the right to exist with a certain dignity, which has sometimes been forgotten by those who have the power to grant or withhold academic independence.

The responsibility for the situation – and the blame, if that is the proper word – was not entirely that of the governments concerned. Both governments and the Catholic Church ought to have discouraged the founding of so many colleges across the country. Recent years have seen changes in both positions. Charters have been forthcoming from governments outside Quebec for institutions with a fair chance to grow. And the recent 'position paper' of the world's Catholic universities calls for long-range planning and wide consultation before launching new Catholic foundations.

Governments in the early days made small subsidies to all colleges. In the Maritimes, payments of varying amounts were made until the demise of the short-lived University of Halifax in 1881. In Ontario, or Canada West, subsidies were discontinued in 1868. Quebec made one or two *ad hoc* subsidies to Ottawa College, but these were by way of assistance in view of that institution's service to French-speaking

13 Robin S. Harris, Constance Allen, Mary Lewis, *An Annotated List of the Legislative Acts Concerning Higher Education in Ontario*, Toronto: University of Toronto Press, 1966, passim, but esp. 55–9

Canadians. Governments in the west have, until quite recently, taken no cognizance of the existence of denominational colleges.

The present situation in regard to government subsidies, inadequate as it is, is better than at any time in the past. The change came during the forties when the federal government's department of veterans' affairs made supplementary grants to universities and colleges that opened their facilities to returning servicemen. No distinction was drawn by the department of veterans' affairs between one kind of institution and another or between one faculty and another. Assistance was given on a per capita basis as the best way of the department's not becoming involved in the strictly educational operation which was the concern of provincial governments. When Mr St Laurent in 1951, following the publication of the *Report of the Royal Commission on National Development in the Arts, Letters and Sciences* (the Massey Commission), promised federal aid to all Canadian universities and colleges approved by the provincial departments of education, and implemented his promise in 1952, the same principle was followed. This was the first time that Catholic and other denominational colleges all across Canada received unrestricted operational grants from a government on the same basis as provincially-supported universities. This situation obtained until 1967 when federal grants were discontinued and the tax revenues which provided them were turned back to the provinces for the support of education at their own discretion.

Policy now affecting subsidies to Catholic universities and colleges from provincial governments varies from one part of Canada to another. From the point of view of denominational colleges, discrimination is avoided only in Nova Scotia.

Nova Scotia's policy was established in three stages. The first stage, quite unofficial, came with the formation in the early sixties of an association of the presidents and chancellors of English-speaking Catholic universities and colleges of the Maritimes. Active in this association were D.C. Duffie, Sister Francis of Assisi, C.J. Fischer, J.A. Sullivan, and H.J. Somers. The association succeeded in calling attention to the urgency of the situation. The second stage came when the association was extended to include Mount Allison, Dalhousie, Acadia, the University of New Brunswick, St Joseph's University (but not Collège Ste Anne or Memorial University of Newfoundland), and was reorganized as the Associated Atlantic Universities (AAU) with Colin MacKay of New Brunswick as president, H.D. Hicks of Dalhousie as vice-president, and H.J. Somers, just retired from the presidency of St Francis Xavier, as permanent secretary.

The third stage came in 1964 when the Nova Scotia government's committee on university grants, consisting of N.A.M. MacKenzie (chairman), Arthur Murphy, and E.L. Goodfellow, issued its 53 proposals covering government aid, institutional co-operation, and utilization of the potential of the newly-formed AAU. Since that time the Catholic universities of Nova Scotia have enjoyed the support of the government of Nova Scotia on an equitable basis, that is, receive operational and capital grants on the same terms and by the same weighting formulas as other universities. Grants to the seminaries (Pine Hill, King's, Holy Heart) are on the basis of those for undergraduate divisions. New Brunswick has a different but similarly equitable arrangement.

The situation in Ontario, though vastly improved over the 1868–1967 period, is still highly exclusive. Church-related colleges may opt for grants identical in dollars with the 1966–7 situation under the federal grant system; and special arrangements obtain within the University of Toronto. But the government adheres adamantly to the no-grants, no-recognition policy, save the flat 50 per cent of one unit per student formula which technically meets the old commitment made by the federal government.

A key to the Ontario attitude is perhaps to be seen in the nomenclature of one of the province's most efficient educational bodies: that known in 1962–3 as 'the committee of presidents of provincially-assisted universities and colleges of Ontario' but now called 'the committee of the presidents of universities of Ontario.' Church-related universities are without representation, and are, so far as the committee's nomenclature is concerned, without existence as universities in Ontario. This fossilizes the hard line taken by the Ontario government since 1868. Ontario must not seem to acknowledge that Church-related post-secondary institutions exist.

For an institution like the University of St Michael's College, which has since 1906, tried committedly and trustingly to function within the provincial university, non-existence at the level of the secretariat of the presidents of the universities of Ontario, and near non-existence in what concerns the departments of education and university affairs, can only be construed as either public rejection or governmental irresponsibility.

This is not just a question of money. The Ontario government has spent very large sums to take over and develop the universities of Windsor and Ottawa. It would have cost much less to develop the two of them according to their traditional nature and ethic. But this would also have entailed a concession to those universities which do not conform to the established pattern. Surely there must be some other way of coping with the problem of survival and continuity than through a process of legal annihilation and rebirth.

The situation in Quebec is capricious. The government is not generous to its universities. In principle, all may receive operational and capital grants, but by negotiation. Operational grants are negotiated through the Comité des Recteurs or directly with the government; capital grants are directly negotiated. The tendency is to delay such grants until the situation is critical, as was the case with Loyola in November 1968.

In Alberta and British Columbia, operational grants are now made to Church-related institutions, but with great caution. In Manitoba and Saskatchewan, both operating and capital grants are made on a less restrictive basis. In these western provinces, as in Ontario, relations between Church-related colleges and governments have improved during recent years.

The various royal and non-royal commissions appointed have had little to offer on this question of whether governments ought today to assume responsibility for financing all post-secondary education.

The most notable of all recent reports, the Robbins Report[14] to the British prime minister, October 1963, dealt with an English situation in which sectarian universities and colleges did not exist and where it would have been folly to pretend that Oxford and Cambridge and their colleges, given their religious origins and their myriad Church-relationships, could be dropped from consideration. Lord Robbins did what he had to do, ignored the problem in terms of religious affiliations. He spoke of providing 'a satisfactory framework of social life and promoting those close and informal relations between teachers and students that are a characteristic feature of this country's [i.e. Britain's] tradition' (p.24). Robbins's concern was to provide enough places in the universities to meet the coming demand, and he recommended 'that the future should be met by developing present types of institution' (p.49). He feared the static type of institution, that is, the kind which exists but is 'not to be allowed to develop.' 'We do not suggest that all colleges should, in the fulness of time, be universities ... But we think it important for the general health of the system that all institutions of higher education should have some opportunity for development' (p.147).

14 *Higher Education*: Report of the Committee appointed by the Prime Minister under the Chairmanship of Lord Robbins 1961–3, London: Her Majesty's Stationary Office, 1963

This principle has proven to be rather too strong medicine for the reports that have appeared since in Canada. They avoid it one way or another, and in the meantime, the nation's colleges, far from being given a chance to develop, are being forced to the wall.

Highly disappointing in this context was the Bladen Report.[15] In the 'Review of Submissions' Professor Bladen showed that he was aware of the problem when he wrote as follows:

In Ontario and most western provinces, denominational institutions, whether independent or affiliated with public universities, stressed their dependence on federal support; without it, some would face bankruptcy. They receive no, or very small, provincial grants. Their only other sources of income – fees and private endowment – are unlikely to increase appreciably. Some groups questioned whether public funds should be made available to institutions under sectarian control. McMaster University, the University of Windsor, and more recently the University of Ottawa were often quoted as examples of changes to that lay control which should, perhaps, be prerequisite of public support. In answer to this, the 'private' religious colleges claimed that they are entitled to parity of treatment from both the Federal Government and the provincial governments provided they do not exclude students or select faculty on religious grounds, that they require no compulsory religious observance, and that they maintain satisfactory academic standards. One denominational university pressed for government financing entirely from federal sources to overcome this discrimination.[16]

Bladen did not raise the principles stated in the Robbins Report: 'this country's traditions,' 'health of the system,' 'developing present types of institution,' 'opportunity for development.' His recommendations, moreover, discreetly excluded reference to Canada's private, post-secondary institutions.

Although the Bladen Report does not say so, members of his commission took the position during the hearings that private institutions were raising economical issues which were really internal to the larger, complex institutions concerned. If St Michael's, for example, had a financial problem, the place to solve it was within the University of Toronto. How welcome such a statement would have been in the report had the commissioners chosen (or been allowed, as the case may be) to make it! The Bladen Report did the universities of Canada a great

15 *Financing Higher Education in Canada*: Being the Report of a Commission to the Association of Universities and Colleges of Canada – and its Executive Agency the Canadian Universities Foundation, Vincent W. Bladen, chairman, Toronto: University of Toronto Press, 1965

16 Ibid., 39

favour in strongly endorsing formula financing; and it would not likely have harmed the colleges if federal aid had continued. But its recommendations in the context of exclusively provincial financing of higher education have been disastrous for them.

Other reports are not better. The Duff-Berdahl Report, which deals primarily with governance, not financing, isolates the problems of the Church institutions in chapter 11, 'Universities and the Churches,' and limits itself to a few comments on the structure of federated and affiliated colleges in their various universities and expresses the pious hope that such colleges 'will survive and flourish.'[17]

A recent brief to the AUCC's Commission on the Relations between the Universities and Governments (the Rowat-Hurtubise Commission) by a special committee to advise on the problems of the Church-related institutions of higher learning in Canada, goes into the problem more seriously.[18] This brief recognizes that Church-relationship is changing, that governments are even now supporting religious education in their own provincial universities, that sectarian indoctrination is no longer a serious threat to education in Canada, and that Church-related colleges are quite defensible on such bases as structural diversity and continuing identity.

The brief makes six recommendations to governments, three to Church-related colleges. To governments it recommends: that Church-related colleges be integrated into the provincial system; that there be an initial and continuing examining of policies of Church-related colleges; that the conditions under which support is available be stated; that such support be extended to both instructional and service functions, and to capital aid; and that ministerial training (where involved) be supported on a basis comparable to the supporting of other professional training.

To Church-related colleges the brief recommends: that they state and define their aims and purpose; that the public at large have representation on their boards and that they be publicly accountable; that they pursue a policy of further integration and consolidation.

These are reasonable recommendations and their implementation could create equitable conditions in which Church-related colleges could operate more effectively in the interest of the people of Canada.

17 *University Government in Canada*: Report of a Commission sponsored by the Canadian Association of University Teachers and the Association of Universities and Colleges of Canada, Sir James Duff and Robert O. Berdahl, commissioners, Toronto: University of Toronto Press, 1966. Quotation is from p.85.

18 Brief to the Rowat-Hurtubise Commission on the Relations Between Universities and Governments, 18 Apr. 1968. With appendices prepared as late as Nov. 1968. Reported in *University Affairs* vol.10, no.6 (July 1969), 22–3.

SCHOLARSHIP IN THE CATHOLIC COLLEGES

It is not uncommon for friends and foes alike of Catholic colleges to question the integrity of their scholarship. Three charges are basic and recur: that Catholic scholarship is too authoritarian, that it does not enjoy academic freedom; and that it is scarred by the anti-intellectualism of the communities which support it. It would be folly to claim that these charges are without substance. They have been dealt with in many places.[19] Those who make them have been sometimes thinking of the limitations which the acceptance of revelation places on the objective presentation and the uninhibited pursuit of knowledge; sometimes of the pressures which the hierarchy and religious orders can bring to bear on ecclesiastical institutions; sometimes of the tolerating, by the Catholic constituency, of colleges which win few competitive awards, maintain wretched libraries, and have an undistinguished professoriate.

Without rehearsing the replies evoked by these charges, let it only be observed that learning in general proceeds by assumptions even where revelation is rejected; that all colleges and universities have to cope with outside pressures, some of which are unhealthy; and that awards, libraries, and qualified faculty usually accompany material affluence. Catholic scholarship is sometimes hampered by orthodoxy, harried by Rome, chancery, or moralistic lay theologians, or crushed by almost unbearable poverty; but not more seriously than is much denominational and secular scholarship by contemporary myths,[20] by non-academic boards, departments of government and the voting public, or by the extravagance of the empires in which it is endlessly vesting itself. Documents emerging from the CAUT and other associations make all this quite clear. Frank Underhill, Canada's outspoken social and political historian, for example, in one of his many pleas for academic freedom, points out that 'the equalitarian democracy that distinguished this continent ... has had from the start a strong anti-intellectual element in its makeup.'[21] The nub of the issue is not whether learning and the inadequacy of its pursuit are sometimes under attack from within and

19 The subject has been surveyed recently; see Christopher Jencks and David Riesman, *The Academic Revolution*, New York: Doubleday, 1968, ch.21, 'Catholics and Their Colleges,' 334–405. See also Frank L. Christ and Gerard E. Sherry, eds., *American Catholicism and the Intellectual Ideal*, New York: Appleton-Century-Crofts, 1961. For further bibliography, see Jencks-Riesman.

20 Langdon Gilkey, 'Modern Myth-Making and the Possibilities of Twentieth-Century Theology,' *Theology of Renewal*, ed. L.K. Shook, New York: Herder and Herder, 1968, I, 283–312. Gilkey identifies the contemporary myths: the myths of cosmic evolution, of Marxist dialectic, and the gnostic myth that knowledge gives control, freedom, and self-fulfilment.

21 Frank H. Underhill, 'The Scholar: Man Thinking,' in *A Place of Liberty*, ed. George Whalley, Toronto: Clarke Irwin, 1964, 64

without but how the academic community copes with its problem.

Canadian scholarship has thus far passed through two phases: an earlier one in which greatness was reckoned to be in a man's life and civility rather than in his publications; and a second phase when greatness was felt to consist in the demonstrated mastery of scholarly techniques exercised in an environment of scholarly resources.[22] The scholar in the Catholic college has moved more tardily from the first to the second phase, not, unfortunately, because of his sense of values, but because of distractions placed in the way of his study – high school teaching, pastoral work, dormitory and proctoring duties – and because he has been isolated from library holdings and deprived of the incentive that comes from graduate teaching.

Publication is a sticky kind of touchstone, though not an entirely invalid one, for judging scholarship. The chronicles in the preceding sections of this study pay only passing attention to publication, usually only to indicate the development of a given post-secondary institution or the atmosphere prevailing in it. When attention was called to publication by religious sisters – St Michael Guinan, Corona Sharpe, Maura Geoffrey – there was no intention either of providing a full picture or of excluding Judith Anne, Francis Nims, Francis Xavier, Geraldine Thompson, Mary Agnes, and others who have also published; or when Lebrun, Kissane, and Dozois were singled out as publishing scholars on the staffs of major seminaries, it was not to suggest that no others have published, even though it is a fact that very few others actually have; and when detailed attention was paid to publication by professors of the Pontifical Institute of Mediaeval Studies, it was not to make a comparison with other professors but to indicate the nature of the Institute's work.

Two points ought, however, to be forthrightly made: that the overall picture of publication by the staffs of Canada's English Catholic colleges and universities is not impressive; and that failure to publish, where it occurs, is usually related to their isolation from graduate studies. This last point must be kept in mind in analysing the bibliographical sections of the two volumes on the humanities in Canada prepared by professors Priestley and Wiles in 1964 and 1966.[23]

These volumes give the names and works of professors in Canada teaching in the humanities and social sciences. Of 575 publication

22 Roy Daniells, 'Literary Studies in Canada,' in *Scholarship in Canada 1967*, ed. R.H. Hubbard, Toronto: University of Toronto Press, 1967, 31

23 F.E.L. Priestley, *The Humanities in Canada*, Toronto: University of Toronto Press, 1964; R.M. Wiles, *The Humanities in Canada: Supplement to December 31, 1964*, Toronto: University of Toronto Press, 1966

entries (not allowing for duplication of names) in the first volume and 758 in the second, 68 and 133 respectively are from private Catholic institutions. These figures 68 and 133 are misleading on the broad national scene as they include large concentrations in Toronto and Ottawa, that is, where there are research institutions geared to publication. Besides, the Ottawa figures include many items that belong in a French rather than an English assessment. Also included in the figures are publications by some Windsor professors whose writings came out of Assumption before the founding of the present University of Windsor.

The comparative picture is not good. The faculty in the English-speaking Catholic colleges are not for the most part productive scholars. The picture is even less good when such matters as bulk, continuance, and recognized calibre are probed. This disappointing feature of Catholic college scholarship is also reflected in the membership rolls of the Royal Society of Canada. In 1968 the society listed seven such members, six from Toronto (four of these from the Institute) and one from Antigonish.[24] Were the statistics extended to include the natural sciences and the professional areas they would be less, not more favourable.

It is time that attention was given to this situation by those responsible for it, that is, by the administrators of the English Catholic colleges and universities, by the graduate schools of large Canadian universities, and by governments and their departments of education and university affairs. Not one of these can shuffle off responsibility. Catholic college administrators have to give more prudent consideration to proper salary scales, teaching schedules, administrative and extra-curricular chores, and to pastoral assignments. Large graduate schools cannot be possessive and exclusive about their courses and their staffs; they are quite justified in not wishing small colleges to be offering competitive graduate programmes, but they ought to be ready within reason to allow good scholars from these same colleges to give courses and seminars in their division: much of the University of Toronto's extraordinary success as an internationally recognized graduate school has come from its openness on this point – a long-standing openness, going back to the twenties and the policies of Dean George Sidney Brett, and one not encountered elsewhere in Canada in any comparable way. Governments and departments of education must for their part come to recognize that the providing of conditions favourable to true graduate work

24 *Calendar 1968–1969 Annuaire: The Royal Society of Canada* lists the following members from the English-speaking Catholic Church colleges: Donald J. MacNeil (ob. 1968), Armand A. Maurer, H. Marshall McLuhan, J. Reginald O'Donnell, Joseph Owens, Anton C. Pegis, Richard J. Schoeck.

by able scholars should be a normal service rendered to competent citizens, not one to be given or withheld or bartered on some antiquated confessionally-distorted basis. The service at stake here is not of any given agent or purveyor of learning but of learning itself.

The somewhat lower scholarly achievement by men located in Canadian Catholic colleges is related not only to their assignments but also to the library conditions in which many of them have to carry on their work. Many of the institutions here chronicled are without a library in the scholarly and research sense of the word, and are without provisions for the kind of mobility by which such a lack may be circumvented.

Strictly speaking, no college should be located far from large pertinent book collections or library centres. A suitable library centre is one with a minimum of 500,000 volumes, chosen with some discrimination, containing a wide range of periodicals and serials, and with at least modest archives attached. There are at most 17 such centres in Canada, ranging from Toronto with over 8,000,000 items to St John's, Regina, and Waterloo with about 500,000. Intervening are Montreal, Ottawa, Vancouver, Quebec, Victoria, Edmonton, London, Halifax, Winnipeg, Kingston, Hamilton, and (in view of the proximity of Detroit) Windsor.

Most Catholic colleges and universities in Canada are located in the above centres, notable exceptions being Notre Dame of Nelson, Notre Dame of Canada, St Thomas, and St Francis Xavier. For the colleges concerned this may not be too serious, but for the two universities – St Francis Xavier and Notre Dame of Nelson – it unquestionably is. The chronicles of these two institutions reveal the special efforts under way to cope with this situation. It is imperative that their efforts to create respectable university libraries be successful. An institution like St Francis Xavier, with its rich history and its national and international significance, should not be left to shoulder this load on its own. Its case should be seen to require special consideration by the national hierarchy, the federal government, and large foundations.

The related and serious problem is the extent to which the English Catholic colleges and universities of Canada maintain and develop a large enough collection to sustain moderately advanced scholarship. An examination of the two most recent studies of library facilities, the Williams Report and the Downs Report,[25] reveals that not one Catholic college or university library has holdings that reach the arbitrary mini-

---

25 E.E. Williams, *Report on Resources of Canadian University Libraries for Research*, Ottawa: NCCU, 1962; and Robert B. Downs, *Resources of Canadian Academic and Research Libraries*, Ottawa: AUCC, 1967. These reports show how inadequate are all university libraries in Canada, a factor which mitigates unfavourable criticism of Catholic university and college libraries.

mum established by librarians for contemporary universities. Table 1 selects for the six largest libraries of English Catholic colleges and universities data adapted from the Downs Report.

Order by enrolment	Enrolment 1966 (1969)[26]	Volumes held in 1966	Rank among Can. univ. lib.	Library Expend. 1966–7	Per cap. in $	Per cent of total expend.
1 Loyola	4794 (3680)	80671	33rd	282,000	32	6.0
2 St FXU	1937 (2669)	96729	29th	153,000	38	3.5
3 USMC	1779 (2052)	118054	27th	145,000	62	9.9
4 SMU	1037 (1562)	62992	39th	108,000	51	6.6
5 MSVU	610 (642)	64517	38th	64,600	66	6.0
6 NDU	596 (514)	19795	51st	98,028	78	8.4

The table calls for a few comments: 26 Canadian university libraries surpass in numbers the largest collection in a Catholic institution (USMC), although only 12 of them have larger enrolments than the largest Catholic institution (Loyola). Although they are all in a 'building' situation, none compares favourably with the 'building' libraries in percentage of total expenditure assigned to the library: Simon Fraser 26.1, Brock 25.0, York 17.2, Windsor 10.6. Marianopolis (not in the above chart), spending 11.1 per cent of its operating fund on its library, has the best ratio of any Catholic institution.

The above statistics change upward from year to year. However, they are very far from meeting minimum requirements for the scholarly needs of a university professoriate. Neither Williams nor Downs can speak complimentarily about the overall picture.

Mollifying slightly the larger situation, which is unsatisfactory, are some of the finer details noted by Williams about the character of special collections in Catholic college libraries. Loyola, for example, has a strong collection in African history (Williams, p.225); Xavier College possesses a Cape Bretoniana collection of 8000 items (p.236); Mount St Vincent has the beginning of a fine collection of books on women (p.267) and a small and unusual collection of 69 books with fore-edge paintings executed between 1767 and 1850 (p.242); St Francis Xavier has a collection of Gaelic items and of books on Scotland, and a fine section of social science periodicals (pp.243,265) gathered for the Coady Institute. Two special collections are excellent by any standards – the philosophical library of St Paul's University (which falls outside the

26 Enrolment figures for 1969 are from *University Affairs*, vol.10, no.8(Oct. 1969), 3; it is quite possible that the Loyola figures, which include night and continuing-education courses of several kinds, may have been differently calculated in the two sources.

present survey) and the mediaeval materials held by the Pontifical Institute of Mediaeval Studies, Toronto (p.25 and passim).

In addition to these features noted by Williams, mention should be made of the theological collections at Holy Heart, Loyola, and Toronto (St Michael's, Regis, St Augustine's), the recusant and ecumenical collections in St Michael's, the Moreana materials and the J.J. Leddy collection in St Thomas More College, Saskatoon, and the rare items brought together by Athol Murray at Notre Dame, Wilcox.

Strangely enough, the Catholic institutions under review are quite deficient in archival materials of special interest for religious studies; also in Catholic newspapers and journals, and in local history; and lamentably weak in a communications system: they neither know one another's collections, nor have ever considered even a joint book and archival catalogue. In only too many ways they continue to operate under pioneer conditions.

The foregoing remarks on scholarship in English-speaking Canadian post-secondary institutions are intended as a factual and objective statement of a situation that is less than ideal. Yet one must insist that the deficiencies they highlight are the easiest of all deficiencies to remove because they are so essentially material. The same colleges and universities which are for the time being falling short of reaching this particular ideal are coming much closer to attaining other ideals more important in themselves and far more satisfactory to those who pursue them. They are striving, for example, to witness in countless ways the eternal and the temporal presence of a transcendent God; they are striving too, to achieve a practical orientation of all learning to that God; they are seeking by their concern about God to confer a valid sort of finality on all human activity and especially that of the mind.

Catholic post-secondary institutions are not unique in doing these things; they may not even be necessary for getting them done. Yet the institutions are with us, they have a respectable history, and they have valid if limited potentialities. They should probably be preserved. They do keep us in touch with one very important aspect of learning: that although learning has its own ends and its own laws, and is properly sought for those ends and according to those laws, it resides in man himself and somehow shares his ends too, including those traditionally called his supernatural ends. Because Catholic institutions are particularly effective in maintaining this kind of awareness, important both for learning and for man, they ought at some sacrifice to be maintained in whatever form turns out to be practical and possible.

Perhaps this continuance could be tied to a puzzling statement of

Jesus recorded by Luke (8:18): 'So take care *how* you hear.' Jesus did not say *what* you hear. He was concerned with what Marshall McLuhan likes to call percepts or the medium, rather than with concepts. Concepts too are valid, but imperfectly so until rightly learned, that is, until learned in relation to God. Only those who learn in the fully human medium, the *how* medium, the God-context, have learning. In fact, it is they who make it to be true learning. For those who grasp this fact, the rest of Jesus's text contains no enigma: 'For anyone who has will be given more; from anyone who has not, even what he thinks he has will be taken away.' The Catholic college and university are not to be praised where they fail, but only where they in some small way succeed, only where they preserve the integrity of learning. For what they achieve, they deserve survival, which is open to as many forms as man's ingenuity can propose.

INDEX

ABBREVIATIONS for Religious as used in this index

cfc	Congregation of Christian Brothers (Irish Christian Brothers)
cjm	Congregation of Jesus and Mary (Eudists)
cm	Congregation of Priests of the Mission (Lazarists, Vincentians)
cnd	Congregation of Sisters of Notre Dame
cr	Congregation of the Resurrection (Resurrectionists)
csb	Congregation of Priests of St Basil (Basilians)
csc	Congregation of the Holy Cross
csj	Congregation of Sisters of St Joseph
csm	Congregation of Sisters of St Martha
csp	Congregation of St Paul (Paulists)
cssr	Congregation of the Most Holy Redeemer (Redemptorists)
fcsp	Congregation of Jesus and Mary: France
fsc	Brothers of the Christian Schools (Christian Brothers)
ibvm	Institute of the Blessed Virgin Mary (Loretto Sisters)
ocarm	Order of Carmel (Carmelites)
ofm	Order of Friars Minor (Franciscans)
ofm cap	Order of Friars Minor Capuchins (Capuchins)
omi	Oblates of Mary Immaculate (Oblates)
op	Order of Friars Preachers (Dominicans)
opraem	Order of the Premonstratensians (Norbertines)
osb	Order of St Benedict (Benedictines)
osu	Order of St Ursula (Ursulines)
pss	Priests of St Sulpice (Sulpicians)
rscj	Society of the Sacred Heart
rsm	Sisters of Mercy
sa	Franciscan Friars of the Atonement
sac	Society for the Catholic Apostolate (Pallotine Fathers)
sc	Sisters of Charity of St Vincent de Paul, Halifax
scsl	Sisters of Charity of St Louis
sj	Society of Jesus (Jesuits)
snjm	Sisters of the Holy Names of Jesus and Mary
ssa	Sisters of St Anne

Abbot, D.C. 193

Aboulin, Jean Joseph Marie, csb 279, 280

Académie St Thomas d'Aquin, Quebec, PQ 88

Acadia University, Wolfville, NS 58, 61, 62, 81, 422

ACLS Newsletter 419n

Actorie, Joseph Marie Julien, general csb 137

Aeterni patris, encyc. of Leo XIII 161, 211

Agricultural College, Tuxedo, Man. 321

Albert College, Belleville, Ont. 150n

Alexander, W.J. 144n

Alfred, Bro., fsc 358, 359

Allen, Elliott B. csb 380, 384, 386

Allen, Francis V., auxiliary bishop of Toronto 195

Allen, Thomas V., priest of Halifax 60

Aloysius, Bro., fsc 355, 360–2, 364, 365

American Association of Theological Schools 206

American Catholic Philosophical Association 214

Amyot, J. 167

Anderson, James Thomas Milton, premier of Sask. 379

Andrew, Geoffrey C. 378

Andrieu, Michel 217

Angelicum University, Rome 160, 220

Anglin, Gerald F., csb 345